Victor A. Nilsson

Sweden

Victor A. Nilsson

Sweden

ISBN/EAN: 9783337723941

Printed in Europe, USA, Canada, Australia, Japan

Cover: Foto ©ninafisch / pixelio.de

More available books at **www.hansebooks.com**

SWEDEN

BY

VICTOR NILSSON, Ph.D.

AUTHOR OF "LODDFAFNISMAL, AN EDDIC STUDY"

ILLUSTRATED

NEW YORK
PETER FENELON COLLIER
MDCGCXCIX

COPYRIGHT, 1899,
BY
PETER FENELON COLLIER.

CONTENTS

	PAGE
INTRODUCTION	5

CHAPTER I
SWEDEN IN PREHISTORIC AND EARLY HISTORIC TIMES—ARCHÆOLOGICAL FINDS AND CLASSICAL TESTIMONY 11

CHAPTER II
DAWN OF SWEDISH HISTORY—HEIMSKRINGLA AND YNGLINGATAL . 33

CHAPTER III
THE VIKING AGE—ANSGAR, THE APOSTLE OF SWEDEN . . . 44

CHAPTER IV
EARLY CHRISTIAN ERA—STENKIL'S LINE AND INTERCHANGING DYNASTIES 64

CHAPTER V
THE MEDIÆVAL STATE—THE FOLKUNG DYNASTY 80

CHAPTER VI
UNIONISM VERSUS PATRIOTISM—MARGARET, ENGELBREKT AND CHARLES KNUTSSON 100

CHAPTER VII
UNIONISM VERSUS PATRIOTISM—UNCROWNED KINGS OF THE STURE FAMILIES 115

CHAPTER VIII
REVOLUTION AND REFORMATION—GUSTAVUS VASA 130

CHAPTER IX
REFORMATION AND REACTION—THE SONS OF GUSTAVUS I. . . 161

CHAPTER X
PERIOD OF POLITICAL GRANDEUR—GUSTAVUS II. ADOLPHUS . . 192

CONTENTS

CHAPTER XI
PERIOD OF POLITICAL GRANDEUR—QUEEN CHRISTINE . . 220

CHAPTER XII
PERIOD OF POLITICAL GRANDEUR—CHARLES X. AND CHARLES XI. . 242

CHAPTER XIII
PERIOD OF POLITICAL GRANDEUR—CHARLES XII. 268

CHAPTER XIV
PERIOD OF LIBERTY—THE ARISTOCRATIC REPUBLIC 310

CHAPTER XV
GUSTAVIAN PERIOD—GUSTAVUS III. AND GUSTAVUS IV. ADOLPHUS . 343

CHAPTER XVI
THE CONSTITUTIONAL MONARCHY—CHARLES XIII. AND THE EARLY BERNADOTTES 365

CHAPTER XVII
PARLIAMENTARY REFORM—CHARLES XV. 391

CHAPTER XVIII
PROGRESS AND PROSPERITY—OSCAR II. 414

LIST OF ILLUSTRATIONS

Frontispiece—Charles XII. in the Battle of Pultowa . . .
Gustavus Adolphus D. G. Rex Svec. Goth . . . . .
The Battle of Pultowa . . . .
Battle of Warsaw . . . .

INTRODUCTION

THE kingdom of Sweden occupies the eastern and larger part of the Scandinavian peninsula, covering an area of one hundred and seventy thousand six hundred and sixty square miles, with a population of somewhat more than five millions. Sweden is of nearly the same width, from east to west, throughout her whole length. If the country were divided into four equal parts, the southernmost part would correspond to the district of Gothaland, the next to the district of Svealand, consisting of most of what is north of the lakes Venar and Vetter and what is south of the Dal River, while the two remaining parts together would make up the district of Norrland. Gothaland, in ancient times called *Sunnanskogs* (South of the Woods), consists of the old provinces Scania, Bleking, Smaland and East Gothland by the Baltic, Halland and Bohuslæn by the North Sea, and West Gothland of the interior. Svealand, or *Nordanskogs*, consists of the provinces Sœdermanland and Upland by the Baltic, south and north of Lake Mælar, respectively, Dal, Vermland and Dalecarlia on the Norwegian frontier, and Nerike and Westmanland of the interior. Norrland consists of the provinces of Gestrikland, Helsingland, Medelpad, Angermanland and Westerbotten by the Gulf of Bothnia, a branch of the Baltic, and Herjedal, Jemtland and the Lapmark on the Norwegian frontier. A great number of islands form part of the kingdom, of which the two largest, Gothland and Œland, are situated in the Baltic. One-twelfth of the area, or as much as the whole state of Denmark, consists of water.

Sweden is politically united with Norway and ruled by the same king, these united kingdoms forming the largest realm in Europe next to Russia, Sweden herself ranking as the sixth in size.

Sweden is a country which offers striking varieties in scenery and conditions. In the southernmost province of Scania, an ancient home of culture, the nightingale and the stork dwell in the fertile plains, and the walnut, mulberry and chestnut trees render ripening fruit. Central Sweden is a wooded plateau, rich in rocky hills and inland seas. Although barren lands occupy large areas, these parts are characterized by a loveliness and picturesqueness which are still more pronounced in the northern provinces along the coast. Only in the inner mountainous regions of Norrland is the scenery of real grandeur where the white-capped giants appear in vast groups, or in isolated peaks of six thousand to seven thousand feet in altitude, where a hundred glaciers with glacier rivers, moraines and erosions cover a surface almost as large as the glaciers of Tyrol, and where, in the turbulent course of mighty rivers, are formed tremendous waterfalls, one of them, The Hare's Leap, being the largest in Europe.

Geologically considered, Sweden is situated around the centre of the ancient Scandinavian land-ice, and in the greater part of the country only two of the geological series, the oldest and the youngest, are represented. Thus the uneven, undulating surface of the Archæan rocks, on which almost the whole country is firmly set, is in general covered with quaternary deposits of gravel and clay. The mountains are rich in iron ore, the streams and lakes in fish, the woods in game, but the soil, itself of a good quality, unfortunately rich in stones. This last-mentioned circumstance, together with the rather severe climate, which yet is a good deal milder than might be expected, especially in the southern and western parts of the country, makes agriculture, which is the most important industry, profitable only on the extensive plains of Scania, Upland and West and East Gothland. Still barley and rye are cultivated within the Polar Circle, ripening in remarkably short time under the nocturnal light of the Midsummer sun. Dense forests cover Sweden in the very same latitude in which Greenland is clad by eternal ice. The short summers are of a surpassing loveliness. In Norrland there is a Swedish *læn*, or governmental district, of the size of the State of Ohio, on which, between the 5th of June and the 11th of July, the sun never sets. If the earth was perfectly plain and even one would be able to see the sun above the horizon continually during this period. But these northerly regions are very mountainous, and consequently you will have to climb a high peak in order to see the wonderful sight of a sun which stands still when it should set, and which marks the difference between night and day only by a rolling motion in the horizon. There is no country in the world where so many places for such observation are reached so easily as in Sweden. One may travel the whole distance from the southernmost point of the country to the very base of a mountain, Gellivara, Sweden's Klondike, from which the midnight sun can be seen for thirty-seven nights in succession. But although the sun itself is visible only from the mountain peaks above the Polar Circle, the nocturnal light steeps the whole realm in midsummer-night's dreams of magic colors and reflections.

The Swedish people are of Teutonic stock and have lived in the land they still inhabit for at least four thousand years, during this entire period not having assimilated other nationalities, or at least to no extent worth mentioning, so that the Swedish nation is of an origin far purer than any other at present existing.

The kingdom of Sweden is the most ancient of the states still extant in Europe, for all historical monuments prove that the Swedes have kept to about their present territory, perfectly independent of foreign nations, probably for a long time divided into lesser communities, but for the past twelve hundred years united in one single realm. The languages spoken in the Scandinavian North belong to the Teutonic family of Indo-European languages, and seem to have been one and almost homogeneous up to the time of the Viking Age (about 700–1060), when various dialects commence to be distinguished. The old uniform language has been preserved in Northern loanwords in the Finnish and Lap languages and in about one hundred of the oldest Runic inscriptions. The early Old Swedish, from the Viking Age to somewhat later than 1200, did not differ much from the Old Norse (the Old Norwegian and Old Icelandic), while the difference from the Old Danish was almost imperceptible. The sources for the study of this language period are about two thousand later Runic inscriptions and nearly one hundred Old Swedish loanwords, almost all proper names, in the Russian language. The classical period of Old Swedish falls between 1200 and about 1350. Its most important monuments are the provincial laws and a manuscript collection of saintly legends, called Codex Bureanus. The language of this period offers a number of dialects, of which only one, the Gutnic, is strictly defined. In the next period of Old Swedish, from 1350 to the Reformation, a universal language for the whole country is distinguished. The so-called Oxenstiern manuscripts and Codex Bildstenianus are the chief sources of our knowledge of this language period, mostly of religious contents. Modern Swedish dates from the Reformation, its later period being counted from the publication of the state law in 1734. The Swedish language seems to be based chiefly upon the dialect of Sœdermanland, with influences from other dialects. Among the Scandinavian languages, Swedish ranks next to the Icelandic in point of purity, and is the foremost of them all in point of beauty.

The Swedes are a hardworking, industrious and intelligent race, not fully conscious of their own rich endowment and slow to push their individual claims. In moments of danger and distress, this people give evidence of an active heroism, which offers a great contrast to their usual quiet and peaceful demeanor. The Swedish nation is endowed with an unusual inventive power, which has placed it in the first rank of scientific research, having produced a quota of initiative spirits, as originators, founders and innovators of sciences, which is considerably larger than that of any other modern country, in proportion to the population. The national temperament is, like the soil, composed of extremes. With the serene quiet and almost sullen tranquillity goes a patience of extraordinary endurance which, when it gives in, surprises by the passion which takes its place. To the melancholy trait in the Swedish character is contrasted a great desire for the pleasures of life and exuberant animal spirits. Under a quiet surface, the Swede conceals a rapid comprehension and an almost morbid sensitiveness, sometimes causing people of other nationalities to judge him slow of intellect or perfidious, when he is only slow of action or indisposed to show his feelings. The most valuable inheritance from his ancestors is his moral courage, while the ancient Northern trait of self-restraint is often carried to an extreme. Akin to both is his dignity. He possesses great musical and improvisatorial gifts which complete his lyric-rhetorical temperament.

There are some 6,000 Laplanders and some 20,000 Finns living in the furthest North, and foreigners to the number of about 20,000 dwell in Sweden, mostly Norwegians, Finns and Danes. More than 99 per cent of the population consists of native Swedes, and 99.9 per cent belong to the Lutheran state church or the Protestant denominations.

The principal towns are Stockholm, the capital, with 300,000 inhabitants, enchantingly beautiful in situation, on the mainland and islands at the outlet of Lake Mælar into the Baltic; Gothenburg, with 120,000 inhabitants, the chief commercial centre, at the mouth of the Gotha River, by the North Sea; Malmœ, with 60,000 inhabitants, in Scania, by the Sound. The university towns of Upsala, in Upland, and Lund, in Scania, have 25,000 and 17,000 inhabitants, respectively.

HISTORY OF SWEDEN

CHAPTER I

Sweden in Prehistoric and Early Historic Times—Archæological Finds and Classical Testimony

THE Swedes, although the oldest and most unmixed race in Europe, realized very late the necessity of writing chronicles or reviews of historic events. Thus the names of heroes and kings of the remotest past are helplessly forgotten, and lost also the history of its earliest religion and institutions.

But Mother Earth has carefully preserved most of what has been deposited in her bosom, and has repaid diligent research with trustworthy and irrefutable accounts of the age and various degrees of civilization of the race which inhabited Sweden in prehistoric times. Thus it has been proved that Sweden, like most other countries, has had a Stone Age, a Bronze Age, and an Iron Age. But there is absolutely no evidence to prove the now antiquated theories of various immigrations into Sweden by different races on different stages of civilization. On the contrary, the graves from the remotest times, through all successive periods, prove by the form of the skulls of those buried in them that Sweden has, through all ages, been inhabited by the same dolichocephalic, or long-headed, race which constitutes the overwhelming majority of her people to-day.

Sweden, physically considered, is not of as high antiquity as some countries of Europe. Yet it has been inhabited during the last four thousand years, at least. In the quaternary period the Scandinavian peninsula was a centre of a glacial movement which spread its disastrous influences over Western Russia, Northern Germany and Holland. In that period no vegetable or animal life was possible in Sweden. From the fact that the earliest stone celts found in Sweden and Denmark are not polished, archæologists were led to suppose that the Stone Age of the North was contemporaneous with the Palæolithic civilization in Western Europe. But this standpoint has been found untenable, because it has later become evident that the fauna surrounding the earliest inhabitants of the Northern countries was ours and not a quaternary one.

The oldest types of finds of *the Stone Age* in the North have been discovered in the refuse-heaps on the Danish coast. These refuse-heaps, consisting of stone implements, shells, bones, etc., do not occur in Sweden, but the implements characteristic of them are found scattered over some parts of the southernmost Swedish province of Scania. The shape of these earliest finds is exactly the same as of those of the later Stone Age, the only difference being that the former are not polished. But there are transitions between the classes, and the act of polishing must be regarded as an important phase of progress.

The Stone Age of Sweden is quite remarkable. If the remains of the earlier period are scanty, the finds from the later one are all the more numerous. With the exception of Denmark and a part of North Germany, there is no European country which can boast of such rich and beautiful relics from the later Stone Age as the southern part of

Sweden. The finds in the other countries mentioned are almost exactly like those of Sweden from the Stone and the Bronze Ages, both as far as implements and skulls are concerned, proving them to have been settled by the same race.

The weapons and implements from the Stone Age consist of axes, daggers, spearheads, arrowheads, saws, and knives of flint; axes, gauges, handmills of stone; fishhooks and arrowheads of bone; earthenware, etc., etc. The graves of this period are dolmens, passage-graves, and stone cists, the last mentioned either uncovered or covered with a barrow. The different forms of burial places seem to indicate four successive stages of the period. Through their existence it becomes probable that the inhabitants of Sweden during the Stone Age had fixed dwelling places.

A dolmen is a grave-chamber of which the walls are formed of large, thick stones set up edgewise, covered with one huge block of stone as a roof, all the stones being rough outside and smooth inside. The passage-graves are built in the same way, but are larger and distinguished by a long covered passage leading to it. These graves are surrounded by a low barrow, upon the top of which the huge roof-stones were originally visible. Dolmens and passage-graves occur in Sweden in considerable numbers along the coast of Scania, on the plains of West Gothland and in Bohuslæn, more sparsely in other parts of West Gothland and in Halland, with stray cases of graves of a similar construction in Nerike and Western Sœdermanland. It is important to note the regions in which these graves have been found, for they must be identical with the parts of the earliest settlements. Such graves are also very common in Denmark, while only one has been found in Norway.

The stone cists resemble very much the chamber of a

passage-grave. They are larger and four-sided, and built of somewhat thinner stones. Stone cists standing partly visible above the barrow constitute a form peculiar to Sweden, occurring in great numbers in West Gothland, Bohuslæn, Dalsland and Southwestern Vermland, while the covered stone cists appear in the same provinces and in Nerike, East Gothland, Smaland, Bleking and the Island of Gothland.

During the Stone Age the bodies were buried unburned, in a recumbent or sitting position. By the side of the dead body was usually placed a weapon, a tool, or some ornaments, sometimes also earthenware vessels, now filled only with earth. These vessels may once have contained food. The elaborate graves seem to indicate a belief in a future life. The food, if any such was placed by the side of the dead, would not necessarily point to the fact that such a future life was imagined merely as a continuation of earth life. The heathen Scandinavians of a later age believed that the dead remained for some time in their burial place before reaching their ultimate destination. For their possible wants during this intermediate state food was left with the dead body.

The total number of relics of stone found in Sweden is 64,000. Of these only 4,000 belong to Svealand and Norrland, while of all the rest found in Gothaland 45,000 belong to Scania alone.

In a much later age the Scandinavians were regarded as pure barbarians. For this reason it is important to observe that graves from the Stone Age show that the Swedes in that remote period had several domesticated animals, the dog, horse, ox, swine, sheep, and, perhaps, also the goat. Hence they were certainly a pastoral people, not living exclusively by hunting and fishing. But whether they practiced agriculture cannot be decided in the present state of our knowledge. The fact that the very oldest graves are found in the most fertile districts of Southern Sweden seems to speak in favor of the supposition that agriculture was known and appreciated.

Of metals, even of gold, the people of the late Stone Age were entirely ignorant, also of the art of writing. Hence no monuments of their language will ever be found. Still it is highly probable that the Teutonic ancestors of the Swedes began to settle in the land from the beginning of the Stone Age.

It is true that some skulls, very much like those of the Laps, have also been found in the graves of the Stone Age; but it must be borne in mind that these burial places, impressive through their size and the amount of work and mechanical skill necessary for their erection, can be believed to have been originally intended only for kings or chieftains, and their families. It was probably a custom, as in later heathen times, to bury with such distinguished people a number of slaves, dead or alive. The presence of skulls of a non-Scandinavian type can thus be explained, without the necessity of accepting the theory of an early mixture of two races.

In the northern part of Sweden have been found relics of stone, usually of slate, which do not appear to have belonged to the people of the dolmens or passage-graves. They bear a close resemblance to those found in Finland and in other countries inhabited by Laps, Finns and peoples related to them. This seems to prove that these so-called Arctic stone implements are relics of the Laps and belong to the time when this people was still ignorant of the use of metal. Judging from the number of relics found on the coast, from Westerbotten to Gestrikland, and in Dalecarlia, the Laps dwelt also in somewhat more southerly parts of Sweden than at the present day. So far south as in the middle provinces, no Arctic stone relics have been found, still less in any of the southern provinces. This seems to indicate that the Laps and the Swedes did not dwell in the same parts of the country during the Stone Age, and their intercourse, if any, must have been of a very accidental and casual nature.

That the Stone Age lasted a very long time in the North is proved by the fact that it reached a far higher development there than anywhere else in Europe. The best authorities think that it must have ended rather before than after 1500 B.C., or 3,500 years before our time.

The Bronze Age followed upon the Stone Age. Flint exists in Sweden and was easily found. There are also copper mines, but their working is of comparatively modern date. The copper of the Bronze Age must have been brought from abroad, and tin, necessary for the production of bronze, is foreign to Scandinavia. The knowledge of the working of any metal proves an immense progress. Yet there are strong grounds for the opinion that the beginning of the Bronze Age in Sweden was not connected with any great immigration of a new race, but that the inhabitants learned the art of working bronze by intercourse with other nations. The resemblance of the graves during the last part of the Stone Age and the early part of the Bronze Age points most strongly to such a conclusion. From Asia the knowledge of bronze, and the higher civilization dependent on it, had gradually spread itself over the continent of Europe, in a northerly and northwesterly direction, until it reached the coasts of the Baltic.

The Bronze Age of Sweden began about 1500 B.C., and lasted for a thousand years, or until the beginning of the fifth century before Christ. The period has been divided into an Earlier and a Later Bronze Age, a division which has been questioned as to its absolute correctness. The works from the former are decorated with fine spiral ornaments and zigzag lines. The graves generally contain remains of unburned bodies. The antiquities of the Earlier Bronze Age, almost without an exception, appear to be of native workmanship. They are distinguished by artistic forms and point to a highly developed taste in the working of bronze. They generally surpass in this respect the relics of the Bronze Age found in almost all other European countries. The works belonging to the Later Bronze Age are characterized by a very different taste and style of ornamentation, though even they are often the result of great skill. The spiral ornaments are no longer predominant, but the ends of rings, knife-handles, and the like, are often rolled up in spiral volutes.

During this period the dead were always burned. Buttons, sword-hilts, and other works of bronze were sometimes decorated with pieces of amber and resin inlaid. Objects are also often found overlaid with thin plates of gold.

Remarkable are the rock-carvings from this period. The Swedes of the Bronze Age understood, by a kind of picture-writing, how to preserve the memory of important events, although an alphabet of any kind was unknown. The rock-carvings have been found abundantly in Bohuslæn (formerly a part of West Gothland) and East Gothland, but also occur in Scania and other parts of Sweden. At the time of the arrival of Cortez in Mexico the Aztecs were exactly on the same standpoint. In spite of their high civilization, they were in the Bronze Age and possessed a picture-writing, but were not acquainted with an alphabet. In Sweden, as in Mexico, there certainly once existed an oral tradition necessary for its interpretation, which, now lost, leaves little hope for their present or future explanation. Yet they throw considerable light on Swedish civilization during this remote period. Thus they show that horses were already used for riding and driving. Cattle are represented. In pairs these are harnessed to a plow, which is being driven by a man. Boats are depicted, generally very large ones, without masts, but with thirty pairs of oars or more. They are usually unlike at the two ends, sometimes adorned with an animal's head in the high and narrow stem, sometimes with a similar decoration also in the stern.

The rock-carvings tell us nothing of the dwellings or the dress of the Swedes in the Bronze Age. All the instruments and tools necessary for the construction of wooden houses existed and appear to have been in use. The material was ever abundantly supplied by the Swedish forests, but it was not strong enough to withstand the influence of time. All the more surprising it is that articles of dress from such a remote period as the Earlier Bronze Age, 1000 B.C., should have been preserved to our time. Still such is the case, thanks to a combination of exceptionally favorable circumstances. These garments are of wool of a very simple substance; some have been worn by men, others by women. The man's dress consisted of an unbrimmed cap of thick woven wool, a wide circular mantle, a kind of tunic, kept together with a woollen belt, and some narrow strips of wool which probably covered the legs. In a man's grave was found a shawl of wool with fringes. The woman's dress consisted then, as it does now, chiefly of two garments, a jacket with sleeves and a long robe, the latter held together with a belt of wool, ending in ornamental tassels. Large mantles, of mixed wool and cow hair, were used as wraps. The women wore splendid bronze ornaments, such as finger-rings, bracelets, torques and brooches. From the finds it becomes apparent that many women in those days carried weapons, a dagger often being found at the side of the body.

Besides swords and axes of beautiful workmanship, fish-hooks, sickles and the different parts of harness have been found; also vessels of gold or bronze, evidently used for temple service. The Swedes of the Bronze Age were not acquainted with the art of forging the heated metal, but they possessed much technical skill in the art of casting. When the implement was taken out of the mold it was dipped in cold water, and very often the surface was ornamented by means of punches made of bronze. Their good taste was as highly developed as their skill. That the work was done in the North is proven by numerous finds of the very molds in which weapons and agricultural implements were cast. During the Stone Age only Gothaland and parts of Svealand were inhabited. The finds of the Bronze Age prove that the limits of the population were about the same during this period. The southern provinces continued to be the more thickly settled. Twenty times as many finds have been made in the soil of Scania as in the rest of the country. Norrland was hardly settled to any extent until the Iron Age, and has offered comparatively few finds from the Bronze Age, the total of which for the whole of Sweden amounts to about 4,000.

The Iron Age followed upon the Bronze Age. It lasts to this very day, we ourselves still living in the Iron Age; but the term is generally applied to that part of the period which commences with the close of the Bronze Age, and ends with the fall of heathendom. During the Iron Age, the Swedes first became acquainted with iron, silver, brass, lead, glass, stamped coins from foreign lands, and learned how to solder and gild metal. Archæologists have divided the period into two main parts, the Earlier and the Later Iron Age, both with subdivisions. The Earlier Iron Age includes the time from the fifth century B.C. to about the beginning of the fifth century A.D. The first half of the Earlier Iron Age is characterized by swords with both blades and sheaths made of iron, thin crescent-shaped knives, brooches of iron, collars, and decorative plates overlaid with bronze. The graves resemble those from the end of the Bronze Age, containing burned bones in urns, or laid together in a heap. This circumstance makes it more than probable that the first introduction of iron in the North was not connected with any immigration of a new people. The finds of the earliest Iron Age are not very rich, but they prove that the people who have left them behind had been subjected to a very strong influence from the Gallic tribes living close to the south of the Teutonic area of population. Then came the second half of the Earlier Iron Age, characterized by a strong Roman influence. It commences with the extension of the Roman empire toward the North, about the beginning of the Christian era, and winds up with the beginning of the fifth century, when Teutonic migrations and invasions put an end to the power of Rome. In the hostile or friendly relations between Romans and Teutons the Swedes were not involved. But by the peaceful ways of commerce the influence of Rome penetrated to the people of the North. Great numbers of Roman coins have been found in Sweden, and also vessels of bronze and glass, weapons, etc., as well as works of art, all turned out of workshops in Rome or its provinces. Out of about 4,760 Roman coins of this time found in Sweden, no less than 4,000 were found in the remarkable Island of Gothland, in the southern half of the Baltic, 90 in the neighboring island of Œland, 650 in Scania, but only 23 on the mainland of Sweden, excluding Scania. About 250 were found in Bornholm, 600 in Denmark, but only 3 in Norway. It becomes evident from these finds that there existed a regular traffic over the Baltic, through Germany, between the Island of Gothland and the Roman provinces, from the epoch of the Marcomannic war down to the time of Septimius Severus. Similar finds have been made on the southern shore of the Baltic, showing that the traffic came from the southeast, along the valleys of the Vistula and the Oder.

One of the most important discoveries of this period was the art of writing, which the inhabitants of the North seem to have acquired soon after the beginning of the Christian era. The earliest alphabetic symbols in Sweden, and the only ones used there during the whole of heathen times, were *runes*. These were probably invented a little before the Christian era by a South Teutonic tribe, in imitation of the Roman writing which the Teutons received from one of the Celtic tribes living just to the north of the Alps. The Roman characters were adapted for the use of inscriptions in stone and wood, the curves being changed into straight lines. The Runic characters, in use among all Teutonic tribes, were twenty-four in number; these older runes were, by the Scandinavians, later simplified and reduced to sixteen. There is a number of inscriptions in older runes in Sweden, dating from about 300 to 500 A.D. They are found chiefly on stones and gold bracteates, also in England, France, Germany, Wallachia and the west of Russia. All belong to about the same date, and are of Teutonic origin. The early Runic inscriptions do not contain any accounts of historically known persons or events. Yet they are of the greatest historical importance, for they show that during the Earlier Iron Age, in the fourth and fifth centuries, the language of Sweden, and consequently also the people, were Teutonic. These inscriptions in Sweden and neighboring countries give samples of the earliest known form of the Northern language, which is considerably different from its descendants, the Old Swedish, Danish, Norwegian and Icelandic, but very much resembling the language spoken by the Goths on the Danube during the same period.

The Later Iron Age commences with the fifth century and stretches to the beginning of the eighth century A.D. When Italy had been overrun by the "barbarians," the centre of the old civilization shifted to Byzantium, and there are many traces of an active intercourse with the capital of the Byzantine rule in the finds made in Swedish soil. Most of these finds consist of gold coins of the fifth century, the majority of them having been found in the islands of Œland and Gothland. The stream of gold coming from Byzantium must have been quite considerable, having its source in the tribute which many of the Byzantine emperors had to pay to the Goths on the Danube.

They are the very same emperors whose names appear on the coins found in Sweden. The great number of costly and beautiful ornaments of gold found in Sweden, and dating from this period, must have been made out of Roman and Byzantine coins, melted down. One of the largest hoards of gold ever found in Europe was discovered in the Swedish province of Sœdermanland. Its weight was twenty-seven pounds, and it contained several ornaments of consummate workmanship.

Remarkable are the graves from this period, discovered in the province of Upland. They are barrows containing the more or less mouldering remains of a large boat in which the dead man has been buried unburned with his weapons, horses, and other domestic animals. The swords found in these graves are of iron with hilts of beautiful designs in gilded or enamelled bronze. The shields and helmets are often of elaborate workmanship. Unlike the swords, which mostly, or perhaps always, are of foreign, generally of Celtic make, these ornaments and weapons are of domestic origin.

It appears, from the many beautiful and artistic finds in Swedish soil, as if the inhabitants have benefited by their situation, aside and outside of the rest of the world. Continual migrations subjected the tribes of the continent to repeated changes and to a never-ceasing series of new and heterogeneous impressions. The tribes of the North remained on the same spot, and their whole development was slower but more consistent. The foreign influences penetrated slowly and gradually, without crushing the old civilization. The industrial arts blossomed not so often in the North as in the South, but steadier, giving a clearer expression of the national traditions and peculiarities.

These circumstances make the study of Northern antiquities of absorbing interest.

Before the end of this period, not only Gothaland and Svealand, but also the coast of Norrland, as far north as the province of Medelpad, were inhabited. As a whole, the first part of the Later Iron Age forms a transition between the Earlier Iron Age and the Viking Age, the archæological finds of which we must leave aside to take up the threads of the earliest history. The Viking Age is exceedingly rich in stones with inscriptions in the later runes, some of these inscriptions being quite lengthy, and containing strophes of alliterative verse in Old Swedish.

Before entering into an account of early Swedish history, let us gather what information the classical writers of history have to give in regard to the countries of the North, or rather whatever of such information that has been preserved to our day.

The Scandinavian countries are for the first time mentioned by the historians of antiquity in an account of a journey which Pyteas from Massilia (the present Marseille) made through Northern Europe, about 300 B.C. He visited Britain, and there heard of a great country, Thule, situated six days' journey to the north, and verging on the Arctic Sea. The inhabitants in Thule were an agricultural people who gathered their harvest into big houses for threshing, on account of the very few sunny days and the plentiful rain in their regions. From corn and honey they prepared a beverage (probably the mead). By Thule is no doubt meant the Scandinavian peninsula, or rather the western coast of it. Pyteas also tells of the land of amber, or the southern shores of the Baltic, where the *guttones* are dwelling. As the northern and southern shores of the Baltic from the very earliest period seem to have been inhabited by the same race which has shared the same development and civilization, there is every reason to recognize the name *guttones* as identical with the one given to the inhabitants of the Swedish Gothaland and Island of Gothland.

Several centuries pass without any notice of Scandinavia in the classical literature. In the still preserved manuscripts of the geographical work by Pomponius Mela, written in the middle of the first century A.D., is found a reference to Codania, a large and fertile island inhabited by Teutons. Codania is likely some scribe's misspelling of Scandinavia.

Pliny the Elder, who himself visited the shores of the Baltic in the first century after Christ, is the first to mention plainly the name of Scandinavia. He says that he has received advices of immense islands "recently discovered from Germany." The most famous of the many islands situated in the Codanian Bay was Scandinavia, of as yet unexplored size; the known parts were inhabited by a people called *hilleviones*, who gave it the name of another world. When he speaks of the British isles, Pliny again gives notice of islands, situated opposite Britain in the Teutonic Sea, without suspecting their identity with Scandinavia. He mentions Scandia, Nerigon, the largest of them all, and Thule. Scandia and Scandinavia are only different forms of the same name, denoting the southernmost part of the peninsula, and is yet preserved in the name of the province of Scania. Nerigon stands for Norway, the northern part of which is mentioned as an island by the name Thule. It is not surprising to find the classical writers ignorant of the fact that Scandinavia was not a group of large islands, but one great peninsula, as the northern parts were as yet uninhabited and their physical connection with Finland and Russia unknown.

Tacitus is the first who mentions the Swedish name. In his work "Germania," of such great importance for the knowledge of the ancient Teutons, their conditions and institutions, and written about 100 years after Christ, the Baltic is described as an open sea called the Süevian Sea, shut out from the west by the Danish mainland of Jutland, by the Romans called the Cimbric Peninsula. The eastern shore is the country of amber. The Swedes are by Tacitus called Suiones, and he speaks of them thus:

"Next occur the communities of the Suiones, seated in the very sea, who, besides their strength in men and arms, also possess a naval force. The form of their vessels differs from ours in having a prow at each end, so that they are always ready to advance. They make no use of sails, nor have they regular benches of oars at the sides: they row, as is practiced in some rivers, without order, sometimes on one side, sometimes on the other, as occasion requires. These people honor wealth; for which reason they are subject to monarchial government, without any limitations or precarious conditions of allegiance. Nor are arms allowed to be kept promiscuously, as among the other Teutonic nations: but are committed to the charge of a keeper, and he, too, a slave. The pretext is that the sea defends them from any sudden incursions, and men unemployed, with arms in their hands, readily become licentious. In fact, it is for the king's interest not to intrust a noble, a freeman, or even an emancipated slave, with the custody of arms."

These remarks by Tacitus, in all their brevity, are of great importance. Boats, exactly corresponding to the description as given, have been found in Swedish graves of this period, and that they were used for river traffic, to bring the gold and products of Rome and Byzantium up the Vistula and Oder, is evident. The great opulence in dress and temple service of which the archæological finds bear witness, and of which later writers also speak as characteristic of the Swedes, is a proof of the wealth that at all times has attended naval dominion. Thus far all the statements being fully corroborated, one cannot but place great importance upon those that follow. The Roman historian tells us that, on account of the honor which the Swedes held for wealth, they were subject to a monarchial government, without any limitations; that is, the crown was hereditary, not elective. This coincides in every way with Swedish conditions of political affairs, such as we know them from later times. The important conclusions to be gathered from the statements of Tacitus, are that the Swedes already at the dawn of the Christian era held the political supremacy in the Scandinavian peninsula, or at least in its eastern and southern parts, and that the various lesser communities stood in allegiance to the hereditary king of the Sviar (Svear), or Swedes in a limited sense, the inhabitants of Svealand.

The psychological conclusions made by Tacitus, on the basis of his own statements, hold good of the Swedes of to-day as well as of those of 2,000 years ago. They still honor wealth and a monarchial government and consider the sea their best defence against foreign foes.

Ptolemy, the Alexandrine geographer of the second century after Christ, speaks of the Scandinavian islands, situated east of the Cimbrian peninsula. The fourth and most easterly of these is the one originally called Scandeia.

He enumerates six tribes which inhabit it, the names being unrecognizable, except the one of Gutai, Gauts or Goths, by him for the first time mentioned as dwelling in Scandinavia.

To this information, gathered from classical authors, nothing is added for the next four hundred years in regard to the countries of the North. Only in the sixth century, when Rome has succumbed before the Gothic invasions, and the Teutonic tribes have divided between themselves the provinces of the West Roman empire, new information about Sweden is given by a Byzantine author, Prokopios, a contemporary of emperor Justinian. He mentions Scandinavia by the name Thule, and says he bases his statements upon information obtained from people "who come from there."

Prokopios says that in the immense island of Thule, in the northern part of which the midnight sun can be seen, thirteen large tribes occupy its inhabitable parts, each tribe having its own king. One of the largest tribes is the Gauts (the Gœtar, or the inhabitants of Swedish Gothaland). These tribes very much resemble the people of southern Europe, with the exception of the Skee Finns, who dress in skins and live from the chase.

Prokopios tells a remarkable story about an immigration to Sweden of Herulians, a Teutonic tribe closely connected to the Goths on the Danube. In the beginning of the sixth century, it happened that the Herulians, after an unsuccessful war with the Longobardians, were divided into two branches, of which the one received land from the emperor Anastasius south of the Danube, while the other made a resolve to seek a home in the Scandinavian peninsula. When they had passed the Slavs, they came to uninhabited regions, whence they continued to the country of the Varinians, and later to that of the Danes. The Danes granted them a free passage and the use of ships, in which they crossed to the island of Thule. Here the Herulians went to the Gauts and were well received by them. Some decades later the Herulians in South Europe were in want of a king. They resolved to send messengers to their kinsmen who had settled in Sweden, hoping that some descendant of their old royal family might be found there who was willing to assume the dignity of king among them. The messengers returned with two brothers who belonged to the ancient family of rulers, and these were escorted by two hundred young Herulians from Sweden. That this immigration really took place there is no doubt. The district of Sweden where these kinsmen of the Goths settled was early distinguished from the surrounding ones, inhabited by the Gauts of Sweden, through the peculiarities of its laws and customs, of which some survived into the commencement of the nineteenth century. This district forms the southern part of the province of Smaland, called Værend, its inhabitants Virdar, and the adjoining province of Bleking.

The Gothic historian Jordanes, or Jornandes, called Master Ardan, who was a contemporary of Prokopios, has taken upon himself to explain the reason of the strange resolve of the Herulians to seek a home in Sweden. He speaks of the traditions of the East Goths, which tell of their descent from the people of the North. Similar traditions also have existed among the West Goths, Longobardians, Gepidæ, Burgundians, Herulians, Franks, Saxons, Swabians and Alemannians. Thus Jordanes: "In the North there is a great ocean, and in this ocean there is a large island called Scandza, out of whose loins our race burst forth like a swarm of bees and spread over Europe." The island of Scandza, he says, has been *officina gentium, vagina nationum*—the source of races, the mother of nations. And thence also the Goths have emigrated.

Material is lacking to prove the historical truth of the Teutonic traditions which point to Scandinavia as the cradle of the Teutonic tribes. But Jordanes, the first historian of Teutonic birth who speaks of Scandinavia, stands at the cradle of Swedish history, and, as a modern historian has expressed it, his shadow throws an umbrage across the whole field of Swedish historical research. The mistake, based upon Jordanes' history, of identifying the Swedish Gauts with the Goths has caused a great deal of mischief and ridiculous chauvinism, Gothic and Swedish history and royal lines being mixed up or put in connection with each other.

In leaving aside the Teutonic traditions of the island of Scandza, or Scania, as the cradle of the race, let us quote a remark by Tacitus which seems to point to the conclusion that such traditions were current already in the first century of the Christian era: "I should think that the Teutons themselves are aborigines, and not at all mixed through immigrations or connections with non-Teutonic tribes. For those desiring to change homes did not in early times come by land, but in ships across the boundless and, so to speak, hostile ocean—a sea seldom visited by ships from the Roman world."

The Old English poem of Beowulf must also be mentioned among the sources which throw light on early Swedish history. Whether the Geátas of Beowulf are identical with the Jutes of Denmark, or with the Gauts of Sweden, is a much disputed question. Although, phonetically, the Old English name Geátas corresponds to the Old Swedish *Gautar*, it seems most plausible to suppose that by this term is meant the Jutes, and not the inhabitants of Swedish West or East Gothland. This accepted, the poem does not contain much about the Swedes. But the information, therein given, of the Swedish kings is of great value, because it renders the service of a firm chronological support to the facts gathered from another source. This source, of vastly greater importance, is the Ynglinga Saga, or rather the poem around which it is spun, in Heimskringla, of which more in the next chapter.

The first information of the religion practiced by the inhabitants of Scandinavia is given by Prokopios, who says that they worshipped many gods and spirits of the sky, air, earth, sea, and also some who were supposed to dwell in springs and rivers. Offerings were constantly made, the chief ones being of human beings, for which the first prisoner made in a war was destined. This sacrifice was made to "Mars," who was the highest god. The statements of Prokopios without doubt are correct. The Scandinavian war-god who corresponds to the Mars of classical mythology was Tyr. Odin, originally the ruler of the wind, became the highest god during the Viking Age. He is an aristocratic god, the god of the select few, whose cult succeeded that of Tyr as the cult of the latter had succeeded that of Thor, the thunderer, as the highest god. The idea of a supreme God was probably unknown until the contact with Christianity, or at least not common. Thor, the peasant god, is probably the oldest of the gods of Teutonic mythology, the representative of stern power and law-bound order. Thor was the most popular god of the Swedes, to judge from the great number of ancient Swedish proper names of which his forms a part. Besides Thor, Odin and Frey were the most honored. All the other gods and goddesses mentioned in Old Norse literature were probably known, but few of them much worshipped in Sweden.

CHAPTER II

Dawn of Swedish History—Heimskringla and Ynglingatal

SNORRE STURLESON, the great historian and poet of Iceland, of the earlier half of the thirteenth century, is considered to be the author of the history of the kings of Norway which, after the first words of the first chapter, has been called Heimskringla. As an introduction to the work he has put the saga of the Yngling kings of Sweden, of whom many of the Norwegian kings were supposed to be descendants. The Ynglinga Saga is a paraphrase to the much older song of Ynglingatal, a poem composed by the Norwegian poet Thiodulf of Hvin (who lived in the latter part of the ninth century) in praise of the supposed Swedish ancestors of the Norwegian king Ragnvald. The Ynglings were probably not identical with the kings of Upsala, who were of the race of the Skilfings, but of South Swedish or Danish origin. It is either out of ignorance, or out of sagacity, that the poet selected the Upsala rulers as originators of the Norwegian line of kings, but he has been unfortunate in the choice of a name for the dynasty. The poem itself is a trustworthy historical document, at least as far as the times are concerned which come comparatively close to the time of its own composition, the first part containing many traits of a mythical character. The saga spun around it is far from trustworthy. Of the poem evidently the first, or first few, strophes are missing, but the "historian" supplies the vacuum with stories of the gods Odin, Niord and Frey, whom he, according to the ideas of his time, changes from gods into historic kings, the first who ruled Svithiod (Sweden). Among learned men in Snorre's day there was a craze for tracing the pedigree of all nations of any renown back to some of the heroes of ancient Troy. Snorre serves us a saga of Odin's migration from Troy which, besides being confuse, would appear only ridiculous, if it had not wielded about as highly disastrous an influence upon correct conceptions of Swedish history as the work by Jordanes. This migration saga is found in a still more elaborate form in an introduction to Snorre's Edda, and is responsible for the erroneous opinion held by earlier Swedish historians, that the Swedes had migrated from Asia under the leadership of a chief who called himself Odin, and that the Swedes and the Gauts were, if not of different origin, at least of a habitation of differing age, in their present locations.

Based upon the information found in Ynglinga Saga we will give a review of the history of the early kings of Sweden, although the first dozen, and more, of these kings are of a doubtful "historic" character. At the dawn of history, Sweden was, like most other countries of Northern Europe, divided into petty communities, each ruled by a king. These communities seem to have been nearly identical with the "lands" or later provinces into which Sweden is yet divided, although the administrative divisions are different. In spite of the fact that it is about 1,200 years since these communities were united into one single realm, the inhabitants preserve to this day their respective peculiarities of customs and language.

The most important among the chieftains of Sweden was, since time immemorial, the king of Upsala, who conducted the sacrifices and temple service at Upsala, the oldest and most celebrated place of heathen worship in the Scandinavian North. Originally, he had under his rule only one-third of the present province of Upland, the chief settlement of the Sviar, or Swedes in a limited sense. The Upsala kings belonged to the ancient royal race of Skilfings (or "Ynglings," according to Snorre), who traced their origin from the gods. The founder of the dynasty as accepted by Thiodulf and others was *Yngve*, who is said to have built the great temple at Upsala, moving thither the capital from the older Sigtuna and contributing to the temple all his lands and riches. Yngve's son was *Fiolner*. King Fiolner was drowned by accident in a huge vessel full of mead, during a visit paid to King Frode in Denmark.

His son *Sveigder* disappeared during a journey which he made in order to find Odin, the old. Both the names Fiolner and Sveigder appear to be mythical. Sveigder's son *Vanlande* was a great warrior. He is said once to have taken up his winter abode in Finland, which, together with several archæological finds, point to an early intercourse between Sweden and Finland. *Visbur* succeeded his father Vanlande, marrying the daughter of Aude (the Rich), whom he afterward left and took another wife, bringing on himself a curse by so doing. Visbur's sons fell unexpectedly over him, burning him in his house. *Domalde*, his son, succeeded him. During a great famine in Svithiod he was offered to the gods in order to obtain good seasons. Domalde's son and grandson, *Domar* and *Dygve*, both reigned and died in peace. *Dag*, the son of Dygve, was so wise a man that he understood the language of birds. *Agne*, the son of Dag, was the ruler after him. One summer he invaded Finland with his army. When the Finns gathered there was a great battle, in which Agne gained victory, subduing all Finland. The daughter of a conquered chief, Skialf, was carried back to Sweden as his bride. But after a drinking feast, Agne was hanged in a tree by Skialf and her men. The place where this happened was called Agnefit, and is said to be identical with the site of Stockholm, the later capital of the country. *Alrek* and *Eric* became kings after the death of their father Agne. They got into a dispute one day while out walking. Having no weapons, they assailed and killed each other with their horses' bridles. Their successors, *Yngve* and *Alf*, the sons of Alrek, shared a similar fate, killing each other in the royal hall by the high-seat. After them *Hugleik*, the son of Alf, became king of the Swedes. On the Fyrisvols, the plains by the river Fyris in Upland, Hugleik was killed in battle against a famous sea-king Hake, who subdued the country and became king of Svithiod. The saga mentions that this Hake was a brother of Hagbard, whose love for the king's daughter, Signe, cost him his life. This love story is one of the most famous in the North and much spoken of in saga and song. The spot where Hagbard was hanged in a tree is still pointed out. When Hake had ruled as king for three years, *Jorund* and *Eric*, the sons of Yngve, returned with warships and warriors. They had grown up and become famous by conquering the king Gudlaug, of the Haleygians in Norway, whom they had met in Denmark.

Now they met King Hake and his army at the Fyrisvols. In the battle, Eric was killed and Jorund fled to his ship. But King Hake was himself so grievously wounded that he ordered a warship to be loaded with his dead men and their weapons, and himself to be placed upon it. The sails were hoisted and the ship set on fire, and out it flew, with the dying king on board, between the skerries to the sea. Jorund now became king in Upsala. When he was one summer marauding in Jutland, he met a son of King Gudlaug, in the battle with whom he was overpowered, captured and hanged.

King *Aune* or *Ane* was the son of Jorund. He was a wise man who made great sacrifices to the gods. Being no warrior he lived quietly at home. Twice he fled from Upsala, on account of Danish invasions, remaining in West Gothland twenty-five years each time, and holding sway at Upsala for an equally long time between his periods of exile. He lived to become 110 years of age. The secret of his longevity was that he sacrificed one of his sons to Odin every tenth year, and was granted in return a decade of prolonged life. When about to sacrifice his tenth son, the people interfered, and he died from old age. The last ten years of his life he was very feeble, drinking out of a horn like an infant. He was buried in a mound at Upsala.

King *Egil* was the son of Ane, and, like his father, no warrior. Under his reign and that of his son, king *Ottar*, Sweden suffered a good deal of trouble from Denmark. The Danish king Frode had helped Egil against the revolt of one of his subjects, and demanded from his son a scat, or tribute, in return. Ottar fell in battle against the jarls of Frode. Both he and his son *Audils*, who ruled Svithiod after him, are mentioned in Beowulf as Ôhthere and his son Eadgils of the royal Swedish line of the Scylfingas (Skilfings). This fact gives to Swedish history its first reliable date. The Danish king Hugleik, a contemporary of King Ottar, died in 515 A.D., which renders with a certainty Ottar's reign as falling in the first part of the sixth century. Audils ruled for a long time and often went on viking expeditions to Saxonland, Denmark and Norway. In Saxonland, Audils captured the household of King Geirthiof, among whom was a remarkably beautiful girl, called Yrsa. The king married her, but she was afterward taken to Denmark by King Helge of Leire after a successful plundering expedition in Svithiod. Helge had a son by her, Rolf Krake, but Yrsa returned to her first husband, after being told by Queen Alof, the wife of Geirthiof, that Helge was her father and Alof her mother. When Rolf Krake later became king his men once helped King Audils in one of his expeditions in Norway. King Rolf's men did not receive the compensation promised them, and Rolf came to Upsala to demand it for them. King Rolf was warned by his mother Yrsa that Audils was not well disposed, and he and his men made in haste for their ships. King Audils and his men started out in their pursuit. Then Rolf took a horn filled with gold, a recent gift of his mother, emptying its contents on the plain. Audils and his men stopped to pick up the gold, and Rolf thus made his escape. Rolf Krake is one of the most famous of Danish heroes. In the poetic language of the Old Northern literature, gold is often called "the seed of the Fyrisvols" or "Rolf Krake's seed." As King Audils once rode around the hall at a sacrifice his horse stumbled and fell, and the king was killed.

Eystein, the son of Audils, ruled after him and was succeeded by his son *Yngvar*. Eystein was never able to defend his people against the Danes, while Yngvar was a successful warrior, both at home and abroad. But one summer when he was fighting in Esthonia he was killed by the Esthonians. He was buried in a mound close to the seashore.

Anund was Yngvar's son and successor. He went to Esthonia to avenge his father, ravaging the country and returning with great booty. In his time there were fruitful seasons in Svithiod. On this account, and because he made many roads, cleared the woods and cultivated the new land, he became one of the most popular of early Swedish kings. He was called *Brœt-Anund*, viz., Anund Roadmaker.

Ingiald, the son of Anund, became king in Upsala after his father. He was the most remarkable of all the Ynglings (Skilfings), for, through violence and cunning, he united all the communities of Sweden into one realm. When his father died, the king at Upsala was certainly the supremely powerful ruler in Svithiod, but not the only one, for there were many district-kings who were to a great extent independent. There were not only kings in East Gothland, Sœdermanland, and Nerike, but in Upland there were, besides the Upsala king, also kings in each of the three "lands" into which this province was formerly divided; viz., Tiundaland, Attundaland, and Fiedrundaland. Ingiald ordered a great feast to celebrate the fact that he had come to the throne after his father, and invited seven other kings, all of whom were present, except Granmar, king of Sœdermanland. When the Brage-bowl, on which promises were made, was carried in, King Ingiald made a solemn vow to enlarge his dominions by one-half, toward all the four corners of the world, or die. In the evening Ingiald set fire to the hall, and all the six royal guests perished with their followers. Ingiald took possession of all the dominions belonging to the unfortunate kings. In the next year he surrounded the hall in which King Granmar found himself at the time, killing him and taking his land in possession. "It was a common saying," Snorre tells us, "that King Ingiald had killed twelve kings and deceived them all under pretence of peace; therefore he was called Ingiald Illrade (the evil-adviser)." His daughter, Asa, was of the same disposition as her father. She was married to Gudrod, king of Scania, but had to flee from the land after having caused the death of her husband and his brother. When it was learned that King Ivar, nephew of Gudrod, had entered Svithiod with an army, Asa counselled her father to set fire to the hall of the king after his men were drunk and asleep. Thus perished Ingiald Illrade with his daughter, very much in the same fashion in which he had killed so many of the petty kings.

For the centuries following upon Ingiald's death, Snorre has a very short, or almost no account to give about Sweden and her rulers. What can be gathered from other sources, principally from late Icelandic sagas, is not trustworthy, mythical and fictitious elements being discernible.

After Ingiald, *Ivar Vidfamne* (the Far-stretching) is said to have ruled Sweden, "also Denmark, Saxonland, all of Austria and one-fifth of England." One account has it that Ivar was the head of a new dynasty in Sweden. As he was originally king of Scania, perhaps these were the real Ynglings. Another source claims for the succeeding Swedish kings descent from the old race of the Ynglings (viz., the Skilfings). Ingiald's son Olof, according to Snorre, fled to the woods of Vermland, until then uninhabited, and later came to Norway. But it is a misunderstanding of Thiodulf's lines which causes Snorre to say that King Olof was buried close by the Lake Venar, in Vermland. The province of Vermland was inhabited much earlier than in Olof's time, and the Olof who became the founder of a Norwegian dynasty was probably a Danish prince.

Harald Hildetand of Denmark is said to have succeeded Ivar, and to have ruled over as much territory as his mother's father. Several sources speak of King Harald and the battle of Bravols, in which his life was ended and which battle generally is taken as a historic milestone, marking the opening of the Viking Age. It was fought somewhere about the year 740. King Harald had become old and almost blind. In Svithiod and West Gothland, the kings Sigurd and Ring (by the sagas made into one hero by the name "Sigurd Ring") ruled under Harald, while he reigned himself over Denmark and East Gothland. The relations were good at first, but their aspect soon changed. After great preparations on either side, Ring met Harald on the plains of Bravik in East Gothland. The battle was a long and bloody one and the most renowned in song and saga. King Harald, too old to take an active part, mounted a chariot, which carried him into the midst of the fight. When King Ring at last saw the chariot empty, he understood that the aged king had fallen and gave the sign that the battle should come to an end. King Ring caused the remains of his fallen foe to be burned with great pomp and ceremony on a pile with his horse, weapons and many a costly treasure of gold and silver. King *Ring* was said to have been ruler of Sweden and Denmark after King Harald. The sagas mention the hero, *Ragnar Lodbrok,* as his son and successor. While this great viking and sea-king appears to have been a historic personage in the earlier half of the ninth century, it is impossible that he could have been identical with King Ring's son *Ragnar*, or that he or his sons ever were kings in Upsala or Sweden.

With the first attempts to introduce Christianity into Sweden (of which more later) a more definite knowledge of Swedish rulers and conditions is gained. When Ansgar, the apostle of Sweden, visited the country for the first time, about 830, the ruling king was *Biœrn*. Shortly afterward King *Anund* is mentioned. He fled from his land, but was reinstated with the help of the Danes. King *Olof* was on the throne at the time of Ansgar's second visit to Sweden, about 850. These kings must have been of the same family as those who held the throne up to the middle of the eleventh century, for their names all occur again in the line of later Swedish kings, the reigns of whom fall in the broad light of history.

We have seen how Ingiald Illrade joined the various communities into one single realm. Although there is doubt whether this realm from the start embraced all Sweden, there is no historical evidence or any reliable traditions whatever to show that Sweden was ever divided into smaller kingdoms after the death of King Ingiald. When Ansgar reaches Sweden he travels through half of the country in order to reach the commercial centre of Birka, where the king of Sweden is dwelling. No other king, great or petty, is spoken of, while the contemporary Icelanders mention jarls (earls) in Gothaland, which proves that the once independent kings in that district were made away with.

Of particular importance is the account of a journey

which a certain Wulfstan made to the North, at the close of the ninth century. This account is given in an Old English translation of Orosii Historia, credited to King Alfred of England. Thus it runs: "Wulfstan said that he went from Schleswig to Truso in seven days, that the ship was all the way running under sail. Wendland was on his right, but Langeland, Lolland, Falster and Scania on his left, and all these lands belong to Denmark, and then Bornholm was on our left, which has a king of its own. Then after Bornholm, the lands of Bleking, Mœre, Œland, and Gotland, were first on our left, and these lands belong to Sweden."

Wulfstan's account, besides furnishing evidence to prove the political consolidation of Sweden, also gives a good idea of the size of the country in this period. The once independent province of Scania, which had kings of its own, already belongs to Denmark. So does also the province of Halland, while Bohuslæn belongs to Norway. Dal and Vermland are contested provinces between the kings of Sweden and Norway, while great parts of Norrland are yet uninhabited, except by Laps, who ramble from one place to another, without a fixed dwelling place. In King Alfred's Orosius, Danish Jutland and Swedish Gautland (Gothaland) are alike called *Gotland*, which recalls the supposition of the majority of modern scholars that Gotland was in the earliest times the common Teutonic name of the North, and Goths the common name of its Teutonic inhabitants.

CHAPTER III

The Viking Age—Ansgar, the Apostle of Sweden

"IN the North there is a great ocean, and in this ocean there is a large island called Scandza, out of whose loins our race burst forth like a swarm of bees and spread over Europe." These were the words the Gothic historian Jordanes put on parchment, inspired by the popular traditions of a Teutonic migration from the North. Historic evidence is lacking to prove or disprove the truth of these words. But they may be applied to the phenomenon which has given its name to the *Viking Age*.

The Viking expeditions seem to stand in connection with the great Teutonic migrations, at least to be related to them in nature. The Teutons of the North were not directly affected by the migrations, but at the close of the eighth century the same restlessness and desire of expansion appear to have taken possession of the Northmen as in earlier times of their relatives in more southerly lands. And it was a timely move, for the energy and strength with which these had in their time suffused Europe were dying out. Europe was in need of new blood and iron to wake her from her anæmia and to build up new institutions. The North was freed from a turbulent and lawless element and was brought in closer contact than ever before with the learning and culture of the world. For centuries the Northmen had through their southern kinsmen been in contact with continental culture. But now they came out to see for themselves, to make themselves a place in a wider and richer world, or to bring home from there what they most desired of beauty, riches and culture. They were not delicate as to means. Violence was with them as natural as their freedom of individuality was indispensable. Yet they were to play a most important part in the cultural development of Europe, furnishing her with institutions of imperishable iron and changing the darkness of the Middle Ages into an era of chivalry in spirit and in deeds.

The Viking expeditions were always undertaken by free men, and were in the North, from remotest times, considered not only an honest but an honorable occupation. Slaves and freed men were excluded. The leaders—often kings or their sons—were always men of noble descent or of importance. As the Viking expeditions took on larger proportions, they became more and more organized; from random expeditions, undertaken by individuals, they developed into national undertakings, led by the king or his chieftains, not for a pastime, but in completion of a national policy. On account of this latest aspect, it is but just to divide the field in which the Northmen were active according to their respective nationalities. With such a division applied, the Viking expeditions to the West, to Britain, France, Portugal and Spain do not pertain to Swedish history, for they were planned and undertaken principally by Danes and Norwegians. It is true that there were many Swedish participants also in these expeditions, as the sagas and the memorial stones on Swedish soil tell us; also true that some of the later Swedish provinces, like Bohuslæn[1] and Scania, sent out their large contingents of Vikings and sea-kings to the West, and that one of the oldest Swedish homes of culture, West Gothland, had an appropriate channel to the West, by way of the mighty Gotha River, through which without doubt many a Viking expedition was sent; yet the leaders were in a majority of cases Danish or Norwegian chieftains. For similar reasons the Viking expeditions to the East belong by right to Swedish history. In them the participants and chieftains were Swedes, to an overwhelming majority, and, from time immemorial, Swedish districts from which the expeditions were started.

To Russia the Swedes first went on marauding expeditions; but after the countries of the North had been shaped into three large monarchies, they came to Russia upon special invitation, in order to found there a realm of strong and consistent government. This becomes evident from the testimony of the Russian historian Nestor, a monk in Kief, who lived in the latter part of the eleventh century. About the founding of the Russian empire by the Swedes he has the following remarkable statements:

"In the year 6367 (after the creation of the world, which is the 859th after the birth of Christ) the Variagi (or Varangians) came across the sea, taking tribute from the Tchud and the Slavs," etc.—"In the year 6370 (862 A.D.) they chased the Variagi back across the sea, giving them no tribute and commencing to govern themselves, but it turned out badly with legal affairs, tribe rose against tribe, caus-

---

[1] The ancient name of this province, Viken, probably is the key to the disputed etymology of the word *Viking*.

ing strife, and a rebellion was started. Then they said between themselves: 'Let us seek a prince who will govern us and reason with us justly!' And they went across the sea to the Variagi, to the Russians, for thus were the Variagi called, just as others were called Sviar, others Nurmanni, others Anglii, and others Goths. And the Tchudi (the Slavs of Novgorod), the Slavs, the Krivitchi and the Vessi said to the Russians, 'Our land is great and fruitful, but it lacks order and justice; come and take possession, and govern us!' And three brothers with their followers were selected, and they took the whole of Rus with them and came. And the oldest, Rurik, took his abode in Novgorod, the second, Sineus, his in Bielo-Jesero, and the third, his in Isborsk; his name was Truvor. After two years Sineus and his brother Truvor died. Rurik then took the whole power into his hands and gave towns over to his men, giving to one Polotsk, to another Rostof, and to a third Bielo-Jesero. And into these towns the Variagi have migrated; the earlier inhabitants in Novgorod were Slavs, in Polotsk, Krivitchi, in Rostof, Meri, and in Bielo-Jesero, Vessi."

That the Variagi were of Swedish descent, and that it was they who gave the name of Russia to the Slav countries, is proved beyond the possibility of a doubt. A most weighty argument is the large number of Swedish names in the list of Variag princes who reigned in Russia. It would not have been possible for Nestor to devise the more than one hundred leading names of Swedish origin which occur in his chronicle. Furthermore, it has been shown that there are fifteen Swedish loanwords in Russian. This is very much. Great and powerful nations have left behind a good deal less in modern languages, the Vandals three words, the Burgundians four or five, the Herulians one. Although the Swedes in Russia had no literature in their ancestral language, they have left behind more words than the majority of Teutonic tribes founding states and nations. The Old Swedish equivalents to some of the most important proper names which meet us in early Russian history are as follows: Rurik=Hrœrekr, Sineus=Signjótr, Truvor=Tryggve, Oleg=Helge, Olga=Helga, Igor= Inge, Ingvar.

For two hundred years after Rurik, all the leading men in Russian history carry Swedish names, and all the czars of Russia were the descendants of Rurik, up to the year 1598. The emperor and historian Constantine Porphyrogenitus, speaking of Russia, makes the distinction between the Slavs and the Russians proper. In his description of the cataracts of the Dniepr, he gives to each the Russian and the Slav name, and these Russian names are nearly all understood by reference to old Swedish roots. Examples are Gellandri (Gellandi)=the Noisy, Eyfórr=the Always Turbulent. Luitprand, the Italian chronicler, speaking of the Russians, says: "The Greeks call them Russians, we call them properly Northmen." The annals of St. Bertinus tell how Emperor Theophilus recommended some Russian envoys to Louis le Débonnaire, but how he, taking them for Norman spies, threw them into prison. The first Russian Code of Laws, compiled by Iaroslaf, presents a striking analogy to the Old Swedish laws.

The Slavs must have originally borrowed the name Russian from the Finns, who, up to the present day, call the Swedes *Ruotsi*. The name is in Sweden connected with a part of the coast of Upland still called Roslagen. The etymology of the name is Old Swedish *rodr* (rudder) and *roďsmenn* (oarsmen). Roslagen means "associations of oarsmen." The district is famous for its large peculiar rowboats. By the term Russians, the Slavs originally meant people from Roslagen, later Sweden in general. But when these Russians had become the founders of a new empire, south of the Baltic, it became necessary to devise a new name for the inhabitants of Sweden. This name was found in Variagi. Only the Swedes seeking employment as sworn warriors in the service of the new Russian dynasty, or in the body-guard of the Byzantine emperors, were originally thus called. But when the name of the new nation of Swedes and Slavs became Russians, the Swedes, and the Scandinavians in general, became known as Variagi. The etymology of the word has been given as the Old Swedish *vár* (*sacramentum*) and *væringar* (*sacramentarii*, soldiers bound by oath). The same name applied to Swedes, or Northmen, occurs frequently in slightly altered forms in Greek and Arabic manuscripts.

While Rurik and his brothers were building towns, which probably means the fortifying of ancient villages, two other Variagi, Askold and Dir, who were not of the family of Rurik, went down to Kief, and reigned over the Poliané. It was they who began the expeditions against Byzantium in 865. In speaking of this, Nestor calls the Bosphorus *Sud*, an Old Swedish word meaning a sound. The Bosphorus is also called Sud on a Swedish memorial stone over a man who was killed in a similar expedition.

Oleg, the fourth brother of Rurik, was his successor, his son Igor being yet a minor. He was an energetic man and a great administrator.

Smolensk, Lubetch and Kief were captured, and Askold and Dir put to death. Between the years 879–912, Oleg organized the Russian empire. For the sake of commerce, he tried to preserve peace with the Greeks, but when difficulties arose he called in new armies from Sweden and great expeditions started against Byzantium. But these Variagi were an unruly element, and, in order to satisfy their desire for war and booty, the Russian rulers always let a plundering expedition to the Caspian Sea follow every unsuccessful attack upon Byzantium; also when war with the Greeks was avoided through decrees of peace, expeditions to the Caspian Sea took place.

These expeditions against the Arabs, who inhabited the coasts of the Caspian Sea, were neither in any marked degree successful. Masudi is the first author among the Arabs who mentions the expeditions of the Swedes. They came down the river Volga in their ships. The Arabs describe the "Rûs" as blond and "tall as palm-trees." The burial of a Rûs is described by Ibn Fosslan, who visited Bulgaria in 921. "The hero was burned in a ship with weapons, horses, dogs and a woman." In 965, the Israelite, Ibrahim Ibn Jakub, made a journey to Germany. He tells that the Arabs in his day with Rûs (Russians) meant partly the Swedes of Sweden, "who often came in ships from the West to plunder," partly the Swedes settled in Russia, "who speak the language of the Slavs, on account of admixture with them."

It was the destiny of the Swedes in Russia to exchange their language for that of the Slavs and finally to absorb Slav customs. Such might not have been the case if they had been greater in numbers, or if their coming had been deferred to a later, Christian period, when to a strong form of government would have been added a strong Church organization. Yet their influence was greater than that of the Vikings in any other country, for the Russian empire was entirely a Northern creation.

To follow further the Rurik dynasty would lead us away from Swedish into Russian history. But let us mention that Oleg was succeeded by Rurik's son Igor, who also was a great war-lord, and undertook the third expedition of Russians and Variagi against Byzantium. His widow was the celebrated Olga, who was converted to Christianity and afterward canonized. She reigned during the minority of her son Sviatoslaf, whose conversion she was never able to effect. Sviatoslaf's son and grandson, Saint Vladimir and Jaroslaf the Great, were the Clovis and the Charlemagne of Russia.

After the conquest of Kief, Oleg commanded a tribute to be paid to the Variagi "for the preservation of peace." This tribute to the Swedes was paid up to the death of Jaroslaf, who in 1019 gave assurance to the king of Upsala that it should be paid regularly, Vladimir having neglected to do so. This tribute could be nothing else than a scat paid to the king of Sweden by the rulers of Russia during the ninth and tenth centuries. Sweden possessed in those days a large territory south of the Baltic, which paid scat to the king of Upsala. It was called Austria (*Austerike*), and reference to it under this name is often made in sagas, chronicles and inscriptions. Ynglinga Saga gives incidents of close Swedish connections to Finland and the Baltic provinces, and archæological finds point to Swedish settlements in Finland, already in the prehistoric period. Memories of conquests are preserved in statements by the Icelanders and by Saxo, the Danish historian, about the Austria of which the Swedish kings Ivar Vidfamne, Harald Hildetand, "Sigurd" Ring and Ragnar "Lodbrok" were rulers.

Closest to an exact statement comes Snorre, who says that King Eric Edmundson of Sweden ruled over Finland, Carelia, Esthonia, Courland and "wide over all Austria." These countries belonged to Sweden until King Olof Skœtkonung "let all his scatlands get away from him." The chronicler Rimbert says that Courland, by which he means the Baltic provinces, in 850 belonged to Sweden. Shortly after this date fall, according to Nestor, those of the first Swedish contact with interior Russia (859) and of the founding of the Russian empire by Rurik (862). The Swedish dominion in the Baltic provinces, as well as the early Russian empire, must consequently have held a position similar to the one of Normandie to France and England.

The old Swedish name for Russia was Gardarike, for Novgorod Holmgard and for Byzantium Miklagard, which mean "Country of towns," "Island town," and "Great town," respectively.

Vladimir of Russia, in 980, sent a number of Variagi to the emperor. But already the emperors had probably surrounded themselves with a small standing army of Variagi or Barangoi, as they were called by the Greeks. They were treated with a good deal of respect and consideration, and in the North it was considered a distinction to have served in Miklagard, which even the sons of kings eagerly sought for. Soon not only Swedes, but also Norwegians, Danes and Icelanders were attracted, and Icelandic sources have a good many, in part wildly exaggerated, accounts of the Variagi and their experiences in Miklagard. The Northmen were relied upon to support the tottering empire, and were despatched to the points where the hardest combats were fought. They had officers of their own nationality, and the strictest discipline was maintained.

About the year 1050 a detachment of Variagi were accepted into the body-guard of the emperor, surrounding his person on all great occasions and in public; also keeping watch over the imperial palace. When the emperor died, they had, according to Snorre, the privilege of passing through his treasury, each taking along all he could carry off. Another privilege of theirs was that they were allowed to keep their heathen faith in the midst of the Christian surroundings.

Many and various as the reasons for the Viking expeditions must have been, the principal cause that led to their abolition was the contact with Christianity abroad, and the introduction of its teaching in the heathen North. The first missionaries to Sweden were sent by Louis the Pious, but Christianity was not entirely unknown before their arrival. For centuries, the Swedes had through commercial expeditions stood in direct or indirect contact with the Christian world, and this had brought home some knowledge of "the white Christ" and his gospel of peace. Many Northmen had been baptized while dwelling in foreign lands, and many must the Christian thralls have been who continually were brought into the country. The influence these elements exerted probably could be traced to the ennobling and developing of heathen myths, rather than to direct Christian conversions. And a similar influence of Roman and Greek myths, without doubt, exerted upon the North in earlier historic times.

Ansgar, a learned and pious monk from the convent of Corvey, became the apostle of Sweden. He had spent two years in Denmark as a missionary when called upon by Emperor Louis to visit Sweden. Louis the Pious had received the assurance by Swedish emissaries that the new faith would not meet with any obstacle, and that many were willing to embrace it. Ansgar started in the year of 830, accompanied by Witmar, also of the Corvey convent. They were well received by King Bicern, and were able to comfort many Christians in Swedish captivity, besides converting some of the inhabitants. Among the converts was the powerful Jarl Herger, who for a long period was the chief supporter of Christianity in Sweden. After about a year and a half, Ansgar and Witmar returned to the emperor, who, satisfied with the result of their mission, erected a special archbishopric in Hamburg for the spiritual needs of the North. Ansgar was made the archbishop and, with Ebo, archbishop of Rheims, apostolic legate among Swedes, Danes and Slavs. At the same time, Gauzbert was made the first bishop of Sweden under the name of Simon. He went to Sweden and was well received by its king and people. But a revolt against the new faith soon rose among the heathens, not issuing from the king but from the people. Gauzbert was captured and with contumely escorted out of the country, while his relative, Nithard, was killed, thus becoming the first Christian martyr in Sweden. For seven years the country was without a preacher of the Gospel, until Ansgar sent thither a new missionary, Ardgar, who stayed there preaching until the death of Herger. In the meantime Vikings had destroyed Hamburg, and not before its bishopric had been united to that of Bremen was Ansgar in a position to visit Sweden for a second time. This he effected early in the fifties of the ninth century, coming this time as a kind of ambassador from the kings of Denmark and Germany to give more importance to his mission. The heathen partisans, who recently had accepted the departed King Eric among the gods, resented, and the reigning king, Olof, dared not grant Ansgar the right to preach. The difficulty was solved through the ancient custom of throwing dice. Ansgar was successful in the proceedings, and his cause was then brought before the Thing (or Assembly) for deliberation. The people decided that permission should be granted to preach the Gospel, principally on the grounds set forth by an old man who rose to remind the Thing that the new God had already helped a good many, and that it was a good thing to have him to fall back on when the old gods failed. After having built churches and baptized a great number, Ansgar returned home, leaving behind Erimbert, a relative of Gauzbert's. Archbishop Rimbert was Ansgar's successor, himself visiting Sweden. After his death, the archbishops of the North seem to have ceased taking interest in Swedish missions. The little church, left to itself, soon succumbed. When at last one of the archbishops, Unne, woke up to the necessity of visiting Sweden, he found that the Gospel was forgotten. He was himself surprised by death while in Sweden, and buried in the town of Birka, in 936. Numerous graves of the earlier Christians in Sweden have been found on the site of the old commercial centre of Birka in the island Biœrkœ, in the Lake Mælar, unburned bodies in wooden coffins, and the graves without mounds.

King *Eric Edmundson* was a contemporary of Rimbert. He was engaged in building up a Swedish dominion in Finland and on the southern shores of the Baltic. With King Harald Fairhair of Norway he was disputing the supremacy over the province of Vermland. He was succeeded by his son *Biœrn*, who is said to have reigned for fifty years. *Olof* and *Eric*, Biœrn's two sons, succeeded him, the former dying suddenly at a banquet. His **young son,** *Styrbiœrn* *Starke* **(the Strong), one of the most famous of** Swedish heroes, demanded his share of the kingdom when only twelve years old. When King Eric told him he was yet too young, Styrbiœrn two springs in succession installed himself on the mound of his father, by so doing making claim upon his inheritance, according to old usage. But when he came to the Thing to demand his share in the government he was chased away with stone-throwing. King Eric gave him sixty ships with men and weapons to try his luck in Viking expeditions. Styrbiœrn won great fame during several years of continual warfare in the Baltic, capturing the mighty Jomsborg, a celebrated Viking nest in the island of Wollin, later turning his weapons upon Denmark, where he made the Danish king Harald Gormson Bluetooth a prisoner. He now felt strong enough to attack his uncle, King Eric. Harald Bluetooth was to help him, but failed to do so. Styrbiœrn sailed with a fleet to Sweden; after having landed he burned his ships to make a return impossible. King Eric met him at the Fyrisvols and fought a battle which was said to have lasted for three days. Styrbiœrn fell, and with him the larger part of his army. His uncle, the king, was after this called *Eric Segerscell* (the Victorious). After the battle the king ascended a high mound, promising a great compensation to the one who could compose a song in praise of the victory. The Icelander Thorvald Hialte, who never previously or afterward appeared as a scald, came forth and recited two strophes which are preserved to our day, receiving a costly armlet of gold as reward. This battle—next to the one at Bravols, the most famous in the heathen North—was fought in 988.

King Eric invaded Denmark and took possession of the country, making the son of Harald Bluetooth an exile, to which facts Saxo, the Danish historian, testifies. In Denmark Eric was baptized, the first Swedish king about whom this is said. But upon his return to Sweden he also returned to the old gods. Eric Segersæll was king of Sweden and Denmark until his death, which occurred in 994. His first consort, Sigrid Storrada (the Proud), from whom he later separated, played quite an important part in the history of her time. After the death of Eric, she married the exiled Svend Tjufvuskægg (their son being Canute the Great), who through this matrimony came to the throne of Denmark.

Olof Skœtkonung, the son of Eric and Sigrid, succeeded his father. His surname is supposed to mean "the lap king," but he was no longer a minor at the death of King Eric. King Olof was not a powerful or energetic ruler, like the father. He let go, one after the other, the lands of his crown. Denmark regained its independence, and he lost also the scat-paying dominions south of the Baltic. Shortly after Olof ascended the throne, the Norwegian king, Olaf Tryggvason, had demanded Sigrid Storrada in marriage and obtained her consent. But when King Olaf asked her to become a Christian, she refused to change faith, whereupon he insulted her. Sigrid told him that this should cause his death. Two years later, when Sigrid was the wife of King Svend of Denmark, she prevailed upon her son and her husband to join hands in assailing Olaf Tryggvason, who was expected back from an expedition to the lands of the Vends. The compact was made, and the Norwegian jarls, Eric and Svein, entered it. These all collected an immense fleet, which assailed the unsuspecting Olaf at Svolder, close by the coast of Pomerania. The Norwegian king lost the day and his life. This famous battle was fought in 1000, the kings of Sweden and Denmark also taking a personal part in it. Norway was divided between the victors. The Swedish king received as his share the districts of Drontheim and Bohuslæn. These he granted to Jarl Svein, who was the betrothed of his sister Holmfrid. Fifteen years later they were recaptured by the Norwegian king.

Olaf Tryggvason had been a devout Christian. His sister Ingeborg was married to Jarl Ragnvald of West Gothland, who was baptized and invited Christian missionaries to Sweden. Through such influences King Olof Skœtkonung was at last converted and baptized by Sigfrid, a German missionary, at Husaby in West Gothland, in the year 1008. Sigfrid, who has been supposed to be of English parentage and a bishop of York, evidently came from Germany. He preached for a long period in West Gothland and Værend, in the latter district once being attacked by heathen men, who killed three of his companions. King Olof himself saw to it that the murderers were punished, and Sigfrid continued his noble work without molestation. He was later worshipped as a saint. Among other missionaries who were active in converting the various provinces may be mentioned the Anglo-Saxon St. David, the apostle of Westmanland, the Anglo-Saxon St. Eskil and the Swede St. Botvid, the apostles of Sœdermanland, and the German Stenfi, or Simon, the apostle of Norrland. St. David was a contemporary of St. Sigfrid, while the others were a few generations younger. It was first through influence from England and Denmark, during the reign of Canute the Great, that Swedish conversions became more widespread and general.

King Olof's conversion met with a great deal of opposition, especially in Svealand, which longest remained heathen. Upsala, with its temple, was the heathen stronghold of the North, and there the king had always, as one of his principal duties, to preside over the great sacrifices. King Olof was forced to accept the decision of a Thing which granted him freedom to select some part of the kingdom wherein to build churches and perform the duties of the new cult, but which forbade him to use his influence toward the conversion of his subjects. For this reason Olof dwelt principally in the more and more christianized West Gothland, in the capital of which province, Skara, a bishop was installed. The name of the first bishop was Turgot. Only after more than two centuries of endeavor was the Christian Church firmly established in Sweden, in the middle of the eleventh century; but even at that time the great mass of the people were heathen in name. The heathen party was so strong that it could for a long time, and occasionally with success, keep up the battle against Christianity. It took yet another century before the complete victory of Christianity was an assured fact.

The reasons for the slow progress of Christianity in Sweden were many, the principal one not being an opposition to the Christian doctrines. The superstitious change easily from one cult to another. The sceptics do not believe more in one god than in another. Of heathen sceptics there were a great many in the North who believed in nothing else than their own strength. But it was the Christian morals which were so difficult for the Swedes to accept. Accustomed to great personal liberty, they could not endure the restraint which Christian morals placed upon the individual. The very spirit of Christianity, with its kindliness and meekness, was not attractive to the Northman, who in his own mental and physical force found a tower of strength. The period of the first attempts at conversion was not well chosen. The whole North was inflamed by the Viking rage for war and plunder. Then followed a period of disinterestedness when the good seed was sown but the field neglected. Later the too arduous zeal of the priests called forth criticism and resistance from the Swedes, so tardy in making a decision and so careful in weighing reasons for and against.

To this must be added the great prestige of the Upsala temple as the heathen arc of worship in the North, and the influence of the scalds and saga men of Iceland. Iceland was discovered in 870, and settled principally by Norsemen from the British Isles and from the western coast of Norway, but also to some extent by Swedes and Danes. Sudden and brilliant was the rise of Icelandic culture, and Icelandic scalds overran the whole territory of the North. At the court of every king and jarl these were at home, sometimes in great numbers, and soon to the exclusion of the native poets. For their poetry, both as to contents and form, they were chiefly dependent upon the heathen myths and traditions, and the result of their popularity must have been a perfect heathen revival in those days of growing scepticism. Through intercourse with Christians in Britain, the Icelanders had borrowed many a noble trait, and their taste found admirers in the old North, where such influence must have been felt through centuries of indirect contact with lands of classical or Christian culture. We are told of the great number of southern coins found in Swedish soil. Which travel further and faster, thoughts or coins, and which are the more impressionable? So although it would be unjust to deprive the Icelandic poetry, the impressive and grand Eddic songs and the more artificial court-poetry, of any of its beauty or originality, it is not right to ascribe all the culture, whose blossom it is, to Iceland, or Iceland and Norway, to the exclusion of Sweden and Denmark, or the Teutonic world at large. Good epic poetry has been written all over Teutondom. In Sweden strophes in the very metre of the majority of Eddic poems have been found on tombstones. In the same manner with the contents of the Eddic poems. Granting important exceptions, we think that the heathen myths have been the same in the East as in the extreme West. The very fact that Icelandic court-poetry was accepted and enjoyed by continental chieftains presupposes a thorough knowledge and mastery of the more popular poetry of Eddic songs of gods and heroes.

Hence the revival of heathendom in the North, by which a king like Olof Skœtkonung for a long time was influenced, finding his chief delight in the association with poets and saga men.

In Norway, Olaf Haraldson had ascended the throne, and he put an end to Swedish dominion in the Norwegian districts. This caused strife, and also considerable annoyance to the provinces touching the frontier. Popular feeling rose high in Sweden, when the demands for a peace guarantee with Norway were disregarded by King Olof. Jarl Ragnvald sided with the people, desiring a union between the Norwegian king and King Olof's daughter Ingegerd. At a great Thing held in Upsala, in 1018, King Olof listened to Norwegian emissaries pleading for peace and a royal marriage. Jarl Ragnvald complained of the annoyance caused to his people of West Gothland. King Olof became indignant, but was, through the forcible yet dignified appeal for peace by Torgny, the *lagman* (justice) of Tiundaland, compelled to a promise of peace and a concession of marriage. But the king did not keep his promises. A betrothal was arranged but soon annulled by Olof, and the Norwegian king was in vain expecting his promised bride. At the instigation of Jarl Ragnvald, Olaf Haraldson married King Olof's illegitimate daughter Astrid. As this was done without the consent of her father, Ragnvald dared not remain in Sweden. He went to Gardarike (Russia), where he died shortly afterward, in 1019, his widow, the princess Ingegerd, in Novgorod becoming the wife of the Russian ruler Jaroslaf.

In Sweden, trouble was brewing against the king, who had broken faith with his people, and in order to avoid open revolt King Olof was forced to divide his power with one of his sons, who, although yet a minor, was solemnly elected king. He had in baptism received the name of *Jacob*, which so displeased his heathen subjects that it was changed to *Anund*. King Olof also agreed to maintain peace with Norway, meeting his son-in-law at Konghæll, in Bohuslæn, in 1019, for a peace agreement. King Olof died two years later and was buried by the church of Husaby, where he was baptized. He was the first king who introduced coinage into Sweden. The earliest coins were made of silver by Anglo-Saxons settled in Sigtuma, and resemble closely Anglo-Saxon coins of the same period.

After the death of his father King Anund ruled alone. He entered into an alliance with his brother-in-law of Norway against Canute, who now was king both of Denmark and England. During Canute's absence, Anund and Olaf invaded Denmark. In the subsequent strife between Olaf and Canute, Anund took no active part. King Olaf had to flee to Russia. Upon his return he gathered an army in Sweden, with the help of Anund, and entered Norway through Jemtland. At Stiklastad he met the much superior Norwegian army, and lost his battle and his life, in 1030. After his death, the sentiment in Norway changed radically, and he was worshipped as a saint throughout the North.

Of Anund's reign little is known. Adam of Bremen, an ecclesiastic, whose history of the diocese of Hamburg and Bremen, during the period 788–1072, is one of the most important sources of Swedish history in heathen times, says of Anund: "Young in years, he excelled in wisdom and piety all his predecessors; no king was more beloved by the Swedish people than Anund." The historian gives as his authority the Danish king Svend Estridsen, who as an exile stayed at Anund's court. Anund died in 1050 and was succeeded by his older half-brother *Emund*, surnamed *the Old*. He was the son of a freed woman, the daughter of a Vendish chief. For this reason he had been passed over at the first election. Emund was educated by his mother's relatives, was baptized, but was not much of a Christian. He was popular neither with the new Christian church nor with the people at large. Emund's unpopularity with the masses was caused by an agreement with Denmark in regard to the boundaries when he ceded the province of Bleking. Emund died in 1060. With him the old royal line became extinct. A new line comes to the throne of Sweden, where, with the general acceptance of **Christianity, a new era commences.**

CHAPTER IV

Early Christian Era—Stenkil's Line and Interchanging Dynasties

THE sources of Swedish history during the first two centuries of the Middle Ages are very meagre. This is a deplorable fact, for during that period Sweden passed through a great and thorough development, the various stages of which consequently are not easily traced.

Before th year of 1060 Sweden is an Old Teutonic state, certain y of later form and a larger compass than the earliest of such, but with its democracy and its elective kingdom preserved. The older Sweden, such as it had existed at least since the days of Ingiald Illrade, was in regard to its constitution a rudimentary union of states. The realm had come into existence through the cunning and violence of the king of the Sviar, who made away with the kings of the respective lands, making their communities pay homage to him. No change in the interior affairs of the different lands was thereby effected; they lost their outward political independence, but remained mutually on terms of perfect equality. They were united only through the king, who was the only centre for the government of the union. No province had constitutionally more importance than the rest, no supremacy by one over the other existed. On this historic basis the Swedish realm was built, and rested firmly until the commencement of the Middle Ages. In the Old Swedish state-organism the various parts thus possessed a high degree of individual and pulsating life; the empire as a whole was also powerful, although the royal dignity was its only institution. The king was the outward tie which bound the provinces together; besides him there was no power of state which embraced the whole realm. The affairs of state were decided upon by the king alone, as in regard to war, or he had to gather the opinion of the Thing in each province; any imperial representation did not exist and was entirely unknown, both in the modern sense and in the form of one provincial, or sectional, assembly deciding for all the others. The latter form is one of transition, the modern form the ripe fruit, both brought out by the historic development. In society there existed no classes. It was a democracy of free men, the slaves and freed men enjoying no rights. The first centuries of the Middle Ages were one continued process of regeneration, the Swedish people being carried into the European circle of cultural development and made a communicant of Christianity. With the commencement of the thirteenth century Sweden comes out of this process as a mediæval state, in aspect entirely different to her past. The democratic equality among free men has turned into an aristocracy, with aristocratic institutions, the hereditary kingdom into an elective, or, at least, into one close upon turning into an elective, kingdom, while the provincial particularism and independence have given way to the constitution of a centralized, monopolistic state. No changes could be more fundamental.

For lack of sources the historians were, until quite recently, led to the belief that the change was due to one tribe in gaining the ascendency over another, the political supremacy changing from one part of the country to another. The epoch was called "The Struggle between Swedes and Goths," "The Struggle about the election of kings between Swedes and Goths." Now it is generally admitted that the struggle was between principles, not between tribes. The circumstances sometimes were such that one section or province opposed others, but these divisions never were identical or at all depended upon racial or tribal conditions. It was a struggle between heathendom and Christianity, democracy and aristocracy, provincial particularism and centralized state unity.

The old provincial laws of Sweden are a great and important inheritance which this period has accumulated from heathen times. The laws were written down in the thirteenth and fourteenth centuries, but they bear every evidence of high antiquity. Many strophes are found in them of the same metre as those on the tombstones of the Viking Age and those in which the songs of the Edda are chiefly written. In other instances the text consists of alliterative prose, which proves its earlier metrical form. The expressions have, in places, remained heathen, although used by Christians, who were ignorant of their true meaning, as, for instance, in the following formula of an oath, in the West Gothic law: "Sva se mer gud hull" (So help me the gods). The laws show a good many individual traits and differences, but these are not of such a serious character as to give evidence of having been formulated by tribes of different origin. A remarkable exception is formed by the laws of matrimony and inheritance for the inhabitants of Værend and Bleking, who, it will be remembered, are the descendants of the Herulian immigration in historic times. In lieu of a missing literature of sagas and poetry, these provincial laws give a good insight into the character, morals, customs and culture of the heathen and early Christian times of Sweden. From the point of philology they are also of great value, besides forming the solid basis of later Swedish law. How the laws could pass from one generation to another, without any codification, depends upon the facts that they were recited from memory by the justice (*lagman* or *domare*), and that this dignity generally was inherited, for centuries being carried by the descendants of one and the same family.

Interesting is the appendix to the law of the island of Gothland, the Guta Saga, being the fragment of a history of the island and its first contact with Christianity through a visit by St. Olaf of Norway. The style is the same simple and serene one as in the Icelandic sagas; while the Gutnic dialect, in which it is written, more closely resembles the Gothic of Bishop Wulfila in vowel sounds than the language of any other known dialect. Quite an important appendix is found in the older form of the West Gothic law, consisting of lines of the kings of Sweden, with short but highly valuable accounts of their reigns and characteristics.

Stenkil was the name of King Emund's successor. He was a jarl and married to Emund's sister. The statement that he was born in West Gothland is not confirmed by the authorities. His father's name was Ragnvald, and it seems likely that this Ragnvald was identical with the jarl spoken of above, who died in Russia. Stenkil had close relations with Russia, for his son Inge was called in from that country to succeed his father. If Jarl Ragnvald was Stenkil's father, this only made his selection as king more plausible, being then the half-brother of Isiaslaf of Russia and the brother-in-law of the reigning kings of Hungary, France and Norway. King Stenkil was a devout Christian, but of a sagacious disposition, careful not to offend his heathen subjects by any Christian propaganda. He was a giant in size, and although phlegmatic, an ardent sportsman. Adalvard, exiled by Emund, returned and did active work as bishop of Skara, also converting the population of Vermland. Even among the heathen of Svealand, Christianity got a foothold, Adalvard the Younger being established as bishop in Sigtuna, close by the pagan centre of Upsala. But when he, in conjunction with Egino, of the newly erected bishop's chair of Lund, schemed for the destruction of the heathen temple of Upsala, he was removed by the command of the king, who found that such a plan, if carried through, would prove disastrous to both Church and throne.

During the short reign of Stenkil there was a conflict with Norway, an exiled Norwegian jarl having been granted possessions in Vermland. King Harald Hardrade invaded Gothaland, punishing this insult by a victory over the Swedes. No further complications ensued, perhaps on account of the close family relations of the two rulers.

Stenkil died in 1066, leaving two sons, *Halsten* and *Inge*, both minors. During their minority two men, both named *Eric*, relatives of Stenkil and the old royal line, fought for supremacy, and both fell in the contest for the crown. Hakon of West Gothland took hold of the reins of state and kept them for thirteen years, until King Halsten became of age, Hakon himself dying. Halsten was a devout Christian like his father, but less sagacious, trying to force the new faith upon the heathen of Svealand. For this reason he was dethroned, and his brother Inge called in from Russia. But King Inge was a Christian enthusiast like his brother, and was subsequently driven away by the irate inhabitants of Svealand, who now called to the throne his brother-in-law *Sven*, surnamed *Blot-Sven* (*Sven, the Sacrificer*), of heathen faith. The royal brothers dwelt undisturbed among the Christians, but after three years King Inge, in old heathen style, surrounded and set fire to the domicile of Blot-Sven, who with all his household perished within. King Inge resumed his reign, likely very much in his old spirit, for two other pretenders, although less formidable, appeared: *Olof Næskonung* (*Nose-king*) and a son of Sven, called *Kol* or *Eric Arsœll*. Two papal documents are preserved from Inge's reign. They consist of letters from Gregory VII., making appeals for closer relations between the pope and the Swedish king.

An invasion was made from Norway, whose king, Magnus Barfod, subdued the inhabitants of the province of Dal. King Magnus built a fortified place on the island of Kollandsœ in Lake Venar, close to the shore of West Gothland, but it was captured by King Inge, who set its occupants free, but without their weapons. Two battles were fought at Fuxerna, the Norwegians being victors in the first, the Swedes in the latter. Peace was effected at a meeting between the two kings at Kunghæll in the summer of 1101, when it was agreed that the frontiers should remain as they were before the war. King Eric Ejegod was also present at the meeting, where the betrothal between King Magnus and King Inge's daughter Margaret was agreed upon. On account of the original nature of the meeting the Swedish princess was surnamed Fredkulla (Peace-Maiden).

In 1103 the bishopric of Lund was raised to the dignity of an archbishopric, yet not becoming perfectly independent of the archbishopric of Hamburg-Bremen. The archbishop of Lund received the title of Primas of Sweden, preserved long after Sweden had obtained its own archbishop.

King Inge died in 1111, receiving, by the appendix to the West Gothic law, credit for "having ruled Sweden with manliness, without breaking the law which governed each province." About his brother Halsten, who died before him, the same source says: "He was sagacious and good-natured; the cases brought before him were bettered, and Sweden became worse through his death." At the time of Inge's death, Jemtland was persuaded to pay scat to the Norwegian king, but it remained in connection with the church of Sweden.

Inge's son Ragnvald died before him, and Halsten's sons, *Philip* and *Inge the Younger*, ascended the throne. They were of a more peaceful disposition toward the heathen than their predecessors, Christianity making great progress during their reigns. Philip died in 1118, Inge following him in 1125; his death was said to have been caused by poison. The epitaph over the two runs thus: "Sweden fared well while they lived," in the terse language of the source quoted above. With them the race of Stenkil became extinct in the male line.

In 1123 the Norwegian king, Sigurd Jorsalafare, undertook a crusade to the eastern parts of Smaland, which were still heathen. "Crusades" of this kind were not uncommon during that period, and were hardly anything else than Viking expeditions in Christian disguise.

Great confusion ensued through the extinction of Stenkil's line. *Ragnvald Knaphœfde*, probably the son of Olof

Næskonung, was chosen king, but lost his life through the contemptuous neglect of an ancient custom. The newly elected king should always make a tour of the realm, receiving homage and giving assurance of his good faith to the population of the various provinces. The provincial laws had stipulations as to the nature and number of the *gisslan* (hostages) to meet and escort him through each province. This tour, called *Eriksgata*, Ragnvald undertook without accepting hostages upon entering West Gothland. He was killed at Karleby, in 1130, by the peasants, indignant at what they considered an insult to all the West Goths. These had, moreover, made another choice in Magnus Nilsson, the son of Margaret Fredkulla in her second marriage. Magnus never made claim to the Swedish throne, endeavoring to become king of Denmark, after his father, Nils Svendsen, but losing his life in the attempt.

Sverker, who had married the widow of the younger Inge, was in 1133 chosen king by the East Goths, and the Up-Swedes (in the provinces north of Lake Mælar), having no special choice of their own, also agreed on him. After the death of Magnus Nilsson, the West Goths joined by formally acknowledging King Sverker, who, born in East Gothland, has been supposed to be the son of Eric Arsæll, without solid reasons. During Sverker's reign ecclesiastical matters developed. The old bishoprics of Birka and Sigtuna were changed into that of (Old) Upsala, where the pagan temple seems to have been at last changed into a church. New bishoprics were created in Linkœping, Strengnæs, Westeros and Vexio. The whole of Swedish Finland formed one diocese. The famous Bernard of Clairvaux was asked by King Sverker and his queen Ulfhild to send monks of his order, and several Cistercian convents were founded. The quiet and scholarly monks from France, no doubt, soon began to exert a beneficial influence of importance, through the means of their superior culture. A papal legate, Nicolaus of Alba (later Pope Hadrian IV.), visited Sweden in 1152, meeting all the dignitaries of Church and State for a conference at Linkœping. The legate was willing to give to Sweden an archbishop, but the matter was postponed, since no agreement could be reached in regard to the archbishopric's seat. Measures for the establishment of the Church on a firmer basis and the payment of Peter's pence to Rome were agreed on.

Sverker was a good and peaceful monarch, but seems with old age to have lost some of his authority. A war with Denmark was brought on through an escapade of his son John, who had carried away two Danish women of noble birth. He returned them, and was himself killed by the peasants at a Thing. Yet the Danish king, Svend Grade, had the excuse for an invasion and entered Smaland with an army in the winter of 1153–54. The brave inhabitants of Værend gave him a hearty welcome, and he soon returned to Denmark. It is an old tradition that a woman by the name of Blenda was chiefly instrumental in this result. When the peasants feared to attack the superior enemy, she had a splendid meal spread for the foe. After the Danes had partaken heavily of its eatables and drinkables, they were surprised and routed by their hitherto invisible hosts and hostesses.

King Sverker, now called "the Old," was murdered by his valet while starting for the Christmas matins in 1155 or 1156. The murder was, without doubt, committed at the instigation of the Danish prince Magnus Henricsson, who on his mother's side was a great-grandson of Inge the

Elder, and who in this manner made his first attempt to reach the throne of Sweden.

Already, in 1150, the Up-Swedes had in *Eric*, the son of Jedvard, found a man in their opinion better suited to rule Sweden than Sverker the Old. His mother is said to have been the daughter of Blot-Sven and the sister of Kol, while his father was "a good and rich yeoman." Through a mistake he was named *Eric IX.*, but is more commonly known as *St. Eric*. One source calls him "lawgiver," although nothing is definitely known of his activity in this direction. At the death of Sverker, his son Charles was certainly of age, but the growing fame of King Eric made it useless for him to force his right, and Eric was recognized as king of the whole realm.

King Eric was a warm friend of the Christian propaganda in his own country, and by crusades spread the faith outside of its borders. It was only natural that Sweden should turn its attention to Finland, with which country it had stood in close relations since the remotest period, and where Swedish settlements in all times existed. Accompanied by Bishop Henric of Upsala, King Eric sailed with a fleet to the southwestern part of Finland, or the province now called Finland Proper, where the inhabitants were forced to receive baptism. This crusade must have taken place late in the fifties of the twelfth century. Eric soon returned, but Bishop Henric remained with other priests to have Christianity firmly established. These efforts met with considerable difficulty, and Henric was murdered by one of his converts. He was later worshipped as the patron saint of Finland.

The pious King Eric was attacked by the perfidious prince Magnus Henricsson at East Aros (the present or

New Upsala), in 1160. It is said that Eric was attending mass at the Trinity Church, when he was told of the approach of his enemy. He remained till the service was over, after which he went to meet his fate. He was overcome and slain by the superior force. His pious life and virtues and the miracles which were said to have been worked at his grave made him the patron saint of Sweden, although never canonized by the Church of Rome. His bones are preserved in a shrine of gilt silver behind the high altar in the cathedral of Upsala, and were in Catholic days objects of worship. Oaths were taken "by the power of God and Saint Eric the King," his banner was carried in war, and the city of Stockholm still has his image on its shield.

Charles Sverkersson (Charles VII.) now made valid his claims, the whole people rising to support him against the usurper Magnus. In the following year Magnus was killed by the indignant people. During the reign of Charles some important novelties in Church and State were introduced. Sweden received, in 1164, her first archbishop in Stefan, a monk of Alvastra. The archbishop's seat was first Old Upsala. Instead of jarls in the various parts, there is from this time on a jarl for the whole kingdom at the side of the king, whom he assists in the government of the state, sometimes obtaining a power rivalling that of his master. The first jarl of the realm was Ulf, the second Gutorm. The rivalry noticeable between the different provinces, which all thought themselves called upon to select a new line to rule after Stenkil's, ceased at the death of Saint Eric. What follows is a rivalry of interchanging dynasties. Charles Sverkersson was, in April, 1167, surprised by a pretender to the throne, Knut Ericsson, who deprived him of crown and life, while his little son Sverker was saved and carried away to the queen's uncle, Valdemar the Great of Denmark.

Knut Ericsson was the son of Saint Eric, and ruled Sweden for twenty-five years in peace. In his youth he had made one unsuccessful attempt to reach the throne, after which he fled to Norway. After the death of King Charles he had to fight two pretenders, Kol and Burislev, the latter said to have been a son of King Sverker.

During this period the Baltic and its coasts were continually disturbed by heathen sea-rovers from the southern shores. A fleet of this kind entered Lake Mælar in 1187 and destroyed by fire the town of Sigtuna, which, as a mercantile centre, had succeeded the earlier destroyed Birka. The second archbishop of Sweden, John, was killed by the invaders. The first preliminary plan for the fortification of the present site of Stockholm was probably then laid, in order to prevent further invasions, and a little town commenced to grow up.

Conditions in Finland were not satisfactory. Invasions by Esthonians and Vends were frequent, while the Finns themselves were troublesome and little devoted to the new faith. Bishop Henric's successor was killed, but Sweden continued to send bishops during the next hundred years.

The relations with foreign powers were peaceable, the first known treaty between Sweden and a German prince being entered into by King Knut and Duke Heinrich of Saxony and Bavaria, in regard to trade relations with Lubeck. King Knut died in the winter of 1195. He had four sons, but although he had selected one of them for his successor, "with general consent and through election by the foremost men in Sweden," *Sverker the Younger*, the son of King Charles, succeeded him. That this could take place with·

out serious objection of Knut's sons can only be explained by the influence wielded by the Church and the nobles. The latter had already grown up to strength and importance. Their leader was the mighty jarl, Birger Brosa, who had succeeded Gutorm. He was of the influential family of Folkungs, which, one of the first in the land, soon aspired to the throne. Birger, himself married to a Norwegian princess, gave his own daughter Ingegerd in marriage to the new king, and remained in power.

King Sverker sought the favor of the Church by supporting its claims. In a document of the year 1200, by which he donates some property to the church of Upsala, historians have seen the privileges extended to the Church as an independent power of state, whose members could be arraigned before an ecclesiastic forum only, and whose property was to be exempt from taxation. This is the spirit of the document; but the king had not, at that period, the right to grant such extensive privileges. King Sverker, and probably each of his successors, in turn, gave only an assurance of their sympathy with the Church policy, which was to its full extent an assured victory only toward the close of the thirteenth century.

In 1202, Birger Brosa died, and with him the firm support against the pretenders had fallen. The sons of Knut now made open revolt, leaving their places at Sverker's court. In 1205, Sverker gave battle to them at Elgaros, three of the brothers being killed and the fourth, Eric, fleeing to Norway. But a few years later he returned with an army, and Sverker found it safest to retire to Denmark, whence he returned with a splendid army, which King Valdemar II. Seier, had placed at his disposal. But this army was defeated at Lena, in West Gothland, in 1208, and Sverker returned to Denmark, now turning to the pope, Innocent III., who in vain threatened the pretender with his ban. Sverker entered Sweden with a new Danish army, but was killed at the battle of Gestilren, in West Gothland, in 1210.

Eric Knutsson now came to undisturbed possession of the throne and thus remained until his death in April, 1216, his reign being short and uneventful. He was the first king of Sweden of whom it is known with certainty that he was anointed and crowned, thus placing himself under the protection of the Church. His queen, Rikissa, a sister of Valdemar II., returned to Denmark after his death, there giving life to a son, who was named Eric, after his father. King Valdemar tried in vain to have this royal babe placed on the Swedish throne.

John Sverkersson succeeded King Eric, being, on account of his fifteen years of age, first surnamed the *Young*, later *the Pious*. By confirming and extending the rights of the Church which his father granted he won the favor of the ecclesiastics, and the attempts made by Valdemar to have his consecration prohibited proved futile. Toward the end of his short reign (in 1220) King John undertook a crusade to Esthonia, where he left behind him his jarl, Charles, a brother of Birger Brosa, and Bishop Charles of Linkœping, with a part of the army. These all perished in an onslaught made on them by the heathen in August of the same year, and the ravages by Esthonians continued as before. King John died in the island of Visingsœ, in Lake Vetter, in 1222, like several of his predecessors, and was, like them, buried in the monastery of Alvastra.

Eric Ericsson now became king of Sweden. The royal babe was then six years of age, a halting and lisping little creature. The Church took him under its protection, but there was no powerful man to take hold of the government during his minority. A pretender rose in the person of Knut the Tall, a great grandson of St. Eric, like the king himself. He defeated Eric's troops at Olustra, in 1229. Eric fled to Denmark, where he remained until the short and restless reign of Knut came to an end through his death, in 1232. Eric resumed the reins of government, with the Folkung, Jarl Ulf, at the helm.

Pope Gregory IX., in 1230, gave commandment to the Swedish bishops to rouse the people to opposition against the ravages of the heathen in the Baltic provinces in the further parts of Finland. In 1237 he commands the Swedish bishops to have a crusade started against the heathen Tavasti in the interior of Finland. This crusade took place under the leadership of Birger Magnusson, who converted the barbarous Finns by the sword and erected a fort on the site of the later Tavastehus. Birger, according to Russian testimony, tried to extend the dominion of Swedish supremacy as far as to the river Neva, but was repulsed by the Russians.

Peace had reigned in Sweden for some time when new conflicts ensued. The peasants of Upland made an uprising in 1247, but were conquered at Sparrsætra and punished by heavier taxes. A pretender rose in the person of Holmger, the son of Knut the Tall. He was captured and beheaded in 1248.

A papal legate, Bishop William of Sabina, visited Sweden and arranged, in 1248, an ecclesiastical meeting at Skenninge, effecting the final separation of Church and State, and establishing the former as an independent power at the side of the latter. Archbishops and bishops were now to be elected by the ecclesiastics and not by the king. Celibacy, previously not enforced in the Swedish church, was then introduced, meeting with a good deal of opposition; for the ecclesiastical offices had already commenced getting hereditary, as had in earlier times the combined dignities of Asa priest and chieftain. Birger Magnusson had, shortly before the meeting of Skenninge, succeeded Ulf as jarl of the realm. This converter of the Tavasti was destined to play a most important part in Swedish history, shaping its destiny through the power of his iron will. He was the leader of the Folkung family and party, a nephew of Birger Brosa, and married to princess Ingeborg, a sister of the reigning king. *Birger Jarl*, as he is generally called, effected a satisfactory agreement with Norway at a meeting with Hakon in the summer of 1249, according to which the enemies of one realm should have no refuge, or support, in the other. Besides, it was agreed that the son of the Norwegian king should marry Rikissa, the daughter of Birger Jarl.

King Eric died in 1250, at the age of thirty-four. He called himself Eric III., while in later times, when St. Eric was supposed to have been the ninth king of that name, he has been called Eric XI. He was said to have been peaceful, just and kind.

CHAPTER V

The Mediæval ·State—The Folkung Dynasty

WITH Eric Ericsson the royal line of Saint Eric became extinct. The crown was, on account of his birthright, offered to *Valdemar*, the oldest son of Birger Jarl. He was crowned in Linkœping in 1251. From this period on, a new historic source is found in the rhymed chronicles, of which Swedish literature possesses several elaborate ones of more than 22,000 verses in all. Of these the Old, or Eric's, Chronicle, was written about 1320, and, like all the rest, anonymously. The verses are fine, the language pure and powerful; the portraits of historical personages are roughly drawn but interesting. Unfortunately these rhymed chronicles in general, and the Eric's Chronicle in particular, dwell rather on the description of impressive events of pomp and splendor than on historical facts; and the facts given are not always reliable. The Eric's Chronicle gives a brief review of events during the reigns of Eric and Valdemar; then for the events up to 1319 more fully.

According to the Eric's Chronicle, Birger Jarl wished to succeed Eric, but had to step aside for his son, who was of royal descent through his mother, King Eric's sister.

But Birger Jarl remained the all-powerful, although uncrowned, ruler till his death.

Many of the nobles were not satisfied with the election of Valdemar. They joined forces, gathering hired troops from Denmark and Germany. Birger met them at Hervadsbro and defeated them, capturing the leaders, who were beheaded. Among these were Philip, a son of Knut the Tall, and Knut Magnusson, with others of the Folkung family, which often was at war between themselves when great interests were at stake.

After this battle peace reigned under the powerful and sagacious rule of Birger. An assault upon Denmark by King Hakon of Norway and Birger jointly was planned, but a peace agreement took its place, in 1253. In the further complications between Norway and Denmark, Birger took no part. When later King Christopher of Denmark called upon his northern neighbors for help against revolts in his own country, these were ready to respond; but at the sudden death of King Christopher these plans were frustrated. In 1260 Birger bettered the already friendly relations with Denmark, by arranging the marriage between King Valdemar and the Danish princess, Sophia, whereupon he, himself a widower, married Mechtild, a queen-dowager of Denmark. In Finland, conditions were the same as of yore, pagan tribes and Russian invasions rendering everything unsafe and perilous. Birger renewed the trade agreement with Lubeck, in 1251, with added privileges to Lubeck, but with the stipulation that those of its citizens who settled in Sweden must become Swedish subjects. In 1261 the same privileges were extended to Hamburg. It was at this period that the Hanseatic League was formed between the commercial centres of North Germany. The relations between the league and the Scandinavian countries waxed quite intimate and, at times, menacing to the political independence of the latter. But Sweden derived many benefits through the contact with the reviving culture of Southern Europe, which was brought about through the Hanseatic League; the newly opened mining industry and the prosperity of Swedish commercial centres particularly owing much to this influence. Stockholm became the largest and most important of Swedish towns during the days of Birger, although he was not its founder. Also with England, Birger was carrying on peaceful proceedings; yet their purpose is not known. In 1237, the king of England had granted the merchants of the island of Gothland free trade privileges. Birger was a great and sound legislator, although it is not known with certainty how many of the judicial reforms accredited to him originated in these days. He made the law that sister should have **equal** share of inheritance with brother, and the laws of sanctity of home, Church, Thing and woman, which formed the kernel of a set of laws, later called *Edsœre* (Pledged oath), which every crowned king and his foremost men must pledge themselves to uphold. He tried to make away with the ordeal of walking on, or the handling of, iron as a legal testimony of guiltlessness. Further, he prohibited the custom of self-imposed thraldom.

The only act of Birger's which has been condemned was his attempt to introduce feudalism. His second son, Magnus, was created a duke, and received, at Birger's death, Sœdermanland, with the castle of Nykœping as a duchy. This gave rise to much strife and many conflicts within the new royal branch of the Folkungs, and endangered the unity of the kingdom. Birger, the last jarl of the realm, was the first real statesman of Sweden, whose stern intellect and integrity of character won for his country an honored position among its neighbors, and for himself the admiration of many generations to come. He died in 1266.

The first few years after Birger's death were peaceful. The archbishop's seat was removed to the present Upsala, where work was commenced on the magnificent cathedral. In 1271 the commercial privileges held by Lubeck and Hamburg were also granted to Riga.

Valdemar was a weak and frivolous man, and his licentiousness gave his brother Magnus the idea of pushing him aside, and later deprived him of the loyalty and respect of his people. The difficulties with his brothers ended in open conflict; Magnus and his younger brother Eric turned to Denmark and Germany, where they hired an army, King Eric Glipping of Denmark helping them with troops on promise of good securities. The brothers **invaded** West Gothland and defeated a Swedish army at Hofva, in 1275, while the king with his best troops remained inactive at Tiveden. Valdemar fled to Norway, bringing his son Eric with him. Venturing back into Vermland, he was captured and brought before Duke Magnus. Valdemar went so far as to abdicate his throne, but the meeting ended in an agreement according to which *Magnus* was to become king of Svealand and Valdemar to keep Gothaland. Eric was made a duke, but died in the same year. Magnus was crowned at Upsala in 1276.

King Valdemar did not long remain content with the new state of things. One month after Magnus's coronation he arranged a meeting with him at Lœdœse, over which King Magnus Lagabœte of Norway presided, but without being able to effect an agreement between the brothers.

Valdemar now turned to King Eric of Denmark, and won an ally in him because Magnus had neglected to fulfil his promises. Magnus gained a supporter in Duke Gerhard I. of Holstein, whose daughter Helvig he married in November, 1276.

With the year 1277 war commences between Sweden and Denmark. Magnus invades Halland and Scania, while Valdemar, with a Danish army, enters Smaland, burning the town of Vexio. With King Eric, Valdemar enters West Gothland, capturing Skara. At last the Danes are defeated at Ettak. Early in 1278 peace is made at Laholm, Magnus promising to pay his debt to Eric, leaving the castle of Lœdœse as security. Each promises not to shelter the rebels against the other. Valdemar lost his cause and had to give up Gothaland and his royal title, keeping only his inherited estates. On account of his scandalous living, the nobles insisted upon his imprisonment, and ten years after his abdication he was placed in custody at the castle of Nykœping. He survived all his brothers, dying in 1302. His son Eric was imprisoned at the castle of Stockholm, receiving good treatment like his father. When his cousin Birger was crowned, in 1302, he was set free, spending the rest of his life in Sweden as a private citizen. During Magnus Ericsson's minority he was a member of the king's council. When Magnus was sole occupant of the throne he took the title of "King of the Swedes and Goths," which, occasionally used before, henceforward became the customary one.

A revolt against King Magnus took place shortly after the meeting at Laholm. Some of the nobles were dissatisfied with the favoritism shown foreigners, a complaint which was only too often justifiable, and forever repeated, in the course of centuries, against the Swedish monarchs. Count Gerhard of Holstein was imprisoned, and the Danish knight, Ingemar, killed. The king invited the rebels to him at Gællqvist, where he in an unexpected way made them prisoners, and had them beheaded, in August, 1280, confiscating their property. This incident is characteristic of the time, but there is no other authority for it than the Chronicle. The reign of Magnus was comparatively short, but a happy and glorious one. The relations with the island of Gothland were made closer and more intimate, although the proud independence of its inhabitants remained largely intact. They were to pay increased scat, but continued their government without royal officials. The Guts were of Swedish origin, and their island formed since the ninth century a part of Sweden, but their isolated position and great commercial activity made them almost independent. About the year 1000 they seek for themselves protection from the Swedish king, and after their baptism they turn to the bishop of Linkœping for spiritual guidance. Thanks to its position, halfway between Germany, Russia and Sweden, Gothland gives rise to the most important commercial centre of Northern Europe after Lubeck. The inhabitants of Visby were Germans, to a great extent, and their conflicts with the rural population were frequent. King Magnus appears as an arbitrator in such cases with an authority great enough to impose his conditions. In spite of the inimical relations between Denmark and Norway, Magnus held peace with both.

As a legislator Magnus was even more important than his father, shaping and reshaping laws which furthered the development of the country and wielding an influence upon its jurisdiction reaching down to the present day. At a meeting of nobles at Alnsnœ, in 1280, King Magnus gave solemn pledge to the so-called Edsœre-laws of his father, and made the nobility into a privileged class. All the men surrounding him and his brother Bengt (made duke of Finland), and on their estates, together with the trusted men in the service of a bishop, were freed from paying taxes to the king. The same privilege was extended "to all men who served with a horse, whosoever they serve." The exemption from taxes did not include those due the church or community, but only those due the king. The horse service (*ross*=later *rusttjenst*) meant to provide for a cavalry force of iron-clad men for military service, according to the demands of the time. The nobles saw to it that this privilege was made permanent even after they had discontinued the horse service, and that others were added to it. A law prohibiting *voldgœstning*, the custom of travellers of taking by violence, or without compensation, food and comfort from the rural population, was also made at Alnsnœ, and won for King Magnus the rustic but beautiful surname of *Ladulas* (Barn-lock). "For he wished to place such locks on the peasant's barn, that no one should dare enter but at the will of the owner," wrote Olaus Petri, the historian and reformer. An official was placed in every country town to see to the traveller's comfort, and to his payment for it. At a meeting in Skenninge, in 1285, a law about *konungafrid* (royal sanctity) was made in order to prevent strife among the nobles and to make away with the ancient evil of revenge for bloodshed. This period of royal sanctity, when between men of the most strained relations peace should reign, commenced a fortnight after the king's arrival had been announced at the Thing and lasted until he had by letter informed it of his departure out of the province. The one who abused this sanctity, or only carried weapons, was exiled and his property confiscated. Secret societies among the nobles were prohibited.

Magnus was not only a great legislator, but saw to it that his laws were not broken. Personally he loved splendor and dignity, another trait through which he won the favor of the Swedes, who in all times have been fond of seeing their highest representatives surround themselves with impressive luxury and wealth. Magnus was in this respect the first mediæval monarch of Sweden, who kept a brilliant court, but at the same time was the pious and obedient son of the Church. He augmented the ecclesiastical privileges and founded several convents. In one of these, St. Clara of Stockholm, he installed his daughter Rikissa. Upon his death, which deplorable event took place in the island of Visingsœ, December 18, 1290, he was buried in the Franciscan convent church (the Riddarholm's) in Stockholm, according to his own wish. He was the first monarch to be entombed in this the present Pantheon of Sweden. Three sons survived him, Birger, Eric and Valdemar.

During the reign of Magnus, the development of mediæval institutions took rapid strides. This is noticeable also in the offices of those who surround the king. In the place of the jarl have been set two new dignitaries the *drotsete* and *marsk*, of the king, "the seater of the retinue" and "marechal" or "servant of the horse," respectively. Circumstances heightened the importance of these offices and changed them from court into state positions, the president of the state council and the commander of the army. The *kansler* (chancellor), often a bishop, is another important royal office. The king's council, consisting of bishops, knights and men of social standing, surrounds the monarch at his command and according to his selection, the archbishop being the only ex-officio member. Important affairs of State and Church are decided on at the meetings of nobles, *herredagar*, no one taking part who is not asked, or not agreeable to the king. These meetings later developed into *riksdagar*, at which all classes of the people were represented. Taxes were collected for the king by bailiffs, who in compensation received fiefs, sometimes consisting only of certain estates, in other instances as much as a whole province or district. The right of taxation belonged to the people. Only in extraordinary cases the king was allowed to impose additional taxes, although such were sometimes imposed wrongfully, in spite of a law stipulated by King Magnus Barn-Lock.

Birger succeeded his father Magnus. He was only ten years of age, but his father had placed by his side a man who was to reign during his minority. Marsk *Tyrgils Knutsson* was the second of the great uncrowned rulers of whom Sweden was destined to receive a number almost as large as that of illustrious monarchs. Tyrgils Knutsson followed out the policy of peace and progress which Birger Jarl had commenced and King Magnus continued, making in all the happiest era of the Middle Ages. To Birger Jarl's conquest of Tavastland in Finland, Tyrgils added that of Carelia. Two expeditions were sent to Carelia, in 1293 and 1299, whose savage inhabitants were converted and made Swedish subjects. Viborg was built and formed a stronghold for further operations, while Landskrona, another fortified place, erected by Tyrgils, not far from the site of the present St. Petersburg, was soon lost to the Russians. Through the conquest of Carelia, better times commenced for the Church of Finland, whose bishopric, in 1300, was moved to Abo.

The legislative work of his great predecessors was continued by Tyrgils, who made possible the union of the various "lands" of Upland into one judicial district. The first justice was Birger Persson, who was at the head of the work of preparing a common law for the whole province (in 1296). Neutrality was preserved during the conflicts between Norway and Denmark. King Eric Menved of Denmark was, in 1296, married to King Birger's sister, the pious Princess Ingeborg. In 1298 Birger was married to Eric's sister Margaret in Stockholm, over the lavish splendor of which event the poet of the Chronicle goes into ecstasies of delight and felicitous description. Both these unions were prearranged by King Magnus, and the princess Margaret had been educated in Sweden for the purpose of becoming its queen.

The king was now of age, but Marsk Tyrgils continued for several years at the helm. His relations to the Church show what a wise and vigorous statesman he was. When in the name of the king the privileges to the Church were once more granted, as by his predecessor, Tyrgils made the important exceptions that the Church should fulfil for its possessions the same military duty as all others in the country, and that certain large fines should be reserved for the king. The ecclesiastics took quietly to these restrictions at first, but soon an open conflict ensued. Another and greater one arose between the king and his brothers, Eric, duke of Sweden, and Valdemar, duke of Finland. It resembles very much the conflict between their uncle Valdemar and his brothers. In both cases there was a weak and deceitful king who was inferior, if not in wretchedness, at least in courage, to one of the brothers. After the first conflict was ended, the dukes selected Marsk Tyrgils for their prey. In March, 1305, Tyrgils saw the king grant to the Church the important privileges held back until then. In December of the same year the king and his brothers came upon Tyrgils unprepared. He was imprisoned, and in a shameful manner dragged to Stockholm, travelling night and day through the cold of winter, probably by some fraudulent legal process found guilty of treason, and beheaded, February 10, 1236. As a climax to this foul political murder, Tyrgils Knutsson was buried on the place of execution. Later, his body was removed to the church of Riddarholm and placed at the side of King Magnus, whose son he had served so faithfully.

The conflict between the royal brothers burst into flame again, revealing some of the darkest and most shocking scenes of deceit, treachery and villany found in Swedish history. The strife commenced in April, 1304, for the first time, and continued, with few and short intermissions, until the autumn of 1318, with broken oaths and pledges, which were renewed and broken again, alliances and royal betrothals formed, ended and renewed, kingdoms and duchies divided and redivided, endless intrigues, rebellion and mutual invasions. The kings of Norway and Denmark, with their armies, and several German princes and hired troops, became actors in this bloody tragedy, which ended in the annihilation of the principals. The most dramatic incidents are known as "the Play at Hotuna" and "the Feast of Nykœping," both taking place during the short intervals of peace. The former was enacted September 29, 1306, when the king invited his brothers to him at Hotuna in Upland. They accepted the invitation, only to carry the king and queen away as captives, forcing the former to give over to them his kingdom and his power, only leaving him the royal title. "The Feast at Nykœping" was held the night between December 10 and 11, 1317. The king and queen invited the dukes to the castle, seized them in the night and threw them into a dungeon, where they both perished after six months of hunger and neglect. Birger did not derive any benefit from his fearful crime. The whole country rose against him and he died, after several years of exile, in 1321. Birger has generally been held forth as the responsible party in the crimes and evils of the conflict, but his brothers seem to have been guilty in about the same degree. Duke Eric was one of the most brilliantly gifted princes of his age, and jealousy on the part of the king was the spark that kindled the fire. But the bad example set by their father of depriving an older brother of his throne, and the great possessions and independence of the dukes, were the underlying causes. The destruction of both the contending parties was an unexpected solution and a great gain for Sweden, whose fate appeared sinister, with the prospect of dismemberment or dissolution, the dukes holding their vast possessions as heirlooms.

During the conflict Norway had sided with the dukes, Denmark with the king. Duke Eric was married to Ingeborg, only child of King Hakon of Norway, and Duke Valdemar to his niece of the same name. *Mattias Kettilmundsson* was, in June, 1318, elected drotsete and regent. He led an army against Denmark in the interests of the duchesses, invading Scania and defeating the Danes near Hessleholm. November 11th of the same year peace was made in Rœskilde between the kings, Eric and Birger, on one side, and King Hakon and the heirs of the dukes, on the other. May 8, 1319, King Hakon died, and *Magnus Ericsson*, the young son of Duke Eric, inherited the crown of Norway, and July 8th of the same year he was elected king of Sweden at Mora in Upland.

For the attainment of this end Magnus's mother, Duchess Ingeborg, and seven Swedish councillors had worked with great activity. They had taken part in shaping the first Act of Union of the North in June, 1319, and from Oslo, in Norway, hastened to have Magnus elected at the Stone of Mora, where the Swedish kings since time immemorial were nominated. The Act of Union stipulated that the two kingdoms were to remain perfectly independent, the king to sojourn an equally long part of the year in each, with no official of either country to accompany him further than to the frontier. In their foreign relations the countries were to be independent, but to support each other in case of war. The king was the only tie to bind them together.

There was another Magnus whose candidacy was spoiled by this union. He was the son of King Birger, already, as a child, chosen king of Sweden in succession to his father. Magnus Birgersson, a prisoner at Stockholm, was beheaded in 1320, to make safe the reign of his more fortunate cousin. King Magnus was only three years old, and Drotsete Mattias Kettilmundsson presided over the government during his minority, the nobles of the state council having great power and influence. Both in Sweden and Norway the nobility had by this time attained a supremacy which was oppressive both to the king and the people, not so much through their privileges as through the liberties they took. Their continual feuds between themselves disturbed the peace of the country.

In 1332, King Magnus took charge of the government. He was a ruler of a benign and good disposition toward the common people, whose interests he always furthered. But he lacked strength of character and was not able to control the obnoxious nobles. The provinces of Scania and Bleking suffered greatly under Danish rule, which was changed into German oppression when handed over to the counts of Holstein as security for a loan. The people of Scania rose in revolt and asked for protection from King Magnus. At a meeting in Kalmar (in 1332) both provinces were united to Sweden. But the king had to pay heavy amounts in settlement, which were increased when Halland was procured in a similar way.

King Magnus was, at his height of power, one of the mightiest monarchs of Europe, having under his rule the entire Scandinavian peninsula and Finland, a realm stretching from the Sound at Elsinore to the **Polar** Sea, from the river Neva to Iceland and Greenland. In 1335 King Magnus rode his "Eriksgata," when he announced that no Christian within his realm should remain a thrall, thus practically abolishing the remnants of slavery. In the following year he was crowned with his queen, Blanche of Namur.

Magnus took great interest in legislation. During his minority the provincial laws were revised. The king himself accomplished the great and noble task of having these united into a state law (*landslag*), appointing a committee of three justices to do the work. The clergy was consulted, but refused to have ecclesiastical laws made for the whole kingdom. The state law was first considered in 1347, and was put in practice in 1352, being both a digest and an elaboration of the ancient provincial laws. In many an instance of foreign or domestic conflicts, the people, through its enforcement, found help and shelter from the national spirit of this law.

To the financial difficulties which beset the reign of King Magnus and made his life a burden the great plague was added. "The Black Death," in 1350, came from England to Norway and spread with great rapidity and the most disastrous consequences throughout the North. In certain parts of Sweden one-third of the population perished, in other parts even a greater percentage, the plague raging with equal violence throughout all classes of society. King Magnus had for a long time contemplated revenge against the invasions made by the Russians into Carelia. He undertook an expedition, under the pretext of a crusade, which ended badly, the Swedish fleet being shut in by the Russians and saved only by means of digging a canal. The king was severely criticised for this crusade, which was construed as a punishment for his sins, and, besides, largely increased his debts. The pope was among his creditors, who, upon non-payment, placed Magnus under his ban.

The union with Norway was not a happy one. As a minor, Magnus dwelt most of the time in Norway, but later principally in Sweden. This was contrary to the Act of Union, the state of things in Norway, furthermore, necessitating the almost continual presence of the king. For this reason his son, *Hakon*, was chosen king of Norway, in 1343, Magnus remaining in power until Hakon became of age, and his older son, *Eric*, chosen king, or heir-apparent, of Sweden, in 1344. It appears that King Magnus was in favor of this separation and had preconceived it in giving to his older son the Swedish name of Eric and to the younger the Norwegian name of Hakon, both equally characteristic of the royal lines of the respective countries. The two young kings caused their father considerable annoyance; but, upon the early death of Eric, Hakon entered more into harmony with King Magnus. Valdemar Atterdag, the crafty and enterprising king of Denmark, took an active part in the conflicts, pretending to support Magnus, while simultaneously depriving him of Scania, Halland and Bleking, which he captured almost without resistance. He landed in the island of Gothland, plundering Visby in a treacherous way. Upon his departure, his ships perished in a storm, the plundered treasures going down with these, the king himself escaping with difficulty. Valdemar arranged a marriage between his little daughter Margaret and King Hakon of Norway. Several Swedish nobles of great influence considered the treachery and impudence of Valdemar and the weakness of Magnus as going too far. They offered the Swedish crown to Albrecht, the son of King Magnus's sister Euphemia. The offer was accepted by Duke Albrecht of Mecklenburg, the father of the young Albrecht, in behalf of his son. He made a sudden assault upon Stockholm in 1363, capturing it. At the Stone of Mora, Albrecht the Younger was chosen king of Sweden. Magnus was defeated and made a prisoner at Enkœping.

King Magnus was taken to Stockholm and there imprisoned for some time, heavily laden with chains. King Valdemar deserted his cause, but the common people of Svealand, with whom Magnus had always been exceedingly popular, rose in order to free him. Soon King Hakon reached the very gates of Stockholm with a Norwegian army, whereupon Magnus was released. But he had to abdicate his throne, leaving for Norway, where he died, through an accident, in 1374.

Albrecht was the rightful king of Sweden. At the death of Eric he became heir-apparent to the Swedish throne, but for having sped on the course of events in his own interest, neither he nor his father acquired any popularity. They surrounded themselves by a great number of Germans, who, through their licentiousness and overbearing manner, enraged the people. The country was practically in the hands of a few Swedish nobles, among whom the drotsete, Bo Jonsson Grip, through his high office and his immense wealth, bore the supremacy. Bo Jonsson is said to have been the wealthiest man who ever lived in the North, his possessions, fiefs and castles being of an astounding number, the most famous among the latter being Gripsholm in the Lake Mælar. He loaned money to the king against new castles and fiefs in security, and held Albrecht in the most humiliating relation of dependence. His enemies he persecuted without mercy, killing one before the high altar in the Franciscan church of Stockholm. When Bo Jonsson died, in 1386, the king tried to better conditions by confiscating to the crown some of his possessions. But he met with opposition from the nobles, who claimed that he did so only to enrich his German favorites. The king was helpless against his councillors, to whom he had handed over all his power. They were in possession of all the fortified castles, and if one of them died, the king had no right to select a successor without their permission. The executors of Bo Jonsson's will ended by offering the crown to Margaret, Valdemar's daughter, and queen-dowager of Norway. She accepted, promising the nobles that they should remain in undisturbed enjoyment of their great privileges. Margaret sent an army into West Gothland, consisting of men from all three of the

Scandinavian countries, under the command of the Swede, Eric Kettilsson. King Albrecht met with an army to a great extent composed of German troops, and was defeated and made a prisoner at Falkœping, February 24, 1389. Albrecht was imprisoned at Lindholm, in Scania, for seven years, later returning to Mecklenburg.

To the Folkung period belongs one of the most remarkable and renowned of Swedish women, herself, on her mother's side, a Folkung, St. *Birgitta*, the daughter of the legislator and first justice of Upland, Birger Persson. Her parents were both pious and devoted to ascetic practices. As a child she had visions, the holy Mary appearing to her. When thirteen years of age she was married to Ulf Gumundsson, later justice of Nerike, also a pious man, with whom she made a pilgrimage to Spain. Birgitta lost her husband shortly afterward. At the Swedish court, where she was the highest functionary of Queen Blanche, she had seen political life at close range, gathering a deep and strong indignation against the mighty and powerful in the world. Her husband's death moved her deeply, and the religious mysticism of her youth now burst forth with increased strength, her visions becoming numerous and important. That she believed in them herself there is no doubt, and she made the world believe her. At first she hurled admonitions and curses against King Magnus and his court; but the wretchedness of the whole world attracted her to its spiritual centre, Rome, where she lived for twenty-three years in continual and open protest against the vices of the popes and priests. She died in Rome, in 1373, at the age of seventy, after a pilgrimage to Jerusalem, seeing the two great ambitions of her life fulfilled: the pope returning to Rome from Avignon, and her creation, the order of St. Salvator, sanctioned by the pope. Birgitta was canonized by the pope in 1391, through the influence of Queen Margaret.

Birgitta was the greatest political-poetic genius of the mediæval North. Her revelations fill eight volumes. She wrote them in Swedish, and had a priest translate them into Latin. Some of her original Swedish work is preserved. Birgitta appears to have thought in artistic images, and these images are of plastic form, often of consummate beauty, sometimes witty, sometimes avowedly comic, always effective. The melancholy charm of Sweden's nature suffuses all her writings and renders to her peculiar mediæval mysticism a national temperament. From Swedish sceneries and animal life she borrows her most beautiful images.

St. Birgitta has by some been considered as a reformer before Luther, but not quite correctly. Luther reformed the institutions; Birgitta aimed at reforming their upholders, and used against the pope and the priests a language almost as strong as Luther's. Some of her ideas were not strictly in harmony with the Catholic dogmas; she insisted on a close personal union with God, without the mediation of priests or saints, fought for a universal knowledge of the Bible and the preaching of the Gospel in the popular vernaculars, and considered the sale of indulgences a mortal sin. Four hundred and seventy convents of her order, in which men and women were to collaborate for the instruction and spiritual guidance of the people, were after her death founded in the Scandinavian countries, Germany, Esthonia, Poland, Italy and the Netherlands, one existing in England up to the time of Elizabeth. The mother institution at Vadstena, in East Gothland, was of the greatest importance to the cultural development of Sweden and the North.

VALDEMAR IV. SACKING THE TOWN OF WISBY

Norway.

One of the greatest libraries of the Middle Ages was reared, and the first book-printing establishment of Sweden founded there in 1490. Within its walls a considerable literary activity prevailed, the religious literature of the time being copied, or translated into Swedish, and many original works written. The Swedish language, used by the Birgittine school of writers, tried, by approaching Danish forms, to establish a common literary language in the North, the Norwegian having approached the Swedish during the time of the close relations between the courts of the two countries. These efforts, for a time furthered by political relations, were unfortunately soon to be abandoned forever.

Birgitta was a great genius in fetters. Her rare gifts were kept back in their development through the idiosyncrasies of her period. She was of an indomitable, aristocratic spirit, always remaining the noblewoman to whom it was natural to speak the truth to the princes of State and Church, because she considered herself their equal through the best blood of the North, of which she had her share. This religious mystic was a true child of her aristocratic age, which gave to Sweden two parallel lines, sometimes identical, of great legislators and weak and indulgent princes.

CHAPTER VI

Unionism versus Patriotism—Margaret, Engelbrekt and Charles Knutsson

QUEEN MARGARET, the successor of Albrecht, for the first time in history united the three Scandinavian countries and their dependencies under one rule. Born in a prison in which King Valdemar of Denmark had placed his consort, Queen Hedvig, there remained in the character of Margaret something of the rigor and chill of her uncomely birthplace. When she was seven, she was engaged to King Hakon of Norway, and married to him at eleven years of age. In Norway, her education was continued for several years after her marriage under the stern supervision of Dame Martha, a daughter of St. Birgitta, who often applied corporal punishment to the young queen. Margaret early gave evidence of self-control and power of reflection, and her mind developed at the expense of her heart. Her son Olaf became king of Denmark upon Valdemar's death, in 1375, and king of Norway upon that of Hakon, in 1380. Upon his death, in 1387, Margaret succeeded him, and two years later laid Sweden under her sceptre.

Albrecht was captured, but the Germans still were in possession of several Swedish strongholds. These yielded to Margaret, one after the other, except Stockholm. In the capital, the German influx of soldiers and merchants had made the foreign population exceedingly large. They now acted as oppressors. A secret league was formed which captured a great number of prominent Swedish citizens, who were cruelly tortured with wooden saws and then thrown into an old shed on the islet of Kæpplingeholm. The shed was ignited and the poor prisoners suffered a terrible death. German freebooters, especially the Vitalen or Victuallen Brotherhood, who provided the fortress of Stockholm with victuals, were plundering in the Baltic and Lake Mælar, and were the allies of the Germans of Stockholm. Margaret was powerless against them until she entered into an alliance with the Hanseatic towns. This ended the war; Stockholm surrendered and peace was made, in 1395. The plunders by sea-rovers in the Baltic were put an end to during Margaret's reign, but cost heroic efforts and much money, while the influence of the Hansa grew into menacing proportions.

Margaret was anxious to place the dynasty of the North firmly within her line of descent. In 1389, she selected her sister's grandson, Eric of Pomerania, then six years old, her successor, and he was thus proclaimed in Norway. In 1395, Eric was chosen king of Denmark and, in 1396, of Sweden. At his Swedish coronation in Kalmar, in 1397, Queen Margaret, who remained at his side as the real ruler, had the outline drawn of an *Act of Union*, which should forever unite the three Scandinavian kingdoms under one ruler. Each country was to preserve its constitution, laws and traditions unmolested, but they were to support each other in times of war. When a king was to be chosen, representatives of equal numbers from each country were to meet in Halmstad, the sons of kings to be favored by choice. This Act of Union was never carried into effect, according to legal forms. The sketch or outline of it, such as it is still preserved, was signed by representatives of the three countries, although not in equal numbers; but why Queen Margaret never allowed it to be enlarged into a legally binding document is not known. Her favorite idea was therein embodied, and she appeared to have an all-powerful influence over those necessary to carry it through.

Margaret made it her object to strengthen the crown and reduce the power of the nobles. She cared naught about keeping her promises to the latter, confiscating their castles and possessions, and annulling their privileges. When they complained, reminding her of her promises in her letters to them, she replied: "Keep my letters; I shall certainly keep your castles." All nobles created by Albrecht were entirely deprived of their privileges if they could not prove their due qualifications. The majority of forts erected during the war were pulled down. No taxes were longer imposed, except through written order of the government. These reforms were all rigorously carried out, according to the "Restitution of Nykœping" of 1396. Margaret succeeded in a remarkable way in reducing to normal proportions the power and influence of the Swedish nobility. The nobles, who were all-powerful and absolutely unyielding in Albrecht's days, bowed to her gracefully and received meekly her severe conditions. An explanation can be found in the fact that they had no leader of authority and power among them, after the death of Bo Jonsson Grip. Further, Margaret was careful not to fill the important offices of drotsete and marsk, when vacant, thus making the personal presence and interference of the sovereign necessary on all important occasions.

The love of the Swedish people should have been Margaret's reward for her abolition of aristocratic oppression, if she had not been in a position which necessitated the imposition of heavy taxes. The existence of the common people was made weary and troublesome through the payment of the "queen's tax," the "stake tax" on each hearth, the "rump tax" on each head of cattle, and, worst of all, the "Gothland's release." Bailiffs, often of foreign birth, collected these taxes with great severity. When the queen became aware of the complaints against her and her bailiffs, she asked in a letter to the archbishop that the people would forgive her in God's name. "Some of it one has not been able to better; some we and they might well have bettered, although what is done is done." Without doubt, there was due reason for the heavy taxes in the unsettled relations with other countries which existed during Margaret's reign; the support of the Hansa and a war with Holstein, commenced by King Eric, were expensive. The island of Gothland had been captured by the so-called German Order in the last days of Albrecht's reign. When the island was redeemed through the payment of Swedish money, Margaret made the mistake of installing there a Danish bailiff, and it thus for a long time remained a Danish province. Margaret believed in the Union and counted no Scandinavian a foreigner in either country. But it was contrary to Swedish law to install foreigners as bailiffs and vassals, and as she appointed a great number of Danes to Swedish fiefs, and never a Swede to Danish positions of the same or equal importance, the Swedish complaints, on this point, were justified.

Margaret was as severe toward the ecclesiastics as toward the nobles. But when she noticed the forebodings of powerful resistance, she made important concessions. She was anxious to observe religious practices, joining the convent of Vadstena as a "worldly sister," kissing the hands of all the monks and nuns on that occasion. She took interest in the conversion of the Laps, sending a baptized woman of their race, by the name of Margaret, to preach the Gospel among them.

The war with Holstein concerning the possession of Schleswig had been brought to an armistice, and the queen sailed to Flensburg to conduct further negotiations. While still on board of her ship, death surprised her, in 1412.

Margaret has been called the Semiramis of the North and well deserves her widespread fame. During her reign, the Northern countries, through her wisdom and strength, enjoyed a degree of order which they missed both before and after. She put an end to the foreign influence which had governed Sweden. Yet her rule was a disappointment, and the Union also. She paved the way for a new foreign influence, by making a German prince her successor and by leaning too much on the Hansa. The aristocratic oppression was crushed by her, but she introduced the oppression through royal bailiffs. She promised to preserve the old territory of Sweden unmolested, but placed the island of Gothland under Denmark. The Union of which Queen Margaret was the champion her successors were not able to grasp or uphold in the spirit of her good intentions. To Sweden it came in an inauspicious time when it was not fit to receive it. Foreign oppression had irritated the people to resistance, and discontent was to give life to patriotism.

Sweden had recently developed into one joint constitutional body, the various provinces giving up their ancient laws for a state law, in which the old individual traits were gathered and recognized. We know how Sweden was settled, not by various tribes, but by pioneers who, from the old home of culture, Scania, penetrated to the wilderness above, settling one district after the other, which, one by one, developed into provinces, little states by themselves, later united into one realm with a common king. One by one these provinces had taken the lead in the political and cultural development, often the youngest before the oldest. Thus the Swedes, a younger branch of the Gauts, gave their name to the country and furnished the rulers, the Guts of the island of Gothland securing the commercial supremacy of the sea, and the Rus of the outskirts of Upland founding the Russian empire. Now it fell upon Dalecarlia, the most recently settled of Swedish provinces, to save freedom and independence to a newly regenerated state which was awakening to the consciousness of its solidarity of interests, aspirations and duties. From Dalecarlia came the first great political leader. From there he and his later successors received their chief support.

Engelbrekt Engelbrektsson is the earliest and greatest of the patriotic heroes of Swedish history. To the glory of his deeds and the noble simplicity of his character the death of a martyr gives added lustre. Engelbrekt was born at Kopparberg, in the mining district of Dalecarlia, where there were many German settlers. Possibly his early ancestors were among them; but for three generations at least they had been native-born Swedes, Engelbrekt's father, as he himself, belonging to the Swedish nobility, although not of the influential families. Engelbrekt had received the chivalric education of his time at the courts of the great nobles, being next in rank to a knight, *væpnare* (squire), at the opening of his career. He was small of stature, but eloquent, courageous and of a lofty mind. The integrity of his character was absolute; his personal necessities were few and plain.

King Eric was a highly educated and refined man, not without a certain ability, but entirely without discernment and patience for the various demands and conditions of the countries over which he was set to rule. His foreign bailiffs in Sweden, mostly Danes, with a fair sprinkling of Germans and Italians, were still less in sympathy with his Swedish subjects. They tried to manage them as they did the Danes and the inhabitants of more southern countries, for centuries accustomed to slavery, ignorant of the ancient spirit of independence of the Swedish yeomanry, abated but not suppressed. When oppression no longer kept within reasonable bounds, the Swedish patience came to an end, and first in the youngest and most solitary parts of the country.

The most hated of Danish bailiffs was Jœsse Ericsson, of Westmanland and Dalecarlia. After having confiscated the horses of the peasants, he is said to have harnessed the men to plows and the women to grain-loads, once suffocating five peasants. Engelbrekt felt compassion for the misery of the suffering people and accepted the commission to seek the king, to make complaints in their behalf. He appeared before King Eric in Denmark, demanding punishment of the cruel bailiff and offering to go into prison or surrender his life if not speaking the truth, as was the custom of the time. The king gave him a letter to the Swedish council of state, demanding an inquiry which was promptly made. When Engelbrekt for a second time appeared with the corroboration of his statements from the Swedish councillors, the king sent him away in a fit of impatient rage. Upon his return, the Dalecarlians rose in a body, selecting Engelbrekt as their leader and marching south to Westeros. The councillors met and promised to have justice done in the case. But things remained the same until the following spring, in 1434. At midsummer the Dalecarlians commenced operations. The fort of Borganæs and the castle of Kœping were destroyed. Engelbrekt asked the people of Westmanland to join him, which they did to a man, the nobles also joining upon evidence of the determination of the popular leader. In Upsala, Engelbrekt found the people of Upland ready to join, and he made clear to the great multitudes the mission he had undertaken. He now felt strong enough to take a hand in the affairs of state; with the consent of the leading nobles reducing the taxes by one-third. Engelbrekt called upon a young, high-spirited nobleman, Eric Puke, to bring Norrland to revolt and destroy the forts of that district, which commissions Puke fulfilled to the letter, thereupon reinforcing Engelbrekt with his men. In the meantime, the people of western Sœdermanland rose by their own determination, destroying Gripsholm; the bailiff of the castle escaping with his treasures in boats over Lake Mælar. In Vermland and Dal the people followed these examples of revolt. The commander of the Stockholm fortress agreed upon an armistice, other castles surrendering or promising to surrender.

Engelbrekt met the council of state at Vadstena, escorted by 1,000 men of his best troops. Without fear or haughtiness, he pleaded the cause of his country, advising the councillors in firm and eloquent words to see to it that the foreign oppression came to an end. The council hesitated, Bishop Knut of Linkœping stating that the oath to the king could not be broken. To this Engelbrekt answered that the king had pledged many oaths but kept none, for which reason the people were freed from their oath. Upon a wholesome demonstration of force the councillors gave in and dictated a letter in which they broke their pledge to King Eric, yet giving as an excuse that they were compelled to do so. The revolt had now spread to all parts of the kingdom, at least 100,000 being armed to meet the emergency. But so carefully and quietly was the work of liberation performed that no harm was done in the parts where the peasant armies were moving. After having entered Halmstad, Engelbrekt returned to Westeros, where the army was scattered, but soon gathered again upon the report that the king with a fleet was approaching Stockholm. Upon his arrival, the king found Stockholm enclosed by a peasant army and returned to Denmark, forced to agree to an armistice. At a meeting in Arboga, Engelbrekt was elected regent. This was the first meeting in which representatives of the merchant class and the yeomanry took part, being thus the first *riksdag* or parliament composed of the four Estates — noblemen, ecclesiastics, burghers, and yeomen.

King Eric promised, upon his return to Stockholm, to govern the country according to its laws and through Swedish men, appointing Krister Nilsson Vasa drotsete, and Charles Knutsson Bonde marsk. But so badly did he keep his promises that he was once more dethroned. The nobles hastened to elect Charles Knutsson regent, but through pressure which the peasants brought to bear it was agreed that he should share his power with Engelbrekt and lead the siege of Stockholm, while the latter should free the country from the bailiffs reinstalled by the king.

Upon his second tour through the country, Engelbrekt was seized by illness, but being called to Stockholm by an important state affair, he started over the lakes thither from Œrebro. One evening he stopped at an islet in Lake Hielmar for the night. When he saw a boat approach with Mons Bengtsson on board he staggered on a crutch down to receive him. This man sprang ashore and assaulted Engelbrekt, who tried to ward off the blows of the axe with his crutch, but failing to do so he was killed on the spot, in April, 1436. The perpetrator of this beastly murder was a son of a noble with whom Engelbrekt had been engaged in some controversy which he had recently settled to the satisfaction of both parties. The murderer escaped; but, although shielded from punishment by Marsk Charles Knutsson, he was shunned by everybody, his high-born and wealthy relations for several centuries refusing to carry the proud family name (Natt och Dag) upon which he had brought shame.

The memory of Engelbrekt is one of the most honored and most beloved in Swedish history. He waged the first battle against the oppression which foreign intrigues had brought upon his country, and saved from the peril of slavery the ancient freedom and independence of the Swedish people.

Through a remarkable coincidence, a cousin of Engelbrekt's murderer, Nils Bosson, a young follower of the popular hero, who took his mother's family name of Sture, was to become the father and grandfather of two of the most revered of Engelbrekt's successors; Nils Bosson himself being as sympathetic and upright a type of nobleman as any time or country has produced.

Charles Knutsson, after Engelbrekt's death, was the most influential man in Sweden. But he was a very different man. Belonging to the highest aristocracy, he was himself of great wealth, highly talented, well read, and a great traveller. He was exceedingly handsome, dignified, amiable, eloquent, and possessed a voice of unusual charm and strength. But he was a prey to ambition, determined to make his way to the throne, but little careful in the selection of his means toward that end. He aroused the suspicion and hatred of Eric Puke, whom he irritated to revolt only to get him in his power. This noble but headstrong man was executed for treason, while Drotsete Krister Nilsson, who signed the death-warrant in the interest of Charles, himself was persecuted by the latter and deprived of all his fiefs save one. Charles showed great severity in punishing the peasants, who were Puke's supporters, four of them being burned alive; thus losing the popular sympathy, while becoming an object of envy in the eyes of the nobles. These recalled King Eric, who was again found impossible and soon dethroned also in Denmark.

Christopher of Bavaria, a nephew of Eric, was elected to succeed him (in 1440) by the nobles of Denmark and Sweden. He was a good-natured man, who allowed the aristocrats of Sweden to rule as they pleased, only keeping an eye on Charles Knutsson. Christopher died in 1448. During his reign a new state law was issued in 1442, called "King Christopher's land's law," although the king probably had very little to do with its form or stipulations. It offered a few improvements, but in general so closely resembled the older state law that the one was often mistaken for the other and both remained valid until 1736.

Charles Knutsson (Charles VIII.) returned from Finland, which duchy had been held under his supremacy, four months after Christopher's death, and was by an overwhelming majority elected king of Sweden. Shortly after his coronation at Upsala he was elected king of Norway and crowned at Drontheim, in 1449. His reign opened with a lucky expedition to the island of Gothland. But in the following year King Charles lost both Gothland and Norway to Christian of Denmark, with whom the Unionist party of Sweden entered into secret plots against the king. Invasions and intrigues followed. Christian invaded Smaland, East Gothland and Vermland, to which Charles responded by an invasion of Scania, destroying the old town of Lund with nineteen of its twenty churches, the cathedral alone being spared. Christian took revenge by an invasion of West Gothland, capturing Lœdœse. Another Danish army marched through East Gothland, but met defeat at Holaveden through an onslaught made by Swedish peasants. The valiant Tord Bonde, a cousin of King Charles, took the Danes by surprise, recapturing Lœdœse. An armistice of two years was agreed on, in May, 1453.

In the battle against open and secret enemies things turned out badly for King Charles. The best supporter of his cause, his cousin Tord, was murdered by a Danish traitor in his service, in 1456, and a new and dangerous enemy was encountered in the Church. The king had confiscated to the crown a number of estates which the Church had gained in an illegal way. While preparing for an expedition to Œland, and having instructed the archbishop to gather troops for him, Charles learned that this man, Jœns Bengtsson Oxenstierna, had turned against him. The archbishop deposited his ecclesiastical robe at the high altar of the Upsala cathedral and started, sword in hand, with his forces to meet the king. Charles tried to surprise him, but was himself caught in a trap and met his enemy on the ice of Lake Mælar. The encounter proved a defeat to Charles, who in haste stored his treasures in a convent in Stockholm and sailed for Dantzic.

Christian of Denmark was called in by the archbishop and chosen king of Sweden. Christian was a sagacious ruler, but his great need of money, incurred by the redeeming of Schleswig and Holstein, made him unpopular. As the easy-going Christopher had been surnamed "Bark-king," on account of dearth experienced in Sweden during his reign, when the people had to mix bark with their flour, thus Christian, on account of his avidity, was called "The Bottomless Purse." During Christian's war with Russia, the archbishop was commissioned to collect the increased taxes, but failing to do so, to the full extent demanded, he was imprisoned at the command of the king. This caused indignation.

Kettil Karlsson Vasa, a nephew of the archbishop, and the bishop of Linkœping, revolted and defeated the king and his army at Haraker's church, in Westmanland, in 1464. The victors then marched on Stockholm. The popular opinion of the country demanded the reinstallation of King Charles. The peasants wanted him "because Sweden was of old a kingdom, not a regent's land or a diocese." King Charles returned in the same year, but soon left the throne again on account of a conflict with Bishop Kettil. This latter turned to Christian, promising a safe return to the crown if he set free the archbishop. Christian immediately did so, the worthy bishops commencing operations against Charles, who, defeated and forsaken by all, abdicated his throne, January 30, 1465. The once upon a time richest man of Sweden was now deprived of all, Christian having taken his hidden treasures. He retired to Raseborg, a castle in Finland, which after some hesitation was granted him. "We have," wrote he, "in such manner departed from Sweden, that never longeth us to return thither the third time." He also complained of his misery in the following strophe of assonance verse:

> While I was lord of Fogelwick
> Then I was both mighty and rich,
> But since made the king of Svea land
> I am a poor and unhappy man.

Great confusion reigned in Sweden during the next two years. Bishop Kettil, who styled himself regent, tried to conduct the government in common with the archbishop, but the great nobles did their own pleasure. At last one of them, Ivar Axelson Tott, who had the island of Gothland in fief, joined the party of Charles, marrying his daughter. His brother, Eric Axelson, was made regent. Nils Bosson Sture had been repeatedly asked to accept this dignity, as also the crown, but he refused. He and Sten Sture, of the original Sture family, who led the army under Bishop Kettil at Haraker, now made possible the second reinstallation of Charles, in 1467, the ambitious archbishop dying in the same year. But Charles was old and weary of the vanities of life, for which he had made so many sacrifices. It was only the valor and strength of the two Stures that made it possible for him to keep the crown and to die in the purple, in 1470. He designated Sten Sture as his successor at the rudder of state, but warned him not to seek the crown. "That ambition," he said, "has crushed my happiness and cost my life."

Charles is very sympathetically dealt with in the New Rhymed, or Charles Chronicle, probably written by one of his men, who flatters him, as did the Old Chronicle the ill-fated Duke Eric. Still the Charles Chronicle and its continuations, the Sture Chronicles, are very important historic sources of these periods of Unionism versus Patriotism, from Margaret to Gustavus Vasa. The less reliable Prose Chronicle and the later historic works by Ericus Olai, Johannis Magnus and Olaus Petri, also throw light upon them. What all of these have in common is a fiery patriotic spirit, entirely lacking in the placid and artistic lines of the Old Chronicle as compared to the New. With the seeds of patriotism were sowed those of national hatred against a foreign foe. That the Dane and not the German was destined to be this national enemy was disastrous to the Union of the North, but probably a gain for the cultural development of Sweden. This period is rich in shorter poems on political men and conditions, all of a strongly democratic flavor. Among these the song about his friend Engelbrekt, by Bishop Thomas of Strengnæs, occupies a high place, but a still higher one the Song of Liberty, by the same high-minded patriot.

CHAPTER VII

Unionism versus Patriotism—Uncrowned Kings of the Sture Families

STEN STURE THE ELDER was chosen regent by the council of state and elected by the people at the Riksdag of Arboga, in 1471. For more than half a century following upon the reign of Charles VIII., Sweden was governed by uncrowned kings, with the intermission of a few years. These regents had not any republican ideals in mind, nor were they secretly coveting the crown. Their ambition was simply to uphold a strong and firm national government by means of which foreign lordships could be made impossible, the people enjoy their rights and their liberty, and the government increase in power and authority at the expense of Church and nobility. The policy laid down by Sten Sture the Elder, and strictly adhered to by him and his successors, was of the broadly democratic spirit of Engelbrekt. This policy was strengthened by the high esteem in which the regents were held. Yet their position was a very difficult one, for although enjoying the full confidence of the people, they were regarded with envy and suspicion by the aristocracy, who never could be persuaded but that these noble uncrowned rulers were secretly scheming for obtainance of the royal crown.

Sten Sture had the good fortune to inaugurate his reign

with a glorious victory over King Christian, which put an end to Danish invasions during a whole generation. Christian arrived at Stockholm with a fine fleet and a magnificent army, taking his position at Brunkeberg, close to the north of the capital. Here a long and fierce battle was fought, October 10, 1471. Sten Sture commanded a large army of peasants, attacking Christian's fortified position from the north, supported by Knut Posse, with burgher troops, from the south. At the third attack victory was won, Nils Bosson Sture arriving on the battle scene with an army of Dalecarlians. King Christian was wounded in the mouth; the famous Danish Oriflamme, Dannebrog, was captured, being surrounded by five hundred corpses of select Danish knights. Through the prestige of the great victory at Brunkeberg, Sten Sture managed to give Sweden ten years of undisturbed peace and comfort. Encouraged by the victory over the foreign invaders, the city of Stockholm took the lead in ridding the towns of undue influence, caused by the supremacy of German commerce. The town laws held a stipulation that half the number of councillors in each town council should be Germans. A petition headed by the burghers of Stockholm and circulated through the towns was acted upon, the council of state abolishing by law the stipulation in question. Free markets were established in the commercial centres Kalmar and Sœderkœping, and a new commercial town was founded on the Gotha River, to be called Gothahamn, although the name was changed to New Lœdœse. In spite of the supremacy of the Hanseatic League, commerce was good, the iron mines of Dalecarlia, Westmanland, Nerike and Eastern Vermland growing in importance, and silver being produced by various mines in Dalecarlia.

Lord Sten gave careful and loving attention to the needs of the yeomanry and the common people. He kept an open and watchful eye on the bailiffs, and carried out the demands of justice with severity. Many farms, desolate and neglected during the times of war, were brought under cultivation. Lord Sten made no decision in any matter of importance without consulting the yeomen and the burghers, as well as the nobles, at *Riksdagar*, the parliamentary nature of which was further developed. With a firm hand he held the nobles down to order and the requirements of a national democratic policy. The powerful brothers Ivar and Eric Tott especially caused him annoyance, the former holding the island of Gothland, the latter the duchy of Finland, in fief. It came to open hostilities with Ivar Tott who, defeated and deprived of his castles, fled to Denmark, taking revenge by turning the much contested island over to said power.

Lord Sten was a very pious man, but he held the ecclesiastics under strict surveillance on account of their unpatriotic tendencies. But he collaborated with them for the establishment of a state university at Upsala, in which the archbishop, Jacob Ulfsson, was greatly interested. Sanctioned by the pope, the university was opened in 1477, with great ceremonies. One of its earliest professors was Ericus Olai, the author of the first but rather uncritical work of Swedish history, Chronica Regni Gothorum, written in awkward mediæval Latin, but in a style attractive through its vivacity. Latin was chiefly used by the learned and literary men. The cloisters and the cathedrals had schools where the young people were trained for the learned professions, chiefly the Church. For a university education, the institutions of Cologne, Prague, Leipzig and Bologna, but chiefly Paris, the greatest of them all, had been sought. The Swedes had three *collegia* in Paris, and the Scandinavians held there an honored position as scholars, the Swedes three times filling the office of rector or president of the Paris university, the highest dignity of learning in the world. Ingeborg Tott, the wife of Sten Sture, was a great friend of learning, having books printed at her expense and collecting a large library in the convent of Mariefred, founded by Lord Sten.

The peace of the country was disturbed by a war with Russia. Attacks on the castle of Viborg had been made shortly after the battle of Brunkeberg, but warded off by Eric Tott, who in return invaded Russian territory. After his death the valiant Knut Posse was made commander of Viborg. The Russians, in 1495, made a violent attack upon the castle, damaging it considerably. But Posse led the defence with superior skill, repulsing the enemy with astounding force. This deed has become famous in popular traditions, both Swedes and Russians crediting Posse with an alliance of a supernatural order. The regent himself twice headed expeditions to Finland, forcing a new Russian army to retire over the frontier. Affairs were going badly on account of unsafety in Finland, and dearth and intrigues in Sweden. The council of state accused Lord Sten of not doing all he could for Finland while secretly fanning the discontent of the commanders, who made personal sacrifices of time and money by remaining with the army. It came to hot words between Lord Sten and the commander Svante Sture, the son of Nils Bosson. He returned home, although Lord Sten told him he was a deserter in so doing, "fleeing from the banner of state." Svante Sture, who with Posse had made a glorious inroad upon Russian territory, now joined the aristocratic enemies of the regent, calling in King John (Hans) of Denmark. John succeeded Christian in 1482, and commenced intriguing for the Swedish crown. The Swedish nobles were anxious to have this good-natured monarch for ruler. Lord Sten was too sagacious to openly oppose them, when they, in the so-called *Recess of Kalmar* of 1483, declared *John* king of Sweden, the king promising the island of Gothland to Sweden, and all old privileges to the nobles. By means of skilful diplomatic operations, Lord Sten delayed matters to such an extent that it took fourteen years before John II. was king of Sweden in anything but name. But the time was ripe for Svante Sture's open conflict with Lord Sten. The council, the archbishop leading, broke their faith with the regent, offering King John the crown. He came with an army to Stockholm, taking his position at Brunkeberg. An army of Dalecarlians marched upon the capital at the solicitation of Lord Sten, who awaited them with another army. The operations took an unfavorable turn on account of misapprehended movements, Lord Sten with difficulty saving his life. King John understood that a continued struggle would lead to his ultimate defeat and made peace. Lord Sten retired, but with the greatest fiefs given to any Swedish man; viz., the whole of Finland, with large possessions besides. When the king entered Stockholm, in October, 1497, it was at the arm of Lord Sten, to whom he said jestingly: "Have you now prepared everything well for me at the castle, Lord Sten; the table set with meat and ale, so that my guests may make merry?" Lord Sten answered in the same light spirit, pointing to the Swedish nobles who had joined the royal retinue: "That these know best who stand there behind you. They have it all both baked and brewed." Later the king remarked: "Lord Sten, it is a bad inheritance you have bequeathed on me in Sweden; the peasants whom God created slaves you have made into lords, and those who shou... have been lords you try to make slaves." At his coronation in Upsala, the king bestowed knighthood upon many Swedish nobles (something that had been beyond Lord Sten's authority to do), upon his return to Denmark appointing Lord Sten to take the reins of government with three state councillors at his side.

King John's reign in Sweden was of short duration. He failed to return the island of Gothland to the Swedish crown and lost his prestige through an unsuccessful war in Ditmarschen. Svante Sture, who had not been dealt with according to his expectations, declared war upon the king and joined Lord Sten, who was in an unenviable position and glad to shake off the Union with Denmark, which he did, in 1501, when made regent for the second time. With a peasant army siege was laid to the castle of Stockholm, held by the energetic Queen Christine, who capitulated after a heroic struggle. Three days later King John appeared with an army, but returned, seeing that he came too late. Lord Sten retained Queen Christine at Vadstena for some time, later escorting her to the Danish frontier. Upon his return he was taken ill and died suddenly at Jœnkœping, December 14, 1503. With him the older or original line of the Sture family became extinct. Lord Sten was the greatest ruler since Margaret, and his rule, being of a more patriotic and democratic tendency, was of greater benefit to Sweden than hers.

Svante Sture succeeded Sten. He was of the younger Sture line, the son of the noble patriot, Nils Bosson, who in the time of Charles VIII., as the friend of Engelbrekt and Bishop Thomas, had taken stand against the archbishop and the nobles, backed by the Dalecarlians, who adored him. Lord Svante was a very quick-tempered man, which led him into the conflict with Lord Sten. Unlike the regent and his own father, he never had experienced what Danish oppression meant, which accounts for his unwise decision in joining the Unionists. The war with Denmark lasted eight of his nine years of reign, which proves him an able soldier and a stanch patriot. His position from the start was less favorable than that of his predecessor, who could reign in the glory of his early victory at Brunkeberg.

Lord Svante had in *Doctor Hemming Gad* a patriotic adviser of rare attainments and great learning. He had studied in Rostock, was for twelve years Lord Sten's representative in Italy, and later bishop of Linkœping, although never sanctioned and finally placed under ban by the pope. Hemming Gad was the first democratic agitator of Sweden, a warm admirer of the Stures, and a good soldier. His statecraft he had evidently learned in Italy with her traditions of Machiavelli. His literary style is very characteristic, the language of a learned ecclesiastic with the oaths of a soldier. Those of his writings which are still extant prove a great love for the common people, a love which was returned by them. Having organized the revolt against King John, he evinced great slyness and presence of mind at the death of Lord Sten. To preserve its secrecy until Svante was forewarned and in possession of the castle of Stockholm, he had a man dress in the clothes of the deceased regent and continue the journey to the capital with Sten's retinue.

The Unionist party was as ready as ever to offer the

crown to King John, their representatives agreeing to pay a yearly tribute until he or his son Christian was chosen king. This agreement was made in 1509, but it called forth a storm of indignation from the patriots and the people, and was never considered by the government. Lubeck opened hostilities against Denmark and was joined by Sweden, the Unionists recommencing deliberations whenever it looked favorable for Danish interests. Lord Svante made sure of peace and safety for Finland before taking up the conflict with the Danes. On the eastern shore, Hemming Gad led the operations against the town and castle of Kalmar, held by the Danes. The town was soon captured, but the castle not before the end of 1510. Ake Hansson (Natt och Dag) fought with great valor and considerable success against the Danes on the western and southern frontier, until this "Tormentor of Denmark," as he was surnamed, was killed in battle in 1510. On the sea the Danes were superior, a fleet under the command of Otto Rud and Soren Norrby plundering Abo in Finland. But when Lubeck's fleet appeared the Danes were forced back. Peace was made, but soon broken. Lubeck sent a fleet to invade the coast of the Danish isles; Hemming Gad, with several Swedish ships, taking part in the expedition. Denmark did her best to crush Swedish resistance by inducing Russia to break the peace, the emperor to declare Sweden the arch enemy of the German empire, and the pope to place her under ban.

More unfortunate to Sweden than these intrigues was the fact that King John in his son Christian had an able warrior and a great organizer. Prince Christian put down a revolt in Norway against Danish oppression, entering West Gothland with a superior army. The Unionists assembled to force the regent to abdicate, but he firmly refused to do so. A rebellion seemed imminent, Lord Svante hastening to Westeros to confer with the people of the mining districts. Shortly after the opening of the meeting, Lord Svante died quite suddenly, after a stroke of paralysis, in January, 1512.

The council of state selected Eric Trolle, a learned but unfit man of the Unionists, to succeed Lord Svante. But the popular opinion condemned him, and the council was forced to choose Svante's son as his successor.

Sten Sture the Younger was barely nineteen years of age at his father's death. Knighted when only five, he early distinguished himself as a warrior, winning fame for his chivalric spirit and noble character, and, like his illustrious namesakes, his father and grandfather, becoming the idol of the people. And he deserved their idolatry. More resembling his grandfather in the sweetness of his disposition than his sterner predecessors, he was as great a warrior as his father, to which he joined the sagacity and power of self-control characteristic of the elder Lord Sten. As a youth, he was made regent of a country in war, distress and peril. He was called away by death when only twenty-seven, leaving behind the memory of not one evil deed to soil the glory of his fair name, although continually placed in trying and dangerous positions of strife, rivalry, envy and rebellion. He made his will respected by high and low with a temperance in spirit and methods worthy of the highest admiration and the devoted love of the people. The young Lord Sten had a tender heart for the lowly and the suffering, never fearing to wring their rights from the oppressors, whosoever they were. He took great interest in the pursuits of peace, during the intervals allowed by his successful exploits in war.

In spite of the plague and other contagious diseases, which, together with the destruction of war, ravaged the country, he left it in a better condition than he received it. In many ways more farseeing than his contemporaries, his name will live on for centuries as one of the most beloved in Swedish history.

With the younger Lord Sten, other new actors appeared upon the stage of Scandinavian history. Christian II. succeeded his father upon the throne of Denmark and Norway. In Sweden, Archbishop Jacob Ulfsson retired and was succeeded by Gustavus Trolle, a son of Lord Eric. The new archbishop was of a hateful and jealous disposition. He resolved to avenge the treatment his father had received at the hands of Lord Sten and the Swedish people by placing Christian on the throne. The young regent made no less than four attempts to win over this formidable enemy, but all in vain. He opened up a court at Stæket, in Upland, more brilliant than that of Lord Sten, and accepted subsidies from Denmark. At last, fully aware of the secret deliberations going on, Lord Sten surrounded Stæket and called a Riksdag at Arboga, in 1517, where it was resolved that Christian should never become king of Sweden, and that the siege of Stæket should be continued. Christian sent a little army to support his ally, but Lord Sten met it at Ladugardsland, outside of Stockholm, completely routing it. A new Riksdag was called at Stockholm before which the archbishop appeared upon truce. His language was haughty and disdainful. He said he was in his full right to support King Christian's claims with mitre and sword, the pope sanctioning his policy; and to the pope alone he was responsible. The indignant Riksdag resolved that the archbishop should be deprived of his seat, being guilty of high treason, and that his castle should be burned. The resolution was written down and signed by all the bishops, none daring to oppose the yeomanry. Bishop Brask, of Linkœping, managed to conceal in the wax of his seal a paper with the words: "To this I am forced by necessity." The archbishop returned to defend Stæket, but soon had to flee with his followers. It was only by using all his authority that Lord Sten could save his enemy's life from the irate people. Trolle was forced to resign his seat and was imprisoned in a convent at Westeros, while his castle was torn down. Lord Sten wanted to appoint a successor to Trolle, but Bishop Brask objected that the pope might not consent to his removal. To this Lord Sten uttered the following manly words, hardly in touch with the policy of Rome: "I think that our most holy father, the pope, and the canonic law should not tolerate as the leaders of the Church, and as the precepts or mirrors to the people, men who are infested by open treason, in particular against their own country." The Church tried various means to gain a settled condition of things. When Sten refused the royal crown from its hand, he was at last placed under ban.

The hostilities with Denmark recommenced. King Christian appeared with a fleet and an army, in June, 1518, laying siege to Stockholm. His attacks were valiantly repulsed, and Christian, fearing to be encircled by his enemies, marched away in a southeasterly direction, taking a firm position at Brennkyrka. A Swedish army met him from the south and gave battle one of the last days of July, 1518. It was a fierce conflict, ending with a victory for the Swedes. The chief banner was carried by the squire Gustavus Ericsson Vasa, who five years later was to become king of Sweden. Christian returned to attack Stockholm, once more in vain. He was to sail for Denmark, but was kept back by storms, great suffering being experienced by his men. Christian was forced to open deliberations, making very high demands. But Lord Sten refused to hold a meeting, postponing it to the following year. A few days later, King Christian sent word that he wanted the regent to visit him in his ship on important affairs. Lord Sten, always good-natured and ready to accept peace, thought that the king had changed his mind and was ready to go. But the burgomaster and council of Stockholm prevailed upon him not to go, sure that it would bring him into the enemy's hands. Lord Sten took their advice and arranged for a meeting on land, sending six Swedish nobles as hostages to the king at his demand. Among these were Dr. Hemming Gad and Gustavus Ericsson Vasa. For two days Lord Sten waited in vain for the king to appear. Then he learned, to his dismay and indignation, that King Christian had sailed to Denmark, taking the hostages with him as prisoners, October 4, 1518.

Christian collected all his forces and resources to crush Sweden. The whole of the following year was spent in preparations. Sweden was placed under ban by the pope, and Christian made himself his representative, the one who was to fulfil the heavenly punishment. In January, 1520, a large Danish army invaded Smaland and West Gothland. Lord Sten made an appeal to the people and gathered a peasant army, with which he met the superior force of the enemy at Bogesund, in West Gothland. The Swedish forces were arranged in line on the frozen surface of Lake Asund. Lord Sten rode in front of the line, encouraging his men, but was seriously wounded during the very first engagement and carried from the field. After two vain attempts, the Danes were victorious in overthrowing the Swedes. These gathered in the wooded hills of Tiveden for a last heroic resistance, which was broken; the Danes taking possession of the provinces to the north. Lord Sten, mortally wounded, died on the ice of Lake Mælar during his journey to Stockholm. Christian continued his march on Stockholm, the castle of which was heroically defended by Lord Sten's consort, Christine Gyllenstierna, who also tried by support and exhortations to encourage other strongholds not yet surrendered to resist the Danes. The castle of Kalmar was defended by another heroic woman, Anna Bielke. But Christian won, through persuasions and deliberations, what he could not take by violence. His operations were carried on by Dr. Hemming Gad, who, for reasons unknown to history, had changed his old patriotic views and become a friend of Christian. In September, 1520, Christian won Stockholm by peaceful agreement. The 4th of November he was crowned by Trolle, the reinstalled archbishop. At this occasion it caused considerable surprise that only Danes and Germans were knighted, the herald proclaiming that the country was won by sword, for which reason no Swede could be thus honored. This was in striking contrast to Christian's proclamation of having ascended the throne by right of his descent from St. Eric. Worse things were to follow.

The 7th of November a great number of Swedish nobles were called to the castle of Stockholm, where they were brought before a tribunal, the king presiding. The archbishop asked for remuneration for the sufferings caused him during Lord Sten's reign. A jury of bishops and nobles convened. Christine Gyllenstierna was the first to answer to the accusations, holding forth that the Riksdag of Arboga was responsible for the action taken against Trolle and bringing the signed document in evidence. The king answered by announcing that all who signed were under the ban of the pope; Bishop Brask was the only one acquitted, producing his written slip of reservation from under his seal, besides Bishop Otto of Westeros, who supported Trolle in his claims. In the evening all the accused were imprisoned and judgment passed on them the following morning.

In the morning of November 8th, a solemn procession of convicts started from the castle to the grand square, hedged in by soldiers and executioners. The bishops Mattias of Strengnæs and Vincentius of Skara, in their ecclesiastical robes, came first, followed by thirteen noblemen and thirty-one town councillors and burghers of Stockholm. In the square, a Danish councillor of state from the porch of the court-house asked the masses not to be frightened. The archbishop, he said, had three times on his knees implored the king that justice should be done. Bishop Vincentius replied with great courage that the king had committed treason against the Swedes and called down divine punishment on him for such deeds. Two of the Swedish nobles followed the bishop with short addresses, admonishing the people not to believe in false letters and promises and to put down such tyranny as soon as within their power. King Christian, who from a window of a house facing the square looked down on the spectacle, now gave a sign for the executions to commence. First the bishops, then the state councillors, nobles and burghers were beheaded, among whom were two brothers of Christine Gyllenstierna and the father and brother-in-law of Gustavus Ericsson Vasa. Many burghers were captured in the street, or in their homes, and brought in to be executed, others being killed on the spot. Not less than eighty-two persons were that day executed, the number being increased during the following days by people killed in various ways. Olaus Petri, the reformer, who was an eyewitness, in his history gives a graphic description of the terrible scenes. He adds: "Yes, this was a horrible and cruel murder, such as no other prince who carried a Christian name ever committed before." The corpses were burned, the remains of Lord Sten and one of his sons being taken from their graves and thrown into the flames. Christine Gyllenstierna, and the mother and sister of Gustavus Vasa, were with several other ladies carried to Copenhagen and thrown into a miserable dungeon. The mass murder has been called the Carnage of Stockholm, but it was extended also to Finland—where Dr. Hemming Gad was executed at Raseborg—and to the provinces. Christian marked his return through the Swedish mainland to Copenhagen by executions and mass murder everywhere; six hundred are estimated to have been killed through his order during his short stay in Sweden.

Archbishop Trolle had taken a terrible revenge, and Christian thought he had crushed forever the stubborn Swedish resistance. But through this excess of cruelty the Union became insupportable, and the Swedish people resolved to throw off forever the connection with any foreign ruler. In the woods of Dalecarlia a man was hiding who soon was to step forward to lead the work of liberation and independence.

CHAPTER VIII

Revolution and Reformation—Gustavus Vasa

GUSTAVUS ERICSSON VASA, the man whom Providence had selected to save his country from anarchy and ruin, belonged to a noble family of Unionist sympathies, his great-grandfather being Drotsete Krister Nilsson Vasa. But the Vasa family had joined the cause of the patriots during the reigns of the Stures, simultaneously losing some of its earlier importance. The Vasas prided themselves on being the descendants of St. Eric and his line, and of St. Birgitta and the Folkungs. Its coat-of-arms consisted of a simple *vase*, or bundle of sticks. Gustavus Vasa was born May 12, 1496, at Lindholmen in Upland, at the mansion of his parents, Eric Johansson Vasa, state councillor, and Cecilia of Eka, a sister of Christine Gyllenstierna. His earliest years were spent with his mother at Rydboholm, another estate of his father's, beautifully situated on an arm of the Baltic, only ten miles north of Stockholm. When a mere boy he was sent to the court of his granduncle, Sten Sture the Elder, who was childless. King John of Denmark noticed the bright little boy during a visit paid to Lord Sten. Young Gustavus took the command of all the other children at play and appeared to be a born leader. The king called the boy to him and asked him what his name was. Gustavus answered frankly. King John smilingly placed his hand on the boy's head, saying: "Certainly thou shalt become a man in thy day if preserved in life." The king intimated that he wanted to take him along to Copenhagen to supervise his education. But Lord Sten, who did not like this idea, hurriedly had Gustavus sent away, so that he could tell the king upon a second inquiry that the boy had returned to his parents. The young Gustavus was described as "attractive and welcome with everybody." Gustavus was sent to Upsala to study at the age of thirteen. The University of Upsala was at that period in a state of stagnation. The first teacher who came in contact with Gustavus was a Dane named Master Ivar. According to the Prose Chronicle, he was a man who "was mean to everybody and who gave Gustavo drubbings." It seems that the patriotic spirit early woke in the breast of this youth, who already in these days foreshadowed his own mission in the following words: "I will betake myself to Dalecarlia, rouse the Dalecarlians and batter the nose of the Jute." When eighteen years of age, he was accepted as a squire at the court of Sten Sture the Younger, and Christine Gyllenstierna, his own aunt. He followed the younger Lord Sten in all his expeditions of war, taking part in the siege of Stæket and a battle of Dufnæs, and carrying the banner of state at Brennkyrka.

A second time in his life it came to pass that Gustavus Vasa was considered a person whom the Danish king was desirious of carrying away. This time the king was Christian II., who gained his object by treachery and violence. Gustavus was one of the Swedish hostages who were offered to King Christian and by him carried away to Denmark.

Gustavus was handed over to Eric Banér, a relative of

his, who held in fief the castle of Kalloe in Jutland. The latter was placed under a heavy fine in case he allowed his prisoner to escape. Gustavus received a kind and generous treatment. He ate at the table of the lord and was allowed to wander at liberty in the close neighborhood of the castle. But the danger that menaced his country never left him in peace. He heard repeatedly of the great preparations made by Christian II. to crush the resistance of Sweden, and of the acts of violence to be perpetrated. Gustavus remained at Kalloe for a year, when he resolved to flee from a captivity which had become insupportable. One morning at sunrise, Gustavus Vasa put on the garb of a peasant and disappeared from the castle. He made good speed, reaching a seaport and escaping to Lubeck with a merchant vessel. In this friendly Hanseatic centre Gustavus expected armed support. Such was not granted, but he was shielded against Danish pursuit. Eric Banér arrived, having followed up his tracks, but his demands to have Gustavus surrendered were refused. After eight months of delay in Lubeck, Gustavus obtained leave and arrived in Sweden on board a German ship. He landed at Stensœ, a promontory outside of the town of Kalmar, while Christian II. was laying siege to Stockholm. Gustavus was resolved to do his utmost to rouse the people to active resistance against the invaders. The castle of Kalmar, next to that of Stockholm the firmest stronghold of Sweden, was in charge of Anna Bielke, the widow of the last commander. Gustavus strengthened the courage of the inhabitants of town and castle, but finding it impossible to accomplish anything for the defence himself, and unsuccessful in his attempts to bring the hired German troops up to a point of enthusiasm for the Swedish cause, he left Kalmar and continued his way through Smaland. But the population of this province had no patience to listen to his appeals for a revolt. The peasants answered him that if they remained faithful to the Danish king they were never to be in want of herring and salt. Some of them in their indignation sent arrows flying after the young patriot. In September he reached the Terna estate in Sœdermanland, where his sister and her husband, Joachim Brahe, resided. Lord Joachim had just received an invitation to be present at the coronation of King Christian in Stockholm. The attempts made by Gustavus to persuade the couple to abandon their intended journey to Stockholm were futile. Reaching his paternal estate of Ræfsnæs in Sœdermanland, he remained there in concealment for some time. He visited the old archbishop Jacob Ulfsson, who, after his retirement, lived in the neighboring monastery of Mariefred. The old prelate tried his best to persuade him to seek mercy and grace of King Christian, but the resolution of the young squire to free his country was only strengthened into an iron-cast determination. One of the servants who had followed Lord Joachim to the capital managed to make a safe return to tell Gustavus the terrible news of the Carnage of Stockholm. He was also told that a high price had been placed on his own head.

Gustavus at once prepared for flight. Accompanied by a single servant he secretly left Ræfsnæs one day toward the end of November, travelling on horseback northward to Dalecarlia. He arrived at Kopparberg in Dalecarlia, where he had his hair close cropped and put on peasant's clothes. Putting an axe over his shoulder, he went about looking for employment. The first man whom he tried was Andrew Persson, a wealthy mine owner at Rankhytta. Gustavus found employment with him, taking part in the threshing. But the other servants soon detected that the new man had a carriage and habits different from their own, and they commenced to watch him closely. They noticed that he was not accustomed to the work, and one of the servant girls saw a collar of silk above the coarse blouse. Andrew Persson called before him the suspect, and was highly surprised when recognizing in him a comrade from the time of his student days at Upsala. He was favorably disposed, but was afraid of sheltering Gustavus, advising him to flee to the less thickly settled parts of the province, and to change often from one place to another. Gustavus continued his way in a westerly direction, following the shore of a lake named Runn, and arrived at Ornæs the following day. He knew he had an old comrade and friend in the owner of the place. This man, Arendt Persson, received him in the most hospitable manner, but was in his heart desirous of obtaining the price placed upon the head of the young squire. Gustavus went to bed in the attic, not suspecting treachery. The host himself accompanied him to his resting place, according to the mediæval custom. This done, Arendt travelled in great haste to one of his neighbors, the much-respected Mons Nilsson of Aspeboda. Arendt asked him to assist in capturing Gustavus Vasa; but Mons Nilsson flatly refused, taking no pains to hide his indignation. Arendt left and went past his own home to Sætra, which was the residence of the Danish bailiff. He started for Ornæs the following morning, accompanied by the bailiff and twenty men ready to capture the fugitive. But Arendt's wife, Lady Barbro Stigsdotter (Swinhufwud), had not been inactive. Her suspicion was aroused when she noticed her husband travelling back and forth to disappear in the direction where the bailiff resided. She divined that the safety of her guest was threatened and decided to take action. Lady Barbro went to the attic, roused her sleeping guest and told him of the impending danger. Gustavus let himself down to the ground by means of towels fastened to the window-sill, assisted by Lady Barbro, who had a horse and sleigh in readiness for him, in charge of a faithful servant. He reached the residence of John, the priest of Sværdsjœ. Arendt was enraged when he found that Gustavus had made his escape. It is said that he from that day refused to ever see Lady Barbro again.

The priest of Sværdsjœ held Gustavus in concealment for three days, but advised him to seek a more secure hiding place. He sent Gustavus to Swan Elfsson, a hunter to the king, who dwelt in Isala, a short distance from the church of Sværdsjœ. Gustavus had hardly reached this place before the men sent after him by the bailiff arrived. Gustavus stood by the oven warming himself after the ride. The wife of Swan Elfsson was busy baking bread. The men entered, asking if any stranger had been noticed in the neighborhood. The woman of the house saved the situation by resolutely dealing a blow with the bread spade to Gustavus, who was turning his back to her. In an irritated voice she said: "Why dost thou stand here gaping at the strangers? Hast thou never seen people before? Get thee at once out to the barn and do some threshing." The men did not suspect in the snubbed servant the noble fugitive for whom they were looking. But Swan Elfsson was not sure of the safety of his guest if he remained in Isala. So he concealed Gustavus in a load of hay and left his house with the great unsettled districts as his destination. He met some Danish spies on the way. These suspected the peasant and pierced the load of hay with their lances repeatedly. Gustavus was wounded in the leg, but kept his breath and lay perfectly still. The spies were satisfied that everything was right and told Swan Elfsson to move on. But the peasant noticed that blood was dripping from his load, leaving scarlet tracks on the snow. He quickly drew his knife and cut his horse a deep wound in one foot. After a while the spies noticed the bloody tracks. They returned and commanded Swan Elfsson to halt, inquiring about the blood. Swan Elfsson pointed to the injured foot of his horse and succeeded in making them believe that the horse had met with an accident.

Swan Elfsson left Gustavus at the village of Marnæs, situated in the Finn woods, where he was received by other hunters. These escorted the noble outlaw to a place further away in the woods, where he for three days remained in concealment under a big fallen fir tree. The peasants in the neighborhood brought food to him. The still hunt seemed to be at an end, and so Gustavus risked a visit to the church of Rettvik, situated on the eastern shore of Lake Siljan. He spoke to the yeomanry collected around the church after divine service, reminding them of the stanch patriotism and manliness of their ancestors, and imploring them to save their country from destruction. The yeomen of Rettvik gave a satisfactory answer, telling him that they were ready to resist the Danes. But as they had not heard the opinion of the people of the other parishes, there was nothing to be done for the moment.

Gustavus continued his way to Mora, one of the most densely populated parishes of Dalecarlia and situated on the northern shore of Lake Siljan. The priest of the parish was afraid to hide the outlaw, but confided him to a peasant, Tomte Mats, in the village of Utmeland. Gustavus remained for several days concealed in a vaulted cellar, which was reached only through a hole in the floor of the cottage above. One day the bailiff's men entered to search for Gustavus. The woman of the house was busy brewing the Christmas ale. She saved Gustavus by quickly placing a big barrel over the hinged door, which covered the opening to the cellar. One of the holidays during Christmas Gustavus addressed the peasants of Mora when coming from church. He stood on a small hill near the churchyard. The noonday sun was shining brightly over the snowy landscape and a fresh northerly wind was blowing. Gustavus spoke in a loud voice and with great eloquence. He asked the men to reflect on what kind of government foreigners always had given Sweden, and to remember what they had themselves suffered and risked for the liberty of their country. He thought that the memory had not died either of the deeds of violence perpetrated by Jœsse Ericsson or of the deeds of heroism done by Engelbrekt Engelbrektsson. He then told them of the treacherous villany of King Christian and of the Carnage of Stockholm. "My own father," he said, with tears in his eyes, "rather wished to die with his brethren, the honest lords, in the name of God, than to be spared and live in dishonor after them." If the Dalecarlians wanted to save Sweden from thraldom, he was ready to offer himself as their leader in the name of the Almighty. The speech of Gustavus made a deep impression upon the men of Mora, and some of them were anxious to rise at once. The majority ruled, deciding that no action should be taken before the other parishes of Dalecarlia had been heard from. They advised Gustavus to seek a safer hiding-place further up in the woods. Gustavus left Mora utterly discouraged, seeking the paths that led along the Dal River into desert wilds.

At New Year of 1521 Lars Olsson, a soldier who had done good service in the times of the Stures, arrived at Mora, bringing particulars of the doings of King Christian. He told the peasants that the king had ordered gallows to be erected at every sheriff's residence to mark the way of his Eriksgata. The peasants were touched to the quick and regretted having sent away the young nobleman. Lars Olsson advised them to call him back. Two expert ski runners were sent after Gustavus Ericsson, and after a ride of a night and a day through the woods, they overtook him close by the Norwegian frontier, which he was ready to cross in despair.

Gustavus returned to Mora and was made the leader of the peasants in that locality. With these men he started his work of liberation, which was the commencement of one of the most remarkable of revolutions that the world ever saw. In the beginning of February, 1521, Gustavus marched southward with a few hundred men. At Falun he captured the bailiff of the mines, confiscating the royal taxes. Returning to the starting point, he left it again, with an army of 1,500 men. Entering Norrland, where he was joined by the peasants of Gestrikland, and the burghers of Gefle, while the people of Helsingland asked for time to consider the matter, he learned upon his return how one of his commanders, Peder Swensson, had won a glorious victory over a Danish army 6,000 strong at the ferry of Brunnbæck, by the Dal River. Gustavus began training his troops, enforcing severe discipline and providing them with better arrows and longer lances. He declared war upon Christian in a formal way and marched on Westeros, where the Danish troops had centred. The town and castle were captured in spite of a force of superior Danish cavalry.

Gustavus shifted his army into divisions which marched in various directions to capture the castles of surrounding provinces. The people of Upland reinforced the Dalecarlians, who were sent home to tend to their sowing. The Upland forces captured the archbishop's seat during his absence, and were joined by Gustavus at Upsala, who made an exceedingly severe speech to the ecclesiastics, asking them to decide their nationality, whether they were Swedes or not. They asked permission to consult Archbishop Trolle, which was granted. "I will bring the reply myself," said Trolle, starting from Stockholm with a splendid body of German troops. Gustavus was near being taken by surprise, but gathering troops he fought the archbishop, whose force met with a crushing defeat, and he escaped with difficulty to Stockholm.

At midsummer, 1521, Gustavus arrived at Brunkeberg, laying siege to Stockholm. The capital was strongly fortified, and Norrby with a Danish fleet supported and relieved it. Twice the Danes routed the Swedish troops with the intermission of one year, but Gustavus provided reinforcements. He travelled through the country, visiting the forces who laid siege to the various Danish strongholds, these surrendering one by one. It was not a chain of glorious exploits, this work which Gustavus carried to a successful end, but one of infinite patience and sagacity, saddened by the news that the revengeful Christian had ended the lives of his captive mother and sister in the miserable Danish dungeon. Bishop Brask was scared into submission, turning his castle Stegeborg and part of his troops over to Gustavus, who at a Riksdag at Vadstena was elected regent in August, 1521.

Gustavus entered into an alliance with Lubeck, and it sent a fleet to Stockholm, thus encircling it also from the sea. Norrby left with his ships and was nearly caught in the ice in the following spring. In Denmark, Christian's reign came to an end. With his usual violence he attacked the nobles and the ecclesiastics in order to better the conditions of the peasants, for whom he had a tender sympathy. In so doing, he brought the nobles to open revolt against his rule. He left his throne in April, 1523. Now Gustavus found the opportune moment to accept the Swedish crown offered him. He called a Riksdag at Strengnæs, in June, 1523, where Gustavus was chosen king of Sweden "by the councillors of state with the consent of the common people." At this occasion a tax was agreed on to pay the German troops engaged in the siege of Stockholm, and to Lubeck for its timely support. In that very month Stockholm surrendered, and Gustavus held his proud entry into the capital on the eve of Midsummer day.

The position of the king was a most difficult one. The crown was ruined through the previous state of anarchy and the expense of war. The Church was in undisturbed possession of its wealth, but not willing to yield any of its power or income. Christian was preparing a plan by which to recapture his lost crowns. Norrby, who had aspirations of becoming Christian's regent in Sweden, tried to persuade Christine Gyllenstierna, lately set free from her prison, to marry him in order to obtain the prestige of the Stures. The common people, whom Gustavus so recently used to free the country, grew restive and rebellious when he could not at once grant them guarantees of comfort and prosperity in return. In a marvellous manner Gustavus understood how to face the situation and how to use to the utmost the resources within reach.

When the outlawed youth of twenty-four spoke of revolt to the peasants at Mora, Martin Luther was burning the ban placed on him by the pope. There were several warm friends of Luther in Sweden, principally Olaus Petri, himself a pupil and friend of the German reformer, his brother, Laurentius Petri, and Laurentius Andreæ. Olaus was a soul of fire and enthusiasm. He was lacking in self-control, but possessed a power which if not restrained would have led him and his work of reform further than the goal set by Luther. The two Laurentii were, like him, men of learning and, in addition, of greater sagacity. The king took interest in these men. He was contemplating a reduction of the ecclesiastical power, and they were to prepare the soil by freeing the people from undue respect for the Roman Church and its worldly power. Laurentius Andreæ was made the king's chancellor, and Olaus Petri secretary to the town council of Stockholm, later pastor of the Cathedral Church. Olaus preached in the Stockholm Cathedral fiery sermons against Rome and the pope, responded to sometimes by irate monks, sometimes by various projectiles from the audience. Gustavus took pains to fill the vacancies of the Church, which were many, by appointing able men. But he made two serious mistakes in making Master Knut, dean of Westeros, archbishop, and Peder Sunnanvæder, formerly secretary to Svante Sture, bishop of Westeros. He came in possession of a correspondence, which proved that Bishop Peder tried to bring the Dalecarlians to revolt, and when accusing him and finding Master Knut on the side of the defence, Gustavus deprived them of their new dignities. The king commanded that a new bishop should be appointed and himself selected Johannes Magni as archbishop. This prelate, a very learned man, was the representative of Sten Sture in Rome, returning to his native land as a papal legate. Gustavus had a rupture with him when, according to his instructions, he demanded that Trolle should be reinstated as archbishop. Archbishop Johannes was lacking in moral courage; brushed aside by the tide of Reformation, he retired to Rome, where he died after writing the history of Sweden in Latin, *Historia de Gentibus Septentrionalibus*. Master Knut and Peder Sunnanvæder turned their steps to Dalecarlia, fanning the brewing malcontent and opening connections with Norrby, who styled himself the betrothed of Christine Gyllenstierna and made ready to attack Gustavus from the sea. Berndt von Melen, a German commander, in whom Gustavus placed much confidence, was to chase Norrby away from his stronghold, the island of Gothland, but turned a traitor, joining Norrby instead, in 1524. Gustavus called a Riksdag at Westeros, in 1525, resolved to use his diplomacy to the utmost. Upon receiving a letter from the Dalecarlians, in which they stoutly swore off their allegiance to him on account of heavy taxes, foreign influence and disregard for the Church, the king offered to abdicate. The representatives at the Riksdag persuaded him to remain, whereupon the king sent the Dalecarlians a sagacious letter, promising to improve the state of things as much as possible, but pointing out the two prelates as traitors in conspiracy with the Danes. The Dalecarlians were pacified, Knut and Peder finding it safest to leave for Norway. In the following year the king met the revolting peasants of Upland at Old Upsala, where he in a fiery speech unfolded his policy toward the Church. The peasants resented; they wanted to keep their monks and their masses. The king commanded one of his followers to make a speech in Latin, the peasants shouting that they did not understand. "Why do you, then, love so dearly your Latin mass?" the king asked them smiling. A few days later Gustavus made a crushing speech against lazy and worthless ecclesiastics before the chapter of Upsala. The archbishop was sent away on diplomatic errands to Poland and Russia never to return. After his departure Bishop Brask became the chief representative of papal interests. He was patriotic, but never yielded an inch of the worldly power of the Church except to force, opposing the Reformation with his whole strength.

The king followed up his policy by demanding for the crown two-thirds of the ecclesiastic tithe and by placing the ecclesiastics under the duties of *russtienst*, in 1526. The ex-prelates, Knut and Peder, were, upon the king's request of an extradition, given up and sentenced to death for high treason. The king arranged for their triumphal entry of mockery into Stockholm in a most humiliating fashion, for which he has been criticised; also for the consummate manner in which the judges were appointed and judgment passed. But he set an example of warning to obnoxious and intriguing prelates that was appreciated by his contemporaries.

Gustavus gained the triumph of his policy by the famous Riksdag of Westeros in 1527. It was nothing else than a coup d'état, a revolution, which, with the establishment of the Reformation, gave his throne solidity and resources. The Diet was called under the pretext of taking measures against a new revolt in Dalecarlia and for the regulation of dogmatic questions. There were present sixteen state councillors, four bishops, one hundred and twenty-nine knights and nobles, one hundred and five peasants, besides various priests, burghers and miners, but no representatives from Finland or Dalecarlia. In the great hall of the monastery the meeting was held, opening with a written address by the king, read by his chancellor, in which the situation of the country was set forth. The king refused to continue at the government, asking to be remunerated for personal losses and expense, and given a fief like any ordinary bailiff responsible to the crown. Only if fundamental reforms were made would he remain, not being able otherwise to cover the inevitable deficit of the treasury. Bishop Brask responded with the statement that he for his part was in duty bound to the king, but that Rome and its demands must, in the first place, be obeyed; showing by his remarks that he understood that the question was one of reducing the ecclesiastical power. The king rose and said in a burst of passion: "We have no further desire, then, to be your king. Verily, we had counted on quite another treatment at your hands. We now no longer wonder at the perversity of the people, since they have such advisers. Have they no rain, they blame us for it. Have they no sun, likewise. For dearth, hunger and plague we are responsible, as if we were not a man, but God. Yea, though we labor for you with our utmost power, both in spiritual and in temporal affairs, you would gladly see the axe upon our neck, but no one dares to grasp the handle. Monks and priests and all the creatures of the pope are to be placed above us, though we have little need of them. In a word, you all would lord it over us. Who under such circumstances would desire to govern you? Not the worst wretch in hell would wish the post, far less any man. Therefore we, too, refuse to be your king. We cast the honor from us, and leave you free to choose him whom you will. But be so kind as to let us leave the land. Pay us for our property in the kingdom, and return to us what we have expended in your service. Then we declare to you that we will withdraw never to return." With tears of anger and emotion the king left the hall, leaving the assembly in consternation.

After four days of pandemonium and deadlock, the representatives decided to give in and ask forgiveness of the king, who long disregarded the appeals made for his return. When re-entering he was greeted by commotion and the humblest demonstrations of respect and repentance. The next day, Midsummer day, votes were taken upon his propositions, each Estate of representatives sending up their vote with a written construction of the propositions. These were then revised by the state councillors in their final form, called "Westeros Recess," with amendments called "Westeros Ordinantia." The startling revolutionary stipulations of the "Recess" were chiefly these: Authority for the king (1) to take in possession the castles and forts of the bishops, whose retinues he was to fix as to numbers; (2) to dispose of the superfluous income of the clergy and to superintend the administration of the monasteries; authority for the nobility to resume title to all their property which had come in the possession of the Church since 1454; authority to have the Gospel preached all over the country in undefiled purity. Among the "Ordinantia" the most important were: (1) Vacancies in the parish churches were to be filled by the bishop under the supervision and right of suspension of the king; (2) the king was to fix the amount of revenue due the bishops, chapters and clerks, and be entitled to use the surplus for the crown; (3) the priests were in secular suits to be responsible to secular courts; (4) the Gospel should be read in the schools. The king asked the bishops in person to surrender their castles, to which demand they all agreed.

We may feel inclined to smile upon the drastic manner in which Gustavus enacted this important drama of Revolution, but must bear in mind his solitary position. He had no statesmen of ability at his side, nor men of great intellect and power to sustain him. He stood alone, and few knew as yet his superior qualities as a statesman and an organizer. The tame opposition, soon yielding to the appeals of the burghers and peasants, can only be explained through lack of leaders. Ture Jœnsson (Tre Rosor), the aristocratic chief of the opposition, was a vain and cowardly man. Bishop Brask, the head of the clergy, was old and more of a diplomatist than a man of action. The latest stanch Romanist, he gave up his cause, finding a pretext to leave the country and dying in his self-imposed exile. The ecclesiastical reforms were definitively arranged at a church meeting at Œrebro in the following year.

It was one of the evils which beset the reign of Gustavus that revolts constantly occurred in various provinces and for various reasons. Dalecarlia took the lead. The inhabitants were not able to bear the distinction won by their great patriotic services in the times of Engelbrekt, the Stures, and Gustavus. Their complaints were mostly unreasonable, sometimes ridiculous, as when they tried to prescribe the kind of cloth and colors to be used at court, and so forth. There was no fable, however stupid, which was not readily believed by them and the responsibility placed on the

THE BATTLE OF PULTOWA

Sweden

king. Particularly was everything eagerly swallowed which spoke of injustice committed against the descendants of the Stures. A daring pretender took advantage of this fact. He was born of the lowest peasant class, serving on an estate in Westmanland, where he had stolen a sum of money from his master. Appearing in Dalecarlia, where he claimed that he was a son of Lord Sten and Christine Gyllenstierna, he gained a great deal of support among the yeomen, who cried with him like children when he spoke of his noble father and asked them to pray for his soul. The false pretender had his instructions from Peder Sunnanvæder; he married in Norway a woman of noble birth, and, upon his return to Dalecarlia, surrounded himself with a regular court. An end was put to his career by a letter from Christine Gyllenstierna, written at the request of the king, in which she told the Dalecarlians that her son Nils, whom the pretender impersonated, had recently died, and that an impostor was misleading them. The false Nils Sture answered by claiming that he was born before marriage, the would-be-reason why his mother did not acknowledge him. This even the Dalecarlians found was a stretching of truth. The pretender, who had been stamping coins with his image and held the demeanor of a ruling prince, fled to Norway and thence to Rostock, where he was captured and beheaded. No blood was shed during this period of revolt; but the king, who was crowned at Upsala in 1528, proceeded from his coronation to Dalecarlia with an army of 14,000 men. He commanded the Dalecarlians to meet him, and forgave them after a severe sermon of reproach, making them surrender the chief supporters of the "Daljunker," who were executed on the spot.

No better was the outcome of a revolt prepared by some

nobles of West Gothland in the following year. They tried in vain to make the population join with them. The king managed to obtain their secret correspondence, and had the guilty ones arraigned before a meeting at which he scrutinized and repudiated the false charges made against him. The nobles asked forgiveness and were pardoned, with the exception of two, who were beheaded. But the originators of the revolt had fled. They were Ture Jœnsson and Bishop Magnus of Skara. The former joined the deposed King Christian, who, in 1532, prepared an attack on Sweden in his attempts to recapture his crowns. With him were other such distinguished traitors as Gustavus Trolle and Berndt von Melen. Gustavus I. sent a splendid army to meet Christian near Kongelf. Christian withdrew in disappointment, leaving Ture Jœnsson behind in the streets of Kongelf, minus a head. Christian was imprisoned by his uncle, Frederic of Denmark, and died in captivity.

In order to pay the debt to Lubeck it was decided at a meeting at Upsala, in 1530, that the bells of the churches should be taken to be melted down. Concessions to do so were asked and obtained from the various communities. But upon the surrender of the bells discontent grew up. In Dalecarlia it came to revolt and open violence. The people refused to give up their bells or took the surrendered ones back with force. Threatening letters were sent to the king, who at first pretended to ignore the whole matter. Christian was preparing his last attack, and prudence seemed advisable. The inducements made by the Swedish traitors to support Christian's claims were scornfully repulsed by the Dalecarlians, who still continued with their insulting letters to the king. Gustavus answered them in a peaceful way. In 1533, at New Year, he suddenly appeared with an army in Dalecarlia, where the revolters also this time received a severe reproach and were forced to give up their leaders. These were executed, and that ended the last revolt of Dalecarlia.

In the following year Sweden was forced into a war which lasted up to 1536, the so-called "Feud of the Counts," the chief participants being the counts of Holstein, Oldenburg and Hoya. Sweden sided with Christian of Holstein, who fought for his rights to the throne of Denmark after his father Frederic, being opposed by the other counts and by Lubeck. Hard and repeated pressure was brought to bear on Svante Sture, a son of Lord Sten and Christine Gyllenstierna, to appear as a pretender against Gustavus; but the noble youth, who was sojourning in Germany, firmly withstood these temptations. His mother had married John Turesson, a son of the traitor Ture Jœnsson, who was as able a man as his father was a bad one, being the successful commander of a Swedish army which invaded the Danish provinces held by the count of Oldenburg. A Swedish fleet, created through sacrifices of nobles and peasants, distinguished itself repeatedly. The war ended in the defeat of Lubeck.

Gustavus had, since the end of the work of liberation, crushed the power of the Church, punished the revolting peasants, kept the aristocracy within bounds, and put an end to the supremacy of Lubeck. But he went still further, trying to deprive the Church of its last vestige of authority, to introduce a minute administration of the provinces and to enforce the absolute power of the crown. To these plans he was led by two foreign advisers, Georg Norman and Konrad Pentinger. But it must be said to the credit of the king that their influence vanished when he saw that their "reforms" were not acceptable to the people. From this period of his reign, one noteworthy and wholesome measure remains, the reintroduction of the former hereditary order of succession to the throne. It was formulated and accepted at the Riksdag of Œrebro (Jan. 4, 1540), memorable also through death sentences pronounced upon two of the apostles of the Swedish Reformation. The king had long regarded his chancellor and the two brothers, Olaus and Laurentius Petri, the latter archbishop of Upsala, with suspicion. The climax was reached when a conspiracy by German burghers of Stockholm against the king's life was discovered, and it was proved that Olaus Petri and Laurentius Andreæ were conscious of its purport, without making it known to the king. They were condemned to death, Archbishop Laurentius being forced to take a seat as one of the judges, but pardoned at the request of the burghers of Stockholm, on the grounds that the ministers had received their knowledge on the pledge of secrecy through confession. Laurentius Andreæ lost his position as the king's chancellor. In the following year each church in the country was presented with a copy of the complete translation of the Bible, the work of the two reformers.

The greatest, most serious and most expensive of peasants' revolts was that called the Dacke Feud (1542 and 1543), after its leader Nils Dacke, a peasant born in Bleking, emigrated to Smaland, which became the scene of his revolt. The peasants were resolved to make war on the royal bailiffs, the nobles and the new religion, and found in Dacke an excellent leader, ferocious, daring and of some military ability. The forces sent by the king to meet him were repeatedly routed. The king was seriously alarmed, particularly since the revolt attracted attention abroad and was encouraged by Emperor Charles V., in the interests of the deposed Christian, his brother-in-law, and by several German princes. The emperor wrote to Nils Dacke a letter, preserved to this day, although it never reached its destination, in which Charles, with pride, recalls his Gothic (that is, according to the views of his time, Swedish) origin: "Sumus et nos de gente Gothorum." Nils Dacke's plan was to place Svante Sture on the throne. He wrote him a letter to this effect, which the noble Sture handed over to the king, together with the messenger who brought it. After much effort the king gathered an army of considerable strength, which was ordered against Dacke, who was defeated at Lake Asund. He fled and was pursued by the troops into Bleking, where he was captured and shot. This revolt cost Gustavus dearly, but was a good lesson in regard to the more immature of his reforms, against which it, to a great extent, was directed.

Now the storms and trials of his reign were at an end, and Gustavus allowed to gather the fruit of his wise management, which itself grew wiser with his old age. In 1544 the Union of Succession of 1540 was confirmed at Westeros. In matters of finance Gustavus laid the foundations of the modern state. The bailiffs were multiplied and made to give close accounts of the revenues. Fiefs granted to nobles before were now kept by the crown. The great nobles who held fiefs were placed under stricter control. The bloody Christian did useful work for the crown by ridding it of many unruly heads. The privileges granted by Westeros Recess were enforced, but the king saw to it that the nobility received back only what was properly due. But when the crown was concerned, property was taken from the Church to the greatest tension of these privileges, and likewise for the king's private rights, by means of which less scrupulous tactics both the state and the king were enriched. The former came in possession of 12,000 farms, the latter of 4,000, in his case called "inherited estates." As Gustavus was a great economizer, he left a treasury replete with money and uncoined silver, in spite of elaborate pomp on state occasions, expensive royal marriages and wooings, and a feud with Russia. From which of the two treasuries in his care expenses were paid, Gustavus was not overparticular. He set a good example as a practical farmer and agriculturist, the dairy at Gripsholm standing under the personal supervision of the queen, with twenty-two less ladylike assistants.

Gustavus created the nucleus to a standing army of hired troops, of natives and foreigners, about 15,000 in numbers, and provided Sweden with a considerable and well-equipped fleet. He encouraged the mining industry by supporting the silver mines of Sala and the copper mines of Falun. He introduced the working of iron, according to new methods, calling in German experts whose work he superintended in person. Putting an end to the supremacy of the Hanseatic commerce, he made treaties of commerce with the Netherlands and France, making Helsingfors in Finland the centre of the trade with Russia. On the western coast he founded the new town of Elfsborg, and ordered the inhabitants of New Lœdœse to move thither. To the common people Gustavus held an attitude which shows evidence of love and confidence. Many of his letters and messages to them abound in hints at practical methods in farming. The schools were improved and partly reorganized through the spirit of Reformation, while the University of Upsala lost in importance and prestige, the students again going abroad.

The war with Russia, commencing in 1554, and marked by mutual invasions, offered no aspect of importance, and was ended by a treaty of peace in 1557.

The founder of the famous royal line of Vasa was, personally, a man of prepossessing appearance, tall, and of commanding presence, having blond hair and beard, sharp blue eyes, full lips, rosy cheeks and a fine frame. He was fond of costly garments, and the styles of his day were becoming to him. Gustavus was of an amiable and cheerful disposition, although of a quick temper. He had a rare gift of winning the goodwill and confidence of all classes by addressing everybody according to their compass of intellect and conversation. He was fond of music, and played and sang. The lute was his favorite instrument, which he liked to play in his evenings of solitude. Gustavus possessed a rare intellect and a remarkable memory. Well aware of his own weakness to give way to his quick temper, he generally postponed all decisive action in matters of importance until sure of his full power of discernment. He was not a brilliant genius, but a typical prince of the Renaissance epoch, never afraid of taking action in instances without a precedence, or of the consequences of his actions. His letters and addresses evince an unusual degree of common sense, clothed in a language of manly vigor, terseness and humor, and are fine specimens of the modern Swedish, such as it meets us in this its period of rejuvenation, brought about by the spirit of the Reformation. There is something in the oral and literary eloquence of Gustavus Vasa which makes it easy to believe that he was a descendant of Birgitta. **Gustavus did** not possess the fine erudition of his sons, who were considered to be men of learning in their time, for he early left his university studies for the court and the war; but he was able to pass such good opinions upon subjects of art and science that he astonished many who had made these a special study. He had the power of recognizing people whose faces he once had noticed after ten to twenty years of absence, and was also skilled in divining what character dwelt behind every face. What he once heard he never forgot. Where he had travelled once he could never mistake the road, and knew not only the names of the villages but also the names of the peasants whom he had met. His life was led by the unswaying principles of an earnest piety and high morals. His nephew, Peter Brahe the Elder, who in a chronicle has given the above picture of Gustavus Vasa, adds: "*In summa*, God had bequeathed him, above others, with great ability, high intellect and many princely virtues, so that he was well worthy of carrying sceptre and crown. For he was not only sagacious and kind above others, but also manly and able. He was sharp and just in passing sentences, in many cases being charitable and merciful."

The royal court was characterized by a joyous and elevated spirit. Every day after dinner all the courtiers collected in the dancing hall. The lady of ceremonies then entered with the ladies of the court, and the royal musicians dispensed music for dancing. Every other or third day the king went out hunting or horseback riding with the gentlemen and ladies of his court. The youths of the nobility once a week held exhibitions of fencing and other knightly sport, the king taking an interested and active part. Those who excelled received prizes in the form of rings of gold or chaplets of pearls and led the dance of the evening.

Gustavus I. was three times married. His first consort was young neurotic Catherine, princess of Saxony-Lauenburg, whom he married while the "Revolt of the Bells" was going on in Dalecarlia, and who died four years later, leaving him a son, Eric, of her own hysteric temperament. Shortly after the death of Catherine, the king married a young lady of the highest Swedish nobility, Margaret Leijonhufvud, with whom he lived in a long and happy union, ended by her death in 1551, and blessed by ten children, among whom the sons John, Magnus and Charles. Lady Margaret had been in love with the oldest son of Christine Gyllenstierna, Svante Sture, whom she renounced, and who married her younger sister Martha. Queen Margaret was a tender and high-minded woman, who won the love and absolute confidence of her royal consort, on whose quick temper she exerted a quieting influence, comforting him in hours of trouble and distress. She preserved as queen the plain and severe habits of her youth, having a personal superintendence over the dairies of the royal castles, especially those of Gripsholm and Svartsjœ. She was interested in brewing, baking and other household affairs, often making with her own hands the clothes of her children. When the king referred to Queen Margaret, he always called her "our dear mistress of the house." The king remained a nobleman of his day in the purple. Royal splendor was displayed on great occasions only. Simplicity was the principle of every-day life. When entertaining his friends, the king took great pains to please and arranged many details himself. Upon one occasion of this kind at Gripsholm,

Queen Margaret carried in the sweetmeats and cookies, while the king served the wine and asked his guests to be glad and make merry.

Queen Margaret was suddenly taken ill while partaking in a pleasure trip on Lake Mælar, and died in 1551, after a touching farewell to her consort. In the following year the king married the young Catherine Stenbock, a daughter of Gustavus Stenbock, an intimate friend to the king, and Lady Brita Leijonhufvud, a sister of Queen Margaret. In the lives and fate of Catherine and Margaret there are several remarkable coincidences. Like Queen Margaret, Catherine was secretly in love with some one else when the royal proposal was made. Strange enough the object of Catherine's secret affection was, like Margaret's, a son of Christine Gyllenstierna, Gustavus Johnsson Tre Rosor. This young man was the grandson of conceited Ture Jœnsson and the son of able John Turesson, the second consort of Christine Gyllenstierna. The family name was Tre Rosor, after the coat-of-arms, which consisted of three roses. As her aunt Margaret must renounce the hero of her dreams, so also Catherine. Like his half-brother, Svante Sture, Gustavus Tre Rosor married the sister of his first love, and this marriage, like that of Svante, turned out a happy one. There was a last coincidence in the life of the two queens. When Margaret heard that the royal sponsor was coming, she knew his errand and concealed herself in an oak chest in a distant part of the castle of Ekeberg. Catherine, upon a similar occasion, ran down in the gardens of Torpa and hid herself behind a bush. The third marriage of the king was a happy one, in spite of the great difference in years between the consorts. The clergy tried to raise objections, holding that Gustavus and Catherine were too nearly related to make the marriage a legal one. After some severe pressure these objections were finally dropped.

Queen Catherine thus expressed the state of her feelings after her marriage: "Gustavus is dear to me, but I shall never forget the Rose."

The king gave scrupulous attention to the education of his children. They were brought up in simplicity and sternness, but received a manifold training and a great amount of instruction. While they were studying at Upsala, hams and butter were sent them from the royal estates to make part of their breakfasts and suppers. In spite of these patriarchal endeavors, Eric and John grew up to be typical Renaissance princes, fond of extravagance and luxury. The king wrote once to Duke Magnus: "Our dear Lady Catherine sends thee five shirts which thou must bear in mind to take good care of; *item*, to keep thy head clean and not ride or run too much." When his sons grew older, King Gustavus used to admonish them orally before the hearth or at the table, or by letters. His wise counsel recalls the terse and sharp advice of Havamal in the Edda: "Ye shall weigh all matters carefully, perform them quickly and stand by it, putting nothing off to the morrow; counsel not followed up in due time is like clouds without rain in times of dearth." "To speak once and stand by it, is better than to talk one hundred times." "Surround ye ever with able men of pure living; one shall believe of ye what one knows about them." Duke Eric early caused him trouble by stubbornness, defiance and vanity. Duke John, the oldest child of Queen Margaret, long remained his favorite, but ended by causing him grief through disobedience and secret conspiracy with Eric.

In his old age, King Gustavus suffered through failing health and melancholy. He complained because the fate of his country seemed uncertain on account of the unstability of his sons, and because his old friends, like John Turesson and Christine Gyllenstierna, passed away before him, leaving him alone in the world.

When King Gustavus felt that the end was drawing near, he sent word to the four Estates or representative classes of the country, the nobles, clergymen, burghers and yeomen, to meet him at Stockholm around the Midsummer of 1560. He made known to the Estates his will, which his sons pledged themselves by oath to fulfil. Eric should inherit the crown, according to the will, but the three other sons were to receive duchies which they should govern with a good deal of authority. It became evident that the king had taken pains to provide liberally for his sons. But it appears as if he intended to make them all responsible in the maintenance of the work of their father, by distributing the power between them.

When the Estates had collected in the hall of state the old monarch entered with his sons. After greeting those present he delivered his farewell address:

"I respect the power of God, which with me has reinstalled the ancient royal line on the throne of Sweden. Ye have without doubt learned, and those of you who are somewhat advanced in years have seen for yourselves, how our dear fatherland, already for ages in distress and misery through foreign lordship, at last suffered the same through the grim despot King Christian, and how it pleased God to liberate us from this tyranny through me. For this it behooves us, high and low, master and servant, old and young, never to forget that same divine help. For what of a man was I to set myself against a mighty king, who not only ruled three kingdoms, but who also was related to the powerful emperor Charles V. and the noble princes of Germany. But God has performed the work, made me the worker of his miracle, and been my help and comfort during a reign of forty years, the cares of which have hastened me on with gray hairs to the grave. Forsooth, I could liken myself to King David," and the tears came to his eyes, "whom God from a shepherd made to a reigning king over his people. I could not divine that glory, when I in woods and desert fells must needs conceal myself from the bloodthirsty swords of my enemies. Grace and blessing have in a wide measure been granted both me and you through the knowledge of God's true Gospel, also in the shape of material abundance, which is evident all through the land, thank the Lord. If during my reign anything good has been accomplished, give ye God the glory of it. But for what there has been of failure and fault, I beg you, as faithful subjects, to forbear and forgive. God is my witness that it has not been by meanness, but by human weakness, that I have not been able to do better. My ambition has always been the improvement and welfare of the people of my country. I know full well that I have been a severe king in the eyes of many. Yet that day shall come when the children of Sweden willingly would dig me up from under the sod if that they could. My time soon is at an end. I need not in the stars or other signs search for my last moment; my body is to me the trustworthy messenger that I soon shall stand before the severe King of kings, to give account for the glorious but earthly crown of Sweden which I have worn."

The Estates listened with great emotion to the words of

the old monarch. After the king had ceased speaking and his will had been sanctioned, Gustavus left the assembly supported by his sons and nodding his farewell to those standing near. Three months later he was taken ill, and September 29, 1560, the great liberator, revolutionist and organizer of his country expired.

CHAPTER IX

Reformation and Reaction—The Sons of Gustavus I.

ERIC XIV. succeeded his father in 1560, commencing his reign under the most brilliant of auspices. But the old King Gustavus had foreseen that his sons would cause danger to the realm which he with infinite care had built up. After his forty years' work of construction followed forty years of destruction which his elder sons brought to bear upon it. Fortunately, that work was so solid that it withstood this bravely, to rise rejuvenated when loving hands anew were laid to it.

King Eric was one of the most gifted monarchs of his time, handsome, eloquent, learned, a fine linguist, a musician and artist. But his sharp reason carried him to the excess of suspicion, his artistic temperament into hysterics, and he was vain, overbearing, quick-tempered, licentious and cruel. His leaning toward mysticism made him devoted to astrology.

Eric's first ambition was to reduce the power of the dukes, convoking a Riksdag at Arboga, in 1561, where the "Arboga Articles" were formulated for such purpose, the dukes being forced to acquiesce. In order to reduce the distance between the dukes and the nobility, King Eric, at his coronation—celebrated with a lavish display of pomp at Upsala in June of the same year—instituted hereditary dignities of counts and barons. Svante Sture, Peter Brahe the Elder and Gustavus Johnsson Tre Rosor were created counts, the first and third one the sons of Christine Gyllenstierna, Peter Brahe being a cousin of Gustavus Vasa. Among the barons were Sten Leijonhufvud, Gustavus Stenbock, relatives of the dukes, and Clas Kristersson Horn (of Aminne). Only small fiefs were given with the new dignities, which were nothing but an outward sign of the distinction existing between a higher aristocracy already extant and the lower nobility. In order to strengthen his connection with the nobles, Eric made the estate on which a noble fixed his domicile exempt from *russtjenst*. He was jealous of his power and dignity, for which reasons he held sharp supervision over his officials. He instituted a supreme court, consisting of twelve men of low birth, who every three years made a tour of the country to hold court in the name of the king. These justices were the creatures of Eric, and soon brought on themselves discredit and hatred through their servile and cruel acts. Among these justices was Gœran Persson, an able and powerful man, revengeful and cruel, who soon rose to be the favorite and influential adviser of his master.

Eric was intent upon making a great match, wooing Elizabeth of England, Mary Stuart of Scotland, Renata of Lothringia and Christine of Hesse, with more or less success, overlooking Margaret of Valois, who was anxious to marry him. His mistress, Carin Monsdotter, a child of the people, but beautiful and of a noble character, for whom he had formed a secret attachment, finally was made his queen.

The German Order which held Esthonia and Livonia suffered during this period considerably through Russian invasions. The town of Reval, with a large part of Esthonia, was ceded to Sweden in 1562, upon the receipt of a loan, Eric immediately giving his attention to the depressed and enslaved peasants of that section. Later the grandmaster of the Order turned Livonia over to the king of Poland, who, in need of money, placed seven castles of this province at the disposal of John, duke of Finland. John had tendered a loan to the Polish king and married his sister Catherine. Eric considered these negotiations as harmful to his royal authority, and he asked his brother to give account of them in person. John refused, making the royal emissaries his prisoners. The Swedish Riksdag condemned John to death for high treason, and an army was despatched to Finland, which carried back Duke John and his consort as prisoners. John's sentence was commuted to imprisonment at Gripsholm, proud Catherine choosing to share the fate of her husband (1563). The prison life of the ducal couple at Gripsholm was not an unpleasant one. They enjoyed a great deal of liberty and luxury at the splendid castle in Lake Mælar, King Eric sending his brother a copy of Boccaccio's "Decamerone" in German, to read for a pastime. The duke read the work and translated it into Swedish. The room called "king John's prison," which is still preserved with the artistic decoration which Duke Charles later bestowed on it, served as sleeping apartment for the prisoners, and there Catherine gave life to two children, one of whom was to become the founder of the Polish line of Vasa kings. It is said that Duke Magnus became a prey to the disposition of insanity latent in his family, by being forced to sign the death sentence of his brother John, King Eric being anxious of having him share the responsibility. Magnus lived until quite an advanced age, but was never cured of his mental ailment. Even in his best hours he was not of very bright intellect. While sojourning at the castle of Vadstena, by the Lake Vetter, he had the vision of a mermaid, who coaxed him to follow her. The duke jumped from the window of his apartment into the moat below. He did not sustain any serious injury, but the incident made the unhappy prince famous in tradition and song.

In May, 1560, a war commenced with Denmark which, with several intermissions, lasted for seven years. It has been called The Seven Years' War of the North. About the same time that Eric became king of Sweden, the young ambitious Frederic II. ascended the throne of Denmark. In the days of Gustavus I., Christian III. had appropriated the Swedish emblem of three crowns for the Danish seal of state, as if by this proclaiming that the Union was considered still extant or that it could be re-established at the opportune moment. King Gustavus had protested, but with no result. When King Frederic kept up the irritating fact of preserving the Swedish emblem, King Eric answered by placing the emblems of Denmark and Norway in the Swedish seal of state. This made things worse and served as a nominal cause for war. The principal interest at stake was the supremacy in the Baltic provinces. The diocese of Œsel, which had accepted a Danish protectorate, was governed by a brother of the Danish king, who had entered into an alliance with Poland against Sweden, Denmark also joining it.

In May, 1563, a Swedish fleet, commanded by Jacob Bagge, left Sweden to bring Princess Christine of Hesse, the promised bride of King Eric. A Danish fleet met them, at the island of Bornholm, and greeted the Swedish ships with some shots from their sharply loaded cannon. The Swedes returned the fire and a naval battle followed, which ended in a defeat for the Danes, who lost their flagship. When Jacob Bagge arrived in Rostock, where he was to meet the princess, her father was found unwilling to let her sail on account of the insecurity brought about by the commencing naval hostilities. This would under ordinary circumstances have enraged the vain and sensitive king, but Eric forgot his rage in his delight at the naval victory. Jacob Bagge was rewarded with a triumphal entry into Stockholm upon his return. He entered the city on foot with a golden chain round his neck, followed by his sub-commanders and surrounded by the banners taken during the battle. The prisoners followed, in chains and with shaved heads. The king's fool was dancing in front of them, playing on his fiddle. A Danish herald soon afterward reached Stockholm, declaring war with great pomp and ceremony on behalf of his royal master. The city of Lubeck sent a messenger to Stockholm on a similar errand, but was not received by the king. "Since he is sent by the mayor and council of his town and other similar lardmongers, let him be heard and answered by the mayor and council of Stockholm," was the royal order.

Jacob Bagge was ordered to sea with the Swedish fleet later in the summer of the same year. He met the united fleets of Denmark and Lubeck at the island of Œland, in the Baltic. A terrible battle ensued, which lasted until the fleets were separated by the darkness of the night, without victory being won by either side. Jacob Bagge started out with his fleet again in the spring of the following year, commanding a new flagship, "The Matchless," which carried two hundred cannon, most of them made out of church bells confiscated by Gustavus Vasa. A new battle was delivered between the islands of Gothland and Œland. The majority of the Swedish ships had by a gale been separated from the admiral and his flagship, but Jacob Bagge fought valiantly for a whole day, continuing the battle the next morning. A catastrophe brought it to a close. "The Matchless" caught fire through some act of negligence, a barrel of powder exploding between the decks. Jacob Bagge then surrendered, and was taken on board one of the ships of Lubeck. The enemies took possession of the "The Matchless" in order to plunder it, but the immense ship exploded with a tremendous roar, sinking with everybody who was on board. Jacob Bagge did not long remain in Danish captivity. He returned, to be greeted with the greatest distinction, and died as governor-general of Stockholm.

The war on land was at the beginning carried on only through mutual invasions, both sides giving proofs of cruelty and vandalism. Elfsborg surrendered to the Danes. A Swedish army, commanded by King Eric in person, entered the province of Halland, pillaging and plundering and laying siege to the town of Halmstad. King Eric suddenly raised the siege, when news came that King Frederic was approaching with an army. The Swedish troops scattered in various directions, one division being met and defeated by the Danes. The whole of Northern Norway was invaded by Swedish troops and temporarily subjugated. The entire kingdom of Norway was very near being altogether absorbed by Sweden. This would have been a happy solution of the Scandinavian question. Norway would have become one in language with Sweden and would have shared her glorious epoch of political grandeur which was to follow. The best families of Norway would have been entered side by side with the Swedish nobility at the knightly chapter-house of Stockholm, and the countries would have had their later democratic and cultural development in common. But King Eric was too restless and undecided to make any lasting conquest, or union, possible. When Claude Collard, a young French nobleman, who was the conqueror of Northern Norway, was taken by surprise and captured, King Eric, to avenge this, devastated forty church parishes in Norway. The Danes invaded and plundered the provinces of West Gothland and Smaland, while the Swedes pillaged Bleking and Scania. The king had given orders that the population of a whole district should be killed. He wrote later about the fulfilment of this cruel command: "God granted luck, so that thousands of men were killed on the road and in the woods." The province of Scania was devastated to a distance of one hundred miles from the Swedish frontier. A new invasion into Halland was made, in 1565, when Duke Charles, then fifteen years of age, commanded the artillery. The town of Varberg was attacked, but valiantly defended by the Danes. The young duke upon this occasion gave the first proof of his indomitable energy. He led the attack and persuaded the Swedes, by word and action, not to give it up. At last the walls were taken, the town being pillaged and burned. All men who could carry arms were killed, except a force of one hundred and fifty men of hired troops who entered Swedish service. A young French captain, Pontus de la Gardie, of a noble family of Languedoc, was among the latter. This man and his descendants were destined to play an important part in Swedish history.

Clas Kristersson Horn was made commander of the Swedish navy after Jacob Bagge, in which position he covered his name with glory. He won a naval battle at Œland (in 1564) which lasted for two days. In the next year he added several victorious battles to his record, among which the principal ones were fought at Buchow, by the coast of Mecklenburg, and at the island of Bornholm. When he went to sea in the spring of 1566 no enemy dared appear. The united fleets of Denmark and Lubeck at last started out, but were defeated by Clas Horn at the island of Œland after a vehement battle. The vanquished fleets were caught in a gale in which sixteen ships perished with seven thousand men. Clas Horn with his Swedish fleet was master of the sea. In the following year no fleet appeared to meet his. The efforts of Gustavus I. to set the Swedish fleet in good order thus proved to be of the greatest consequence.

The Danes were superior in the hostilities on land during the latter part of the war, thanks principally to their eminent commander, Daniel Rantzau. He made an unsuccessful attempt to recapture the town of Varberg, but gained, at Axtorna, a battle over a superior Swedish army (in 1565). When Rantzau saw the Swedes approaching for an attack, he held prayer with his troops, whereupon he arranged them for resistance. The Swedish infantry captured the Danish stronghold and artillery, but the hired German troops of the Swedish wings turned into flight. Rantzau made an attack upon the deserted infantry, and was victorious when nightfall ended the battle. The Swedes lost thirty cannon, and Nils Sture, the son of Count Svante Sture, was able to save the banner of state only by severing it from the pole and hiding it on his person. In the following year, Rantzau pillaged Smaland and West Gothland, and in 1567 he penetrated as far as East Gothland, where he was very near being caught in a trap by the Swedish troops. **The interior struggle of Sweden caused hostilities to cease for some time.**

The sad fate of his brother Magnus also befell King Eric. Evidences of approaching insanity were frequent and brought on horrible consequences. By licentiousness, mysticism and astrological speculations his mind became unsettled. It had been predicted that a blond man would dethrone him. Eric at first made his brother John the subject of his suspicions. After the duke's imprisonment he suspected a rival in Nils Sture, who also was a blond. Eric accused him of ill behavior in the battle of Axtorna. The king's court sentenced him to death, but Lord Nils escaped with a contumelious entry of mockery into Stockholm, on a miserable horse, and a crown of straw on his head. But frightened at the indignation aroused by his shameful act the king tried to undo it, and sent Lord Nils on an embassy to Lothringia, to bring the king's proposal to Princess Renata.

In the commencement of 1567, the king had several of the nobles arrested, on the suspicion of conspiracy, and carried to the castle of Upsala, where a Riksdag was convoked. Nils Sture arrived with the consent and betrothal ring of Princess Renata, but was thrown into prison. The king asked the Riksdag to pass a sentence of death upon the accused nobles. When this was refused, he was seized by fear and rage. Rushing into the prison of Nils Sture, he wounded him in the arm. Lord Nils drew out the weapon, a dagger, kissing its handle and returning it to the king, with a prayer for mercy, but was killed by the soldiers at the command of the king. Eric's disposition immediately was changed, and he darted into Count Svante's prison, begging forgiveness at his feet. The aged Sture's answer was that he would forgive all, granted that no harm was done to his son. The king fled in despair from the castle and town, followed by some of his soldiers, one of whom he sent back with an order to kill all the nobles, "except Lord Sten." As there were two by that name, these were spared, but Count Svante and his son Eric Sture, Abraham Stenbock and Ivar Ivarsson were killed. The Riksdag was forced to pass sentence for high treason upon the murdered men, at the instigation of Gœran Persson, whose perfidious advice had continually inflamed the sickened brain of his master. King Eric was for several days missing, and at last found wandering about in a peasant's garb. Cared for by Carin Monsdotter, he slowly regained his reason, showing evidence of repentance by declaring the murdered nobles innocent and promising to compensate their families. During this spell he set free his brother John and dismissed Gœran Persson. But soon his evil disposition returned, and the resolution of his brothers to free the country from his rule must be acknowledged as a beneficent one. The nobles were brought to revolt, when Eric, in July, 1568, proclaimed Carin as his consort, and had her solemnly crowned Queen of Sweden. The dukes John and Charles were at first unsuccessful in their efforts, the king defeating their troops repeatedly. But in 1569 Stockholm was captured, Gœran Persson killed and the king forced to abdicate. The sentence passed upon Eric, by the Estates of the Riksdag, stipulated that he should be "imprisoned, but sustained in a princely manner, for the rest of his days."

Eric was at first held imprisoned in his own apartments at the royal castle, but was transferred to two of the vaults, called the "apartments of Lord Eskil." They had served as a treasury during the reign of Gustavus I., but now stood empty. Queen Carin and her children were his company. After an unsuccessful attempt at flight, one room was taken away from him and the windows in the remaining one reduced in size. The table of the royal prisoner was well provided for, but he was unmercifully treated by his warders. The cruel Olof Stenbock once deprived him of all his clothes. In a struggle which followed, he shot Eric in the arm and let him remain senseless in his blood for several hours. Some of the members of the former body-guard of Eric once attempted, but in vain, to set free the unhappy prisoner. In 1569 Eric was removed to Abo in Finland, where he was locked up in a secure prison. Two years later he was taken to Castellholm, in the archipelago of Aland, for fear that the Russian czar would liberate him by violence. Shortly afterward he was removed to the lovely castle of Gripsholm, where he had spent some of the happiest days of his youth, and where he once upon a time held his brother John imprisoned. At Gripsholm there is a gloomy dungeon which is said to have served as the prison of King Eric, but this is not authentic. Eric was treated comparatively well while at Gripsholm, enjoying the company of his family, a good table and plenty of servants. The recording books of the castle from this period speak of "the court of King Eric." King John was, in the meantime, irritated by Russian hostilities and intrigues, the old supporters of Eric joining in the latter. The appeals of Duke Charles for the improvement of the condition of his poor imprisoned brother roused the suspicion of the king, who fostered dark plots against the prisoner. Eric was removed from Gripsholm and its pleasant associations, separated from his family and put in hard prison at Westeros. The warders received instructions to take his life if necessary. The state council and the archbishop sanctioned this order of the king. The last prison of the unhappy King Eric was Œrbyhus, where he suddenly died, exactly at a time when King John's fears of a revolt had reached a climax. Rumors that Eric had been poisoned were current, and Duke Charles also gave utterance of his belief that such was the case. In spite of the wars, cruelty and evil deeds of King Eric XIV., the Swedish people of his time had a good deal of devotion for him and his faithful consort. The country enjoyed good years during his reign and profited by the wise measures of his father.

Gustavus, the son of Eric XIV. and Carin Monsdotter, was born, in 1568, at Nykœping. When Queen Carin was separated from her imprisoned consort, her children, Gustavus and Sigrid, followed her to Finland, where she resided at Abo. In 1575 the young prince was harshly taken away from his mother, at the command of the state council, and sent to Prussia. The jealous and uneasy King John made him the subject of cruel persecutions. In spite of these he received a fine education, and is known to have embraced the Catholic religion. He was kindly received by King Sigismund of Poland, his cousin, at whose coronation in Cracow he is said to have been present, in the disguise of a beggar. A relation of intimate friendship existed between the outlawed prince and Emperor Rudolph of Austria, both of whom were devoted to the study of alchemy. King John refused to listen to the appeals for grace and support which Gustavus repeatedly made to him. Gustavus was not allowed to see his mother until the year of 1596, when the two had a touching meeting at Reval. He later made his home in Thorn, but left for Russia, in 1600, upon an invitation from Czar Boris. He was received in Moscow as a reigning prince; but when he refused to appear as a pretender to the Swedish throne, he was imprisoned. At the fall of Boris, Gustavus was set free, but again put in prison by Dimitri. At the fall of the latter, in 1607, Gustavus once more regained his liberty, but died in Casijn, in the same year. This unhappy Gustavus Ericsson Vasa was a man of fine erudition and pure morals. He was a dreamer and of a sensitive disposition, being an ardent Catholic and fondly devoted to the country which had outlawed him.

Sigrid Vasa, the daughter of Eric XIV., was twice married to members of the Swedish nobility. Ake Henricsson Tott, her son of the first marriage, was a distinguished warrior in the times of Gustavus II. Adolphus. Queen Carin died, in 1612, beloved and highly respected, at the beautiful estate of Liuksiala in Finland, given her in fief by King John.

John III. succeeded Eric, without sharing his power with his younger brother Charles, as he had promised. John was as learned and highly talented as Eric, and as vain, restless and unreliable. But while Eric was a mystic and a sceptic by turns, John was a Catholic, or leaning toward Catholicism, and a hypocrite who, under the pretence of meekness and piety, tried to hide his vanity, bad temper and utter selfishness. Like Gustavus I. and all his other sons, John was devoted to the fine arts, particularly to architecture, with an ardor that reached the vehemence of a passion. He planned a vast number of churches and castles, which he completed, utterly regardless of cost. The Swedish Castle Renaissance which was established by John and his brothers is influenced by contemporary Flemish art, severe and majestic in outline, graceful and profuse in interior decoration. Good specimens of it were the earlier castles of Stockholm and Svartsjœ, the castle of Vadstena remains so and, to a great extent, the beautiful and memorable castle of Gripsholm.

At his coronation, John issued hereditary privileges to the nobility. *Russtjenst* became no longer essential. Legal offices were preserved for the nobles, the king's supreme court being abandoned. John's policy was to win the support of the aristocracy against Charles, who, indignant and sulky, kept within his duchy, consisting of the provinces of Sœdermanland and Vermland, with the town of Œrebro in addition.

In 1570, an unsatisfactory peace was made with Denmark, Sweden ceding all the Norwegian and Danish territory in her possession, together with the island of Gothland, and agreeing to pay something like one hundred and fifty thousand dollars for the return of Elfsborg, held by the Danes. A friendly relation to hostile Poland commenced with John's reign, but a long and bloody war with Russia began in 1570. The Russians tried repeatedly, but in vain, to capture Reval, plundering and killing the population of Esthonia, who remained faithful to Swedish rule. Henric Horn and Clas Tott won laurels for their heroic deeds, while the war was changed into more modern methods and to a successful issue by the Swedish general Pontus de la Gardie, who captured the provinces Keksholm and Ingermanland and the town of Narva.

John III. had set two goals for his ambition: to return the Swedish church to Catholicism and to make his son Sigismund king of Poland. The latter he reached at the death of King Stephan in 1589, Sigismund succeeding him upon the throne. The former ambition John never attained, after years of stubborn and unreasonable perseverance giving up this pet idea. John made some attempts to bring order in the confused conditions of the church, but left it in a worse state of confusion than he found it. The crown and the aristocracy had deprived the church of nearly all its property and withheld its income from it. Archbishop Laurentius Petri complained of the miserable state of things, the ministers often being useless wretches and the service in some churches impossible to uphold for sheer lack of money. In 1572 the ecclesiastical matters were arranged at a meeting in Upsala, when a new church law was introduced, demanding higher qualifications for the ministers, who were to be elected by their congregations, and enforcing a school law. Laurentius Petri died in 1573 and was succeeded by Laurentius Petri Gothus. The new archbishop willingly subscribed to a set of rules, laid before him by the king, which reintroduced monasteries, worship of saints and the ceremonies of the Roman church. Jesuits were invited to the country, but met with little encouragement from the people. The very climax of John's reactionary movements was formed by the introduction of his ritual, Liturgia, which was nothing else than an adaptation of the Catholic ritual. It was accepted by the Riksdag of 1577, but Charles refused to accept it for his duchy. The king had many conflicts with his brother, the latter always giving in to his wishes, except on this point. Ministers and university professors who refused to conform to the new ritual, or attacked it, were sheltered by the duke and, in many instances, given high offices. The king grew angry, but the duke remained firm and unyielding. When Queen Catherine died, in 1583, John's Catholic fervor suffered a relapse, and ceased altogether after his marriage to young Protestant Gunilla Bielke, in the following year. He stubbornly stuck to his Liturgia for some time yet, but exiled the Jesuits, and dismissed with contumely ministers who had joined the Roman Church. During the last years of his reign, he said it was best to leave everybody a free choice in religious matters, regretting his Liturgia—which he once considered the gem of his own theological system —because it had caused so much trouble and confusion.

Sweden suffered a great deal through the slack and unsteady government of King John. He spent unreasonable sums on his court and his craze for architectural marvels, while always short of funds for the necessities of war and internal improvements. Commerce and industries suffered and were brought to a standstill by dearth, hunger and pest. The population decreased; the towns were made bankrupt and many farms abandoned. Bad and greedy officials and the recommencing war with Russia increased the evils. After unsuccessful attempts to have his son leave Poland, where he had met with many difficulties, John entered into more intimate relations with his brother, who came to wield a beneficial influence on the government. John III. died 1592, malcontent and tired of life, his death being little regretted by the people.

One of the most famous love episodes of Sweden dates from the reign of John III. It has no bearing upon the affairs of state, but is not devoid of value as an illustration of the history of civilization, giving us a glimpse of the private life of the nobles of that period and the standard of morals of their lives. The episode is told by Countess Anne Banér in a manuscript by her hand with the title: "In the following manner my blessed mother's sister, Lady Sigrid Sture, lady of Salestad and Geddeholm, related what took place when Lord Eric Gustafson Stenbock carried away our blessed mother's sister, Magdalen Sture, from Hœrningsholm."

The dowager-countess, Martha Sture, resided at the castle of Hœrningsholm, enlarged to a four-story structure and fortified with four corner towers by her consort. She was a sister of Queen Margaret, the second queen of Gustavus I., and was married to the renounced lover of that sister, Count Svante Sture. The countess was called "King Martha," partly because of her stern power and great authority, partly because it was known to have been her ambition to see her husband's family grace the throne of a country which their forefathers had ruled as uncrowned kings. She had lived to see her husband and two sons killed by the insane Eric XIV., but she had yet two sons who would carry high the glorious name, on which there was not a stain of any kind. There were five daughters, Sigrid and Anne, married to members of the influential Bielke family, and Magdalen, Margaret and Christine, as yet unmarried. There was another young lady at Hœrningsholm, besides the daughters, the little Princess Sigrid Vasa, the daughter of King Eric XIV. and Carin Monsdotter, who had received a home with the stern "King Martha" while her mother was following the tracks of the deposed monarch from prison to prison.

Between Magdalen Sture and Lord Eric Stenbock a passionate love sprang up. Lord Eric was a very fine young man, of an influential family and the brother of the queen-dowager, Catherine, third consort of Gustavus I. But, unfortunately, he was the nephew of Countess Martha, and, as a cousin of Magdalen, considered to be too closely related to her to make a marriage possible. Countess Martha was unwilling to listen to any appeals, and she was strengthened in her resolution by the old Archbishop Laurentius Petri, who still held the same opinions as when he, once upon a time, refused to grant his consent to a marriage between

King Gustavus I. and young Lord Eric's sister, because she was a niece of Queen Margaret. The years passed by, but no change came in the stubborn resistance of "King Martha." Christmas eve of 1573, Lord Eric visited Hœrningsholm to remain until New Year. He brought with him costly presents which he offered as New Year's gifts to Countess Martha, her daughters, chaplain and servants. He left to return on Palm Sunday with his sister Cecilia, the wife of Count Gustavus Tre Rosor. One morning a few days later, Lady Sigrid Bielke, who was visiting her mother, entered the so-called rotunda, a large room in one of the towers which Countess Martha and her daughters used as sleeping apartment. She was surprised to find her sister Magdalen kneeling and in tears. Lady Sigrid greeted her: "God bless you, you have a good deed in mind!" "God grant it were good," answered Magdalen, rising. "Certainly it is good to make one's prayers amid tears," Sigrid said. Magdalen caught the hands of her sister and said: "My darling sister, if all the rest forsake me, you will not turn away your faithful heart from me." Sigrid found the words and emotion of her sister strange, but did not suspect anything. "Why do you use such words to me?" she answered. "I do not believe that you are going to make an evil-doer out of yourself; there are none in the Sture family who have carried themselves in a way to make us turn our hearts away from them." Tears came again to the eyes of Magdalen, but Sigrid was called into an interior room by her mother. Magdalen went to play with one of her little nieces, when Lord Eric entered. "Dear lady," he said, "would you like to see the horse that I have given you? It is now waiting in the court." Magdalen rose and left, escorted by her cousin. They met two of the women of the household, whom Eric commanded to follow them. A horse and sleigh stood in the vaulted entrance. Magdalen was placed between the two servants, while Eric took his position back of them on the runners, holding the reins. In the castle court they met the chaplain and several of the servants, who thought it a pleasure ride and let them pass. When they rode down on the frozen lake, the two servants in the sleigh grasped the importance of the situation for the first time, and commenced praying Lady Magdalen to return. Lord Eric silenced them by displaying his short musket. A few moments later they were surrounded by a force of one hundred men on horseback, who formed an escort. They were a loan to Lord Eric by Duke Charles.

The excitement at Hœrningsholm was great when the elopement was discovered. Margaret Sture happened to look through the window at the moment when the sleigh reached the lake. At her outcry Countess Martha and Sigrid joined her. The old countess fainted on the stairs when making for the court, and Sigrid was ordered to follow up the eloping couple. Countess Cecilia found her aunt on the stairs and hastened to assure her of the mortification that she felt at the daring and unsuspected deed of her brother, also expressing some surprise at the bad manner in which it was accepted. But then the old countess became wroth, exclaiming: "Go to the devil, and may God punish both you and your brother! And if you have any part in his scheme of robbing me of my dear child, betake yourself after him, so that no shame or dishonor may happen." Countess Cecilia hastened to her sleigh and reached Sværdsbro, where her brother was stopping, ahead of Sigrid.

When Lady Sigrid arrived at Sværdsbro, she was admitted through the lines of soldiers only after some difficulty, finding tailors and seamsters busy cutting and sewing precious stuffs for clothing for Lady Magdalen and her servants, "for she left with uncovered head such as she went and stood in her mother's house." Sigrid tried to persuade her sister to return to her mother, who in her great sorrow was willing to forgive all if she only came back. Magdalen sat silent for a long time. Finally she said: "If you can vouchsafe me, that the lady, my mother, will grant that we shall belong to each other, since I have so dearly pledged myself to him, I shall return." This Sigrid could not do, and Magdalen added, weeping sorely: "The last complication is then as bad as the first." Lord Eric entered with his sister Cecilia. When Sigrid asked where he intended to bring Magdalen, he answered: "To Visingsœ, to the Countess Beatrix, my sister, where she shall remain until we obtain the consent to marry of the lady, her mother." It was arranged that Cecilia should accompany Magdalen, and Sigrid try her best to win her mother's consent. Magdalen sent home to her mother a piece of horn of the fabulous unicorn; "the only thing I have carried with me from my father's house," she added. This horn, which really was taken from the incisor of the narwhal, was in those days generally thought to be authentic and of miraculous power.

Countess Martha was, in her grief and dismay, taken ill. She soon gathered strength enough to write to King John, her nephew, pleading her cause. King John at once took action in the matter, calling Lord Eric to account, and issuing a command to all ministers of the kingdom, prohibiting them to unite in marriage the two cousins. Eric Stenbock was on his way to Stockholm when he received the order of the king. Upon his arrival at the capital, he was imprisoned and deprived of all his offices. But Lord Eric had powerful friends in Duke Charles and the Stenbock family. As the king himself did not wish to be without his service, he was soon set free and reinstalled in his offices. He succeeded in obtaining the goodwill of the whole Sture family, but "King Martha" remained irreconcilable. More than a year had passed since the elopement. One day Lord Eric suddenly appeared at the castle of Visingsœ. He made, with Magdalen and his aunt, Lady Anne, a journey into the province of Halland, where a Danish minister joined the two cousins in marriage. The wedding was celebrated at the home of Eric's father, Baron Gustavus Stenbock of Torpa. But Lady Magdalen was not happy. She grieved because of her mother's hostile attitude, and continued to dress in black colors, as she had done ever since she left her mother. Duke Charles, the queen-dowager, the royal princesses, and all the members of the state council, yea, the king himself, wrote letters to the indignant countess, whose ire was rather increased than diminished thereby.

Finally, after another year and a half, "King Martha" gave in to the tears and prayers of her daughters. Lady Magdalen returned to Hœrningsholm after three years of absence. She was not allowed to come up to the castle at first, but had to dwell in the building occupied by the baths. As the winter was approaching, and Lady Magdalen was soon to give life to a child, her brothers and sisters prevailed upon their mother to receive Lord Eric and his wife at the castle. The event was arranged in a conspicuous way. Countess Martha was seated in the place of honor in the great hall of the castle, surrounded by her daughters and sons-in-law, when Lord Eric entered with

Magdalen. When the mother saw her pale and thin features, she was moved to tears, exclaiming: "Thou unhappy child!" Magdalen approached her on her knees, and the countess embraced her, stammering her forgiveness between tears. Magdalen remained at the castle, where she bore her husband a son, who was called Gustavus. Lady Martha invited the king, the duke and the princesses to be present at the baptism, at the same time granting Magdalen an equal share of inheritance with the other daughters. Lady Magdalen continued to dress in mourning as a self-imposed punishment for her disobedience to her mother. One day she was preparing to leave for a wedding, when her mother asked her the reason why she dressed thus. When "King Martha" learned why, she took a costly cross of diamonds intended for the bride and placed it on her daughter's breast, telling her to put aside her black dresses. From that day joy and happiness seemed to return to Lady Magdalen, who commenced to put on lighter colors and to wear diamonds. Of Magdalen Stenbock—a child of these Stures, who so often had protected and preserved Sweden—Count Magnus Stenbock was a lineal descendant, he who during the reign of Charles XII. saved his country in the hour of its greatest peril and distress.

Sigismund, the son and successor of John III., was not apt to become more popular than his father. Born at the pleasant prison of Gripsholm, which yet was a prison, he was of a cold, unsympathetic disposition, a king of few words and hard to approach. At John's death, Sigismund was twenty-six years of age and had reigned several years in Poland. Charles stepped to the front as the head of the government until Sigismund's arrival.

The Protestants, fearing the worst from their new Catholic king, decided to take firm and early action. The duke ordered a Riksdag at Upsala in February, 1593, the deliberations being held by the clergy alone. The Liturgia was abolished with the majority of Catholic church ceremonies, Luther's catechisms, L. Petri's ritual, church visitations, etc., being reintroduced. Abraham Angermannus was elected archbishop, and decision made for the re-establishment of the Upsala University. The duke had not been present at the deliberations, and appeared displeased because not consulted. He, who was secretly accused of being a Calvinist, pointed out more Catholic ceremonies to be abolished, whereupon the decisions won the sanction of the duke, the state council and the bishops. By this act the Lutheran Church was re-established, the Augsburgian Confession being laid down by the meeting as its corner-stone. When this action had been taken, the chairman, Nicolaus Bothniensis, a young Upsala professor, exclaimed: "Now Sweden has become *one* man, and we all have *one* God."

In August, 1593, King Sigismund arrived in Sweden, surrounded by Jesuits and Polish nobles, and with a sum of money wherewith to pay the expenses of a Catholic revival. To the demands made to sign the decisions of the Upsala meeting he gave a flat refusal. The conditions in Stockholm grew perilous, Jesuits and Lutheran ministers preaching denouncements upon each other in the churches and conflicts between the Polish troops and the populace taking place. In January, 1594, Sigismund, accompanied by the state councillors and the members of the Riksdag, came to Upsala for his father's funeral and his own coronation. Duke Charles arrived with 3,000 men, whom he quartered in the neighborhood. He dismissed the papal legate, Malaspina, and his Jesuits from the funeral procession, be-

fore it entered the cathedral, and told the king, in behalf
of all, that no coronation would take place before the con-
fessional liberty of the Lutheran Church was confirmed.
The Estates declared themselves ready to sacrifice their lives
for the pure faith. The king still refused his sanction,
whereupon the duke replied that the Riksdag would be dismissed within twenty-four hours if he insisted. Sigismund
gave in, upon the advice of the Jesuits, who told him that
pledges to Lutherans were not binding. Sigismund was
crowned and returned suddenly to Poland.

The king had left matters in an unsatisfactory condition,
placing six governors with great authority in various districts, but leaving the government to be conducted by the
duke and the state council in common. This little pleased
the energetic Charles, who soon called a Riksdag at Sœderkœping, in 1595, forcing the councillors to sanction this act
and follow him to the Riksdag. In Finland, the governor,
Clas Fleming, had tried to have a peace agreement with
Russia postponed as an excuse to keep the navy and army
at his disposal in the interest of the king. At Sœderkœping, Charles had himself chosen regent, the last vestige
of Catholicism abolished, and the punishment of Fleming
decided on. In consequence, the Catholics were dealt with
in a merciless way through the instigation of the archbishop, whom the duke called an executioner on account
of his recklessness. The convent of Vadstena was closed,
its eleven nuns scattered and its property confiscated. In
Finland a bloody revolt against the oppression of Fleming
cost 11,000 people their lives. It was called the "War
of Clubs," on account of the rude weapons used by the
peasants. The state council refused to consent to Fleming's
punishment, whereupon the duke suddenly resigned. But

he convoked a Riksdag at Arboga, in 1597, at which the councillors and nobles were absent, also the burghers. The peasants and clergy were abundantly represented and cheered the propositions of the duke to the echo. It was then decided that the king should be asked to return, until which event the duke was to remain regent, and that peace should be restored in Finland. Fleming died in the meantime and was succeeded by Arvid Stolarm, who also was one of the duke's enemies. The Riksdag at Arboga was the first in the deliberations of which the state council had not taken a part. The councillors were disposed to punish the duke; but, not agreeing as to means, they left the country to seek the king.

King Sigismund arrived in the summer of 1598 with an army of 5,000 Poles, gathering a good deal of strength by reinforcements from Gothaland. The duke had his stronghold in Svealand, the Dalecarlians rising to join him. The Uplanders warded off an attempt made by Stolarm to land with his army; they were led by Nicolaus Bothniensis, the Upsala professor, who called his exploit "a crusade." The two princes met in East Gothland, near Stegeborg. The duke and his peasant army were surrounded by the king's cavalry, and would have been doomed if not for the outcry of one of the king's followers that his subjects would be killed on either side. The king gave order to stop the attack, feeling pity at the sight. The duke was deeply moved by this act and offered to leave the land with his family. But the deliberations which followed were without result.

On the 25th of September a battle was fought at Stongebro, near Linkœping, ending in the defeat of the royal army. An armistice followed. The conditions of peace were that the king should remain in Sweden, dismissing his foreign troops, and take charge of the government. No one should be punished except five of the nobles, to be placed before a jury of ambassadors. The king agreed to the conditions, but soon left Sweden never to return. A meeting of nobles and clergymen, in 1599, accepted him as reigning king if willing to return within four months. In July, a Riksdag was called at Stockholm, which declared Sigismund dethroned and his son Vladislav king if sent to Sweden to be educated in the Lutheran faith. Sigismund took no heed of these stipulations, planning to regain his throne by force.

Charles followed up the punishment with such unprecedented severity that it has left a stain upon his memory. Three nobles were beheaded after Kalmar was taken, and proceeding to Finland, the duke applied capital punishment to a wide extent, in more than twenty cases at Abo alone. At a Riksdag in Linkœping, in 1600, the duke appeared as an accuser against the five imprisoned nobles and several others, eight state councillors being among them. The accused, thirteen in number, were sentenced to death for high treason, but the majority were pardoned upon confession of guilt. The councillors Gustavus Banér, Eric Sparre, Sten Banér and Ture Bielke were beheaded. They were all men of learning and great ability, who had faithfully served their king. During John's reign they had already suffered years of imprisonment for intrigues against a hereditary kingdom and a strong government.

Charles IX. was chosen king at the bloody Riksdag of Linkœping, and his son Gustavus Adolphus heir-apparent. The hereditary rights of Duke John, second son of John III., were acknowledged, and a duchy, consisting of East

Gothland and Leckœ Castle, granted him; but he was passed over as too young and too closely related to Sigismund. Measures to strengthen the financial administration and the army were passed.

Sigismund prepared, by alliances with Catholic powers, to gather support, Charles turning to England and France for the same purpose. A conflict was unavoidable, and Charles decided to invade the disputed province of Livonia, which he captured, only to be ousted by the Polish general, Zamoisky. The castle of Volmar was long and heroically defended by the Swedes under Jacob de la Gardie, a son of General Pontus, and Charles Gyllenhielm, an illegitimate son of Charles IX. After their surrender the former received for five years a tolerable treatment, the latter a most severe one for twelve years. After attempts to place conditions on a better footing in Finland, where the peasants had long suffered through aristocratic oppression, Charles increased the army still further and invaded Livonia once more, in 1604. He met with a crushing defeat at Kerkholm, close by Riga, at the hands of the Pole, Chodkiewitz, losing 9,000 men. But the Poles did not understand how to use their victory, and the centre of the conflict changed to Russia.

On Russian territory, the troops of Sigismund and Charles were to meet. The line of Rurik became extinct in 1598, its last descendant, Dimitri, being murdered. Great complications ensued with usurpers and two "false Dimitris" in succession. Sigismund supported the false Dimitris in order to gain ground and place the royal line of Vasa upon the throne of Russia after that of Rurik. Charles sided with Vassili Schuisky against the second false Dimitri. In 1607 an agreement was made that Sweden, upon the receipt of the province of Kexholm, should send an army to Russia to support Czar Vassili. In 1609, a small Swedish army, consisting of Swedes, Finns and some hired troops, entered Russia, under command of Jacob de la Gardie. It was received at Novgorod with the blaze of cannon and tolling of church bells. A victory was won at Tver over the pretender, but further progress was impeded by mutiny among the hired troops, the stubborn Finns returning home. With his 1,200 faithful Swedes, reinforced by hired troops to 5,000, De la Gardie made a daring march eastward to Moscow, scaring away the Polish army, attacking it and making a triumphant entry into the Russian capital. Sigismund was at Smolensk, and met De la Gardie at Klusina, winning the battle on account of renewed mutiny of the hired troops in the Swedish army. De la Gardie was given free leave with 400 men, upon pledge not to support Czar Vassili, and later captured the promised Kexholm, while Sigismund's son Vladislav for a short time became czar of Russia.

Although the short reign of Charles IX. was filled with continual warfare, the king never for a moment lost interest in the peaceful development of the country. He continued his father's work in furthering the mining industry, and tried to build up the commerce and trade relations. He founded the city of Gothenburg, on the western coast, in the island of Hising, opposite Elfsborg, also founding the towns of Karlstad, Christinehamn, Mariestad and Philipstad. The aristocracy looked upon his administration with coldness. It received sanction of the privileges granted by John III., but nothing more, except in return for additional *russtjenst*. The peasants were his favorites and he was surnamed the "Peasant King." To the Church, Charles stood in a good relation, supporting its re-established Reformation with his whole authority. Also the University had in him a patron, although he severely criticised the too conservative spirit in both, exchanging a series of pamphlets with the archbishop on theological questions, firm in his Calvinistic tendencies. To make the government stronger it was stipulated that four members of the state council were always to hold the four principal offices, with the titles of drotsete, kansler (chancellor), admiral and treasurer. The greatest economy was enforced at court and throughout the whole system of government, various minor country offices being established for the enforcement of order, justice and economy. The king was liberal only with severe orders and harsh words, the artistic tendencies of his youth succumbing to the cruel necessities of his reign.

In private he was as severe as in public life. His first consort, Maria of the Palatinate-Zweibrucken, had a quieting influence upon him, but the second, Christine of Holstein, stern and sharp like the king, strengthened the harshness and violence of his disposition. During the last years of his reign, Charles gave his attention to the critical European situation, desiring to join the Netherlands, England, France and the Protestant German princes into an alliance against the forming Catholic league. This man, so assured of his power to reign and so unscrupulous as to his means, was very careful not to do any act of importance without the sanction of his people, and for a long time refused to be called king. In 1604 he agreed to accept that name, but was in 1606 ready to cede it to Duke John. Still, after his coronation he admitted the hereditary right of his nephew, who was a good-natured man without the qualifications of a ruler. At the Riksdag of Norrkœping, in 1604, the crown was made hereditary among the descendants of Charles, also in the female line, provided that the monarch confessed the Lutheran faith and had not accepted the government of, or residence in, any other country.

The stress placed upon Charles was greater than his originally strong health could carry. In 1609 he suffered a stroke of paralysis, which deprived him of his full power of speech. He still stood firm at the head of the government, with Prince Gustavus Adolphus, now sixteen years of age, at his side, who took part in the affairs of State and spoke for the paralytic king. The young and ambitious Christian IV. of Denmark thought that the opportune moment was come to turn down the rising power of Sweden. He declared war, in April, 1611, in spite of the efforts made by King Charles to avoid the conflict, pointing to Germany, where their joined forces would be needed. Christian captured the town of Kalmar, while its castle withstood his attacks, being handed over to him by treason. In his wrath and disgust, Charles sent word to Christian to meet him in a duel face to face, which the latter refused to do in a letter of abusive contempt. Gustavus Adolphus had made a dash into Bleking, capturing the store of provisions at Christianopel. In the autumn, the war came to a temporary standstill.

Charles started for Stockholm from Kalmar, but was taken ill during the journey and died at Nykœping, October 11, 1611, surrounded by his sons and councillors. To his death-bed came the news that Jacob de la Gardie had captured the important city of Novgorod, and that the Russians offered the crown to either of his sons, Gustavus Adolphus or Charles Philip. With Charles died the only worthy son of Gustavus I. Vasa. In strength of intellect and stern power, he stands first among Swedish rulers. Devoted to the work of his great father, he educated the Swedish people, through hardships and sacrifices, to its political grandeur.

CHAPTER X

Period of Political Grandeur—Gustavus II. Adolphus

GUSTAVUS II. ADOLPHUS is the greatest figure of Swedish history, revered and beloved as one of the noblest of heroes, a genius in whom the qualities of the great statesman and warrior were blended with the faith of a man ready to sacrifice his life for the loftiest of causes—religious liberty. Gustavus Adolphus was, by his own triumphant deeds and through his school of discipline, which turned out men worthy to follow up his work, destined to bring his country up to the fulfilment of its mission in the history of human progress, and to open for it an era of glory and political grandeur which its limited resources made it impossible to preserve, but which was fruitful of results for its later cultural evolution.

The secret of Sweden's success in solving the stupendous conflict between Catholicism and Protestantism, between reaction and progress, rested in the fact that this little country was eminently ready to wage a war for religious liberty. It had been more perfectly rejuvenated by the spirit of Protestantism than had, at the time, any other country. The mediæval state, completed later in Sweden than on the continent, also gave way there sooner and more completely than elsewhere. The yeomanry, never fully suppressed, had preserved its old **spirit of independence,** fostered and guided by patriotic leaders of the nobility, with or without a crown. The population was suffering, hungering, bleeding, but free, indomitable, and devoted to its once more hereditary kings of Swedish birth and to their new faith, which had made strong in them their old individuality of views and life.

When Gustavus Adolphus ascended the throne, the country was in the greatest peril and distress, and had many a lesson to learn before entering the universal conflict of the Thirty Years' War.

Gustavus Adolphus was born, Dec. 9, 1594, at the castle of Stockholm. When six years old, he followed his father to devastated Finland, returning through Norrland, for the settlement and future of which territory great plans were made. At ten, he was ordered to be present at the deliberations of the state council; at thirteen, he received petitions and complaints, rectifying wrongs and soothing suffering. His father said of him, in speaking of the fulfilment of great works, placing his hand on the curly blond head: "*Ille faciet.*" The prince received a severe and carefully supervised education, led by Johan Skytte. He acquired knowledge of a considerable number of languages, probably all in a mechanical way, except the Swedish and German, with both of which he was made equally and thoroughly familiar, speaking and writing the latter language with greater ease and perfection than the emperor Ferdinand, or Maximilian of Bavaria. In the sciences of economics and war he was well read, himself inaugurating novel theories in both. In him the best traits of the Vasa dynasty were admirably blended and enlarged. He possessed an acute intellect, far-reaching views of almost prophetic discernment, a mastery and patience in detail, and an indomitable strength of will. To the ceaseless and painstaking care of the welfare of his subjects, characteristic of his father and grandfather, were in him added a harmony of endowment and a gentleness of disposition which made him their superior. In him the turbulent blood of the Vasas was held in noble self-restraint. After his rare outbursts of passion, he made good his faults in a most royal manner. His youth was not without the temptations which beset all richly endowed natures, but they were vanquished as he grew up to the importance of his grand mission. He stood in the paternal attitude to his people so becoming to his grandfather, but lacked the fiery democratic tendencies and the sympathy for the untitled, unpretentious and lowly, so strong in his stern father. To his relatives he was as gentle as to his subjects, treating his resolute and ambitious mother, Christine of Holstein-Gottorp, with love and respect; on her demand sacrificing the love of his youth and intended bride, Ebba Brahe, who became the consort of victorious Jacob de la Gardie. Also to his brother Charles Philip he stood in an exemplary relation; but firmly refused to grant him privileges for his duchy of Vermland which could be injurious to the country at large.

Gustavus Adolphus was a man of commanding presence, tall and of a heavy frame. The color of his face was clear and light, his eyes blue, his hair and beard blond. Foreign contemporary authors called him "the golden king of the North." He carried his head high, and his open, frank eye, and the clear voice of manly resonance, gave added charm to his noble appearance. Gustavus Adolphus possessed a majestic dignity of bearing coupled with the unfeigned kindness of a noble heart.

Charles IX. had left his son the Danish war as an inheritance. It was carried on in the provinces of the frontiers, and consisted chiefly in small conflicts, which caused fatigue and detriment without being decisive. The Danes entered the interior of Smaland during the first days of the year 1612. Gustavus Adolphus, in his turn, moved from the fort of Ryssby into the province of Scania, destroying by fire the town of Væ and several castles belonging to the wealthy nobility. During a smaller conflict which then took place, Gustavus Adolphus was in imminent danger of his life.

The Swedes had made a camp for themselves at the cemetery of Vittsjœ, when suddenly surprised by a force of Danish cavalry. The Swedes fought with determination, but found it necessary to leave their camp. They took a firm stand on the frozen waters of the adjoining lake, but were forced to leave that position also. A tumult ensued, during which the ice gave way on the spot where the king found himself, for the moment, alone and without an escort. Per Banér, a son of Gustavus Banér, who was executed at Linkœping at the command of Charles IX., perceived the king in the moment of greatest danger, and hastened with Thomas Larsson, a trooper from Upland, to rescue him. When in safety, the king at once unbuckled his silver belt, and, handing it to the trooper, said: "I shall remember thee with a piece of bread, which neither thou nor thy children shall ever find lacking." Thomas Larsson received in the following year a farm in the province of Westmanland, which has remained in the possession of his descendants to this very day. Per Banér received in fief the estates which had been in the possession of his uncle, Sten Banér, also executed at Linkœping, and rose to the dignity of a state councillor during the minority of Queen Christine.

It was the ambition of Christian IV. of Denmark to cut Sweden off from any communication with the North Sea. As Bohuslæn and Halland both were parts of the Danish dominion, there was only the small strip of territory surrounding the mouth of the Gotha River to conquer. The island of Hising constituted the larger part of it, and was the site of the new town of Gothenburg, which was defended by the fortress of Elfsborg. The town of New Lœdœse was situated on the opposite shore, some few miles up the river, defended by the fort of Gullberg. The Danish king approached Gullberg from Bohus, having with him a smaller force, which he considered sufficient in numbers. Gullberg was only a poor little nest, but it was valiantly defended by Morten Krakow and his wife, the stanch Lady Emerentia Pauli. One day the Danes made a violent attack. The ladders which they placed against the walls were crushed by heavy beams which the Swedes let fall down on them. In spite of this, the Danes succeeded in forcing the gates of the place. The position was a critical one for the Swedes. The commander had met with an accident and was unable to lead the defence. But Lady Emerentia resolved to take the command. She gave orders to the wives of the soldiers to fill up the vaulted passage of the gates with barrels, washtubs, timber, etc. When the Danes stormed on in a compact body, they were received by a downfall of scalding-hot lye, which the women kept pouring down on them from behind their barricade. The daughter of Lady Emerentia thus graphically describes the effect: "They lay in the vault and around the gates like scalded hogs." Lady Emerentia had placed two pieces of artillery on the top of a small building fronting the gates. They were loaded with broken horseshoes and the like and sent out a disastrous fire. The few surviving Danes fled hurriedly for their lives, leaving Lady Emerentia in proud possession of the fort. A second attack which was made later on proved as futile as the first. King Christian then gave command to abandon the plan of taking the fort. The Danish army collected in a field in front of Gullberg. But Lady Emerentia was vigilant. From the walls of the fort she espied a man of prepossessing appearance who rode a white horse. "Shoot that man!" was her immediate command to the nearest soldier. The shot took effect, killing the white horse, whose brains and blood spattered the king. For the man on horseback was King Christian. "That devilish crow does never sleep!" exclaimed the king, referring to the commander.

King Christian turned on New Lœdœse, killing without mercy all the male inhabitants of the town. West Gothland was invaded, the province appearing to be an easy prey because the Swedish army, commanded by Duke John, had just left it to march into Halland. But the bailiff of Hœjentorp called on the peasants to rise, which caused the Danes to recede. The Danes next made an attack on the fortress of Elfsborg, commanded by Olof Strole. Elfsborg was defended with heroism, but when fire threatened to destroy the towers, Olof Strole at last surrendered. On account of their valiant conduct the commander and his men, who were reduced to 200, were granted free passage with their music and banners. The able Morten Krakow of Gullberg had been promoted to the fortress of Vaxholm. His successor surrendered Gullberg to the Danes shortly after the fall of Elfsborg. King Christian planned a series of invasions in the year 1612, but, thanks to the vigilance of Gustavus Adolphus, he failed to accomplish the desired effect.

Gustavus Adolphus wanted peace with Denmark, and such was made at Kneroed in 1613, after a war of mutual invasions and without any decisive battles or conquests of territory. The frontiers were to remain the same as before the war; the Danish king was allowed to keep the emblem of three crowns, but had to resign his claims upon the Swedish crown. The fortress of Elfsborg remained in the hands of the Danes for six years, until $1,000,000, an exorbitant sum in those days, was paid for it. It cost the people of Sweden very dear to pay this sum, sacrifices being made by the king and his friends to contribute to it. But Elfsborg, the only approach to the North Sea, was indispensable. It was returned in a miserable condition, and Gothenburg, on the opposite side of Gotha River, destroyed. Gustavus Adolphus ordered Gothenburg to be moved to its present site, on the mainland, and endowed it with extensive commercial privileges, encouraging Dutch merchants to settle there.

The war with Russia began once more in 1614. Gustavus Adolphus not having been found willing to accept the crown for his brother Charles Philip, the negotiations were dropped. Count de la Gardie resumed control of the movements, although the king was present in person. The Swedes won a great victory at Bronitz and captured the fortress of Augdof. An attempt to take Pskof was unsuccessful, Evert Horn, the hero of a hundred battles, losing his life; but the Russians were willing to make peace. Through the honorable peace of Stolbova, in February, 1617, Russia gave up all claims on Esthonia and Livonia, and ceded to Sweden Ingermanland and Kexholm. This cut off the Russians from the Baltic, fixed the Swedish frontier on the lakes Ladoga and Peipus, and left Sweden in peace with the mightiest of her enemies during almost a century. The armistice with Poland ended in 1616, but after two years of insignificant movements it was continued up to 1620.

Gustavus II. Adolphus with untiring energy continued the work of building up the new state founded by Gustavus I. At the death of his father, the royal youth had won everybody by his gentleness and generosity. His first act was perhaps the wisest of all, in selecting among the councillors the young, highly talented Axel Oxenstierna as his chancellor. This couple have no peers in history, being united by the firmest of friendships and rising simultaneously to the highest ability of statesmanship, the gifts of the one wonderfully supplementing those of the other. The chancellor was cooler and slower than his royal friend. He placed supreme the duties to his country, but was of very aristocratic tendencies, through his influence leading the king still further away from the democratic principles of his father. To the nobility were granted the old privileges, with others in addition, which became menacing to the ancient freedom of the peasantry. The management of internal affairs and all branches of the administration were placed under various departments. They were presided over by the high functionaries and their offices chiefly filled by noblemen. A permanent supreme court was established in Stockholm, with the Drotsete as president, in 1614. In 1623, a supreme court for Finland was established and a governor-general for that grandduchy appointed, who was also to be president of the court. In 1630, a supreme court for the Baltic provinces was established at Dorpat. The Riksdag, governed by the new rules of 1617, was to convene yearly, and to consist of the four Estates of the kingdom: the nobility, clergy, bourgeoisie and yeomanry, each divided into various classes. These latter were as yet not quite distinct or organized, except those of the nobility, who, in 1625, formed a knightly chapter, the Riddarhus, which kept a register of the legitimate noble families of Sweden and Finland and watched over the interests of its members. The Estate of the nobility was divided in three classes, lords, knights and squires. To the first belonged the holders of counties and baronies, to the second those whose ancestors held the rank of state councillors, and to the third the rest of the nobility. As each class had one vote in the Riksdag, the supremacy of lords and knights, called the "higher nobility," was secure, when standing united, over the more numerous third class, the "lower nobility." The king appointed the speaker of the nobility, the *landtmarskalk*, who also was the president of their chapter. The Swedish church had its greatest epoch during the period of political grandeur, being characterized by a remarkable strength of faith and by a praiseworthy energy and earnestness. The clergy, high and low, set beautiful examples of piety, learning and patriotism. It was beloved by the people and spoke in their behalf with authority and courage. Not able to win Gustavus Adolphus over to more democratic views, it won his admiration, and he surnamed the ministers "tribunes of the people." The burghers, touched by the patriotic spirit, developed great energy during this period, trade and commerce having a devoted patron in the king, who, besides the new Gothenburg, founded twelve other towns in Sweden and Finland. The miners occupied

of old an uncertain position between burghers and yeomen.
They were strengthened and encouraged by the personal
interest which the king took in the mining industry. He
visited the mines repeatedly, descending into the bowels
of the earth to inspect the ore and the new methods introduced from abroad by foreign miners. Among the latter
the immigrated Dutchman, Louis de Geer, exerted a beneficial influence upon that industry. The factories producing
clothing and weapons for the army were also encouraged.
The yeomen occupied a difficult, almost desperate position
between the increasing privileges of the nobility and the increasing taxes of the crown. Their burdens were doubled
and their rights reduced; yet sustained by the church, and
believing in the lofty ideals of the king, they persevered,
fulfilling their duties with a high degree of patriotism.

No Swedish king has done so much for education as
Gustavus Adolphus. To the University of Upsala he donated 300 of his hereditary estates, founding its library,
improving its courses, banishing misrule, and appointing his old teacher, John Skytte, its chancellor. He
created the German University of Dorpat in Esthonia, in
1632; later for some time moved to Pernau. Colleges were
established in the larger towns. The king was, through
his thorough studies of Swedish laws and conditions, in a
position to take an active part in the reforms which he
promulgated, never resting long in one place, but travelling from one point to another, where his presence was
most necessary; shaping plans and reforms by his own
judgment, to have them indorsed by the next Riksdag,
and then enforcing them himself. Especially the army
passed through an evolution, thanks to new methods, devised by the king, who was to win his victories through

the introduction of improved tactics and divisions, by means of which the troops were easier to move and the co-operation between the various weapons increased.

In 1618 the "Thirty Years' War" began. The dethroned Frederic of the Palatinate turned, among others, to Gustavus Adolphus for support, which the latter was not able to give in a direct way. But he promised to attack Poland as soon as the armistice was at an end, thereby making it impossible for Sigismund to support Emperor Ferdinand with troops. In 1621, Gustavus Adolphus commenced operations against Poland, taking the command himself. Riga and Mitau were captured, the former important commercial centre regaining its privileges, but sending representatives to the Swedish Riksdag and accepting a Swedish governor. After having conquered Livonia, Gustavus Adolphus entered Courland the following year, when an armistice was agreed to. Gustavus followed the events in Germany with increasing interest, forming the plan of an alliance between the Protestant powers. Learning that the emperor was willing to support Sigismund, Gustavus Adolphus offered to invade Silesia. But as Christian IV. of Denmark was anxious to lead the Protestant forces, Gustavus Adolphus quietly withdrew, resuming action against Poland. After a victory at Wallhof, he entered Polish Prussia, where he was dangerously wounded at Dirschau. The Poles were reinforced by imperial troops, but suffered a defeat at Gurzo; the Swedish general, Herman Wrangel, winning the day. When the considerable reinforcements of 10,000 men joined the Poles, the Swedes receded in good order. A smaller conflict occurred at Stuhm, famous because Gustavus Adolphus was twice in danger of his life during the struggle, which otherwise was of no importance. An imperial trooper caught him by the belt and tried to drag the king with him. According to the report of Axel Oxenstierna, the king loosened the belt and let it go. In so doing, he also lost his hat, which was carried to Vienna and preserved as a token of the "great victory." Another trooper, shortly afterward, caught the king by the arm, aiming at the head with his sword. In the critical moment, Eric Soop, the colonel of a Swedish cavalry regiment, appeared, killing the trooper with a pistol-shot. Gustavus Adolphus referred to this struggle as the "hottest bath" that he was ever in.

In September, 1629, an armistice was agreed to, at Altmark, to last for six years, during which period Sweden was to keep Livonia and the Russian towns of Elbing, Braunsberg, Pillau and Memel. The new acquisition of territory was small, but the revenue from these commercial towns, and from Dantzic, Libau and Windau, was considerable, and went to pay for the army expenses of the German campaign. The new temporary possessions in Prussia were formed into a Swedish governmental section, over which Axel Oxenstierna was appointed governor-general.

What follows belongs to one of the most noted chapters of universal history. The unbroken chain of Swedish victories, the noble character of the king and the severe discipline upheld among his men, who commenced and ended their battles with prayers and hymns, astounded the world. The exalted nobility of Gustavus Adolphus appears to us all the more striking, contrasted with the faithlessness, vanity and cowardice of the contemporary reigning princes of Germany and Denmark. His victories appear all the more remarkable because the greatest warriors of the age—Tilly, Wallenstein and Pappenheim—were his adversaries.

He was received by the people of Germany as a liberator, and his memory is blessed by every thinking German, who admits that the Swedes, Gustavus Adolphus and Axel Oxenstierna, completed the work which the Germans, Luther and Melanchthon, created. The loftiness of the ideals which inspired Gustavus Adolphus have been doubted, but not with justice. He was brought up in a severely Christian home and the sincerity of his piety is unmistakable. His father's clairvoyant views upon the coming religious conflict were familiar to him since his early youth, while he was, through his mother, related in blood to the majority of Protestant princes. Thus apparently predestined, as the greatest statesman and warrior of his age, to take up the cause of his persecuted brethren, he did not do so before the ambitious Christian IV. had utterly failed in his attempts and with contumely been forced to retire. It is not probable that Gustavus Adolphus ever thought of placing the crown of the Roman empire upon his head, but plausible to suppose that he had in view the formation of a strong union of the Protestant countries of Northern Europe.

Before leaving Sweden, Gustavus II. convoked the representatives of his people, holding on his arm his little daughter Christine, four years old, for whom he asked their pledge of allegiance. His farewell speech was touching in its simplicity and the premonition of his tragic end. Not for worldly glory, but to save his country from peril and his brethren from distress, he undertook this risky war. "Generally," he said, "it happens thus that the vessel hauls water until it goes to pieces. With me likewise, that I, who in so many perils for the weal of my country have shed my blood, and yet until this day have been spared through the grace of God, now at last must lose my life. For that reason I will this time commend you, the collected Estates of the realm, to the hand of God, the Supreme One, wishing that we, after this our miserable and burdensome life, according to the will of God, may meet again, to dwell in the celestial and infinite." These words do not resemble the terse, striking speeches of his grandfather, but they bear the stamp of sincerity, and by them Gustavus Adolphus, his work and his purpose, are judged by the Swedish people.

Midsummer Day, 1630, Gustavus Adolphus landed with his troops at the island of Ruden, on the coast of Pomerania. Two days later he proceeded to the larger island of Usedom. His troops consisted of 13,000 men. Gustavus Adolphus was himself the first to land. He knelt on the shore and prayed to God in a loud voice; his prayer moved those surrounding him to tears. When the king noticed it he said: "Do not cry, but pray to God with fervor. The more of prayer, the more of victory; the best Christian is the best soldier." Then he took hold of a spade and commenced to assist personally in the work of building a camp. When it grew dark, the heavens were illuminated by the fire of burning villages, giving evidence of the manner in which the enemy conducted his warfare.

The supercilious Wallenstein had been dismissed by the emperor at the time when Gustavus Adolphus landed in Germany, but his wild hordes were pillaging Pomerania. Yet Gustavus Adolphus had great difficulty in persuading the old duke of Pomerania to accept the alliance he offered him. But when this was done, it took the Swedes only a short time to clear the duchy of its enemies. The young landgrave of Hesse and the free city of Magdeburg were glad to accept an alliance with Gustavus Adolphus. A treaty was made with France, which country promised to pay subsidies to Sweden as long as the German war lasted. Tilly, who was in command of the imperial troops, approached Magdeburg. Gustavus Adolphus sent proper provisions to Magdeburg with an experienced commander, as he could not go himself, because the elector of Saxony refused to let him pass with his army through Saxon territory. Magdeburg was captured by Tilly, who sacked and destroyed it by fire in a most barbarous way.

The discipline and moderation of the Swedish troops formed a great contrast to the reckless behavior of the imperial army. The Swedes left the peaceful inhabitants in undisturbed possession of their lives and property; the strictest order was maintained within the army; each regiment held morning and evening prayers in the open air; gambling, carousing and plundering were sternly prohibited. For these reasons the Swedish king and his army were received by the poor downtrodden people as saviors and liberators. Gustavus Adolphus deeply mourned the fall of Magdeburg, whose fate it had not been in his power to prevent. He took a fortified position at Werben, where the river Havel is joined by the Ube. Tilly entered Saxony with a hostile demeanor, not satisfied with the lukewarm friendship of the elector. Burning villages marked the way of his army. The poor elector, not knowing what to do, in his despair turned to Gustavus Adolphus, whom he had treated so coldly and begged him for help. The king at once was ready to forget past differences, and, joining forces with the elector, he marched toward Leipsic.

Tilly, with 35,000 men, occupied an advantageous position near the village of Breitenfeld, not far from Leipsic, at the summit of a long ridge of sandy hills. The infantry and the greater part of the cavalry were grouped in heavy divisions, forming one single line of battle with artillery behind at the very top of the hills. Tilly himself commanded the centre, while his able and fiery sub-commander, Pappenheim, had the command of the left wing, being in hopes to encounter the Swedish king personally. The Swedish army consisted of 22,000 men, who were joined by 11,000 Saxons.

Early in the morning of September 7, 1631, the Swedes started toward Breitenfeld. Tilly turned pale, it is said, when he saw the order and firmness with which the Swedes marched up to take their positions on the narrow slips of ground between the Lober brook and the reach of the imperial cannon. The Swedes were arranged in a double line of battle, infantry in the centre and cavalry on the wings. Between the squadrons of cavalry divisions of musketeers were placed. The regimental artillery was distributed over a number of places. The king commanded the right wing in person, with John Banér as sub-commander. Teuffel led the centre and Gustavus Horn the left wing. The king had no confidence in the Saxons, for which reason he had arranged them by themselves at some distance to the left of the Swedish army. When everything was arranged, the king rode to the front. With his head uncovered, and his sword pointing to the ground, he prayed: "Almighty God, thou who holdest victory and defeat in the hollow of thy hand, turn thine eyes unto us, thy servants, who have come hither from distant dwellings to fight for liberty and truth, for thy holy Gospel. Give victory unto us for the glory of thy hallowed name! Amen!" The prayer of the king could be heard by almost every man of the army, and all were touched and strengthened by his pious trust in a righteous cause. The Swedes of the right wing were soon attacked by Pappenheim and his cavalry. But the horses of the imperialists were frightened by the flashing fire of the musketeers, and the attack failed to have an effect. It was ended as quickly as it was begun. Pappenheim concluded to make an attempt to surprise the Swedes from the left side. But the king divined his plan. He ordered John Banér with the second line to make a movement by which to turn at an angle with the first and face the attack from the side. Pappenheim was surprised to find a new line facing him. A bloody struggle ensued. Seven times his men made an inroad on the Swedish line and were seven times repulsed, badly damaged by the fire of the musketeers. The Swedes, in their turn, made an attack which scattered Pappenheim's forces from the field in wild flight.

Tilly had with his light cavalry attacked the left wing of the Swedes. His men were mostly made up of Croats and other semi-barbarous people. When repulsed by the Swedes they concentrated their forces to crush the Saxons. These withstood the first assault, but the second routed them completely. The imperialists then made a second attack upon the left Swedish wing, made up of only 2,500 men. Gustavus Horn acted with coolness and great presence of mind. He let the first line close in on the second till it was able to take a firm stand against the heavy force of the attacking enemy. The Swedes never for a moment lost their position, in spite of the frightful onslaught. The king arrived and remained for some time with the left wing. He ordered the Scotch brigade of hired troops to support him. The Scotch had cannon hidden behind their lines. These had a telling effect upon the attacking imperialists, who were thrown back, suffering great losses. Everywhere the battle was fought with frenzy, the clouds of dust and smoke changing the day into night.

The king made sure that the left wing of the enemy's army was engaged in continued flight. Then he commenced an attack with his own right wing upon the imperial artillery, which had kept up a steady fire against the Swedish centre. Tilly's cannon were captured at the first attempt and turned on the imperial troops, causing consternation. Horn opened an attack on his side and the king hastened to support him with his troops. Tilly tried in vain to lead his troops into the battle. Pappenheim had returned and gave brilliant proofs of personal courage. The defeat of the imperial army was unavoidable; it scattered in helpless confusion. Tilly lost his horse and was near being captured himself. Four of his best infantry regiments took a stand and tried to resist the conquering foe. These imperial soldiers, who never had suffered a defeat, preferred death to surrender. Tilly fled at last, followed by only 600 men. After five hours of fighting the Swedes had won a glorious victory. They finished the day with prayer and remained on the battlefield over night, arranged in order of battle. The following morning they entered the deserted camp of the enemy where a rich booty awaited them.

The progress of Gustavus Adolphus along the shores of the river Main to the towns of Frankfort and Mayence was a march of triumph. In capturing Mayence, the Swedes fought the Spanish allies of the emperor. The towns surrendered to violence or by their own consent. Gustavus Adolphus made their inhabitants pledge their fidelity to him and strengthened his power with the rich resources of the Frankish country. Then he turned against Maximilian of Bavaria. Tilly, who was to defend Bavaria, was again encountered and defeated at Lech. He was carried from the battle mortally wounded and died soon afterward. Gustavus Adolphus made his triumphal entry into Munich, with Frederic of the Palatinate at his side. The danger to the crown lands of the emperor was imminent.

Wallenstein was the most famous of German generals. Reticent and secretive, he appeared to be unable to feel mercy. He was devoted to the secret doctrines of astrology, which in him had taken the place of religion. He cared naught for the cause of religious liberty or the fall of the German empire, looking only for occasions to satisfy his own ambition and the means of obtaining power and wealth. He had served the emperor, who had raised him to the dignity of a duke of Mecklenburg, but had been dismissed and deprived of his dignities at the time of the arrival of Gustavus Adolphus on German soil. His downfall was caused by complaints of his insolence and recklessness, made by Maximilian of Bavaria and other German princes. Wallenstein retired to Prague, at the castle of which town he surrounded himself with princely luxury and comfort, scheming for revenge. His plan was to join the enemies of the emperor. He approached Gustavus Adolphus for such purpose, before the battle of Breitenfeld, and was delighted to hear of the defeat of Tilly. Gustavus Adolphus seemed at first inclined to take up relations with Wallenstein, but at the point where an agreement was to be made he suddenly changed his attitude. The king probably hesitated to accept the services of a man who had no other aim than to satisfy his own ambition. The emperor was placed in a bad predicament, at the second defeat of Tilly, for want of an army to defend his lands and a commander to lead it. There was only one way out of the difficulty, and that was to pacify the mortally offended Wallenstein, and to persuade him to re-enter the service of the emperor. The emperor resigned himself to accept this humiliating condition, and Wallenstein agreed to resume command, but only at a high price. The name of Wallenstein was enough to bring thousands of warriors under the imperial banners, and Wallenstein was soon at the head of an army of sufficient proportions. His doctrine was that "the war should support itself," according to which his soldiers were allowed to sack and plunder at will the countries through which they were passing. He cared naught for the recklessness of his subordinates, if they only showed blind obedience to him.

Wallenstein expelled the Saxons who had invaded Bohemia. But he showed disinclination to assist the elector of Bavaria, who was compelled to leave his country. At Eger, Wallenstein was reinforced and marched on Nuremberg with an army of 60,000, prepared to meet Gustavus Adolphus. He was confident of his superior force. "Within four days," he said, "it shall become evident whether I or the Swedish king is the master of Germany." Gustavus Adolphus hastened to relieve Nuremberg, taking his position in the immediate neighborhood of said town. He had only 18,000 men with him, but he surrounded this army with solid fortifications, and Wallenstein dared not risk an attack, in spite of his superior force. Wallenstein took his position at the summit of three steep hills, surrounded by trenches and ramparts. His intention was to cut off the Swedes from all sources of supplies and force them to surrender by starvation. "I shall teach the Swedish king," he said, "a new method of warfare."

For nine weeks the two armies were facing each other. The suffering became great in both camps. The Swedes suffered most, although the inhabitants of Nuremberg tried their utmost to supply them with food. When the provisions were diminishing, the bonds of discipline were loosened. Especially the Germans of the Swedish army made themselves conspicuous by licentiousness and plunder. Gustavus Adolphus decided to try an attack on Wallenstein's camp, in order to put an end to the critical state of things. He was so much more anxious to risk it, as his army had been considerably reinforced and was almost equal to Wallenstein's in numbers. At noon, August 24, 1632, the Swedish army made ready for battle. The attack was first made on Burgstall, the most important one of the three hills occupied by the enemy. The battle was a fierce and bloody one, the whole mountain being clothed in fire and smoke. Several of the most distinguished of the Swedish officers were killed or captured. A bullet passed through the boot of the king; an officer was killed at his side. The Swedes were thrown back on one hand, while on the other, Duke Bernhard of Weimar, one of the German commanders of the king, succeeded in capturing one of the forts built on the Burgstall. But as the day was over and the army exhausted, the Swedes were not able to profit by their success. A heavy rain commenced, continuing through the night. This made it impossible to haul any cannon up to the captured fort, which was then abandoned. The Swedish army returned to the camp. This unsuccessful attack cost the Swedes almost 2,000 men. Gustavus Adolphus wrote in regard to it: "It was too much to be considered a page's trick, but too small to be of real earnest." Wallenstein wrote of it. "Never in my life have I seen a more desperate fire, but I hope that the Swedes have lost their horns in this conflict."

The king broke camp a fortnight later, arranging his army into a line of battle. For four hours he waited for Wallenstein to come forward, but the latter did not risk an attack. Gustavus Adolphus intended to enter Swabia, to complete the conquest of Southwestern Germany. But Wallenstein, who soon afterward also broke camp, invaded Saxony. This caused the king to change his plans. He was obliged to follow Wallenstein in order to protect his ally and to avoid the danger of being cut off from the connections with his own empire. Wallenstein marked his way bv cruel devastation, and the appeals of the unhappy population persuaded the king to take an early decision.

The people of Saxony received Gustavus Adolphus with great enthusiasm, of which they gave evidence in the most exultant manner. People were seen kneeling everywhere on his way, imploringly stretching their hands toward him. The king was not content with their exaggerated devotion. "I fear that God is offended by their vain demonstrations of joy and soon shall show them that the one whom they adore as a god is naught but a weak and mortal man."

Wallenstein was in the neighborhood of Leipsic, at the little town of Lutzen. He had sent away Pappenheim, his best sub-commander, to Halle with a considerable force. Gustavus Adolphus found this circumstance favorable and decided on an attack.

It was the 6th of November, 1632. A heavy mist covered the spacious fields around Leipsic. Wallenstein was, with the right wing of his army, close on Lutzen, the little town being set on fire, in order not to shield a clandestine attack. The flame of the conflagration appeared dull but magnified through the mists of the early morning. In front of the imperial army was the highway. Musketeers were stationed in and above the ditches, which were made deeper and provided with ramparts. The musketeers were so arranged that higher lines could shoot over the heads of the lower ones. Behind them was another chain of musketeers. The artillery was placed partly behind the musketeers, partly on the sides of a hill where some windmills were situated. The cavalry was placed on the wings, the infantry in the centre, both arranged in great square divisions. A courier had been sent to recall Pappenheim, as the army without his force counted only 18,000 men. The Swedish army was 20,000 strong and was arranged according to a plan similar to the one followed at Breitenfeld. It was arranged in two lines. Musketeers were interspersed among the cavalry. The regimental artillery was placed before the front. The king commanded the right wing, Nils Brahe the centre, Kniephausen the second line of the centre, and Duke Bernhard the left wing.

The king, who for the time being had none of his best officers around him, spent the night in a wagon, together with Duke Bernhard and Kniephausen. He rose in the morning, dressed, without armor, in a blouse and a gray coat, and mounted his usual white charger, without having tasted food. He conducted in person the morning prayers of the army, when Luther's psalm, "Eine feste Burg ist unser Gott," was sung. After the song had ceased, the king made a short speech in Swedish, which he repeated in German. He said: "There you have the enemy. He is not now at the top of the hill or behind intrenchments, but in the open field. You know well how eagerly he has sought to avoid a conflict and that he is forced to fight because he cannot escape us. Fight, then, my dear countrymen and friends, for God, your country and your king. I will reward you all. But if you flinch, you know well that not a man of you will ever see his country again." Then the psalm, "Versage nicht du Hæuflein klein," the words of which were written in German by Gustavus Adolphus himself, was sung. The king gave the sign of attack by waving his sword over his head and cried: "Forward in God's name; Jesu, Jesu, Jesu, help us to-day to strive to the honor of thy holy name!"

It was eleven o'clock, and the mists had, to a great extent, scattered. The Swedish centre, with the battery behind, marched toward the highway. The left wing made an attempt to penetrate between the burning Lutzen and the batteries below the windmills. A terrible fire from muskets and cannon met the attacking Swedes. Whole lines of infantry were killed. The left wing suffered in particular. But when the Swedes reached their destination, the centre moved on with great force, cleaning the ditches of musketeers, capturing seven pieces of artillery and making two of the great squares of imperial infantry retire from their position. While fighting the third, the Swedes were surprised by the reserve and cavalry forces of the enemy, and had to abandon what they had taken, retiring into the open field.

The king had, in the meantime, with the cavalry of the right wing, forced the ditches. When notified of the danger in which the centre was placed, he hurried to assist his infantry. At the head of his Smaland cavalry he moved on so quickly that he was separated from the rest of his forces. The king was near-sighted and the mist once more thickening. For these reasons he happened to ride close up to the lines of the imperial cuirassiers. His horse was wounded, and the king himself received a pistol shot in the arm. He turned to one of his companions, Duke Frantz Albrecht, of Sachsen-Lauenburg, with a request to be escorted out of the battle, but was at that instant wounded in the back, immediately falling off his horse. Duke Frantz Albrecht, only thinking of saving his own life, fled from the spot. But a German page, eighteen years of age, who accompanied the king, jumped from his horse and tried to assist the king in mounting it. Some imperial cavalrymen passed by. They inquired for the name of the wounded lord. The page tried to hide his identity, but Gustavus Adolphus answered: "I was once the king of Sweden." One of the imperialists attempted to drag the king with him, but seeing some Swedish soldiers approaching, he sent in leaving a bullet through the wounded hero's brain.

The Swedes had been thrown back from the highway all over the line. The white horse of the king, with empty saddle and stained with blood, was seen galloping before the front. The message of mourning spread with lightning rapidity through the army, causing universal sorrow and anger. The ambition to avenge the death of the beloved king was kindled in every breast. Duke Bernhard at once assumed supreme command when notified of the catastrophe. The sagacious Kniephausen thought the battle lost and considered it best to retire in good order. The duke answered: "Here is not the question of retreat, but of revenge in victory or death." The Swedish line of battle soon moved forward once more and with redoubled strength. The right wing, commanded by the valiant Stolhandske, threw back the imperial troops who had caused the fall of the king. Nils Brahe once more carried the troops of the centre across the highway and captured for a second time the seven pieces of artillery. The left wing, commanded by Duke Bernhard, also moved forward victoriously, capturing the batteries at the windmill and pointing the cannon toward the enemy. When simultaneously some wagons loaded with powder for the imperial artillery exploded with a tremendous roar, the whole army of Wallenstein was thrown into a state of confusion. It was thought that the Swedes had made an attack from the rear. The cavalry fled in great numbers with the cries: "We know the king of Sweden! He is worst toward the end of the day."

But now another cry was heard: "Pappenheim is coming! Pappenheim is coming!" And so it was. Pappenheim arrived with his valiant cavalry at this important juncture. "Where is the king of Sweden to be found?" was his first question. When told that Gustavus Adolphus had been seen leading the right wing, he hurried thither, not knowing the fate that had befallen his royal enemy, and desirous of fighting him face to face. The imperialists recommenced the battle with renewed vigor. The scattered forces of cavalry and infantry were collected once more and were joined by the fresh troops of Pappenheim. The attacking Swedes met a stanch resistance. The latter were almost tired out, but preserved their courage. A contemporary writer says that a battle was never fought in a better way by troops who had for such a long stretch been in the fire. The Swedish losses were exceedingly heavy. The royal standard and several other banners were taken. The able Nils Brahe was killed, and the division of which he was the head fell to the very last man. But Pappenheim, who rushed forward blindly, in his eagerness to meet the king of Sweden, was also killed, according to tradition, by a bullet from Stolhandske. "Pappenheim has fallen! All is lost!" shouted his men, and drew back discouraged. Wallenstein still thought there was a chance to hold the field against the exhausted enemy.

Kniephausen had preserved the second line of battle in good order, resolved to cover the retreat he thought unavoidable. He had sent away smaller divisions to support the first line, but not in numbers enough to disturb the order of his own troops. Now he commanded his men to the front, to fill all the gaps of the first lines. When this was done, the Swedes made a third attack. The evening sun pierced through the mists for a moment, and Wallenstein in this light saw the Swedish army approach in a mighty solid line as at the opening of the battle. He was greatly surprised. This time the Swedes were resolved to conquer or die. Soldiers were heard to promise each other to stand by that resolution. For a third time the Swedes passed the highway and recaptured, after a bloody struggle, the disputed cannon. The wings of Wallenstein's army were both in a state of dissolution. But his centre preserved two divisions which offered a stubborn resistance until sunset, when they were ordered to retreat. The Swedes had won the day, but were too tired to pursue the enemy. Following their custom, they rested over the night on the battlefield they had bought by their blood.

The loss of troops had been heavy on either side, amounting to about 6,000 men altogether, or about one-third of the whole number of men engaged in the battle. The excitement was so great on both sides that no prisoners were made. The corpse of Gustavus Adolphus, bruised

DEATH OF GUSTAVUS ADOLPHUS AT THE BATTLE OF LÜTZEN
Norway.

and mangled, was found during the night under a heap of dead soldiers. A large monumental stone, with inscription, now marks the spot where the hero king lost his life. The Gustavus Adolphus Society of Germany is a living monument to his memory.

CHAPTER XI

Period of Political Grandeur—Queen Christine

CHRISTINE was six years old when she succeeded her father. Her armies stood scattered through foreign lands, surrounded by enemies and faithless allies. Her country was covered with glory, but in direst distress. The most remarkable aspect of her father's greatness now was to become apparent. Gustavus Adolphus had left behind men whom he had educated as statesmen, and generals capable of bringing his work to a successful end. First among the former was the state chancellor, *Axel Oxenstierna*, the friend and adviser of the hero king. He managed to keep the Swedish allies together and to establish harmony and unity of action between the Swedish commanders, supplying funds to carry on the war and strengthening the government at home with his courage and his wisdom. Oxenstierna was a statesman of considerable power before the death of the king; after it he grows in grandeur to carry the burden of unlimited responsibility placed on his shoulders. His coolness and dignity were a source of constant irritation to Richelieu, who said there was "something Gothic and a good deal of Finnish" about his proceedings in diplomatic affairs, while Mazarin said that if all the statesmen of his time were to be put aboard of one vessel, Oxenstierna should be placed at the helm.

The great chancellor always upheld the dignity of his country. When French diplomatists forgot themselves thus far as to use, in correspondence, their own language, instead of Latin, the recognized language of diplomacy in that day, Axel Oxenstierna gave instructions that they should be answered in Swedish.

After the death of Gustavus Adolphus, the war in Germany lost more and more of its original aspect. The cause of Protestantism was dropped out of sight for political interests. The battles of Sweden were, to a great extent, and sometimes altogether, fought by foreign troops; but Swedish were the generals and statesmen who led the operations of the armies and the diplomatic deliberations. The success of Sweden, at first, seemed to have passed away with her great hero king. The imperialists won a great victory at Nœrdlingen in 1634. The young archduke, Ferdinand, had succeeded Wallenstein as their commander-general, the latter having been murdered at the request of the emperor. Ferdinand marched on the town of Nœrdlingen with an army of German and Spanish troops, the experienced Piccolomini being at his side. Duke Bernhard, who with an army had been taking possession of Franconia in his own personal interests, hastened to support the town and was joined by Gustavus Horn, who, with another army, had been stationed in Elsass. Count Horn gave the advice to await reinforcements, but the excitable Duke Bernhard opened an attack on the enemy, which necessitated an immediate battle. After eight hours of hard fighting, the imperialists, who were 30,000 strong, entirely routed the Swedish army of 18,000 men, not a single Swedish regiment being among them. Horn was made a prisoner. Duke Bernhard, who soon afterward with his troops entered

French service, acknowledged his fault, saying: "I was a fool, but Horn a wise man." Sweden lost through this terrible defeat an army and two able generals. The Swedish conquests in South Germany were lost, and the German allies were scattered, the elector of Saxony joining the cause of the emperor. The armistice with Poland came to an end in 1635, and it was renewed for twenty-six years, at the cost of the Prussian seaports, with their lucrative revenues, which had paid for the expenses of the German war. Oxenstierna returned to Sweden to gather means wherewith to continue the war. The ordinary resources of Sweden were drained, and great sacrifices were needed. The Riksdag declared itself willing to "risk life, blood and means, until God grants a peace equal to the dignity of Sweden."

John Banér was the man who re-established the success of the Swedish arms. He resembled Gustavus Adolphus in greatness of mind and ability in war, paying back the execution of his father under Charles IX., by loyalty to the illustrious son of the latter. Banér was a typical soldier of the Thirty Years' War, amiable, but licentious, and cruel to his enemies. An able tactician and strategist of inexhaustible resources, he had distinguished himself in the Polish war and later held many important commands. The death of Gustavus Adolphus stirred this strong man to the very depths of his soul. He left his army in Bavaria and arrived at Wolgast, resolved to leave the army. At the sight of the body of his beloved king, he was overcome by a paroxysm of grief. Axel Oxenstierna persuaded him to resume his command in order to bring the work of their dead master to completion. He marched with his army through Silesia to Bohemia, encamping before Prague.

After the battle of Nœrdlingen he retreated to Saxony, whose deceitful elector he reproached with harsh words. Intrigues by the latter to bring the German troops in Swedish service to mutiny were frustrated by Banér, who had only 2,000 Swedes and Livonians with him. The Saxon army followed Banér into Mecklenburg, but suffered a defeat at Dœmitz. Banér marched eastward and joined the Swedish force, which met him, from Prussia, commanded by Lennart Torstensson. The elector of Brandenburg also declared war on Sweden, Banér answering by invading his country. From the vicinity of Berlin, Banér continued his way through Saxony back to Mecklenburg, his German troops marauding with such cruelty that they were sharply remonstrated with by Banér, who said he found it strange that God did not instantly punish them.

Banér was followed by the united armies of Austria and Saxony, but, having received reinforcements of Swedish troops, he turned on his tracks and met the enemy at Wittstock, in Brandenburg, September 24, 1636. The Swedish army consisted of 20,000 men, while the opposing force was much larger and occupied a favorable position on a hill. Banér won a glorious victory, thanks to a skilfully executed manœuvre. It grew dark, and the right wing of the Swedes was leading an almost forlorn hope against the overwhelming forces, when their left wing, after a difficult roundabout move, attacked the enemy from behind. Of the hostile armies every man was killed except a detachment less than 1,000 strong. The baggage, artillery and banners were taken, even the table silver of the elector and the imperial generals falling into the hands of the Swedes, who by this victory had regained their supremacy on German soil.

Banér had commenced the siege of Leipsic, when, upon news of an approaching army of the imperial allies, he was forced to undertake the famous "Retreat from Torgau," which made him more celebrated than any of his great battles. He with his army was near being surrounded at the river Oder, but saved himself through a series of movements of the highest strategic skill. Cardinal Richelieu wrote that "this retreat, by means of which Banér saved 14,000 men, less a few fugitives and wounded, with cannon and baggage, against an army 60,000 strong, is to be compared to the most glorious deeds in history." The enemy prided itself on having "caught Banér in a bag." "Yes," said Banér later, "surely they had me there, but they forgot to tie the string around."

In Pomerania, Banér received the reinforcements from Sweden which he had awaited, and once more invaded Saxony, where he won a grand victory at Chemnitz, in 1639. The Swedish army invaded Bohemia, cruelly devastating the country. Banér made a daring attack upon Regensburg in order to make the emperor and the whole German diet his prisoners. Sudden thaws frustrated the plans, making it impossible for the Swedes to cross the Danube. A superior force was sent to meet Banér, who saved his army by another famous retreat back to Saxony. On the way Banér was attacked by a fever and died at Halberstadt, in 1641. When the imperialists learned of the death of the Swedish Leonidas, they thought they could easily defeat his army. The Swedes saw the approaching enemy and collected around the coffin of their dead hero, offering solemn pledges to fight for the glory of his name. They then made a sudden attack upon the imperial army, which suffered a thorough defeat at Wolfenbuttel. John

Banér, triumphant in death like his great master, was buried in the Swedish Pantheon of the Riddarholm.

Banér had expressed the wish that Lennart Torstensson should succeed him as commander-general of the Swedish armies. Lennart Torstensson was a greater warrior even than John Banér; no Swedish general, Gustavus Adolphus not excepted, ever reaching higher skill or perfection in the science of war than this crippled hero. Torstensson was of a noble although not influential family. He entered the service of Gustavus Adolphus as a body page to the king, later distinguishing himself as an artillery commander. Torstensson took an honorable part in the battle of Breitenfeld, but made a prisoner at Nuremberg, he lost his health, during one year's captivity, in a miserable dungeon. During his later brilliant career he suffered greatly from rheumatism, and was mostly carried around in a litter throughout the battles which covered his name with undying fame. He was a pious man of a gentle and cheerful disposition, who tried his utmost to reintroduce among his troops the excellent moral behavior and severe discipline which had been lost after the death of Gustavus Adolphus.

Torstensson with rigor suppressed the intrigues against Sweden which were secretly carried on within the army. Brandenburg received a new elector in Frederic William, who, ambitious and far-seeing, entered an alliance with the victorious power of the North. Torstensson now was enabled to invade the imperial crown lands, commencing with Silesia; but finding it necessary to force a battle he met the imperialists at Breitenfeld. October 23, 1642, the second great victory of Breitenfeld was won by Swedish arms. Archduke Leopold and Piccolomini led the imperial army, the latter general fighting as a common soldier to inspire courage by his example, but with no effect. The Swedes captured the baggage, cannon and banners of the enemy, taking 5,000 prisoners and leaving as many dead imperialists on the field. Torstensson conquered Leipsic on the following day.

Torstensson marched through Bohemia and Moravia with the rapidity which characterized all his military movements, and penetrated to the very gates of Vienna, the emperor with difficulty saving himself from being made his prisoner. But suddenly he left and marched through Silesia to North Germany. He had received an order from the state council to attack Denmark. The great chancellor was out of patience with the perfidy and intrigues of Christian IV., who stood in secret connection with every one of Sweden's enemies. No previous declaration of war was made. Torstensson captured the Danish duchies of Schleswig and Holstein before any one could prevent it, his army then taking possession of all Jutland. Gustavus Horn invaded Scania, almost completely capturing the whole province in spite of bands of freebooters among the peasants, called *Snaphaner*.

Denmark was in danger of its very existence, but King Christian IV. did not forget his old wish to destroy the town of Gothenburg, whose growing prosperity caused him envy. He approached Gothenburg with a fleet, and viewed the town from the overlooking mountain of the Ramberg. His demands for a surrender were refused. Patriotic Louis de Geer had ordered from Holland a fleet at his own expense, which was to go to the support of Gothenburg. It did not arrive in time, but King Christian left to meet it, and it later proved of great value in the Swedish movements at sea, joining the Swedish fleet in the Sound. The latter, consisting of twenty-two ships under the command of Clas Fleming, sailed to the Danish waters, capturing the island of Femern, supported by Torstensson. An invasion of the island of Funen was planned, but could not be effected. A great naval battle between the Swedish and Danish fleets was fought July 6th. It caused great loss on either side, without being decisive. King Christian, who commanded his naval forces, lost one eye and received over twenty different wounds. The Swedes kept the place of battle, but sought the Bay of Skiel for repairs, where they were hedged in by the Danish fleet. Clas Fleming encouraged his followers to cut through the line, in which they were successful. A month later he was killed by a shot from the coast of Holstein, where the Danes had erected a fort. The Swedes avenged the death of their valiant commander by destroying the fort and killing its defenders. Fleming was succeeded by Charles Gustavus Wrangel, who saved the fleet to Sweden, returning to Femern in the autumn, joined by the Dutch fleet of Louis de Geer. The Danish fleet was met with October 13th, and at once scattered. The swift-sailing Dutch ships went in pursuit and destroyed all the seventeen Danish ships but two, which brought the news of the disaster to Copenhagen.

King Christian, who had in vain expected support from the emperor, found himself defeated on every point, and had no other choice than to make peace. The treaty was signed August 13, 1645, at Brœmsebro, Denmark ceding the provinces of Jemtland and Herjedal and the islands of Gothland and Œsel. The province of Halland was to remain for thirty years in the possession of Sweden, which country was exempt from duties of toll for the traffic in the Sound. Denmark disavowed all claims of supremacy over

Holstein, the duke of said country two years later formally placing himself under Swedish protection.

Lennart Torstensson had fulfilled his task in Denmark and returned to Germany. At Jueterbogk, in Brandenburg, he met the imperial army, which had been sent to cut off his retreat from Denmark, and entirely routed it. After this victory Torstensson hastened to Bohemia, resolved to "attack the emperor in his heart and force him to make peace." At Jankowitz, in Bohemia, Torstensson administered a new and crushing defeat to the imperialists, in 1645. The emperor, who himself had ordered his army to battle, had arrived in Prague to witness the defeat of the Swedes, which the Holy Virgin had promised him in a dream. He soon learned the news, which was quite different from that expected. The imperial commander-general, five generals and eight colonels were made prisoners by the Swedes, who captured the artillery and baggage of the enemy. The health of Torstensson was at that moment so good that he was able to lead the movements on horseback. He said that such a bloody battle would not be seen for a long time.

Torstensson invaded Moravia, the fortresses surrendering and the inhabitants fleeing in terror. For a second time he stood at the walls of Vienna. The very fortifications which protected the bridge across the Danube were captured by the Swedes. The enemy, whom the elector of Saxony had promised to chase out of Germany, was now knocking at the gate of the emperor, who heard the report with consternation. But Lennart Torstensson was forced to surrender to a perfidious enemy, who came to his door without knocking. His rheumatic ailment returned with such violence that he was obliged to renounce his command and return from the fields where he had led none but victorious armies. He was succeeded by Charles Gustavus Wrangel. The latter had to give up the siege of Vienna, but maintained, in connection with the French, the supremacy in Germany until an honorable peace was won. Upon his return to Sweden, Lennart Torstensson was covered with distinctions, being made a baron and a count on one and the same day. He was appointed governor-general of West Gothland, Vermland, and the lately conquered Halland, with his seat at Gothenburg, where he built himself a palace (still the official residence of the governor of Gothenburg and Bohuslæn). Lennart Torstensson died in 1651, leaving behind the fame of one of the greatest warriors known to history, and a spotless memory.

The treaty of peace of Westphalia was signed in October, 1648. The representatives of Sweden were John Oxenstierna, a son of the great chancellor, and Adler Salvius. Sweden received, as a reward for her decisive and glorious part in the Thirty Years' War, the following possessions: West Pomerania, with the islands of Rugen and Usedom; the western part of East Pomerania, with the island of Wollin; the town of Wismar, with surrounding territory, and the bishoprics of Bremen and Verden. With these German possessions followed three votes at the German Diet. The Swedish government was to receive a sum of several millions to defray the army expenses, of which Queen Christine recklessly ceded the larger part.

Through these glorious conditions of peace Sweden rose to the rank of one of the mightiest of European empires, which held the balance of power in Northern Europe. Her possessions made the Baltic almost an "inland lake of Sweden," and efforts soon followed to make it completely so. Sweden exerted a beneficent influence throughout her large possessions, which, from a cultural point of view, hardly can be overestimated. Her methods of planting the seeds of culture, by establishing Swedish and German universities, and by abolishing serfdom in the conquered lands, are worthy of the highest respect. But with her new political grandeur Sweden acquired formidable enemies; she had not the resources to sustain or defend her great possessions, and the development of the mother country was for a time misdirected by dreams of vain glory.

The government of Sweden during Christine's minority, according to the directions left by her father, consisted of the five highest officials of the realm. Among these the chancellor, through his experience and his former intimacy with Gustavus Adolphus, was the leading spirit, king in all except the name, and deserving the honorable surname of "our greatest civilian," given him by Swedish historians. Unlike the majority of other uncrowned or crowned rulers, he did not use his power to secure wealth or distinction for himself and his family until upon his retirement. Offers to make him a ruling prince of Germany, and the young queen his son's consort, were coldly refused. While the war was going on he strengthened the foundations of the centralization of the state by the government regulations of 1634. At the side of the supreme court of Stockholm another was established at Jœnkœping, for Gothaland, with a state councillor as president. The system of various government departments was enlarged upon.[1] The most important of these was the chancery, in which all business to come before the government was prepared. Departments for commerce and for mining were established. Sweden

---

[1] These were not departments in the sense of bureaus, but *collegia*.

was divided into eleven administrative districts, *læn*, later increased to sixteen, each of these having a governor. Finland was divided into five districts. Count Peter Brahe the Younger, as governor-general of Finland, did more for this neglected country than was ever done before to right wrongs and foster prosperity. Livonia and Ingermanland received each their governor-general, the latter province, by repeated wars brought into a devastated condition, serving as a place of deportation. This system of administration won the admiration of the Continent and was in many instances copied as a pattern of perfection. The Swedish army was considered the finest in the world, and troops better trained or more victorious did not exist. At the end of the Thirty Years' War about 100,000 men were under Swedish command. The majority of these were foreigners, who afterward were enlisted for continual service. Their officers were raised in great numbers to the rank of nobles and endowed with dignities and estates. The army was divided into twenty regiments, seven of which were Finnish. The town and coast population regularly furnished able men for the navy. Much was done to improve the interior communications by means of new roads and canals. A postal route was established between Stockholm and Gothenburg, and others followed. A Swedish postmaster in Hamburg had charge of the foreign mails. Newspapers were published, the government shaping for itself an organ for official announcement which is yet published.

Great improvements were made in the mining industry, thanks principally to the efforts of the noble immigrant, Louis de Geer and his Walloons, who made the mines of Dannemora a source of riches. Weapons and cannon were manufactured not only for the army, but for exportation also. The brass foundries were excellent. The towns began to flourish, especially Stockholm and Gothenburg, through commerce with Holland and the Baltic States. A Swedish colony, planned by Gustavus Adolphus through the South Company, created by him in Gothenburg, was founded in North America. In 1638 two ships, "Kalmar Nyckel" and "Fogel Grip," arrived at the mouth of the Delaware River, where territory was procured through honest purchase from the Indians. The Dutch in neighboring colonies tried to persuade the Indians to oust the newcomers, but the Swedish governor, Peter Menuet, won their goodwill by fair dealing. The members of the colony of New Sweden were honest, upright people, who dwelt in peace with the natives. They accepted a governor appointed by the government, in the person of John Printz, but refused to tolerate among themselves criminals who later were despatched to their colony, and these had to be taken back. New Sweden after a few decades became the prey of the Dutch, but many American families point with justifiable pride to their descent from these honest and industrious Swedish settlers. A Swedish colony on the coast of African Guinea existed between 1650 and 1663, but was through treacherous dealings turned over to the Dutch.

Much was done to build up the educational system, several new colleges were established, and regulations made to instruct the peasants. Peter Brahe founded the University of Abo, in 1640, while in Finland, and the German University of Greifswald, in Swedish Pomerania, was reestablished. Swedish men of learning began to attract attention, such as John Skytte, who was considered the most brilliant Latin scholar of Europe in his day, Stiernhœk, the jurist, Bureus and Messenius, the historians, and

Georg Stiernhielm, poet and antiquarian. The old Icelandic literature was discovered and began to exert a strong influence on literature and science, to a great extent strengthening their chauvinistic spirit. The Swedish poets Stiernhielm, Runius, Holmstrœm, Lucidor and the poetess Brenner, from the Eddic songs, which contain some of the oldest humorous poems in existence, learned how to write in a humorous vein, something entirely unknown in the German and French literatures of that day.

The excellent government, of which Axel Oxenstierna was the leading spirit, had its defects. In its perfect system of administration, which in the main features stands unshaken to this day, there appeared to be no room for the people themselves to be governed. On account of the great allowances made to the nobles it was necessary to increase the taxes of the peasants. Many had to leave their homes and farms for want of resources to pay their taxes; others were forced away from their property by the nobles. There was danger of the destruction of the free, self-dependent yeomanry. A hatred against the nobility grew up. The great lords returned from the wars laden with booty, erected fine castles, and continued the high living to which they had become accustomed while abroad. The power of the nobility was increased by lavish donations from Queen Christine and by the appropriation of other crown lands which the government was forced to sell or mortgage on account of the wars. The clergy were the spokesmen of the peasant class at the Riksdag, every year demanding with greater emphasis a restitution to the crown of its property, which was held by the nobles.

Queen Christine herself took the reins of government, in 1644, at the age of eighteen. She had inherited from her illustrious father some of his genius, and from her mother, Marie Eleonore of Brandenburg, a peculiar nervous disposition. Her mother took no interest in her until the death of Gustavus Adolphus, when a flood of exalted tenderness suddenly was let loose over her. Count Jacob de la Gardie took the lead in opposing the undesirable and unstable character of this relation, Christine being separated from her mother and educated by the Countess-Palatine Catherine, a pious and noble woman, the older sister of Gustavus Adolphus. Greatly offended, Marie Eleonore left the country never to return. Queen Christine showed a remarkable faculty of absorbing knowledge. Well versed in a great number of languages, and well read in various sciences, particularly mathematics, she soon acquired fame as the most learned woman of her time. She was of frank countenance, slept little, cared little for dress, and was passionately fond of hunting and riding on horseback. Queen Christine possessed a sharp intellect, was daring and resolute, but headstrong, fickle, extravagant, and but little particular in her choice of favorites. Her vanity and egotism knew no bounds. At the beginning of her reign she took pains to give serious attention to the affairs of state. The great chancellor had been her instructor in economics and statecraft, but she repaid him by open coldness and secret antagonism. Her ambition to surround herself with scientists of note, particularly foreigners who flattered her vanity by blowing her fame to the four corners of the earth, killed her interest for politics. Later she was seized by the evil spirit of frivolity, abandoning herself to empty pleasures and to excesses of extravagance when her learned admirers were forgotten for unworthy favorites. Among the latter, Count Magnus Gabriel de la Gardie was for a long time all-powerful. The grandson of General Pontus and a daughter of John III., he was the son of Count Jacob de la Gardie and Ebba Brahe, and one of the most brilliant noblemen of Europe. In his youth he formed an intimate friendship with the dauphin of France, later Louis XIV., who throughout his life honored him with the title of "Mon Cousin," or "Mon cher Cousin." His ambition to become Queen Christine's consort was never satisfied, nor was he allowed to accept the rank of a prince from the German emperor, but the queen made him the richest man in her realm. Magnus de la Gardie did not possess the sterling qualities of his ancestors, but was of great patriotism and lavishly liberal toward educational institutions, in this respect without a peer in Swedish history. In 1666 he founded the Academy of Antiquities, which was the first archæological institution in Europe, the Swedish antiquarians of the day, principal among them Bureus and Stiernhielm, doing valuable antiquarian research. In 1664, Count de la Gardie donated to the University Library of Upsala a highly valuable collection of manuscripts and books, chiefly from Iceland. In the collection was also the Gothic Bible translation of Bishop Wulfila in the only copy extant. Liberal with his silver, Count de la Gardie gave to the precious book a silver binding, as he had in earlier years presented to Queen Christine a silver throne (which is still in use). This book has an interesting history of its own.

Codex Argenteus, the silver book, thus called on account of its silver binding, contains fragments of the four Gospels in the Gothic language. The translation was made from the Greek original by Bishop Wulfila (b. 318-d. 388), the apostle of the Goths. The writing is done in so-called encaustum (printing with heated stamps) of gold and silver letters on vellum of scarlet color. This copy is considered to have been made toward the end of the fifth or in the beginning of the sixth century, when the East Goths still held sway in Italy. Its early fortunes are unknown, but it is supposed that the book was found in the possession of the Visigoths (or West Goths) when their empire was seized by the Franks, and donated to the monastery of Verden by some munificent Frankish chief. Here, in the Benedictine abbey of Verden, on the river Ruhr, in Westphalia, the book was discovered at least as early as 1554, when the scholars Cassander and Gualther of Cologne are known to have had copies which can have been made from no other source.

After the outbreak of the Thirty Years' War, the Codex was transmitted to Prague for safety. In the year of 1648, Prague, or rather the older portion of the town, was captured by the Swedish general, Count Hans Christopher Kœnigsmark, who, among the vast treasures of the Bohemian capital, found also the Codex Argenteus which he presented to Queen Christine. All the books and manuscripts of the queen were in the care of her librarian, Isaac Vossius, a learned but eccentric scholar of Dutch parentage. Vossius was at first Queen Christine's teacher of Greek, not a very agreeable position, for the queen called him to the castle at three o'clock in the morning for her first hour. In 1650 he had to leave court and country on account of a quarrel with that light of learning, Claude de Saumaise (Salmasius), another one of the foreign scholars in favor with the queen. In 1653 he was called back, and again took charge of the books of the queen, but soon returned to Holland. Before his departure he gathered several costly books and manuscripts, among which Codex Argenteus, with or without the queen's private permission, taking them with him. In 1670, Vossius came to England, where he died, in 1688, as court chaplain at Windsor. King Charles II. of England said of him: "Vossius believes in anything but the Bible."

When in Holland, the Codex Argenteus passed out of the hands of Vossius after his uncle Franziskus Junius had made a complete copy of it. Junius, called the "grandfather of modern philology," published the first edition of Codex Argenteus at Dortrecht, in 1665, providing the beautiful fac-simile with parallel Old English texts and a Gothic glossary. In Holland the Codex changed hands repeatedly until found in Brabant by Samuel Pufendorff, in 1661, who, in the following year, bought it for Count de la Gardie, paying a sum of something like $1,200 for it.

Once more in Sweden the Codex Argenteus was made the subject of close attention, a new edition of it being published, in 1671, by Georg Stiernhielm, the innovator of Swedish language and literature.[1] That Bishop Wulfila's Bible should ultimately harbor in Sweden does not seem out of place, for of all languages now spoken the Swedish

---

[1] Through the efforts of the Swedish scholar, Eric Benzelius, Junior, a third edition was published at Windsor in 1750. J. K. Kohn's edition dates from 1805, founded on the works of the Swedish scholars Sotberg and Ihre. Of later editions, the one by Professor A. Uppstrœm, of Upsala, of 1854 to 1857, is considered to be the standard one. A fine American edition has, in recent years, been published by Dr. G. H. Balg, of Mayville, Wis. The history of Codex Argenteus, after once for all being placed in the University Library of Upsala, has not been altogether uneventful. In 1834 ten of the 187 leaves were stolen and remained missing for twenty-three years. One of the trusted janitorial attendants of the library had taken them in the hope of obtaining a great sum of money for them, but later dared not dispose of them. On his death-bed he surrendered the stolen leaves.

comes closest to the language of the Goths as crystallized during its classical epoch. The interest taken by Swedish scholars in the book has always been great and fruitful of results, in times when it was thought to be written in the mother tongue of all the Teutonic languages, as well as later, when Gothic was found to be, not the mother, but the oldest sister in the family.

At the Riksdag of 1649 considerable dissatisfaction was directed against the nobility and the extravagance of the queen in deeding over to favorites all the possessions of the crown, in form of counties and baronies. The nobility sided against the queen, desirous of reducing her power. But Queen Christine received gracefully the complaints made, and promised to institute a reduction of taxes and payments. In the following year the commotion increased when the same taxes were asked as in time of war. The queen continued her policy of earnestly considering the requests of the lower Estates, thus gaining the controlling power. The nobility, suffering strife between its various classes, was forced to seek a shelter in the royal power it desired to crush, and humiliated itself before the queen. Christine received a joint appeal from the lower Estates for a restitution to the crown of all property illegally turned over to the nobility, but she managed to have the reform postponed upon promise of some minor privileges and a reduction of taxes. She refused the appeals of the nobility to have the clergymen and others punished who had used hard language against the aristocrats. But the discontent was spreading and turned against the queen personally. The ministers preached against the wrongs and violence of the mighty ones; the nobles and the peasants threatened each other. Peasants in Finland refused to work for aristocratic masters, and a general rebellion seemed imminent. In the meantime Queen Christine was crowned at Upsala amid great display and elaborate festivities, the count-palatine Charles Gustavus, her cousin, being installed as heir-apparent to the throne.

But Queen Christine was not able to still the storm around her. The finances of the crown were utterly ruined by her extravagance, and she dared not take by violence from the nobility what she had given by grace. In 1651 she declared it to be her intention to leave the government, but was persuaded to remain. Her cousin was placed in a very difficult position, apparently taking no interest in what was going on, but following everything with the keenest attention. The son of John Casimir, count of Palatinate-Zweibrucken, and Princess Catherine, he was born at Nykœping in Sweden, in 1622, and designated as the future consort of Queen Christine. Charles Gustavus was educated in simplicity and rigor, and was, as his father before him, utterly neglected by Axel Oxenstierna and the government. He slept in a room without wallpaper, and when through with his lessons he sawed wood with his teacher, Professor Lenæus. Burning with ambition, and perhaps also in love with his brilliant cousin, he proposed to her repeatedly, but in vain. After several years of extensive travel he joined Lennart Torstensson, refusing a command and working himself up through the military degrees. He took an honorable part in the victory at Jankowitz, and was appointed supreme commander of the Swedish armies shortly before the close of the German war. When the opposition against Christine reached its climax a good deal was expected from Charles Gustavus, which he, on account of his singular position, could not undertake to do. A petition replete with abusive language about the queen was sent him, asking him to take hold of the government. Charles turned the document over to the queen. Its author, the promising young Arnold Messenius, and his father, an able historian, suspected as having inspired his son, were accused of high treason, condemned to death and executed.

This act of force produced an impression, and the new taxes demanded at the next Riksdag were granted without opposition. But the queen felt that the discontent was only subdued, not suppressed, and, having no further means to keep up a luxurious court, she did the wisest act of her reign, that of resigning, at Upsala, in June, 1654, Charles Gustavus being crowned the same day. The scene of her abdication was very impressive, Queen Christine carrying herself with noble and lofty dignity, an inheritance from her father which she made use of when she saw fit. Leaving the crown and the royal emblems, one by one, to the Riksdrotset, she descended the throne, from the lowest steps of which she spoke an eloquent and touching farewell to the four Estates of the Riksdag. She suddenly left the country after having secured for herself a princely income. At Innsbruck, the daughter of Gustavus Adolphus joined the Catholic church, thereby, and by her fame as a learned woman, creating a sensation. She died in Rome in 1689, after having made two unsuccessful attempts to regain her Swedish throne, and one equally unsuccessful to succeed the last king of the Polish line of the Vasa dynasty, and was buried in the church of St. Peter.

Among the many learned men who at one time surrounded Christine were Vossius, Heinsius, Salmasius, Huet, Freinshemius, Loccenius, Meibom, Bœclerus, Ravius, Schefferus, and others. The greatest of them all, the philosopher Cartesius (René Descartes), died in Stockholm, in 1650.

After the love-story of Gustavus Adolphus had come to an end, he long felt a disinclination to marry. His sister Catherine is said to have tried to rouse him to the necessity of choosing a consort. His answer was always: "Never mind, dear sister, you shall yourself bring up a son to inherit the crown and continue my work." This son of Catherine became Queen Christine's successor.

CHAPTER XII

Period of Political Grandeur—Charles X. and Charles XI.

CHARLES X. was one of the most ambitious men ever placed upon a throne, and Europe was soon to realize that a new war-lord was come. His ambition, so long unsatisfied and secreted, burst forth with uncontrollable strength, in compass only to be equalled by his rare gifts of mind and heart. Charles Gustavus had suffered a good deal of neglect, coldness and hatred, but when ascending the throne he seemed to have forgotten all this. Oxenstierna died a few months after the abdication of Queen Christine, deeply impressed by the magnanimity and genius of the new sovereign. Charles Gustavus was one of the most highly gifted of Swedish monarchs. He had a great deal of interest in and rare discernment for the requirements of a peaceful development. But reared in the most warlike of times, when a reputation could be made only by winning so and so many "victorias" for the firm establishment of a hero's "gloire," Charles Gustavus thought that only the monarch favored by "Fama" would have the prestige to lead firmly the fate of his people. He often expressed the wish to rest from his campaigns in order to contemplate his work and make it beneficial to his people, but such a rest he never gave himself time to enjoy during his short and remarkable reign.

BATTLE OF WARSAW

Sweden.

Charles burned with desire to gain fame in war, taking for pretext that the king of Poland, by his repeated claims to the Swedish throne, made peace treacherous and impossible. But such was the condition of affairs that something must be done to quiet the malcontent people, restore peace between the quarrelling classes, and reimburse the empty state treasury. At a Riksdag in Stockholm, in 1655, a restitution was proposed by the king and agreed to, according to which all estates which in earlier times had been rendering dues to the direct support of the court, army, fleet, or administration, should be confiscated to the crown; also one-fourth of the estates given away since the death of Gustavus Adolphus, and all estates fraudulently obtained. A committee to enforce the restitution was appointed, to be presided over by the able Herman Fleming. The restitution, far from radical in itself, was not completely carried through, thanks to the opposing nobles. But it proved effective for the moment, the king securing the goodwill of the people, temporary quiet and means to carry on the proposed war, to commence which Charles Gustavus received the somewhat reluctant consent of the faithful people whose financial state was a most despairing one. Charles X. thought in new conquests to find means to better their condition. Shortly after his coronation he married Hedvig Eleonore of Holstein-Gottorp.

John II. Casimir of Poland, the younger son of Sigismund, like Vladislav, styled himself king of Sweden and had claims to Livonia. For this he should be punished. It was not the original intention of Charles X. to make himself king of Poland, but he was probably the first who ever devised a division of that unhappy country. The success of Charles X. was without a parallel. The strong fortresses were captured, the armies surrendered and registered in Swedish service. After two months Charles X. entered the old capital of Cracow, John Casimir fled from his country, and, carried away by the frenzy of success, Charles Gustavus had himself crowned king of Poland. West Prussia was captured, and the elector of Brandenburg, who held East Prussia in fief, and the duke of Courland were forced to become the vassals of Sweden, in 1656.

But Charles X. had roused an enemy that few invaders, however great, have been able to successfully encounter, the spirit of patriotism. The Poles, enticed to revolt by the Catholic clergy, found a leader in the noble Czarniecki, who commenced a war of liberation on the Swedish usurper. King John Casimir returned, and armies were gathered. Charles Gustavus was yet to do wonders of strategy, which aroused the amazement and fear of all Europe, but he was glad, when finding a good excuse, to extract himself from the affairs of Poland. In 1656 he defeated Czarniecki at Golumbo, undertook the adventurous crossing of the river of San, and captured, and recaptured, the capital of Warsaw. The "three days' battle of Warsaw" (18th–20th of July, 1656) is one of the most famous in modern warfare, by which the reputation of Charles X., as one of the greatest warriors of his time, was firmly established. Charles X. had joined forces with the "great elector" of Brandenburg, who up to the last moment was unwilling to risk a battle of 22,000 men against an enemy twice as strong. Charles Gustavus was unyielding and turned it into a great victory. But his position became precarious, Russia, Germany, Holland and Denmark being hostile, joined by Brandenburg, the ambitious "great elector" not being satisfied with the Swedish supremacy in East Prussia. To save himself from the dilemma with untarnished glory, Charles X. decided to fight Denmark, which country had declared war without suspecting the possibility of an attack.

Lennart Torstensson, his master of strategy, had shown Charles X. how Denmark was to be attacked. With an army of only 8,000, but consisting of the choicest and most victorious troops in all Europe, Charles X. hastened in rapid marches through Pomerania and Mecklenburg, recaptured Bremen, and invaded through friendly Holstein all of Schleswig and Jutland, defeating the larger but inexperienced Danish army and capturing the strong fortress of Fredericia.

Yet the new position was as precarious as the one in Poland, and Charles had to use all the skill of his diplomacy to save his little army from an assault by inimical Europe. France and England seemed unwilling to render him effective help. But when the elector of Brandenburg, who had taken upon himself the leadership of Sweden's enemies, turned to the emperor, emphasizing the necessity of crushing the Swedish power in one blow, he received the following surprising answer: "The king of Hungary has no reason to be the enemy of the king of Sweden." Charles had reached a secret understanding with Austria. By this move he gained time. Through what seemed almost a miracle, he was not only to save his army but lead it on to victory after a strategic deed, in originality and daring unique in the history of the world.

The year of 1658 commenced with severe frosts. Charles X. conceived the daring plan of attacking the Danish isles by leading his army over the frozen sounds. He concluded to cross the sound of Lille Belt, opposite the islet of Brandsœ. His quartermaster-general, Eric Dahlberg, an engineer of great genius, ascertained that the ice was safe. One frosty winter morning, the 30th of January, the Swedish army, reinforced to 9,000 men, marched down on the ice, safely reaching Brandsœ at sunrise. A Danish army, arranged in order of battle in the island of Funen, was defeated. While crossing over to Funen, the ice cracked under two squadrons of cavalry, those who followed not daring to proceed. The king himself hurried past the dangerous place, pointing out a safe course, and the troops followed him.

The most dangerous part remained to cross, the much wider sound of Store Belt, in order to reach Seeland. Charles first thought of taking the direct route of two miles, but commissioned Dahlberg to explore the condition of the ice across to the smaller islands to the south. Dahlberg did so, and said he would wager his head for its perfectly safe condition. In enthusiasm, Charles clapped his hands exclaiming: "Now, brother Frederic, we will converse in good Swedish!" In the night between the 5th and 6th of February, the Swedish army marched from Svendborg in Funen over the ice to Langeland. "It was terrible," wrote an eye-witness, "to march through the night over this frozen sea, where the horses' hoofs had thawed down the snow on the ice, which was below two feet of water, and where we, in every moment, were in fear of striking the open sea." At dawn the army landed in Langeland. During the rest for breakfast, frozen beer was chopped and distributed in pieces to the soldiers. The march continued over the still wider sound to Laaland, Eric Dahlberg in front, directing the march. Reaching Grimsted in Laaland at three o'clock in the afternoon, and proceeding to Nakskov, Charles Gustavus was met, at midnight, by the burgomaster and council of said town, who surrendered its keys. The 9th of February, the army stood in Falster, and a few days later was collected at the captured castle of Vordingborg in Seeland. Peace was hastily offered and agreed to on the 17th, and the treaty of peace signed the 28th of February, 1658, at Rœskilde. The conditions were severe, Denmark ceding the provinces of Scania, Halland, Bleking and Bohuslæn, the whole district or diocese of Drontheim in Norway, and the island of Bornholm, and agreeing to hold the Baltic closed to hostile fleets with the help of Sweden. The last clause was a piece of a Scandinavian policy devised by the Swedish king.

Charles X. now prepared to meet Brandenburg and Austria, once more siding against Sweden. It was necessary to keep Holland out from the Baltic, and when Charles X. found Denmark unwilling to keep the conditions of the recent treaty on that point, the war-lord became wrathful, dooming obnoxious Denmark to lose her very existence. But the spirit of patriotism, which so often had saved Sweden in instances of extreme danger, now sided with Denmark, as it had already sided with Poland. King Frederic declared he would die like a bird in its own nest, and roused the patriotism of the population of Copenhagen, which, badly defended, was hurriedly fortified at the news of an intended attack. Contrary to the advice of Eric Dahlberg, Charles X. made no instantaneous attack, but commenced a siege, although he did not bring with him the necessary means. The castle of Kronborg by Elsinore was captured and its cannon used against Copenhagen. The greatest enthusiasm prevailed in the Danish capital; the king slept in a tent by the fortifications, and especially the students and Norwegian sailors distinguished themselves by their valor and patriotism. Charles X. found it impossible to take Copenhagen and retired to some distance from the capital. What caused Charles to retire was the arrival of a Dutch fleet. It had been met by the Swedish fleet, under command of Charles Gustavus Wrangel, the hero of Fredericia and Kronborg. After six hours of hard fighting the Dutch forced the entrance to the Sound. Before leaving, the Swedish king resolved to make a desperate effort to capture Copenhagen, defended by 13,000 troops and by a patriotic population, with his 8,000 Swedes. The attack was made in the night of February 11, 1659, but the city, forewarned by traitors, tendered the Swedes a warm reception, consisting of artillery fire, stones, and scalding hot water. The Swedes lost 600 men and suffered their first and only defeat under the command of Charles X.

The situation was grave. The Swedish army in Jutland was forced to retire; the troops of 5,000 men in Funen were defeated and made prisoners; a revolt took place in Bornholm, and the Danes recaptured the district of Drontheim. The powers united in their efforts to force Sweden and Denmark to a treaty of peace on the basis of the Rœskilde stipulations. Charles still held his head high, declaring that he would crush the fleets of the allies if they tried to interfere in the affairs of the North, striking a sharply discordant note in the concert of the powers. To Denmark he was willing to cede the district of Drontheim, but prepared to occupy that of Akkershus instead, when he was taken ill at the convening Riksdag at Gothenburg, dying February 11, 1660, in the palace erected by his friend Lennart Torstensson.

Charles X. Gustavus was one of the most remarkable

men of his day, whose wonderful deeds of bravery and genius caused amazement through their brilliancy, and anxiety through their recklessness. At the first glance his appearance gave no idea of the real man. He was short, and of an unusually square and clumsy build, with a head of coarse proportions. But there was the fire of genius in his sharp blue eyes; under the black hair, and below the thin black mustache, there was a mouth of firm and resolute lines. In the versatility of his endowment, he stands as one of the first among Swedish kings, the rich gifts of the Vasas and the Wittelsbachs being united in him. As a warrior he was great, yet more of a tactician than a strategist. As a statesman his views were almost as clairvoyant as those of his grandfather, Charles IX., but he gave way to the impressions and impulses of the moment. He failed to make the Baltic a Swedish inland lake, but gained for his country the inestimable gift of a natural frontier to the east and south, by the acquisition of Bohuslæn, Halland, Scania and Bleking, provinces more valuable to Sweden than a whole empire south of the Baltic.

Charles XI. was a child of four years at the death of his father; his country at war with a world, and in a sorely afflicted condition. In the will of Charles X., the queen-dowager, Hedvig Eleonore, was named to preside over the government, with two votes, and the brother of Charles X., the duke Adolphus John, was to take a seat with her as Riksmarsk. This arrangement displeased the nobility, understanding that it was directed against their influence, and they had the duke excluded from the government. The lower Estates of the Riksdag sided with the duke, but soon gave up his cause as they found that he was utterly vain, quick-tempered, and without stability or genius. Lars Kagg, a good warrior, was appointed Riksmarsk in his place. Herman Fleming, the able state treasurer, was removed as disagreeable to the nobility, his ill-health being taken as an excuse, and was succeeded by Gustavus Bonde. Peter Brahe remained Riksdrotset, Magnus Gabriel de la Gardie state chancellor, and Charles Gustavus Wrangel state admiral. Kagg died in 1661 and was succeeded by Wrangel, Gustavus Otto Stenbock becoming state admiral.

The first duty of the new government was to make peace for the bleeding country. This was effected in 1660 through the treaties of Oliva and Copenhagen, and in a most satisfactory manner, speaking high for the diplomatic ability of the governing ones, but also of the ignorance of the powers of the utter helplessness of Sweden, in great contrast to her outward political grandeur. Poland ceded Livonia to Sweden, and Denmark all the territory gained by Charles X., except the district of Drontheim and the island of Bornholm, while Russia was satisfied with the boundaries set by Gustavus Adolphus.

The government, with care and consideration, made the necessary arrangements to have the new provinces intimately connected with the country. Representatives were sent to the Riksdag of 1664, and the University of Lund, in Scania, was founded in 1668. If to this is added that a good deal was done to encourage art and science, principally through Count Magnus de la Gardie, who was the Mæcenas of Sweden, the meritorious deeds of the government during Charles XI.'s minority are enumerated. The less that is said of it in addition, and of its leading men, the better for these. They were men of some patriotism, but, through their exceedingly aristocratic views and lack of stability, unable to further the interests of their country, so badly in need of reform. There was not one of them who possessed the abilities of a statesman. They lived like princes in their counties, each holding court and possessing various considerable castles, all the members of the higher aristocracy upholding the same standard of luxury and power, appointing clergymen and judges, founding towns, and discussing the necessity of having mints and coins of their own. Magnus de la Gardie, count of Leckœ, and married to a sister of Charles X., was the greatest of these lords. Close to him came Peter Brahe, count of Visingsborg, and Charles Gustavus Wrangel, count of Skokloster. The barons approached the counts in their display of wealth. The lower nobility, whose members often served at the courts of the great lords, were not satisfied with this state of affairs. But in the contempt and oppression in which they held the lower classes, they agreed with the higher nobility, who made no secret of their intention to reduce the peasants to slaves. The peasantry, suffering and neglected, became the prey of a superstition which was shared by the more educated members of society, accusations and legal executions of witches becoming numerous.

The government was not agreed between themselves upon many questions and turned to the state council for support. The old privileged class of councillors forced their influence upon the government, and the position between the two became quite intimate, at the same time difficult to define. The state council was as divided in its opinions as the government, which fact had a disastrous influence upon state politics and administration. Great negligence was shown in the various departments, the records of receipts and expenditures being imperfect, and a constant lack of funds existing. Forgery and thefts were committed by high and low officials. Administrative orders were not obeyed. The army and the navy suffered utter neglect.

During such a state of affairs the abominable practice of receiving "subsidies" came into use. The government received, now from one foreign power, now from another, a large sum of money to back its respective interests with the military forces or the diplomatic influence of Sweden. This practice, ignoble in itself, injured the dignity of the state and had a demoralizing influence. Thanks to it, Sweden sided sometimes against, but mostly with, France, her old ally, who, in Count de la Gardie, had an enthusiastic friend. In 1662, Sweden schemed with France for the election of a French prince as king of Poland; in 1667, she formed, with England and Holland, a triple alliance against France. Louis XIV. soon won back the friendship of the government of Sweden, thus having this country as his only ally when reaching the climax of his success. At last the Swedish promises to send an army against the elector of Brandenburg were fulfilled. It was under the command of the old and invalid Count Wrangel, and suffered defeats at Ratenau and Fehrbellin, in 1675. These were of little importance, or extension, in themselves, but they injured the prestige of Sweden, so long supremely victorious on German soil, and caused her enemies to combine their efforts in order to regain their lost possessions.

Charles XI. was declared of age at seventeen, in 1672, when he himself took charge of the government, yet for a few years standing under the influence of Count de la Gardie. King Charles was, as a child, physically weak, and the astrologers had prophesied that he would die an infant. For this reason the queen-dowager, a very ordinary woman, gave all her attention to have her son develop a strong and sound constitution. The child was given its own way in everything, casting aside books and rules for his individual pleasures. King Charles grew up an ignorant self-willed and headstrong youth, who delighted in hunting and reckless riding on horseback. His companions, manners and language were not of the choicest order, and he remained all his life shy and awkward in demeanor. From his thirteenth year he was made acquainted with the routine of state affairs, but he lacked the qualifications to grasp them in detail. He surrounded himself with members of the lower nobility, but was well at ease only among ministers, burghers and peasants. Charles XI. was all his life of an unrestrained temper and an indomitable will, coming to the throne the most ignorant king Sweden had had for centuries. But he was pious, sincere and just, and his morals pure and severe. Through the hardest of lessons, Charles XI. was to develop his great uncultivated gifts, to become the liberator of his people and one of its most remarkable rulers.

Sweden had to encounter many enemies after the battle of Fehrbellin, and a chain of disasters followed, nearly crushing the young king under their weight. Holland, Austria, Brandenburg and Denmark attacked the Swedish possessions, which were all captured, one after the other. Charles was not able to send reinforcements, the navy being in a miserable condition, and when rejuvenated, through strenuous effort, defeated by the excellent admirals Juel, of the Danish, and Tromp, of the Dutch, navy. The treasury was empty, the administration in disorder, and mistrust and strife reigned supreme. But the young king showed that he wanted to be obeyed, and managed, by hard work, to establish order, the Riksdag sacrificing means to organize the defence.

The Danes were successful in their first expeditions on land also, their army having undergone a reorganization. King Christian V. marched into Scania, while his general, Gyldenlœve, invaded Bohuslæn and West Gothland. The hostile fleets captured the islands of Œland and Gothland. Charles XI., in a sinister state of mind verging on despair, at last had his army collected, and entered Halland, where Danish troops were encountered and defeated at Halmstad. This gave courage to the Swedes, who soon thought themselves invincible, when commanded by the young king himself. Charles received reinforcements through peasant troops, and was desirous to meet Christian in open battle. But the Danish army in Scania retreated until forced to meet the enemy near Lund. Here a bloody and decisive battle was fought, more than 8,000 men being killed, and resulting in a victory for the Swedes, who took 2,000 prisoners, fifty-one cannon, and the whole hostile camp, December 3, 1676.

In the following year Sweden suffered two defeats at sea, through the hands of Juel, but won another victory on land, at Landskrona, when the Danes lost 3,000 men.

While Charles XI. fought with the courage of despair, Louis XIV. was supremely victorious over his enemies, soon appearing as the dictator of Europe, when peace was made at Nimwegen, in 1679. Finding Charles XI. resolved not to cede any of his territory, King Louis took a similar standpoint in his behalf, but contemptuously neglected to let the Swedish ambassadors take any active part in the deliberations. Louis XIV. made peace with the emperor,

Brandenburg and Denmark on behalf of Sweden, which country only ceded a small part of East Pomerania to Brandenburg. Charles XI. deeply felt the insolence of the benevolent dictator, and forced Christian V. to sign a treaty of peace at Lund, in 1680, as if Louis XIV. had no part in it. An agreement was made that Charles XI. should marry the sister of Christian V., the beautiful Ulrica Eleonore. Through her gentleness, piety and great benevolence, she soon acquired fame as one of the noblest queens of Sweden. Ulrica Eleonore led a quiet life, seldom being seen at court, where the vain and despotic queen-dowager held the first place. She was never able to win the affection of her consort until during her last illness. King Charles then, for the first time, understood what a treasure he had held unappreciated at his side, and watched over her with infinite care, bringing peace and sunshine into her last days. After her death, in 1693, the king became a prey to deep sorrow and remorse, which threw added gloom over his dark countenance. The queen had been active in upholding a good relation between the Scandinavian countries, often bitterly opposed by the queen-dowager, in the interests of Holstein.

When peace was made, Charles XI. immediately took action in the matter of reform. He saw his country at the verge of utter ruin and the crown unable to help it. The peasants were losing their rights, one by one, and five-sixths of the crown lands were in the possession of the nobles. Brought up in ignorance and isolation, finding rottenness and incapability everywhere, it was no wonder that the king became strongly imbued by the spirit of absolutism, which pervaded all Europe. He followed the example of the monarchs of France and Denmark, learning from them how, by secret agitation and pressure, to make the lower classes fervently appeal to him to take the absolute power in his hand. His principal adviser was *John Gyllenstierna*, a man of old, celebrated stock, but belonging to the lower nobility. Gyllenstierna was one of the greatest and most patriotic statesmen of his day. He first attracted attention as a champion of the lower nobility against the great lords for the restitution of crown lands. Raised to dignities and a high station, he never changed his position to the aristocrats in power, who thought they could win him over by favors. Seeing the absolute impossibility of reform, with the help of the nobles, Gyllenstierna turned to the king, whose whole confidence he won, inspiring him with plans of a Scandinavian peace policy, and a reform through the destruction of the aristocracy. Gyllenstierna died after having brought to the king his bride, a union which was the work of this able statesman.

The Riksdag was convoked to meet October 5, 1680. Everything commenced quietly. No royal proposition was made; but a strong agitation had been set in motion among the four Estates, the three lower ones sending in a petition to make the royal power absolute, to have a restitution of crown lands made, and the government, during the king's minority, brought to answer for their acts. Similar requests were sent up from the nobility, after many stormy scenes at the Riddarhus. Thus, toward the end of the Riksdag, with the petitions in, came the royal propositions which, when accepted, in one blow crushed the aristocracy, as a ruling class, and the antiquated state council, as an institution, and established the absolute power of the king.

According to the resolutions of this memorable Riksdag, which marks a new era in Swedish history, a "grand commission" was selected which fulfilled its duties with the greatest severity. The members of the former government and state council were made responsible for their administration, and themselves, or their heirs, sentenced to pay smaller or larger sums. Two-thirds of the whole amount was afterward given up, but the fines were nevertheless great. Count Nils Brahe, the heir of both Peter Brahe and Charles Gustavus Wrangel, and the wealthiest man in Sweden, had to pay something like $600,000 in fines, an immense sum in those days, and was reduced almost to poverty. The restitution department, assisted by two commissions, did equally thorough work under the pressure of the king. Ten counties and seventy baronies, with a great number of other crown lands of various classes, were confiscated. It cost the higher nobility dearly; Count Magnus de la Gardie, the all-powerful favorite of three monarchs, lost his immense wealth and died on a little estate left him, with one single servant out of his former princely retinue. The work of restitution was carried on without cruelty or injustice.

A second restitution was to follow. The propositions were arranged at the Riksdag of 1682, in the same way as in 1680. This time the lower nobility was to suffer. All crown lands rendering less than $600 a year of income had been spared; now these were confiscated, without exception. In 1686 followed another blow. The dividends on the state loans were reduced, and a stipulation made that holders of bonds must refund what they, up to that date, had received above the new schedule. The same principle was applied in the redemption of mortgaged state lands. These new harsh measures were enforced with a great deal of severity, with incidental cases of injustice. The king showed clemency only to certain parties in stringent need. The discontent of the nobles caused many of them to leave the country, as, for instance, Count Otto William von Kœnigsmarck, son of the conqueror of Prague, and himself the valiant defender of Pomerania against the hostile allies. Their example was followed by many nobles of Livonia, the measures of the restitution entirely crushing the nobility of that province, while its peasants, who were slaves, gained their liberty, and had every reason to bless the Swedish government.

The power of absolutism grew steadily stronger. The king decided all matters alone, and prepared in advance the measures he proposed to the Riksdag, of whose sanction he was as independent as of that of the old state council. All officers and institutions were also changed in name from "state" to "royal" servants and instruments. The university professors were instructed to impress the students with the necessity and divine rights of an absolute ruler. The nobles were alone in their discontent. The other classes, especially the peasants, looked with satisfaction and approval on the work which crushed the enemies of their liberty and prosperity, and submitted willingly to the absolute power because it was in the hands of a patriotic king.

Charles XI. used the revenues of the restitutions principally for the reorganization of army and navy. For the former he reintroduced a system which Gustavus Adolphus had applied, the so-called *Indelningsverk* (work of division), which, elaborated upon and firmly established by Charles XI., became the foundation of the Swedish army system. The whole country was divided into small sections, which were each to support an infantry soldier, or a seaman, and larger ones to support a cavalry soldier. This soldier received a hamlet with earth to till within his section, paying for it by work to the farmers or squires, while these paid for his equipment. In times of war the state paid his expenses. This changed the troublesome army element into useful members of state in times of peace. The officers were given small estates by the crown for their support. The army consisted, at the death of Charles XI., of 65,000 men, well equipped. On the coast of Bleking extensive navy yards were built by Count Hans Wachtmeister and Eric Dahlberg, in a new town called Carlscrona. At great expense, the best fleet ever under Swedish command was constructed by Wachtmeister, who enjoyed the full confidence of the king. His excellent means wherewith to conduct a successful war, Charles XI. used to maintain a dignified peace, of which his country was badly in need. Bengt Oxenstierna held the reins of diplomacy, which had no attraction for Charles XI. The old alliance with France was broken off and close connections with William of Orange established for the maintenance of peace. Sweden regained its prestige, rising to a power whose support was sought by all. When William became king of England, Sweden was a member of the alliance against Louis XIV., but contributed to the great European war only a few thousand soldiers, according to agreement, preserving, together with Denmark, an armed neutrality. Charles XI. lived to the proud moment when the powers selected Sweden as an arbiter in the deliberations for peace in Riswick, a worthy satisfaction gained over the earlier insolence of Louis XIV.

Charles XI. improved the administration by filling the offices of the excellent institutions with excellent men. This he obtained by enforcing the necessity of obeying orders, supplying officials of all ranks, from the lowest upward, with new regulations which must be obeyed, also regulating their salaries. Sweden never had a greater lover of law and order than Charles XI., and he used his absolute power in their interests, trying to remold the old laws to suit modern requirements, and having a new church law, a masterpiece in its line, introduced. The church itself and its men had in Charles XI. an interested friend. New catechism, hymn book and ritual were prepared, and a new translation of the Bible completed, being published after his death. Commerce and mining industries were encouraged, while agriculture improved with the improvement of the financial conditions of the peasants. Charles XI. was not only a "peace king," but a "peasant king," who was ardently devoted to the improvement of the education and financial circumstances of the country population. He was of broadly democratic inclinations, finding his delight in moving among the humble and lowly as one of them. The peasants, who had been brushed aside by the great and powerful, were now brought to the front and took an active and important part in the affairs of state. Charles ruled over them with a stern husbandry, and asked great sacrifices of them for the maintenance of an armed defence; but no king has accomplished more in their true interest than he, or remains more clearly in their memory and traditions. He travelled continually through the country, avoiding the places where he would be received with ceremony, stopping in the houses of the farmers, and enjoying heartily what comfort these offered. In his appearance he was far from prepossessing. His features were not devoid of beauty, but gloomy; his figure strong and vigorous, but not impressive. Through an accident while hunting he became slightly lame. Although dearth and hard times set in during the last years of his reign, causing terrible losses of life through hunger and prostration, he could plainly tell the beneficent results of his administration. Charles XI. took the reins of state when disastrous war ravished a country which seemed doomed to destruction. He left it reformed, reorganized, rejuvenated and prosperous at his death, in 1697.

The Period of Political Grandeur in Swedish history falls within the epoch of the history of art which has been called *Barocco*, an unbalanced offspring of the Renaissance, and a style characterized by great complicity, pretensions and ambitions, a renaissance in wigs of formidable proportions. After the great victories of the Thirty Years' War, it seems as if the interchange of influences between art, literature, science, politics and religion was increased. The whole era becomes a Barocco period of bombast and chauvinism, the climax being reached in the form of the absolute monarchy of the age.

In Sweden, as elsewhere, there was no lack of men of ability and brilliant genius; but, influenced by the spirit of their time, the works of most of them were bombastic and chauvinistic, like the artistic and political aspirations of the era. The artists were, as were at first the scholars, mostly foreigners. The native and imported scholars were characterized by great learning and versatility, but abused their genius by Utopian theories and vainglorious dreams, and violated the laws of history and sound research.

Olof Rudbeck was not only the most learned and brilliantly gifted scholar of his day, but his genius also embodles the eccentricities of the period in gigantic outlines. He was born at Westeros, in 1630, his father being the learned bishop, Johannes Rudbeckius. As a boy, he gave evidence of rare artistic and mechanic talents. He made drawings of exquisite designs, constructed clock mechanisms of wood, and was a skilled musician. His character was proud and violent. At sixteen he was through with his college course and ready to enter the university. The youth could not stand the change from his coarse jacket and fur coat into a coat of broadcloth with buttons such as the students wore, and was for his overbearing manner punished by his severe father with an additional year of college work. At the University of Upsala he caused from the start great surprise by his knowledge in all subjects. He devoted his attention chiefly to natural science, which, in that day, was a neglected study, and soon excelled his professors.

At twenty, Rudbeck made a scientific discovery of great importance, which caused a stir in the whole learned world. By his discovery and theory of the lymphatic ducts, the blood circulation of the human body received a satisfactory explanation. Before the circle of scholars which surrounded Queen Christine, Rudbeck was allowed to demonstrate his anatomical discoveries, in 1652. Queen Christine, who earlier had been an admirer of his beautiful voice and musical abilities, loaded him with praise and gave him the means for a journey abroad. Rudbeck returned, in 1660, to Sweden, and was appointed professor of medicine at the University of Upsala. He planned the first botanic garden in the country, donating it to the university. He had illustrations made of the native plants and commenced a learned work on botany. The first hall of anatomy was erected according to his proposition. As rector of the university, he established several important reforms, in spite of opposition, but supported by the chancellor, Magnus Gabriel de la Gardie, who was his friend and protector. To the stupendous mastery of all sciences, Rudbeck added a skill and cleverness in various branches of practical activity which made him carry, with honor, the nickname of "master at all trades." He was an excellent financier, who succeeded in restoring the sound economy of the university. He built a fish pond, from which the tables of the learned professors were regularly supplied with fish. A book store and a book-printing establishment were erected by him, and for a time run at his expense. He repaired windmills, built houses, provided the university town with water works and street pavement, also arranging its postal service. Rudbeck was one of the finest composers and singers of his day, conducting the musical exercises at the university. He made fireworks and compasses for the Swedish navy, built fountains and organs, was a good poet and painter and an excellent etcher and drawer.

Rudbeck does not owe his great renown to his mastery of any of these trades, arts or sciences, nor to any discovery, reform or invention by his versatile genius. It was his monumental work, "Atland or Manheim," generally called "The Atlantica," which made him world-famous. For centuries one had believed in the statement made by Jordanes, and based upon traditions current among his people, that the Goths who conquered Rome had migrated from the North, and that their ancestors, from the remotest period, were inhabitants of Sweden. Johannes Magnus constructed a line of Swedish kings, beginning with Magog, the son of Japhet, on the basis of which the sons of Gustavus Vasa, Eric XIV., and Charles IX., had accepted their high ordinals. In the time of Rudbeck it was considered a supremely praiseworthy effort to glorify the fatherland by strengthening its claims to a high antiquity. Rudbeck, the remarkable savant and able poet, got his head turned by the political grandeur of his country. He had in his youth read the story of Atlantis, found in Plato. Rudbeck undertook to prove, in "The Atlantica," that the lost island, with its ancient ideal state from which the gods of antiquity were supposed to hail, was identical with Sweden. The work, in four large volumes, was written in Swedish and Latin of parallel columns. The first volume was printed in 1675, Rudbeck having made the types himself. In Sweden the work was greeted with an enthusiasm which had no bounds. The second volume was published by funds which Charles XI. with great generosity placed at the author's disposal. The third volume was dedicated to the youthful Charles XII., a true child of the chauvinistic epoch, who hailed the book with delight. The fourth volume was in press when Upsala was destroyed by fire, in 1702. The aged Rudbeck led the battle against the ravaging element, by supreme exertions saving the university halls, at the expense of his home, his press and manuscripts, and the rest of the town. Rudbeck died in the autumn of the same year.

The elaborate construction which Rudbeck had completed by means of ingenious deductions and learned guesswork succumbed with the political grandeur of Sweden. "The Atlantica," which once had its place beside the Bible on the tables of the mighty ones, was ridiculed and forgotten. On the continent of Europe, where similar books had been written in Germany and Holland, making for these respective countries similar claims, "The Atlantica" was at first received with surprise and admiration, later with doubt and criticism. The work, in spite of its mistakes, proved a foundation for archæological research, which gradually was developed into a science. In order to support the boldest and most impossible theories, the almost unparalleled power of combination of an eminent genius has brought together material which for the first time gave the suggestion of relationship between the Teutonic and the classical languages of Greece and Rome. Rudbeck was also the first to point out the unmistakable resemblance of the Old Norse and classical mythologies, as to the origin of which modern scholars have reached no absolute certainty, but radically different conclusions. The importance which Rudbeck placed upon popular customs and traditions was too great, but it has favorably influenced later students of ethnography and folk lore.

If Rudbeck had limited himself to the demonstration that Sweden has been not the cradle of all races, but the original home of the Teutonic branch of the Aryan race, he might have been able to offer a theory, the truth of which modern science lacks, and forever may lack, the resources to disprove.

Rudbeck had not been entirely without opponents in Sweden. The most noted among them was John Peringskiold, who criticised the opinion expressed by Rudbeck that the Runes were the oldest alphabet of the world. Peringskiold was a fine Icelandic scholar, and the first editor of Snorre Sturleson's "Heimskringla."

A typical and highly valuable illustrated work from this period is the "Svecia Antiqua et Hodierna," by Eric Dahlberg, the renowned quartermaster of Charles X. The text, written by Dahlberg and translated into Latin by several scholars, was never published, the magnificent engravings not before 1716. The latter give an impressive portrayal of architectural Sweden during the reigns of the three Charleses, but are not quite reliable, as some of the castles and palaces in this work are provided with additions and embellishments which were never more than projected.

There is no family who has wielded a greater influence over the Swedish church than that of Benzelius. The founder of the house, Eric Benzelius the Elder, and three of his sons were archbishops of Sweden, and two of his grandsons bishops of the state church. The first Archbishop Benzelius, born in 1632, was the son of a peasant, and took his name from the farm of Bentseby, of Lulea parish, in Norrland, where he was born; he and the three of his seven sons who were archbishops refused to be ennobled, the other members of the family adopting the name of Benzelstierna. The earlier generations of the family produced men of great talent and power, to whom the third one, although consisting of able men, could not be compared. The influence of this family in matters of religion, science and culture was strongly felt during the period of more than one century. The most remarkable member was Eric Benzelius the Younger, one of the most learned, active and patriotic men ever born in Sweden. Like the other members of the family, he perfected his education at foreign universities and made the personal acquaintance of Leibnitz, Thomasius, Malebranche, and other celebrated scholars. He was a historian, literary critic and philologist of merit, writing a history of Sweden and preparing an edition of Codex Argenteus, published in London after his death. He was highly appreciated by Charles XII., and was a friend of Polhem and Swedenborg, being married to a sister of the latter. Eric Benzelius was appointed archbishop, but died, in 1742, before he had entered office.

CHAPTER XIII

Period of Political Grandeur—Charles XII

CHARLES XII., the most famous of Swedish kings, was a boy of fifteen at the death of his father. He was born June 17, 1682, at the castle of Stockholm. The astrologers declared that Sweden was to receive a new war-lord, and that time they were not mistaken. Charles XII. was born in the same year as the absolute monarchy of Sweden, which power he was to abuse in such a great measure. Shortly after his birth, one of the speakers of the knightly chapter house, Justice Gyllencreutz, said while warning against the consequences of an absolute power: "A king may come who follows his own will, being more fond of war than peace, or utterly extravagant. History proves that changes of the constitution generally are beset by dangerous consequences; yea, that they often have brought destruction to the country and its people." These words were prophetic.

The early education of Charles was supervised by his mother, sweet Ulrica Eleonore, who taught him piety, modesty, gentleness and justice by her own example. He participated with earnestness in the morning and evening prayers, kneeling before the only Lord he ever acknowledged as his superior. His mother died when Charles was seven years of age, but the devotion in which he held her he fixed upon his sisters, Hedvig Sophie and Ulrica Eleonore, but especially upon the former. His religious feeling was deep and sincere, and he evinced early a love of truth, justice and pure morals which, like his brotherly devotion, followed him through life. The most remarkable trait in a son of Charles XI. was his power of self-control; but he was his father's superior also in intellectual gifts, such as a ready memory, a good apprehension and a sharp discernment. His faults were early developed, and met, after the death of his parents, no restraint. He was taciturn, unapproachable, proud, self-willed and headstrong. He had from his grandfather inherited an ambition for the vain glory of war, which was led astray by his unrestrained power of imagination. From the age of five he was taught by the learned professor, Andreas Norcopensis, ennobled under the name of Nordenhielm, to whom he was very devoted and under whose guidance he received a good general education. The plain, able scholar influenced the young prince in a wholesome manner. When his teacher asked him how an honest man ought to be, the pupil, then seven years of age, answered: "He should be gentle but of great courage; fierce like a lion to his enemies, gentle like a lamb to those at home." To the question if it were not better to avoid dangers in order to save one's life, the little Charles answered: "No, it would be a shame to live in such a manner."

Charles XI. had drawn an outline of the course which the education of his son was to follow. The first place was given to study of the Bible and the Christian doctrines and the severe practice of religion. The prince was to learn Swedish and German early, to receive instruction in the laws and constitution of his country, and in the science of war, and to be trained in the arts of military drill, fencing and riding on horseback. He soon acquired the faculty of speaking Latin fluently, in the ordinary mechanical way, and learned some French. When his first governor, Eric Lindskiold, tried to interest him in the latter language by pointing out its usefulness in diplomatic intercourse with the French ambassador, the prince answered: "If I meet the king of France I will converse with him in his own language. When a French ambassador comes here, it is more appropriate that he learns Swedish on my account than I French on his." His favorite studies were strategy and mathematics, which he made under the Swedish general, Charles Magnus Stuart. He often said that the one who was ignorant of mathematics was only a half human being. Charles was fond of riding the horses of his father, and followed the latter on his adventurous journeys and hunts. When only twelve years of age he killed his first bear. He early developed the reckless courage which made him so famous. Charles was exceedingly fond of reading the Eddic poems and the old hero Sagas of the North. He said he wanted to resemble the ancient hero kings, and wished he had, like many of them, a brother who would remain at home to rule the country in peace, while he, with his warriors, made a tour of the world. The prescription, made by his father, that the prince should be taught to make a moderate use of his absolute power, was, if carried out, of little consequence. Charles mourned deeply the losses of his mother and of his first teacher, Nordenhielm, which followed close upon each other, seeking, after that, more the company of his father. Charles XI. had a long private conversation with his son shortly before his death, pointing out the men in whom he could confide. Among these Charles Piper occupied a conspicuous place. He remained ever the adviser of Charles XII., but never had his full confidence. The enigmatic king confided in nobody, and passed through life without opening his heart to any one.

Charles XI. had appointed a government to reign during the minority of his son, to be presided over by Queen-dowager Hedvig Eleonore. But the Estates of the Riksdag, at the request of the nobility, declared Charles XII. of age when only fifteen. The young king placed the crown upon his head with his own hands at the coronation, and took charge of the government in November, 1697. Bengt Oxenstierna remained at the head of foreign affairs as the president of the chancery, while Charles took personal interest in continuing the life work of his father, the restitution of crown lands, which still went on. Charles Piper, who had been quite active in obtaining an early majority for the king, was raised to the dignity of a count, and became one of the most influential members of the state council. Charles was not influenced by anybody in spite of his youth. He listened to what the councillors had to say, then announced his resolutions with terse independence. He refused firmly the appeals of the nobility to reduce the demands of the work of restitution. He abolished the practice of torture, in spite of the unanimous vote of the state council to the contrary. When the aged Bengt Oxenstierna was anxious to have annulled a treaty with France, already signed, the young king answered tersely: "You have heard my opinion; I am the one who signed the treaty." Charles took, in general, little interest in foreign affairs, except those concerning Holstein, to the duke of which country his elder sister was married.

The exuberant spirits of the youthful Charles found an outlet in daring exploits and plays of war. The somewhat older man, Count Arvid Bernhard Horn, the commander of the royal body-guard, took an active part in these as the most intimate comrade of the king. They went bear-hunting together, with wooden forks as their only weapon, fought naval battles with hand-spurts, made breakneck rides on horseback, etc. When the king was near being drowned in one of these "naval battles," the only ones that Charles XII. ever fought, he was saved by Arvid Horn, who pulled him up by the hair. When Horn in some other game was badly hurt and taken ill, the king kept the night watch at his bedside. Upon the visits of Duke Frederic of Holstein, the two young princes indulged in escapades of the wildest kind, if one were to believe the reports made by the foreign ambassadors at Stockholm to their respective governments, and chiefly founded upon hearsay. His application to state affairs was almost constant and very arduous, for which reason these reports of the escapades and adventures of the youthful king are probably wild exaggerations, or mere fables.

The reports of a young inexperienced king who gave up his time to sport and pastimes spread abroad, and the enemies of Sweden were led to believe that an opportune moment was come for an attack on the empire which held the balance of power in Northern Europe. Peter the Great, one of the most remarkable men of modern history, was czar of Russia. Engaged in his heroic task of reorganizing his barbarous empire to a modern European state, he was desirous of obtaining harbors on the coast of the Baltic, from which sea he was cut off by the Swedish possessions. August, a cousin of Charles XII., who was elector of Saxony and king of Poland, was anxious to take possession of Livonia. King Frederic IV. of Denmark, also a cousin of Charles, wished to suppress the duke of Holstein, who had gained independence, thanks to the assistance of Sweden. Czar Peter and King August entered into a secret alliance with each other. While negotiations for continued peace with Sweden were still pending, the Russians secretly crossed the boundary in Ingermanland, Saxon troops entered Livonia, and the king of Denmark took possession of Holstein. The Swedish council of state was amazed at this triple danger. Charles simply remarked that it was strange that both of his cousins wanted war, and expressed the hope that God would support him in his righteous cause.

Charles XII. was eighteen years of age when he entered this stupendous conflict. He was tall and slender, but broad-shouldered; he had a sympathetic face, dark-blue eyes, thin brown hair, and a carriage expressing courage and an indomitable spirit. Upon entering actual warfare, Charles renounced all pleasures and comforts. Sharing the severe discipline of his soldiers, he slept in a tent, ate of their rude food, and drank nothing but water. The wig, considered so indispensable in those days, was laid aside, and he dressed, like the men of his body-guard, in a coat of coarse blue cloth with large brass buttons and yellow lining. His long sword was hung at a yellow leather girdle. He wore high boots and yellow trousers made of skin. In battle he was always found where the danger was most imminent.

Charles turned first against Denmark. A Swedish fleet of forty-eight ships joined the naval forces of equal strength which the Swedish allies, England and Holland, had sent to meet it in the Sound. A more powerful combination has

never been seen before or after in Scandinavian waters.
Charles embarked with his troops on one hundred Scanian
ships and landed at Elsinore, August 4, 1699. He was
impatient to reach shore, jumped into the water, which
reached to his arms, and was followed by his troops,
who carried their weapons high above the water. A sudden attack was made on the Danish troops on shore, who
turned and fled. The Swedes made a temporary camp
and prepared themselves for a march on Copenhagen.
King Frederic was struck with terror and hastened to
make peace with the duke of Holstein, who was left in
undisturbed possession of his country through the treaty
of peace at Traventhal. Charles withdrew his troops at
once, although reluctantly, having wished to crush the
power of Denmark. He had maintained the strictest discipline in his camp, and treated the inhabitants of the country with gentleness. The Danish peasants, who abundantly
brought necessary provisions, said to the king: "You do
us no harm because you are the son of our pious Ulrica
Eleonore." The king answered: "What I have done I
have been forced to do. But rest assured that I shall from
this day be the upright friend of your king."

Charles now turned against Russia. With an army of
somewhat more than 8,000 men he sailed for Ingermanland
to attack the invaders, at least five times as many in numbers, who were laying siege to the town of Narva. The
majority of the Russian troops consisted of serfs who were
taken directly from their work and were without any military training. This army of undisciplined serfs was to
a great extent commanded by foreign adventurers. The
news of the approach of the Swedish troops brought consternation. Several of the Russian officers shed tears, while

the czar quickly left his army to gather more troops. The remarkable battle of Narva was fought November 20, 1700. King Charles offered the enemies a battle in the open field, but when they refused to accept or to come out, he attacked them in their trenches, which formed a semi-circle around the town of Narva, with the wings touching the river of the same name. The war-cry of the Swedes was: "With the help of God!" Their attack was favored by a snowstorm, which blew in the faces of the Russians, blinding them. The enemies could tell that the Swedes were few in numbers, but thought that reinforcements must be on the way. The trenches were filled with bundles of fagots, the ramparts were mounted, and the Russians thrown into confusion. The Russian cavalry fled at the opening of the artillery fire. The rest, crushed in between the walls of the town and their aggressors, tried to escape on every side. The Swedes soon had cut the immense Russian line of troops in twain at the centre. The half which consisted of the right wing moved down to the bridge over the Narva River. But the bridge gave way under the weight of the first 3,000 men, who found their graves in the river below. The rest of the right wing was hedged in between the Swedes and the river. The regiments of the Russian guards, who were the most experienced of the troops, fought bravely for some time, but great confusion ensued among the others, the soldiers wanting to kill their foreign officers, whom they blamed for the catastrophe. The chief commander, Duke de Croi, with several other foreigners, for this reason surrendered to the king.

The Russian soldiers of the right wing, abandoned by their superior officers, made heroic efforts to defend themselves behind barricades which they erected for the moment. King Charles hastened to the spot, but was very near losing his life in passing through a swamp. He sank so deep that the water rose to his neck, and he could save himself only by leaving his horse, his sword, and one of his heavy boots behind in the mud. Without in the least improving his condition, the king took another horse and sought his way to the heart of the battle. The Russians were killed in masses, but did not surrender before King Charles had taken a Russian battery, thus depriving them of the last hope of being reunited with the left wing. The latter, who kept in the vicinity of their trenches, had fought with a good deal of courage. At nightfall two officers were sent from the right wing to ask the king for an armistice, which was granted. King Charles spent the night in his wet clothes, by the bivouac fire, on the ground, his head resting in the lap of one of his soldiers. In the morning, before dawn, two Russian generals arrived, demanding free leave for the remainder of the right wing. This was granted, but the superior officers had to remain as prisoners of war. The commander of the left wing also opened negotiations. Free leave was granted them upon the surrender of their arms. It must have been an impressive sight to see the body of 12,000 Russians, with heads uncovered, who passed in line by only half as many Swedes, depositing their banners and arms at the feet of Charles XII. It was a wise plan to keep as prisoners only the superior officers, for the Swedes had not the means at hand to watch and feed so many prisoners as those who were allowed a free leave. In the battle of Narva 18,000 Russians were killed or captured; the hostile camp, baggage and artillery fell into the hands of the victors. Charles XII. made his solemn entry into Narva, where

Te Deum was sung in the cathedral. Charles with his own hand crossed out all expressions of vainglory over the success or disdain of the vanquished which occurred in the official account of the victory to be sent to Stockholm.

In the following year Charles XII. turned against his third enemy, King August. Saxon troops, 10,000 strong, were joined by 19,000 Russians, and had taken a strongly fortified position on the southern shore of the river Dvina. Charles decided to cross the river from Livonia and attack the enemy. The famous crossing of the Dvina was planned in all details by Eric Dahlberg, the venerable hero and engineer from the wars of Charles X. and Charles XI. Baron Dahlberg died not long after this memorable event. It was June 27, 1701. The Swedish infantry was carried across in prams, the cavalry on fleet-bridges provided with wooden walls on hinges, which, when erect, were a protection against the fire of the enemy, and, when let down, formed gangways for the landing. In front of all boats loaded with hay and straw were sent out, which were ignited, sending a thick, disagreeable smoke in the face of the enemy. The artillery in the prams kept up a disastrous fire. Charles XII. was one of the first to land, and opened the attack when only half of his infantry had reached the shore. The Russians soon scattered in wild flight. The Saxons withstood three powerful attacks, but at last followed the bad example set by their allies. The battle was fought and won before the Swedish cavalry had reached the shore. The bountiful provisions of the scattered army were captured. The crossing of the Dvina was executed under the direction of Charles Magnus Stuart and Count Magnus Stenbock.

The victories of the young hero king and his valiant

soldiers aroused the admiration of all Europe, and much sympathy was expressed for Sweden, who had so successfully warded off a deceitful and unjust attack. Charles XII. received offers of peace from his enemies, but he did not accept them. He did not believe that his treacherous neighbors would keep their promises, and he was no doubt right. He ought to have crushed Russia first, but his victory over Czar Peter had been too easily acquired to make him realize the genius, power and resources of this semi-barbarous enemy. Charles considered King August a more formidable opponent, which was a mistake; but his suspicion that the latter would attack him from behind if he entered Russia would probably have proved to be well founded had circumstances permitted. So Charles invaded Poland, resolved to gain by the interior conflict which was disturbing the peace of that country. He wanted to dethrone August and select a prince who would keep faith with Sweden.

The Polish empire had not taken any active part in the war against Sweden, but Charles XII. demanded that the Poles should prove their good faith by dethroning August and by choosing a native king. When they refused, he let his army enter Poland. For four years King Charles remained there, marching from one part of the country to the other. He conquered the Polish capitals of Warsaw and Cracow, and several other fortified places, winning over a considerable group within the nobility. In 1704 the Diet of Warsaw was called, at which the Polish nobles, in the presence of Swedish troops under the command of Count Arvid Horn, were compelled to deprive August of his crown and elect a new king according to the instructions of King Charles. The new king chosen was the noble, but incapable Stanislav Leczinski, who belonged to an aristocratic family of little influence and few connections. He was an upright and highly educated man, but lacked energy. King August was not willing to abdicate, for which reason King Charles pursued him into his hereditary land. The line of march to Saxony went through Silesia, a neutral country belonging to the empire of Austria. As the army of August had been allowed to pass this country, Charles argued that the same right must be granted him and his troops. At the river Oder, Charles was met by a number of persecuted Protestants, who, kneeling and weeping, prayed for his assistance in pleading their cause before the emperor. Charles promised them to do so, and kept his word.

The Swedish army entered Saxony in the year 1706. The inhabitants, who had in a clear memory the acts of recklessness and cruelty committed by the troops of John Banér, fled for their lives, taking along all the property that could be moved. To their great surprise, they saw the Swedes encamp themselves as quietly as in time of serenest peace. No violence was committed. Nothing was taken, except in exchange for money. But a heavy war tax was imposed, which made both August and his people inclined to seek an early end of the war.

Thanks to the means raised in this manner, the Swedish army was provided with an entirely new outfit of clothes and furnished with necessary provisions. Every regiment established a savings bank of its own, in which the soldiers deposited their earnings. The castle of Alt-Ranstædt was the headquarters of Charles XII., situated close by the memorable battlefield of Lutzen. The sojourn of Charles XII. in Saxony was an incident of universal importance to the history of Europe. He had with his soldiers approached the scene of a conflict which was shaking the whole of Western and Southern Europe. The situation was such that it for the moment hung at the point of the victorious sword of Charles XII. The great question was whether he was resolved to take an active part in the universal conflict. Charles was besieged at his headquarters by princes, warriors and statesmen, who came to pay their respects, desirous of winning his favor and of getting an idea of his plans. The Swedish invasion of Saxony was highly beneficial to the interests of France, and Louis XIV. was the first to admit it, anxious to make the stay of Charles as long as possible, because it had caused a standstill in the hostilities against France. The Duke of Marlborough was among the visitors of Charles XII. He brought a letter of courtesy from Queen Anne, who wrote that the letter "came not from her chancery but from her heart, and was written by her own hand." She longed to meet the famous king personally. The duke's errand was to find out whether Charles was to join the fighting forces of Western Europe or to attack Russia. He was glad to learn that the latter move was the one which the king had in mind. Although the two great warriors expressed mutual admiration, neither was sympathetically impressed by the other. Charles XII. thought Marlborough looked "too fine" for a soldier, while the latter thought the rude simplicity of the king an affectation by which to obtain notoriety. On account of the great influx of distinguished visitors, the style of living was quite different at the royal headquarters of Alt-Ranstædt to what it was during the Polish and Russian wars. But the king kept up the heavy military drills and long individual expeditions on horseback, which he thought indispensable. One of the first ones of the latter which he undertook was to visit the battlefield of Lutzen. The king remembered distinctly all that he had read about the famous battle, and made clear to his generals the various positions of the two armies. At Schwedenstein, the place where Gustavus Adolphus fell, he lingered for a long while in silence. At last he said: "I always have tried to live as he did. May God grant me the grace of dying in like manner."

King August was satisfied to conclude a treaty of peace, which was signed at Alt-Ranstædt. He renounced the crown of Poland and recognized Stanislav Leczinski as the legitimate king. August turned over John Reinhold Patkul, a Livonian traitor, who during the reign of Charles XI. had made himself disagreeably conspicuous, and who had been intriguing against Sweden ever since. Charles XII. was, in gentleness and justice, far in advance of his contemporaries, but he made an exception to his ordinary course of clemency in the case of Patkul, who was executed according to the cruel practice of the time. When the Swedish army left their camp, after peace was made, the regiments were for many miles followed by the grateful inhabitants, who, with tears in their eyes, gave evidence of their friendship. The reason was that the good-natured soldiers of the regular army had followed the habits of their country in assisting their temporary hosts in their various rural pursuits. The Swedes were greeted by the people of Silesia with great enthusiasm, out of gratitude for the improved conditions which the emperor had granted them, at the request of the king. Charles XII. thus made good, in a measure, the acts of violence committed by the Swedish army during the Thirty Years' War, and proved that he had at heart the cause of religious liberty.

Czar Peter was now to be punished, when it was too late. The Russians had invaded the Baltic provinces and captured the fortress of Nœteborg, which Czar Peter gave the new and significant name of Schluesselburg. The new Russian capital of St. Petersburg, with formidable fortresses, was founded in 1703. The laborers were carried away by force from the various parts of the immense empire. They died in great numbers of prostration and of fevers, the Swedes also doing their best to impede the progress of the work. The vacancies were rapidly filled by new multitudes. While the Swedish king was fighting in Poland, the provinces of Ingermanland, Esthonia and Livonia were overrun by the Russians, who devastated the country with acts of cruelty. Dorpat was captured and Narva fell after a bloody conflict, being bravely defended by Rudolph Horn. The Russians destroyed the Swedish navy of the Lake Peipus and penetrated to the province of Courland where Charles XII. had left a considerable detachment of troops. The plan of Czar Peter to conquer Courland and cut off Charles from the connections with his empire was frustrated by General Adam Louis Lewenhaupt.[1] He met a formidable Russian force, several times as numerous as his own, at Gemauerthof, near Mitau, which he routed, in 1705.

---

[1] Lewenhaupt is a German translation of the old Swedish family name of Leijonhufvud, and carried by a branch whose members held the dignity of counts. Almost similar is the derivation of Von Rosen from Tre Rosor, etc. During the Period of Political Grandeur, and later, it was a habit of certain branches of the old Swedish nobility to translate or Germanize their names in this way. The burghers and clergymen followed the custom when being ennobled. Archaic spelling was preserved, or adopted, in most cases.

Sweden stood alone in her struggle with Russia. The old alliance with England and Holland was no longer in existence. The continental powers were too busily engaged in the West to assist in checking the rising power of the Eastern giant. For the limited resources of Sweden he was too big already. Charles XII. had with him a stately and well-equipped army of 44,000, which, by contemporary authors, was pronounced to have consisted of the finest soldiers of the world. Charles was to attack Russia from Poland, for the devastated Baltic provinces could no longer support an army with the necessary provisions. General Lewenhaupt was to join him from Livonia with an army of 12,000 men and ample provisions. Another Swedish commander, General Lybecker, was to attack and destroy St. Petersburg, with an army of the same size, from his headquarters in Finland. The total of Swedish troops distributed in various directions amounted to 100,000, the largest regular army Sweden ever had put up. Charles had concluded to engage semi-barbarous allies in a battle against a semi-barbarous enemy. In 1707 he entered into an alliance with Turkey, and, about the same time, another with Mazeppa, an old ambitious Cossack leader who wanted to establish his supremacy over the steppes of Russia. The plans of Charles XII. for the invasion of Russia have often been severely criticised, but competent judges of our day have declared that they were not only elaborate but highly ingenious. They miscarried on account of arrangements which could not be made according to expectations, and on account of Czar Peter's practice of laying bare and waste the parts of his own country through which the invaders were to pass. Furthermore, Charles had sent home to Sweden several of his best generals, such as Arvid Horn and Magnus Stenbock. This was done after the successes in Poland, and was a good thing in itself, for the men mentioned were exactly those who were destined to save the very existence and honor of a country which was deprived of its political grandeur through the heedlessness of King Charles. But without them he was surrounded by inexperienced men only. Charles Gustavus Rehnskiold was the most conspicuous of these, a valiant but reckless man, who only understood certain details of the elaborate expedition.

When the Swedes were approaching Russian territory, Czar Peter made offers of peace which the French ambassador urged Charles to accept. Charles answered: "He does not mean it. He wishes the world to believe that he wants peace and I war." Czar Peter had organized his army through a wonderful exertion of energy, built new fortresses and strengthened the old ones, enforced discipline and gathered ammunition. Able officers had been trained in the repeated conflicts with the Swedes. These took the lead of the army movements.

Charles left Poland with somewhat more than 30,000 men, entering Lithuania and chasing the Russians before him. A last great victory was won by Charles XII. at Holovzin in Lithuania, in 1708. The Swedish army crossed the Dniepr and marched to Mohilev. Charles lingered in this place for a month, anxiously awaiting the arrival of General Lewenhaupt. The latter remained in Livonia during all this time, the letter ordering him to join the central army not reaching him in due time. The march was continued toward Smolensk, but King Charles thought that he could only reach Moscow over that route with the greatest difficulty, and changed his course, marching toward the

Ukraine to join Mazeppa and the Tartars. Mazeppa had been vexed by the long delay, and was, besides, not able to gather the forces which he had promised. Czar Peter captured his stronghold, and Mazeppa reached the Swedish army more like a fugitive than an ally. The expedition of General Lybecker against St. Petersburg proved a failure. Lewenhaupt, who had at last received his order, moved into Russia. At Liesna he met a hostile army considerably larger than his own. After a fierce battle, which involved a great loss of life, Lewenhaupt broke through the Russian lines. He had been forced to destroy the great amount of provisions which he had gathered, and reached the army of King Charles in a very different state than was anticipated. The king found himself in a difficult position, being cut off from all connections with his country and in want of provisions.

The battle of Pultowa, which was fought June 28, 1709, decided for centuries the contest over the political supremacy of Northern Europe. Charles XII., with his army, which had been reduced to 18,000 men, laid siege to the important town of Pultowa, by the river Vorskla. The Russian army, 50,000 strong, under the command of Czar Peter, hastened toward the enemy. The fear of the terrible Swedes was as yet so strong in them that they did not risk an attack, but built a strongly fortified camp. King Charles, with his army in distress, further reduced to only 12,000 men, and in want even of ammunition, saw no other way than to fight. He was himself wounded in the foot and unable to take command in person. General Rehnskiold, who led the cavalry, acted as general commander during the battle, which position he was not able to fill; Lewenhaupt commanded the right wing with decided success. He forced the enemy to abandon three of its seven forts, and saw it once inclined to leave in flight. The left wing of the Swedish army was brought into disorder and receded. King Charles, who suffered greatly from his wounded foot, was carried on a litter between the lines, encouraging his soldiers and dealing out new orders. The litter was soon shattered, and the horse which the king mounted was shot under him. He saved himself by accepting the horse of one of his officers. Rehnskiold, who appeared nervous and confused, offered only a lame assistance with the cavalry. While riding back and forth in his heedless anxiety to be useful, without obtaining his object, he rode into the Russian lines and was made a prisoner. The same fate befell Count Piper, the aged adviser of King Charles. Lewenhaupt kept up his heroic struggle on the right wing, but his forces were greatly reduced by the fire of the Russian artillery. The Swedes had lost the battle. Their infantry had especially suffered great losses. A great number of the ablest officers were killed or made prisoners. As an illustration may be quoted the fact that among the killed were twenty-two officers of the Wrangel family. The Russians made no fierce pursuit, and the remnants of the Swedish army were given time to recede to the shore of the Dniepr where this river is joined by the Vorskla. The change of route toward the Ukraine had been made contrary to the advice of Count Piper; the march to the Dniepr was made contrary to that of Count Lewenhaupt. The Swedish troops were in fact shut in between the mighty rivers, which they lacked the means to cross, and the surrounding mountains, lined with Russian artillery. Charles was unwilling to leave his army, but Lewenhaupt persuaded him to save his life. Mazeppa had crossed the

Dniepr with his troops. Charles followed in the night of July 1st with 1,000 of his men. With 500 Swedes Charles reached the Turkish town of Bender, where he was at first resolved to remain only until his wound was healed. Lewenhaupt, who now was in command, surrendered to the Russians the following morning, with all the rest of the army. This course was inevitable; another battle would only have caused new and useless sacrifices of human lives.

A sad fate awaited the Swedes in Russian captivity. Only a few saw their homes again, after years of suffering. Rehnskiold was among these. The majority, like Lewenhaupt and Piper, died in captivity. Considerable information about the experiences of the Swedish prisoners in Russia is found in their memoirs and note-books, preserved to this day. It appears that the treatment which they received varied greatly, according to circumstances. Czar Peter wished to keep the Swedish captives in the country as long as possible, with the object of favorably influencing his barbarous subjects by their superior abilities and culture. He had commanded clemency in their treatment; but his orders must have been disobeyed, for many Swedish soldiers are known to have perished in the sulphur mines. In Tobolsk and other towns of Siberia, Swedish majors and captains were in great numbers occupied in the humble pursuits of teachers, barbers, tailors, painters and blacksmiths. Some kept shops and others made articles of the Swedish sloyd, in which there was no competition in the market. The pastimes were music and theatricals. There were, among these thousands of prisoners, 9 generals, 17 colonels, 27 lieutenant-colonels, 38 majors, 494 captains, 975 lieutenants, 67 ministers of the Gospel, etc. A good many of these were Swedish subjects of German descent, or foreigners in Swedish service. The prisoners tried their best to make it as pleasant for themselves as possible. They formed a little community of their own in Moscow, with Piper and Rehnskiold as their highest officials. Georg Nordberg, pastor of the body-guards, was made the president of a chapter-house, which held church conferences, issued texts for special services, examined and consecrated ministers. Czar Peter tried to attract some of the ablest officers to him by promises of liberty and remunerative positions. Many of the captives, seeing no prospect of freedom, decided to remain in the country, entered the Greek church and married Russian women. Some who could not endure captivity made a revolt at Kasan, killing the armed troops, and making an attempt to reach their own beloved country. The plot was frustrated and was of sinister consequences, for the Swedish captives commenced from that time, 1711, to be transported to Siberia in great numbers. This was only to move the important work of civilization eastward. The captives, instead of succumbing to the severe climate, unfolded the great energy of their race, cheerfully accommodating their lives to the new requirements and devoting their time to travels for scientific research, or mercantile purposes, in Russian service, or on their own responsibility. They made accounts and maps of undiscovered and unexplored parts of Siberia, gathering results which have been of great importance to later explorers, geologists and ethnographers. Principal among these scientists are Philip John von Strahlenberg, whose great book on Siberia was published in Leipsic in 1730, and John Anton Matérn and Peter Schœnstrœm, his collaborators; John Gustavus Renat, made a prisoner by the Kalmucks, whom he taught the secrets of manufacturing cannon and bombs, and of printing books with movable types; Lorenz Lange, who was secretary of several Russian embassies to the imperial court of China, about which country he has given valuable information; John B. Muller, John Schnitscher and Ambjœrn Molin. Tobolsk was the centre of the Swedish colonies in Siberia, where a peculiar sect grew up among those of deep religious sentiment. A sectarian school, with more than 100 pupils, was established, and the German pietist, Aug. Herrman Francke, for some time supported the movement. Governor Gagarin, who wanted to make himself ruling sovereign of Siberia, arranged a formidable conspiracy. It was discovered, the governor was hanged, and the Swedish captives who were involved in it were sent still further away to Nerschinsk.

If Charles XII., up to the date of the terrible battle of Pultowa, has deserved our sympathy, in spite of his faults and mistakes, it is impossible to look upon him in the same charitable light for the rest of his career. The great defeat and the loss of his army he described in letters to his sister, Ulrica Eleonore, and the state council, as small misfortunes, without consequence, which he was soon to repair. Instead of trying his utmost to obtain peace on the best possible conditions for his poor country, and instead of saving his unhappy army from the miseries of captivity, he made plans for new campaigns and demands for a new army. Czar Peter expressed more correct views of the situation. A few hours after the battle of Pultowa he wrote to Admiral Apraxin: "Now rests at last secure our city on the Neva." And he was right. The period of the political grandeur of Sweden was at an end.

Great was the renowned heroism of Charles XII. and his warriors. Still greater, although less renowned, the

XX 13

heroism with which his poor and neglected country suffered the disasters which these glorious deeds brought upon it. The regular troops of the army created by Charles XI. had not been sufficient. New regiments were, one after the other, created by means of increased taxes and repeated enlistments, until it appeared as if the whole male population was to be sent out in the endless wars, to be killed or imprisoned, and the distressed country doomed to inevitable destruction. Plague, hunger and emigration threatened to make away with those spared from military service. Swedes of the nineteenth century have difficulty in apprehending how the country was able to endure such terrible hardships.

The consequences of the defeat at Pultowa soon became manifest. The enemies of Sweden had formed a better idea of the resources of the country than had its own ruler, and were resolved to profit by it. King August at once declared the treaty of Alt-Ranstædt to be null and void, and entered Poland, where he in a short time recovered his lost authority. Stanislav fled and sought a refuge on Swedish territory. King Charles later gave him his little hereditary land of Palatinate-Zweibrucken. King Frederic of Denmark declared war upon untenable grounds and had an army of 16,000 men invade Scania. Helsingborg was captured without difficulty. Great consternation was caused by this assault upon the unhappy and apparently defenceless country. The state council was brought to despair. The situation was saved by Count Magnus Stenbock, the able general. After having served as quartermaster-general of the Swedish army in Poland, he was sent back to Sweden, being governor-general of Scania at the time when this province was invaded. He had not with him the necessary troops to meet the enemy, but left for Smaland, where he gathered an army of peasants, chiefly consisting of inexperienced but sturdy youths in wooden shoes and coats of goatskins. From Vexio, where he had met his new mustered troops, Stenbock returned to Scania, in February, 1710, obtaining the reinforcements of a few additional regiments, which swelled his army to the number of 14,000 men. The well-equipped Danish force, which, after an expedition into Bleking, returned to Scania, made a good deal of fun of the "Stenbuk og hands Gededrenge" (the mountain buck and his goatherds). Governor Stenbock understood how to gain the confidence and rouse the patriotism of his "goatherds." He was soon sufficiently sure of their ability to risk a battle, which was fought at Helsingborg, February 28, 1710. The Danes, commanded by George Rantzau, were routed, and sought a refuge behind the walls of the town. The Danish losses were 4,000 killed and wounded and 3,000 prisoners, with their camp, artillery and baggage. A few days later the Danes evacuated Scania, returning to Seeland. The victory of Helsingborg was the most glorious of the battles fought by Magnus Stenbock. It saved Sweden in the hour of direst distress, rekindling the hope which the battle of Pultowa had extinguished. It was the last time in Swedish history that the Danes entered Scania as enemies.

The victory at Helsingborg was only one bright star in a night of darkness. In the Baltic provinces the disasters followed close upon each other. Count Nils Stromberg, the governor-general of Livonia, was forced to surrender the town of Riga, July 1, 1710, after having fought the Russians for months with great bravery. The enemies which forced the able Stromberg to give up his cause were hunger and plagues. Not less than 40,000 Russians had lost their lives outside the walls of Riga. Within a few months Duenamuende, Pernau and Reval also surrendered. This made complete the Russian conquest of the Swedish empire in the Baltic provinces. The operations against Finland, begun earlier, were continued with success. The town and fortress of Viborg, which never had been occupied by foreign troops, were captured in June, and Kexholm in September. The country was unmercifully devastated, in spite of solemn promises to the contrary.

That under such circumstances discontent against the absolute ruler was fostered seems only natural. During the first few years of the Carolinian campaign the noise of the great victories was stronger than the voices of discontent and complaint. When the glorious battles were not followed by treaties of peace, the grumbling voices grew louder. The king was at first not the object of the growing discontent, but the state council, which was considered to make greater demands than were necessary. The king was supposed to fight for a righteous cause against treacherous enemies, but the truth dawned on a good many that a government invested with absolute power was the cause of the misery. The battle of Pultowa brought to a mature state the thoughts of a change in the constitution, thoughts which for years had occupied the ablest men of the country. The double government was to a great extent responsible for the bad state of affairs. The king tried to rule with absolute power from his headquarters in Saxony, Poland and the Ukraine, with Piper as his adviser. At home the state council held the reins of government and sometimes acted in direct opposition to the instructions or intentions of the king. Charles XII. was very jealous of his power, and the state council, foremost in which were a few men of the very highest ability, like Count Arvid Horn, was on this account sometimes unable to carry out its best endeavors. Charles by his methods brought confusion and uncertainty into the deliberations and acts of the government, injuring the commonwealth and the principles of an absolute monarchy as well. The king was not able to supervise the details of his administration, and unrighteous officers profited thereby, by their unlawful collections of taxes, causing open revolts of the suffering population in various parts of the country.

The state council took no pains to hide the truth from the king, rather using strong colors in their descriptions of the critical condition in order to obtain the much-sought-for and needed peace, or at least the gratification of seeing the armies of the country used exclusively for the defence of its own possessions. King Charles considered the members of the state council as a body of weaklings, cowards and fools, who painted the devil on the wall because they lacked the courage and endurance to await the final and infallible triumph of his royal arms in a righteous cause. The climax was reached after the arrival of Charles at Bender. The state council commenced to negotiate for peace on its own responsibility. It also convoked a committee of the Estates of the Riksdag to a meeting for deliberations on measures which would better the hopeless conditions of the state and people. King Charles learned of it and sent from Bender a remarkable order, in which he absolutely forbade such meetings, "especially because the last convention of the Estates," he wrote, "had no other consequence than to let them still plainer discover their impoverished condition."

King Charles lingered in Bender, fascinated by the plans made by several Turkish princes of an armed support against his enemies, or at least an escort of troops for his return through Poland. The king succeeded in his efforts to force the sultan of Turkey to an attack on Russia. The Turks, 200,000 strong, made an invasion, according to plans drawn up by Charles, and were successful in completely surrounding a Russian army, commanded by Czar Peter in person, at the shores of the river Pruth. The czar saved himself by a supreme effort, sacrificing all his gold and the jewels of the czarina as bribes to the grand vizier, who commanded the Turkish army. This dignitary let the Russians escape, thus spoiling the plans of the whole campaign. To Charles it was a great disappointment. His hope to see the Russian giant crushed, and the defeat at Pultowa avenged, was gone forever. His plan of reaching Poland with Turkish troops to join Stenbock and a Swedish army was shaken with the loss of confidence in his barbarous allies. The perfidious grand vizier was punished, but the agreement of peace which he had made with the czar was sanctioned by the sultan, in 1711.

The Swedish state council was quite reluctant to obey the repeated orders of the king for a new army, hesitating to impose new burdens upon the suffering people. The king grew impatient and there was no escape possible. Magnus Stenbock, the most popular man in all Sweden, set an example of personal sacrifices which was followed by many others, and a new army of 9,000 men was at last equipped with a navy to carry it across the Baltic to Pomerania. Stenbock landed in the island of Rugen, in September, 1712, and increased his army to 14,000. He abandoned the idea to march toward Poland because the king remained at Bender, and entered Mecklenburg after having skilfully avoided meeting a superior force of Russian and Saxon troops, which followed him at a distance. Negotiations of peace had been commenced before the arrival of Stenbock, between the dethroned Stanislav of Poland, who was then in Pomerania, and King August. This caused a standstill in the operations, an armistice of a fortnight having been agreed to, with a prospect of renewal. The Danes made an end to it, entering Mecklenburg in December. When the armistice was at an end, Stenbock hastened with his troops to Gadebusch, where the Danish army was encamped, by this rapid move preventing the latter from joining the Russian and Saxon forces. Only a detachment of Saxon cavalry had succeeded in reaching the Danish camp. The battle of Gadebusch was fought December 9, 1712, and was the last of the great victories on land that a Swedish army ever won on the Continent. The Danes were crushingly defeated, and their allies found it safest to return to their former fortified positions. The Swedish artillery, commanded by Charles Cronstedt, distinguished itself in this battle against an enemy of superior strength. But Stenbock could not for any length of time keep up the struggle against the armies of three countries, not receiving any support from Sweden, nor sufficient provisions in Mecklenburg. When the Danes burned the town of Stade, Stenbock in revenge burned Altona, toward the end of the year. His army was reduced for lack of provisions, and Stenbock saw no other course to take than to shut himself up with his troops in the fortress of Tœnning, in the possession of the young duke of Holstein-Gottorp. Stenbock persevered in his hopes for support from Sweden, or friendly powers, in vain. Efforts were made in Sweden to send him troops and provisions, but did not prove successful. When death from starvation was impending, the valiant general concluded to surrender. May 6, 1713, it was agreed that Stenbock and his army of 11,000 men should become Danish prisoners, but that they should be exchanged at the earliest opportunity. King Frederic IV. of Denmark dishonestly neglected to fulfil this agreement, repeatedly and flatly refusing to exchange any of the prisoners. The hero of the victories at Helsingborg and Gadebusch at first received a tolerably good treatment in Danish captivity, which later was changed in a horrible manner. After years of cruel suffering, he died in a miserable dungeon, in 1717, one year prior to the death of Charles XII. This great descendant of Eric Stenbock and Magdalen Sture tried to kill the time of his captivity by carving in ivory, some articles of exquisite design by his hand still being preserved.

At the surrender of Tœnning, Sweden lost her last army and her ablest general. Her king dwelt among the Turks in circumstances fraught with increasing dangers, and her enemies on every side stood ready for attack, the country being a prey to discontent and despair. Still her measure of misery and contumely was not filled.

Charles XII. persevered in his strange sojourn at Bender, being a guest who caused the sultan continual worry through his great political influence. The king was resolved to leave Turkey only in one manner, and that was escorted by a Turkish force. He was successful in persuading the sultan to declare war on Russia once more, but Czar Peter hastened to make so many concessions that peace was made before any campaign was begun. King Frederic of Prussia offered Charles an alliance on the condition that he should at once return to Sweden. Charles seemed at last inclined to do so, but then a conspiracy was brought to his notice, disclosing a plan by which the perfidious Turkish princes of his intended escort were to deliver him into the hands of King August of Poland. King Charles refused to leave Poland, and the conspirators effected an order from the sultan to attack Charles with an army of 10,000 men, and bring him, dead or alive, to Adrianople. The order was executed February 11, 1713, Charles defending himself with his few hundred Swedes and some Poles of his escort against the overwhelming force of Turks and Tartars. The house of the king, near Bender, had been strongly fortified for the occasion. When the trenches were taken most of his men surrendered, but Charles remained with fifty Swedes in the house, which was built of wood, warding off the attack and putting the enemy to flight with a heroism vividly recalling the tales of the ancient Sagas. The Turks returned toward evening and ignited the building. The Swedes valiantly continued their struggle, fighting with their swords against the Turks, surrounded by heavy fire and by the smoke of the burning building. The king at last was forced to leave the house and tried to make his way to the neighboring chancery building, which was of stone and better fit to withstand an attack. Charles stumbled and fell, and was at once made prisoner, together with his followers. This peculiar incident, which has been called the Kalabalik, or Popular Tumult, of Bender, aroused universal surprise and dislike. Charles was conducted to a Turkish pasha, who treated him with respect. He was under supervision first at the town of Demotika, later at the palace of Timurtasz, both in the vicinity of Adrianople. Charles considered it incompatible with his royal dignity to call on the grand vizier. For this reason it was given out that he was ill, and in his miraculous stubbornness he persevered in keeping his bed for a whole year! During all this time, Charles followed up his policy of governing Sweden from afar with absolute despotism. He prepared new rules for the chancery, attempting to change the form of administration from one of faculties, or colleges, to one of departments, or bureaus. He made negotiations of peace in the same spirit as of yore, viz., without being willing to make any concessions, and planned new campaigns. For recreation he played chess and listened to music.

In Sweden the peculiar Turkish adventures of Charles XII. were not understood or appreciated, and the country seemed forsaken by all, even by the king, who by many was thought to be insane. The state council saw no possibility of maintaining a government without the consent and goodwill of the people. Plans for a new constitution, a reduction of the royal power and a peace at any cost were in the air. Princess Ulrica Eleonore was called as a member of the state council and a Riksdag was convoked, to meet toward the end of 1713. The Estates declared that they were, in case of necessity, ready to seek peace under the auspices of the princess and the state council, and were in favor of appointing the princess to the regency. Arvid Horn, the leading spirit of the state council, used the utmost of his influence in keeping the Riksdag from the revolutionary acts which would be involved in making Ulrica Eleonore regent, but he saw to it that the declaration of the Riksdag, of intended peace-making through the princess and state council, was communicated to the king. Hans Henric von Liewen, one of the state councillors, was selected to carry this communication to the king, together with letters from the queen-dowager and the state council. Count Liewen gave a full and true account to the king, telling him in plain words that if he did not return home without delay his kingdom would be lost to him.

King Charles at last decided to return to his country. He sent an embassy of seventy-two people to officially announce his departure to the sultan at Constantinople, made a loan of a considerable sum of money, and left Demotika with a large escort. In Wallachia he left the Turks behind, and continued on his way through Hungary and Germany, followed by two Swedish officers. The emperor of Germany, who was desirous of winning over the Swedish king for his plans, prepared a hospitable reception, but Charles passed Vienna *incognito* as Captain Peter Frisk. He rode on, through night and day, taking care of his own horse and never changing his clothes. Charles arrived at the gate of Stralsund, in Swedish Pomerania, in the night of November 11, 1714, accompanied by one officer. In a fortnight he had, on horseback, traversed a stretch of 1,300 miles.

The situation at the arrival of Charles XII. in Stralsund was beset with new dangers and complications. Prussia had ceased to be friendly and was planning to seize the Swedish possessions in Germany. Hanover, united with England under the same ruler, had the same ambition. The dilapidated fortifications of Stralsund were attacked by Saxons and Danes, commanded by their respective kings, August and Frederic. For more than a year, Charles, with admirable heroism, withstood the siege. Once, while the king was dictating a letter to a secretary, the latter sprang to his feet in consternation, a bomb having shattered the roof of the building. "The bomb, your majesty, the bomb!" exclaimed the scribe. Charles answered: "What connection is there between the bomb and my letter?" quietly continuing his dictation. The king found it at last impossible to keep up the defence of Stralsund, leaving it a stormy December night, and arriving safely in the town of Trelleborg, on the southernmost point of Sweden, December 15, 1715.

What a different country that Sweden was which Charles XII. left in August, 1699, at the very summit of her political grandeur, to the impoverished and suffering Sweden in which he had now landed! And what a different man he had himself become during these sixteen years of absence! Sweden had won a new hero king, of greater fame than any of his predecessors or successors, but lost her prosperity for the time being and her political grandeur forever. The people received the king with demonstrations of joy and with reviving hope for an honorable peace. The state council and the intelligent few received him with badly concealed hopelessness and indifference. They knew that although the young ambitious king had changed to a world-famous hero, prematurely aged in victory and defeat, the unyielding stubbornness and the never satiated desire for glory had remained unchanged in Charles XII. Charles was met by a message from the dying queen-dowager, his grandmother, with an ardent prayer for peace. Charles answered to hopes and prayers, to silent indifference and despair, with a command of more money and more troops! He wanted peace, but as he spoke in the same terms as when he was the victorious commander of an apparently invincible army, nobody cared to consider his demands in earnest. The absolute power reached its last stage of development, a military despotism which had no other policy than war, no other administration than the one requisite to maintain and provide the requirements of war. The state council fell in deepest disgrace, and its functions ceased, in 1715.

During the last years of his reign, Charles XII. took no advice of Swedish men. Foreign adventurers and schemers were in charge of the affairs of state, principal among whom was Baron George Henric Gœrtz. This man was a minister of state of the young duke of Holstein-Gottorp, in whose service he remained, and in whose interests, as a successor to Charles XII. on the throne of Sweden, he zealously worked, while developing into the all-powerful minister of the Swedish king. Charles granted him authority to act in his name in almost every branch of the government, interior as well as foreign. Gœrtz was a genius, but utterly reckless. For his acts the king was responsible, not he. Gœrtz was a foreigner and working for the cause of a foreign master. He tried to obtain loans abroad, made compulsory loans within the country, placed a tax on articles of luxury, and put in circulation coins of copper which were a kind of "promissory notes," worthless in themselves, but each representing a Swedish dollar. At first these "coins of need" were issued to the amount of a sensible sum, but were soon increased in number at the command of Charles XII. himself, so that they represented higher sums than the crown could redeem, and thus lost their value. The people refused to take them, while the prices of everything in the market rose to an astounding height. The government, in order to save itself from this difficulty, took possession of all coined money and uncoined silver, and gave the "coins of need" in exchange, perpetrating several other scandalous acts of violence against the rights of private property.

The situation grew almost insupportable. Commerce and industry, injured by the war, ceased entirely because nobody was inclined to sell, only to receive in exchange worthless coins. Wars and hard years combined in creating misery and distress everywhere. The peasants were recklessly treated, and a disregard for moral obligations grew out of the bad examples set by the government. The students and scientists had in great numbers been carried away by the bloody wars, and the interest in the fields of culture was slackened by the power of financial depression. The wealthy and well-to-do saw their means daily diminish, and, losing their interest in public welfare, they tried to save the remnants of their own property. The members of the state council were threatened by investigations which Gœrtz and his friends were scheming to institute against them. In the nobility, the plans for a change of the constitution matured, the leaders in this movement being Count Per Ribbing and the old Gyllencreutz, who had prophesied the outcome of an absolute monarchial government.

Charles XII., in spite of his all-absorbing passion for war, did not lack interest for the pursuits of peace. He encouraged several men of genius, of whom two were eminently worthy of distinction; viz., Nicodemus Tessin, Junior, the architect, and Christopher Polhem, the engineer.

Nicodemus Tessin was born in Nykœping in 1654. His father and namesake belonged to an old Pomeranian family, and had come to Sweden during the reign of Queen Christine. Nicodemus Tessin, Senior, was an able architect, who built the castle of Drottningholm for Queen-dowager Hedvig Eleonore, a moderately gifted but art-loving woman. The latter gathered around herself artists and architects at her castle of Drottningholm, in Lake Mælar, among whom were Ehrenstrahl, a famous artist of German birth, who founded the first school of Swedish painters. The younger Tessin belonged to this circle and was, in their respective times, in the favor of Charles XI. and Charles XII., acting as court architect to both. The work which won for him an immortal fame is the royal palace of Stockholm, an architectural creation worthy of the admiration of all Europe, and, in Sweden, standing unsurpassed to this day. It was planned and commenced by Tessin, but completed according to his plans a hundred years after his death. Charles XI. ordered a reconstruction of the old castle, which enterprise Tessin undertook. Shortly after the death of Charles XI., both the old and the reconstructed parts of the palace were burned, and the body of the king with difficulty saved from the conflagration. Charles XII. ordered Tessin to build an entirely new palace. The work was commenced in 1698, but was gradually abandoned during the war times, to cease shortly before the battle of Pultowa. Charles was highly interested in it and wrote from Turkey to Tessin about his views. Tessin intended to decorate the exterior according to the taste of his day, but Charles raised opposition, finding the severe beauty of the stern yet graceful outlines perfect in themselves. The work on the new palace was recommenced after the death of Charles XII. King Adolphus Frederic was the first who took up his residence within its walls. Tessin rose high on the social ladder. From Turkey, the king made him a count and chancellor of the

University of Lund; after his return to Sweden he appointed him marshal-colonel. Tessin stood in strong opposition to Baron Gœrtz, and after the death of King Charles joined the leaders of the revolutionary nobles. He was of universal fame.

Christopher Polhem was the first of great Swedish engineers and inventors. He was born at the ancient town of Visby, in the island of Gothland, in 1661, and was the son of a merchant, who died when Christopher was a child. When only twelve years of age he had to make his own living. As secretary to a widow of wealth, he early developed his genius as a mechanician, building his own shop of carpentry, sloyd, etc., making watches and devising smaller inventions. His want of a classical education was detrimental to him, and he commenced, when twenty-four years of age, to study Latin with various ministers in the country, in exchange for works of his genius and handicraft. At last he was able to enter the University of Upsala by means of recommendations from his last teacher. Soon after his arrival he created considerable attention and admiration by a proof of his ingenuity. Behind the high altar in the Upsala Cathedral there was a clock of the finest workmanship, devised in mediæval times by a monk of the monastery of Vadstena. It was out of order, and not for a hundred years had anybody attempted to set it right. Polhem undertook to reconstruct the whole work, connecting with the main mechanism all the hands which pointed out the hours of the day, the eclipses of the moon and the motions of the "ruling" planets, according to the system of the astrologers. Polhem succeeded in his task, and was allowed to test his invention of automatic haulers of ore in the mines. The college of mining, before which the invention was successfully demonstrated, accepted it, and Charles XI. appointed Polhem a mining engineer. In 1694, Polhem made an extensive journey through England and the Continent. In Paris he learned that several mathematicians were in vain endeavoring to construct a clock which would simultaneously show the time of the day in various countries and strike the hours at the same time. Polhem announced through the Swedish ambassador in Paris that he was willing to solve the problem. He constructed a model which gave universal satisfaction. Louis XIV had a clock made after this model and gave it as a gift of honor to the Turkish sultan. Upon his return he proposed the founding of a *laboratorium mechanicum*, which in several respects served as a pattern for the later technological institutes of Stockholm and Gothenburg. The youthful Charles XII. embraced the idea with interest, but the promising institution came to a standstill during the wars. Among Polhem's more remarkable inventions was one for the leading of water-power, to be used at considerable distances. Charles XII. said that a man like Polhem was not to be had for several centuries, and that for this reason he ought to be made useful as long as he lived. A task of gigantic proportions was intrusted to him—the construction of a dock for the navy yards at Carlskrona. The great engineer filled it in an admirable way, and was appointed councillor of commerce and ennobled under the name of Polhem, his original name having been Polhammar, which to modern ears sounds just as fine and a good deal more suggestive.

Another gigantic task worthy of the genius of Polhem was the construction of a navigable route from the North Sea across the great inland seas of Sweden to the Baltic, but he was not allowed to finish it. Charles XII. intrusted the work to Polhem, who was to have it ready in five years. In 1718, Polhem commenced by forming an immense sluice, by means of explosions in the rock at Trollhetta. The great waterfalls of said place were to be avoided and the work of completing the sluice was begun, when it was all destroyed by unknown enemies, who dropped beams and planks in the river above, which carried away the dam. The death of King Charles and the impoverished condition of the country made it impossible to continue the work on the great canal system, which had to wait for more than a century for its ultimate completion. With the death of Charles XII. the era of ambitious enterprises came to an end; but Polhem was employed in various works of mechanic improvements in the interest of agriculture, industry and manufactures. Czar Peter of Russia, King George I. of England, and several other monarchs made brilliant offers in order to win Polhem for their countries. He executed several works and inventions abroad, but loved his own country too much to leave it. Polhem exerted a great influence in the interest of his science, both by instruction and by the publication of technical works. Active to the last, he died in 1751. Polhem was a man of a harmonious endowment, amiable and dignified, and preserved his plain mode of living throughout his brilliant career.

Gœrtz led with superior skill the negotiations for peace, while the impoverished country suffered untold miseries as a consequence of his unscrupulous financial schemes. He tried to benefit by the sudden but lasting enmity between Czar Peter and George I., desiring to gain the support of either against the other. The deliberations were held in the archipelago of Aland, with Gœrtz as the representative of the Swedish government. Czar Peter wanted to keep

Ingermanland, Esthonia and Livonia, but was ready to cede Finland, which country he occupied, and to assist King Charles with troops in an attack on Denmark. Norway was to be the compensation for the lost Baltic provinces, and the attack on Denmark was to be made from Germany. Charles XII. had no confidence in the czar as an ally and had commenced the conquest of Norway directly and without his aid. No decision was reached in the negotiations with England.

In February, 1716, Charles XII., from Bohuslæn and Vermland, made an invasion into Norway, penetrating over the Glom River to Christiania. He captured the capital, where he held his headquarters for several weeks, but was not able to take the fortress of Akershus, which, with its artillery, commanded the city. The Swedish army, 10,000 strong, suffered a great deal from want of provisions and through a guerilla war, skilfully conducted by the Norwegians. Charles was in danger of being surrounded by the enemy, and with difficulty retreated to Sweden, over the Strait of Svinesund. The dangers were increased by the Norwegian naval hero, Peter Tordenskiold, who, with some Danish ships under his command, had destroyed a flotilla of Swedish transport vessels. An invasion into Scania by Denmark and her allies was planned for the summer, but did not materialize. King Charles took up his headquarters at Lund.

The war offered no aspect of interest during the year 1717, except some unsuccessful attempts made by Tordenskiold to capture the towns of Strœmstad and Gothenburg. Charles prepared another attack on Norway, and, by draining the last resources of his country, managed to equip an army of 60,000 men. In August, 1718, a smaller army, under the command of Charles Gustavus Armfelt, was sent through Jemtland over the mountains into the diocese of Drontheim. King Charles, with an army of 30,000 men, invaded Norway from Bohuslæn, Dal and Vermland, and took in possession the country east of the Glom River. Within a few days the king laid siege to the fortress of Fredericsten, close by the town of Fredricshall. November 27th the fort of Gyldenlœve was captured, and the Swedes moved their trenches ever closer to the fortress, which seemed doomed to surrender. In the evening of November 30th the king was seen in one of the trenches watching the work of his soldiers, and leaning against the rampart. He remained there a long time, not heeding the appeals of his officers, who grew uneasy on account of the apparent danger to his person. Suddenly his head sank down on his breast. A bullet from the fortress had reached him, penetrating his temples and causing instant death. He met death in the manner he most desired it, although not while engaged in battle.

Charles XII. was of an enigmatic character, which attracts, through its strength and superiority over his contemporaries, but which is repulsive through its tenacity, unyielding sternness and inaccessibility to reason or persuasion. His moral greatness has won admiration. It had its limitations, but was superior to the standards of his time. His ideals were pure and lofty, but, through lack of contact with the realities and facts of life, only assumed a tragic grandeur, without proving beneficent to mankind. His faults were such that his education and experience as an absolute monarch aggravated them. Charles XII. was the most remarkable man of his age and one of the greatest soldiers that ever lived. He was also a great general, although the proper balance between the soldier and the field marshal, perhaps, was to some extent lacking. The influence of his personality and example had a miraculous effect upon his soldiers. He suffered his one great defeat in open battle when wounded, suffering, and not able to exert his usual influence to its full extent.

Charles XII. has been idolized by his countrymen of all ages, who in him have recognized an impersonation of all their chief national virtues, with a few of their national faults, enlarged into the image of a patriotic hero of almost supernatural grandeur. The Swedish people were forced to accept absolute power as a salvation from the impending thraldom of oligarchy. In Charles XII. it saw to what a climax of abuse this power could attain, even in hands which were deemed righteous and free from stains With Charles XII. the political grandeur and the absolute monarchy of Sweden came to an end, although attempts to restore both were to be made. A new phase of her development, with new improvements and new evils, commenced with the reign of Ulrica Eleonore.

CHAPTER XIV

Period of Liberty—The Aristocratic Republic

ULRICA ELEONORE succeeded her brother Charles XII. as the sovereign of Sweden. She was proclaimed queen by birthright, and called the Riksdag, willing to cede the absolute power. When the Riksdag convened a disagreeable surprise met her. The Estates refused to acknowledge her right to the crown, stating that both she and her older sister had deprived themselves of their rights of succession by marrying without the consent of the Estates of the Riksdag. Princess Hedvig Sophie was dead, but her son, the young Duke Charles Frederic of Holstein was in Sweden, ready to claim the throne. Ulrica Eleonore was compelled to yield gracefully. She sent a note to the Riksdag disclaiming her hereditary right, but declaring herself willing to accept the crown, with restriction of the absolute power. She was at once elected queen by the Riksdag of 1719, which then proceeded to pass a new constitution. Such a constitution had been formulated in advance by a new party, chiefly consisting of nobles, who aimed at introducing a royal government, restricted in its power by the state council and the Riksdag. They were successful in their efforts, but unfortunately lost their ablest leaders at the start, Per Ribbing dying soon after the first Riksdag, and Arvid Horn retiring from the government and council on account of a conflict with the queen. Thus the new government did not open up under favorable auspices. Baron von Gœrtz was captured and put to death for high treason without being granted the privilege of an appropriate legal defence. The queen overstepped her limit of power in being the active force in this illegal execution, anxious to rid herself of Gœrtz because he was the ablest man among the supporters of Duke Charles Frederic of Holstein. The duke gave up his chances and left for Russia, where he married a daughter of Czar Peter. The arrangements made to establish order in financial matters were not satisfactory. The management of the war with Denmark was miserable. The army was recalled from Norway and little done to protect the coast from attacks by the Danish fleet under Admiral Tordenskiold. This valiant naval hero, of Norwegian birth, who, during the reign of Charles XII., had made unsuccessful attacks on Strœmstad and Gothenburg, through cunning captured the strong fortress of Carlsten, but was unable to take New Elfsborg. Danckwardt, the commander who surrendered Carlsten, was executed by the Swedish government. The Swedish army of 6,000 men, which had entered the district of Dronthiem by the command of Charles XII., perished from hunger and cold when returning through the mountains of Jemtland. Only a few hundred survived to tell the terrible tale. The Russians sent a fleet to the Swedish shores with 40,000 men, and burned, in two expeditions, twelve Swedish towns in the middle and northern parts of the country. They avoided open battle, and when landing in great numbers were effectively repulsed.

Under such conditions Sweden was anxious for peace. In compensation for various sums of money, Bremen and

Verden were ceded to Hanover in 1719, Pomerania, south of the river Peene, with Stettin, Usedom and Wollin to Prussia, in 1720, and Ingermanland, Esthonia, Livonia, with Viborg and Kexholm, and surrounding Finnish territory, to Russia, in 1721. Denmark had to give up all territory captured from Sweden, but received a sum of money in exchange for Carlsten, in 1720. Thus the Baltic empire of Sweden was swept away. It had been of importance during the time of the German war and for the shielding of new conquests in the Scandinavian Peninsula itself. Now its loss was a gain for Sweden, as it allowed her to concentrate her attention upon the interior development of the country.

The tendency of Ulrica Eleonore to exert more power than was within her authority had created dissatisfaction, and when she commenced an agitation to have her consort, Prince Frederic of Hesse, share the throne with her, the crown was granted him only upon her own resignation from the government.

Frederic I. was crowned in 1720 and Ulrica Eleonore retired from the government. Frederic left the Reformed and entered the Lutheran Church. The crown was to be inherited by his male issues only, in the union with Ulrica Eleonore. He showed a tendency for mixing in the affairs of state to further his own interests, but soon gave in to his easy-tempered, pleasure-loving nature, occupying himself exclusively with his hunts and his mistresses.

The real ruler of Sweden, during the first two decades of Frederic's reign, was *Arvid Horn*, one of the greatest of Swedish statesmen. His was not the work of building up the government of a strong and influential nation, like that of Oxenstierna or Gyllenstierna, nor were his their

grand, far-reaching views. But his mission was to raise
from the dust his bleeding, downtrodden country, and to
reinstall it in the honor and respect, not only of itself but
of the world. Count Arvid Bernhard Horn was an opportunist, but one of the noblest kind, who by means of peace
found the only way in which to protect and further the
financial and cultural development of Sweden. He was
an able soldier and a skilled diplomatist. The son of an
illustrious but poor family, of the Finnish nobility, he entered the military service after a university course at Abo.
He served in foreign armies, but was with Charles XII.
in Stockholm as the best companion of his youth. As the
commander of the royal body-guard he took an honorable
part in the early victories of Charles XII., later being
chosen to fulfil the delicate task of making the Polish
nobles elect Stanislav king, in which he was eminently successful. After a short captivity he was released and returned to Sweden, where he became a member of the state
council and president of the state chancery. In this position he repeatedly sent letters to Charles XII., in which
he described the distress of the country, in eloquent words
pleading its need of peace. Upon his return Charles XII.
removed him from office with the other councillors, although
he was the one who had saved the tottering throne for the
king. Of this Ulrica Eleonore was aware and was glad to
accept his resignation; when reinstated in his position he
found that he could not preserve it with dignity in the face
of the irregularities committed by the queen. Count Horn
was responsible for the exclusion of Ulrica Eleonore from the
government at King Frederic's ascendency, but the latter
was forced to accept Horn in his former position as the controlling power of the government. With due reason, the

peaceful and honorable decades of Frederic's reign have been named the "Period of Arvid Horn."

The new form of government introduced by Ribbing, Horn and others was nothing else than that of an aristocratic republic. The rights of the monarch, reduced in 1719, were still further reduced in 1720. He had two votes in the state council and a deciding vote in deadlock, but besides the authority to appoint councillors from the candidates nominated by the Riksdag, and to appoint all higher officials, no other rights. The government was in the hands of the state council, consisting of sixteen members. The Riksdag decided all questions of taxes and legislation, and settled issues of peace and war. Each of the four Estates was represented in the committees, except in the "secret committee," for international affairs, to which no yeoman could be chosen. Each Estate had its speaker. The president of the chancery was the minister of foreign affairs and consulted the secret committee on important questions, being the only head of a department who was allowed as a member of the state council. The nobility held the balance of power, much to the opposition of the lower Estates, who tried, by repeated agitation, to invest the king with the authority held by him before the days of absolute power. The nobility had done away with its three classes, and, with these abandoned, it was the majority, viz., the lower nobility, who were the governing class. The aristocracy tried its best to regain the privileges enjoyed during the reign of Queen Christine and Charles X., but Horn forced it to be satisfied with those granted by Gustavus Adolphus. The power of the higher nobility was forever crushed by the loss of their immense possessions. The friction between the nobility and the lower Estates of the Riksdag was constant, Horn siding with the former, but keeping them all in check.

Arvid Horn led with superior skill and gentleness the management of foreign affairs. All influences from the powers and from the restless nobles to involve Sweden in a conflict of war were unsuccessful. A treaty was never entered into with any one power without another one formed with a power of the opposite continental party to counterbalance it. Thus England, France and Russia were unable to make Sweden an obedient ally, Horn upholding her independence, maintaining peace and inspiring respect. Utterly refusing to accept the bribes which were freely offered and considered the indispensable means of obtaining diplomatic influence in that day, Horn himself distributed bribes to gain his patriotic purposes. Horn's great mistake was to refer the decision of foreign affairs in which he was opposed by members of the state council to the Riksdag and its secret committee. The latter commenced to act independently in important foreign matters. By signing an agreement with France, through which Sweden lost its former privilege of an independent policy, the committee ultimately caused his downfall, in 1738. Arvid Horn then retired, at the age of seventy-two, and died a few years later.

During Horn's peaceful administration the financial conditions improved, the state debt was reduced and the peaceful trades and industries were furthered. The great deed accomplished was the completion of a new state law which was published in 1734 and is in force to this very day. Arvid Horn was a perfect type of the great Carolin era, of pure and severe morals and modest requirements. In a day of increasing scepticism and levity, he ostentatiously preserved the rigid religious practices of his youth. He showed unreserved indignation at the unworthy and immoral conduct of the king, for which reason strained relations existed between them. Count Horn was of impressive form and carriage, controlling the quick temper of the warrior beneath the smooth and dignified bearing of the statesman.

The decades which followed upon the fall of Arvid Horn were stormy ones and full of miseries. The friends of peace were called Caps and the warlike party Hats. The latter, now in power, commenced a war against Russia, which turned out badly, the Swedes being defeated at Vilmanstrand, in 1741, and at Helsingfors, in 1742. The government and secret committee felt ashamed of their work and had the poor generals, Charles Emil Lewenhaupt and Buddenbrock, executed for their lack of martial skill and good fortune. Peace was made with Russia in 1743, the towns of Fredericshamn, Vilmanstrand and Nyslott, in Finland, being ceded by Sweden, and the river Kymene made the boundary line.

Next the Hats had to face a rebellion. In order to please Elizabeth of Russia, Czar Peter's daughter, they had selected Charles Peter Ulric, her nephew and the son of the duke of Holstein, as heir-apparent to the Swedish throne, to which he was the nearest in right, Ulrica Eleonore dying without issue, in 1741. But when chosen as Elizabeth's successor in Russia, the Hats selected Adolphus Frederic, prince bishop of Lubeck, who on his mother's side was a descendant of Gustavus Adolphus. This caused popular discontent, the people, forgetful of past enmities, desiring to make Crown Prince Frederic of Denmark heir-apparent. The peasants at the Riksdag of 1742 proclaimed loudly their desire of a personal union with Denmark-Norway, which would establish Scandinavia as one solid power against Russia. The peasants of Helsingland and Dalecarlia revolted. They gathered, and marching down to Stockholm, placed the government in a dangerous position by demanding the election of Crown Prince Frederic of Denmark and the execution of the two imprisoned generals. In that very moment peace was obtained with Russia, and the government persuaded the leaders of the rebellion, who had obtained admission to the Riksdag, that Adolphus Frederic must be chosen, since it was a part of the treaty of peace. Later the rebels, 3,500 in number, were forced to surrender. Their principal leader was executed.

The Hats were at first led by Count Gyllenborg, who was succeeded by the brilliant Count Charles Gustavus Tessin, a son of the great architect, Nicodemus Tessin the Younger. Although not a statesman of any higher ability, Charles Gustavus Tessin was able to shake the oppressive influence of Russia. He was assisted by Prince Adolphus Frederic, who said he would rather resign than be a Russian vassal. A war seemed imminent, but was averted, Finland in the meantime being effectively fortified. The unconquerable fortress of Sveaborg was built near Helsingfors, and was the creation of Augustinus Ehrensverd. The Hats were eager in their attempts to encourage industry and manufacture, but did so at the expense of agriculture, and placed immense taxes on imported goods. A pioneer of industry was John Alstrœmer, who, in his town of Alingsos, built factories of various kinds. King Frederic died in 1751.

Adolphus Frederic was a good-natured and gentle man.

He was not averse to an increased royal authority, but was not energetic enough to exert a controlling influence or to push his claims. His consort was the ambitious and brilliantly gifted Louise Ulrica, the sister of Frederic the Great of Prussia. She tried to inspire the king to action. Continually occupied by ambitious schemes, she spoiled them herself, through lack of caution and stability. As crown princess, she stood close to Count Tessin, whom she hoped to win over for her plans. They devised the institution of the knightly orders of the Seraphim, the Sword and the North Star, the credit of their introduction being given to King Frederic I. Adolphus Frederic was forced to subscribe to the same minimum of royal privileges as those enjoyed by Frederic I. At court a party was formed which supported the king, who soon commenced to oppose the state council. In 1755 this went so far that he refused to sign a document from the council. The case was brought before the Riksdag, where, in spite of strong opposition from the peasants, a resolution was passed indorsing the action of the state council. Count Tessin, in friction with the court, resigned from all his positions. The Riksdag tried to reinstall him as governor of the royal princes, but gave in upon the request of Tessin. The Riksdag went to the extreme of having a stamp made of the king's signature, to use in cases where he refused to sign, and also took upon itself to engage and dismiss teachers for the royal princes. At court indignation rose high, and a conspiracy was formed to take possession of the capital, with the state council and the speakers of the four Estates, in order to bring about a revolution with increased power for the king. The conspiracy was discovered, and Count Eric Brahe, Count Jacob Horn and six others of its leaders executed.

A new humiliation to the court was Sweden's alliance with Austria, Russia and France against Frederic the Great of Prussia. The plans laid out by the Swedes were as elaborate as those for the Russian war. But on account of poor equipment and repeated change of commanders nothing effective was done. When peace was made at Hamburg, in 1762, Sweden neither lost nor gained anything. The Swedes had fought no battles, and Frederic the Great said he would call the Swedish invasion of Pomerania a private fight at the frontier.

The great expense of the profitless war gave the Caps an occasion to gain in influence, and at the Riksdag of 1765 they overthrew the power of the Hats, in their turn summarily dismissing the councillors of their opponents. They introduced perfect liberty of the press in 1766, but went too far in their policy of economy, dangerously injuring the new industries by the withdrawal of loans and subsidies. The expensive factories came to a standstill and skilled workingmen emigrated. Popular opinion turned against these repeated changes and the endless strife of the parties, and felt inclined to criticise a Riksdag which had attained such power without giving a prosperous and secure administration in return. Foreign powers, encouraged by the court, tried to gain adherents of their various policies by bribes to councillors and members of the Riksdag, thus demoralizing state politics.

The king received a valuable supporter in the crown prince Gustavus, who in 1767 became of age. He prevailed upon the king to resign when the state council refused to call an extraordinary Riksdag for the granting of added royal authority. The king did so, and the country was without a monarch for six days (December 15-21, 1768). The crown prince notified the presidents of the different administrative offices in Stockholm that his father had ceased to reign. The state council persisted; but had to give in, when the colonels of the regiments reported that they could no longer answer for their troops, since also the paymaster's office was closed. The Riksdag convened in Norrkœping in 1769. The Caps suffered defeat in spite of strenuous efforts made for their preservation by the secret agents of the powers, anxious to see the anarchic condition of the government continue. But the court party failed in the exertions to have the royal privileges augmented. The intrigues of the foreign powers continued, and the crown prince left for France to insure her support in case of war. While the Hats were once more in power, Adolphus Frederic died suddenly in February, 1771.

Gustavus was to put an end to the party strife of the "Period of Liberty," as it has been called. His own reign belongs properly to it, for he reaped the benefit of the seed it had been sowing. The Period of Liberty, with all its faults, forms an important chain in the cultural and political development of Sweden. Its form of government made necessary a varied and active part in public affairs, educating all classes of officials to a high degree of efficiency and the people at large to self-government. The Riksdag, through parliamentary activity and importance, developed an authority which, although too composite to govern itself, was enabled to act as a shield of steel against all abuse of the executive power. The national life never gathered a richer harvest of men of genius who worked for the progress of their country and for that of the world. The heroism of the Swedish people during the preceding period of suffering and distress bore fruit in men like Emanuel Swedenborg, the inventor, naturalist, philosopher and founder of a new religion; Charles Linnæus, the founder of modern botany; Andrew Celsius, Junior, the inventor of the centigrade thermometer; John Ahlstrœmer, the pioneer of industry; John Ihre, the able philologist, and Olof von Dalin, the poet, humorist, and, with Sven Lagerbring, the first modern historian of Sweden. The Period of "Liberty," viz., of an Aristocratic Republic, was the golden era of Swedish science, the latter for the first time becoming of universal fame and of universal importance. The scientists of this period belong to the fathers of modern research, basing their conclusions upon personal observation, in strong contrast to *their* fathers and precursors of the chauvinistic barocco period.

Emanuel Swedenborg, the most remarkable man whom Sweden has ever brought forth, was born in Stockholm, June 29, 1688. His father was Jesper Svedberg, bishop of Skara, in West Gothland, and his mother Sara Behm. The tendency toward mysticism, an inheritance from his father, was noticed in him at an early age. He has told of himself that between the age of four and ten his thoughts were exclusively occupied with religious subjects. While in prayer, he sometimes entered a somnambulic condition, revealing things which surprised his parents, who said that angels spoke through him. As a child, he had the idea of God as one, without any conception of a Trinity. Later he received instruction in the systematic theology of his day. His father gave him a thorough training in the Oriental and classical languages. The early mysticism of the boy was supplanted by a thirst for knowledge of the phenomena of life and nature, coupled to a burning desire to illustrate his reading by practical experiments. Having entered the University of Upsala, he at first devoted himself to the study of the classical languages and literature, later to that of mathematics and natural science. When the university was visited by the plague in 1710, and almost all courses of instruction were interrupted, Swedenborg made a journey for scientific purposes to England, Holland, France and Germany. He returned in 1714, enriched with valuable results. In 1716-18 he published the first scientific journal of Sweden, "Dædalus Hyperboreus," treating subjects of mathematics and physical science. In 1716 he came in close personal contact with Charles XII. at the university town of Lund. The king, being deeply impressed by his great learning and practical ability, appointed him assistant assessor of the college of mining. Swedenborg had, by the scholar Eric Benzelius, been made acquainted with the idea of the old Bishop Brask, of the time of Gustavus I., to "cut up the land" between the North Sea and the Baltic to make a navigable route through Sweden. Swedenborg gave close attention to this scheme, and communicated his plans to Charles XII., who became very much interested in them. Christopher Polhem was selected to build the great canal, and Swedenborg was made his assistant. We know from the sketch of Polhem's life why the great work failed of accomplishment. Swedenborg gave a proof of his superior genius as a practical engineer during the siege of Fredericshall. Tordenskiold made the sea unsafe and had hedged in the Swedish fleet at Iddefiord. The Swedish boats and galleys were then carried overland to the town of Strœmstad, travelling the main road for fifteen miles on rolling machines devised by Swedenborg. After the death of Charles XII., whom he highly respected, Swedenborg travelled to Saxony and Hungary to study the mining industry of these countries. Returning in 1722, he entered for the first time upon his work of the college of mining, becoming assessor a few years later. In 1719 he was ennobled with his brothers and sisters, when the change of name from Svedberg to Swedenborg was made. In 1724 he declined to accept the chair of mathematics at the University of Upsala, dividing his time between his official work and his studies, until 1747, when he resigned from his position with a pension of the same amount as his salary. His religious works were commenced in 1745, and after that time he made repeated journeys to London or Amsterdam to have these printed, as they could not be published in Sweden on account of the strict and highly orthodox censure of that period.

In 1744 the event occurred which Swedenborg in various places of his works has described as the opening of his spiritual sight, or the manifestations of the Lord to him in person. He had not, by geometrical, physical and metaphysical principles, succeeded in grasping the infinite and the spiritual, or their relation to the nature of man, but he had touched on facts and methods which seemed to conduct him in the right direction. He thought that God had led him into the natural sciences in order to prepare him for his later spiritual development. The visions of his boyhood returned, now conceived by a nature enriched by the experiences of a life spent in ardent and scientific research. The great seer remained a man whom everybody loved and respected. People who did not believe in his visions feared to ridicule them in the presence of this august savant. His manner of life was simple, his diet chiefly consisting of bread, milk and large quantities of coffee. He made little distinction between night and day, and sometimes lay for days in a trance. His servants were often disturbed at night by hearing him engaged in what he called conflicts with evil spirits. His intercourse with spirits was often perfectly calm, in broad daylight, and with all his faculties awake. He held that every man and woman has the same power of spiritual intercourse, although not developed in the same degree as it was found in him.

The work which established the scientific reputation of Swedenborg was published, in 1734, in three massive folios, at the expense of Duke Ludvig Rudolph of Brunswick. The second and third volumes describe the best methods employed in Europe and America in the manufacture of iron, copper and brass. The first volume contains a philosophical explanation of the elementary world which has aroused admiration as a beautiful, daring and consistent creation of human genius, worthy of being placed side by side with the works of Newton, and replete with remarkable ideas and anticipations of later discoveries. Swedenborg indicated the existence of the seventh planet forty years before Uranus was discovered by Herschel. He was the first to form an idea of the development of nebulæ from chaotic masses to concrete heavenly bodies, a hypothesis later perfected by Herschel, and the first to offer the theory, later developed by Buffon, Kant and La Place, of the solar origin of the planets and their satellites. As in astronomy, so also in physics and geology he preconceived great discoveries. His experiments and theories in physics have been confirmed by the discoveries of the polarity of light and the galvanometer and its magnetic properties. Swedenborg discovered before anybody else the great importance of magnetism and the fact that magnetism and electricity are manifestations of the same power. He made observations concerning air and water which have been confirmed as to their correctness by Priestley, Cavendish and Lavoisier, who long were supposed to have been the first discoverers. In geology, he was the first to demonstrate that the Scandinavian peninsula, except the southern part of Scania, was a rising continent, proving the earlier level of the sea to have been much higher and the inland lakes to have stood in connection with the sea. Through his remarks on bowlders, he gave rise to the later theories of Berzelius and Sæfstrom of a bowlder period. Upon these researches followed great and remarkable works of anatomy, which, by later anatomists of the first rank, have been declared to be classics in the literature of physiology. His immense work, "Arcana Cœlestia," and other theosophical writings which he has placed as a foundation for the New Church, and on which his present fame rests, were not so celebrated in his days as his scientific works. Like the latter, they were all written in Latin.

The new religion, founded by Swedenborg, more spiritual than the old, has proved equally attractive to the individual and idealistic thinkers of all sects, Protestants and Catholics, Unitarians and Theosophists. Swedenborg made no attempt to establish a sect, and the New Church as an organization is the result of a movement which was started after his death.

In his personal appearance Swedenborg was a middle-sized man of strong constitution. His head was of a fine shape, the color of his face somewhat dark and its expression pensive, but his blue eyes were large and radiant. His disposition was amiable. He was a man of the world, fond of music and society, especially of that of cultured women, and was often seen at court. He had a tendency to stutter when speaking fast, for which reason he used a slow diction, characterized by choice and mature expressions. In his youth, he frequented the house of Christopher Polhem and fell in love with his daughter Emerentia. Both Polhem and Charles XII. favored the idea of seeing them united, the young girl of fourteen giving her consent. But young Emerentia was secretly in love with somebody else, and her health and disposition suffered under the strain. When Swedenborg discovered the truth, he gave his betrothed freedom from her allegiance. He ceased to visit the house of Polhem and never entered any other relation of love.

In 1770, at the age of eighty-two, Swedenborg for the last time visited Amsterdam. John C. Cuno, who then saw him, thus described the impression which the aged visionary and thinker made upon him: "He looked so touchingly pious, and when I gazed into his smiling eyes of a heavenly blue, it always seemed to me that truth itself spoke from his lips." Swedenborg left Amsterdam for London, where, on Christmas eve, 1772, he was struck by hemiplegia. After a few weeks he recovered his speech, and his faculties were clear to the last. The chaplain of the Swedish legation asked him if he had not formulated the doctrines of his new religion in order to gain fame, and if he wished to recall it all before he died. The yet partly paralyzed man raised himself into a sitting position, saying: "As true as it is that you see me here in front of you, as true is also all that I have written, and in eternity you will find a confirmation of it." The chaplain asked him if he wanted to receive the sacrament. Swedenborg answered: "I need it not; for I am already a member of the other world; but your intention is good, and I will with joy receive the sacrament in token of the bond of unity between heaven and earth." Swedenborg died March 29, 1772, and was buried in the Lutheran church of London.

Swedenborg was shrewd in worldly affairs and discussed politics and finance in the Swedish Riksdag for nearly a score of years after his visions and theological writings had begun to occupy most of his time.

If the theological works of Emanuel Swedenborg at first were apt to discredit the results of his manifold scientific research in the eyes of those who did not share his theosophical views, the renown of the great religious thinker in later times has outshone the fame of which, as the versatile scholar and philosopher, he was so eminently worthy. With his younger contemporary, Charles Linnæus (or Carl von Linné), the case was different. There was in his career no radical change to divert or throw an umbrage over the fame he had won as a scientist of the very first rank.

Charles Linnæus, the most celebrated of Swedish scientists, was born at Rashult, in Smaland, in 1707. His father was a minister of a very subordinate charge of the state church. The neighborhood in which the young Linnæus grew up was not fertile, but rich in flowers, which were the toys and comrades of his childhood. He made but little progress at his work in the college of Vexio, being more fond of collecting and examining plants than of studying Greek and Latin. It was the wish of his parents that he should become a minister and the assistant of his father; but the youth had so little inclination to pursue the life or studies of a clergyman that he at last found it necessary to tell his parents so. He had found a friend and protector in Doctor Rothman, a district physician, who encouraged him to follow his ambition of becoming a naturalist and physician. Doctor Rothman supervised his studies in botany and succeeded in teaching him Latin by giving him the natural history of Pliny to study. In this manner Linnæus, who at college showed utter dislike for the classical languages, learned to write and speak Latin with ease. His teachers, who at first had advised his parents to let him quit the book, in order to take up some trade, were made aware of his gifted nature, but as he was found deficient in the regular courses, their recommendation, necessary for his admittance to the University of Lund, was very carefully worded. "The youths in our colleges may be likened unto little trees in a plant school, where it happens, although but rarely, that young trees upon which the greatest care have been lavished do not turn out well, but resemble wild stems, yet, when removed and transplanted, change their wild nature and develop into beautiful trees of agreeable fruit. Likewise, and for no other purpose, this youth is sent to the university, where he may venture into a climate favorable to his growth." There was an accurate but unconscious prophecy concealed in this beautiful "recommendation," which, curiously enough, has chosen the similes which were considered indispensable in the artificial language of the period from the world of plants, when speaking of the future flower king of the North.

The young Linnæus made his way to the university town of Southern Sweden, walking the whole distance from Vexio to Lund, with a heavy knapsack and a light pocketbook. He was in hopes to win the protection of his uncle, the influential dean of the cathedral. Upon entering Lund, he heard all church bells tolling, and, upon inquiry, learned that they rang for the funeral of his uncle, the dean! A

former teacher of his managed to have him enrolled at the
university without having to turn in the diplomatic recommendation from his college. He took his bachelor's degree
and was kindly encouraged by Professor Chilian Stobæus,
at whose house he was stopping. The mother of Stobæus
told him to look after the young man from Smaland, who
was in the habit of going to sleep with his candle left burning, thus liable to "lead the whole house into adventure."
When the learned professor looked into the matter he found
his own works in the hands of the youth, who spent his
nights reading them. After that all the books and the
heartfelt sympathy of the scholar were at the command
of Linnæus.

In 1728 Linnæus, so advised by his earliest protector,
changed his place of study to the University of Upsala,
which at the time was better equipped and provided with
a fine botanical garden. The young scholar endured a
great deal of suffering for lack of funds, his father no
longer being able to provide for his support. His diet was
very light, and he wrapped his benumbed feet in paper to
keep them from peeping out of his ragged shoes. His
father called him home to reconsider his resolution as to
a ministerial calling. Linnæus was ready to leave and
paid a farewell visit to the botanic gardens. He lingered
in melancholy thoughts before a rare flower which he intended to pluck. A harsh voice behind commanded him
to leave the flower alone. Linnæus turned and stood face
to face with the dean, Olof Celsius the Elder. In the interview which followed the young man surprised the dean,
who was an able and enthusiastic botanist, by his exceptional knowledge of plants. Celsius inquired about his
circumstances and ended by taking him into his house and

providing for his future. Shortly afterward Linnæus published a short but important treatise on the sexual life of plants, which he handed in to Professor Olof Rudbeck the Younger. This able scholar was forcibly struck by the ingenuity of the thoughts in the work, which contained the nucleus to the grand scientific system which Linnæus later developed. When, in 1730, Rudbeck obtained a vacation he had Linnæus installed as a lecturer of the botanic gardens. Shortly afterward Linnæus received the commission to pay a visit of botanic research to Lapland, on the plants of which he published a remarkable work. The journey was made on horseback, the young scholar returning deeply impressed by the grandeur of natural sceneries in the extreme North.

Linnæus had to fight poverty and adversity for some time still. His mother, who always had regretted that he should "turn out a surgeon instead of a minister," was elated over his first triumph when opening the field of a new science by his sexual system of plants. He suffered all the more at her death, which he was forced to conceal because he could not afford a mourning garb. Envious comrades put an end to his lectures at Upsala by having enforced, through petitions, an order against the filling of temporary vacancies by men who had not taken the doctor's degree. It was found necessary for Linnæus to go abroad, and some money was subscribed by his friends for that purpose. In Holland he met the learned Professor Boerhave, who, on being made acquainted with his system of botany, which Linnæus then for the first time published, received him with tokens of unlimited admiration and friendship. It was by Boerhave that the continental fame of Linnæus was founded. The latter found, in the arranging of the great gardens of Hartekamp intrusted to him, a work both agreeable and instructive. In London, Linnæus broadened his experience with study of the rich collections of plants and naturalia which were made accessible to him by the celebrated scholar Hans Sloane, later the founder of the British Museum. The letter of recommendation from Boerhave was somewhat different to the one Linnæus had received at Vexio: "Linnæus, who hands you this letter, is the only one worthy to see you, and to be seen by you. Those who see you together look upon two men the peers of which the world does hardly possess." After a stay in Paris, where the greatest scientists of France treated him with distinction, he returned to Holland, to find his friend Boerhave dying in Leyden. Linnæus kissed the hand of the dying man, who insisted on kissing the hand of Linnæus in return, pronouncing him the greater genius, of whom the world should expect and receive more.

Linnæus, the celebrated founder of a new science, returned home as an unknown man. His ability as a physician, acquired at the University of Leyden, and his growing continental fame soon made him distinguished. In 1741 he was appointed professor of medicine at Upsala, but changed chairs with the professor of botany. The study of the latter science was highly developed through the continued research of Linnæus, and became very popular, while giving a great impetus to the study of medicine. The grace and animation of Linnæus as a lecturer caused students and scholars to flock around him in hundreds. The botanic excursions led by Linnæus resembled daily marches of triumphs, the multitude of students escorting their beloved teacher back to the botanic gardens with flowers in their hats and with music of drums and French horns. Sweden, with Upsala as a centre, was for the first time in history considered a home of scientific culture, to which naturalists gathered from all parts of the world, America included. Pupils of ability and distinction were sent by Linnæus to strange and unknown quarters, from which they returned with new and unfamiliar plants, which were examined and classified by the flower king of the North. Linnæus was honored by his contemporaries in such a superlative manner as no one of his countrymen, before or after, and few other scientists of any age or country. Count Charles Gustavus Tessin has the credit of having encouraged him in his work and improved his career upon his return from the Continent. When ennobled, Linnæus changed his name to Von Linné, the earlier form being the more familiar to English readers. King Gustavus III. presented him with the estate Hammarby, where he liked to dwell, surrounded by his flowers and his family, resting from the fatigue caused by the endless stream of distinguished pilgrims who came to visit his flower court at Upsala. The offers of foreign monarchs to have him come and dwell with them were many and liberal. In 1739 he married the love of his youth, Maria Elizabeth Moræus, "and never since felt an inclination to leave Sweden."

Linnæus in many respects resembled Swedenborg, being convinced that his acceptance of truth was the correct one and disliking disputes. Like Swedenborg, he was pious, modest, benevolent and sincere. Of his own exterior and disposition Linnæus has himself given the following characteristic account: "Linnæus was not tall, not small, lean, brown-eyed, light, quick, walked briskly, did everything promptly, disliked slow people, was sensitive, easily moved, worked continuously and could not spare himself. He was fond of good food and drank good drinks, but never to excess. He cared little for exteriors, considering that man should adorn his dress and not vice versa. Faculty meetings were not his delight, or business, for he was made for quite other things, and had other things in mind than those which there were discussed and decided upon." In the preface to the late edition of his principal work, "Systema Naturæ," the following noteworthy paragraph is found: "I saw the shadow of the Supreme Being go past me, and I was seized with respect and admiration. I searched for His footsteps in the sand—what power, what wisdom! I saw how the animals existed only by means of the plants, the plants by means of the lifeless particles, and these in their turn constitute the earth. I saw the sun and stars without number hanging suspended in the air, held by the hand of the Being of beings, the artist of this grand masterpiece."

Linnæus died January 10, 1778, and was buried in the cathedral of Upsala. His botanic system has been superseded by others, but the influence that his researches and discoveries have exerted on the natural sciences and medicine, has not ceased to be benignantly felt, nor have the utmost results of his researches been as yet attained.

Andrew Celsius, professor of astronomy at Upsala, acquired fame as a writer on astronomy and was successful in his efforts to have an observatory built at the university. In 1742 he introduced his invention, the Celsius or centigrade thermometer, which is of almost indispensable practical value in all physical and chemical experiments. Olof Celsius, Senior, the able botanist, Orientalist and patron of Linnæus, was his uncle, he thus being a cousin of Olof Celsius, Junior, whose brightly written histories of

Gustavus Vasa and Eric XIV. were translated into contemporaneous French and German.

John Ahlstrœmer accomplished more for the resurrection of the downtrodden industry of his country than any one else, and therefore justly deserves the name of the Father of Swedish Industry. This man, who occupies an honored place in Swedish history, was born in 1685, of poor parents, at the town of Alingsos, in West Gothland, his original name being John Toresson. He worked himself up in various mercantile positions in Stockholm and other towns, later coming to London, where he engaged in business of his own and became an English citizen. He saw with regret that his countrymen sent their money abroad to obtain articles which they could manufacture at home, and was seized with the ambition to introduce into Sweden the industries which constitute the foundation of England's mercantile wealth.

When Charles XII. returned to Sweden, Ahlstrœmer went there also, trying to win the king to his industrial plans. He did not succeed, but found in Christopher Polhem a man who listened to and appreciated them. Ahlstrœmer intended to return to England, but was captured by the Danes during the journey. On account of his English citizenship he soon regained his liberty, visiting England and the Continent, and carefully selecting everything which he had in view of sending to Sweden as the requisite instruments for his plans. This work sometimes involved great danger, as the buying of looms for hose and ribbon, fulling vats, dyes, etc.; for the great manufacturing countries were keeping jealous watch that the secrets of their industries should not become known abroad. In a town in Holland, Ahlstrœmer barely missed being pelted with stones by the mob. Pursued by the revenue authorities, he managed to escape with his ship, arriving safely in Gothenburg with the valuable cargo and skilled laborers in his employ. Shortly afterward he arrived in his native town of Alingsos, where the industrial enterprises were established. The Riksdag at first was unwilling to grant him the necessary concessions, the clergy especially being averse to allow so many foreign workingmen free confession of their Catholic religion. In 1724 the concessions were at last obtained, and Ahlstrœmer began his course, which he was resolved should result in the fostering of the same industrial activity in his impoverished country, which he, with surprise, had noticed in England and on the Continent.

In establishing his enterprises, Ahlstrœmer exhausted his resources, and when he tried to form a company to keep them going he was met with stubborn resistance, caused by ignorance and jealousy. He succeeded at last in obtaining the financial backing of some wealthy mine owners of Vermland, who took shares in his enterprises. The Riksdag of 1726 encouraged him by placing high protective or prohibitive tariffs on foreign articles which could be produced in the country. In the following year King Frederic paid a visit to Alingsos, spending a whole day in looking over the mills and factories. The king said that he would rather own the stock of goods of Ahlstrœmer than the largest arsenal in his kingdom, and saw to it that his servants were dressed in broadcloth manufactured at Alingsos.

Alingsos saw its population suddenly increase from 300 to 1,800 and entered upon an era of prosperity. Ahlstrœmer's factories formed almost a little town of their own beside the older one. There were twelve looms for the manufacturing of broadcloth, forty-five looms for wool, and, besides, cotton mills, dye works for wool and silk, hose factories, an English tannery and various other industrial works. Also a foundry, with eight communicating shops, where all kinds of household articles of simple and composite metals were manufactured. Alingsos was made a kind of normal school of industry for the whole country. The foreign master workmen, who at the beginning had charge of the factories, instructed in time a great number of native apprentices, who later found employment elsewhere, thus distributing to various parts the experience obtained at Alingsos. Wool was the principal material in the factories, and in order to obtain a refined quality, Ahlstrœmer imported stocks of foreign breeds. He commenced with English sheep, the Riksdag of 1727 granting him the use of the royal estate Hœjentorp for the purpose. Angora goats were later imported and seemed to thrive.

Ahlstrœmer did his country a great service by introducing the cultivation of potatoes. The first shipment of this useful plant arrived in 1723, with workingmen imported from France. As soon as the plant was seen to stand the climate, larger quantities were sent for. Potatoes were cultivated in the vast fields around Alingsos at a period when they were exhibited in the botanic gardens of the Continent as rare plants from Peru. Prejudice at first interfered, but when the soldiers returned home from Pomerania with the habit of eating potatoes, and planted such around their cottages, the popularity of the Peruvian plant was assured. Ahlstrœmer also introduced the cultivation of tobacco and several dye plants. The coal mines, near Helsingborg, in Scania, commenced to be operated at his instigation. When the Academy of Science was instituted, in 1739, Ahlstrœmer was made one of its members. The Academy of Science served originally and in that era of utilitarianism a more practical purpose than later. The Cap administration of Arvid Horn gave comparatively little attention to the enterprises of Ahlstrœmer, having more in view to develop agriculture than industry. When the Hats got into power the conditions were reversed. Count Charles Gyllenborg, the successor of Arvid Horn as president of the chancery, in order to set a good example, always dressed in broadcloth of Swedish manufacture. Ahlstrœmer was made a councillor of commerce, and ennobled, while his bust was placed in the Exchange of Stockholm and medals issued in his honor by the Academy of Science.

Ahlstrœmer was a middle-sized man of a strong constitution. He was amiable, courteous and hospitable, ever ready to conduct visitors through his factories and warehouses. His energy was as great as his kindness, and he refused to recognize an enemy in anybody. The large profits of his plants he mostly spent on other patriotic enterprises, leaving hardly any other inheritance to his sons than an excellent education. During the last few years of his life he suffered the consequences of a stroke of paralysis. He died in 1761, and thus was saved from witnessing the destruction which was caused to the new factory industry and his own works at Alingsos by the reckless policy of the new Caps.

Olof Dalin is the principal poet and writer of the Period of Liberty, strongly influencing not only the creative minds of his own day, but also those who with more or less right have been counted as belonging to the Gustavian Period. Dalin was the son of a minister in the province of Halland and a relative of Professor Andrew Rydelius of Lund, a historian of the older generation, who conducted the course of his studies. He came to Stockholm in 1726, where several positions in various state departments afforded opportunity for study in libraries and archives. Dalin, from the year 1732 to 1734, published a magazine called "The Swedish Argus," which, with the English "Spectator" as a pattern, contained articles on public and individual morals, with allusions to the facts of contemporary life. This publication caused a great stir and became very popular on account of the acute logic and excellent language of its editor. Dalin was appointed royal librarian by the Riksdag, and, on the recommendation of Count Tessin, teacher to the young crown prince Gustavus.

Dalin was an enthusiastic admirer of the glorious epoch of Swedish history and of the character of Charles XII., which caused him to join the party of the Hats. When the latter utterly failed in their attempts to restore the political grandeur of the past, and Dalin witnessed the excesses of the rivalling parties, he joined the secret agitators for an increased royal power. In the literary and artistic circle of the brilliant Queen Louise Ulrica, Dalin was the leading spirit. He was not unaware of the conspiracies and intrigues of the queen, and is supposed to have been the author of several of the sharp notes which the king added to the records of the state council. The Hats, who took offence at his sharp satires, made him resign from his position as the teacher of the crown prince. After the conspiracy of the court party was detected, Dalin was called before a committee of the Estates and by order dismissed from the court. Dalin used the time of his compulsory isolation for the writing of a history of Sweden. This work, which never was carried further than to the end of the Period of Reformation, is characterized by an attractive style, but is not reliable as to facts.

Dalin was allowed to return to the court in 1761. He stood in great favor and was covered with testimonials of appreciation. He died in 1763, at the moment when King Adolphus Frederic was resolved to make him a state councillor. Dalin was the first writer who made Swedish history popular, and exerted, by his poems and his magazine, and by his education of Gustavus III., a considerable influence upon the history of his own time.

In point of scientific research the historical works of Sven Lagerbring have a much higher value than Dalin's history, although they lacked the literary excellence of the latter. Lagerbring, who, born in Scania, was professor of history at the University of Lund, carried his work to the times of Charles VIII. A shorter history of his was translated into French and long formed the chief source of continental knowledge of Swedish history.

As a poet Dalin had a rival in the somewhat younger Hedvig Charlotta Nordenflycht, one of the most interesting characters in Swedish history of literature. Her works, chiefly consisting of lyrics and idyls, show a long chain of development from the taste of the Carolinian period to that of the Gustavian epoch. In her deep emotional nature and enthusiasm for all cultural movements she stands without a rival. Receiving an annuity from the government, she was after many adversities able to maintain a literary salon. The men who met there, like Gustavus Philip Creutz and Gustavus Frederic Gyllenborg, were the founders of an academic style in poetry, as was Charles Gustavus Tessin in eloquence.

John Ihre is perhaps the most highly gifted of Swedish

philologists and the first whose research had a lasting scientific value. He stood at the summit of contemporary European study of language, and rose a head or more higher than the philologists of his own country in that day. The period was characterized by a movement for the purification and analyzation of the language, Dalin expressing his wish to speak the truth to the Swedes in pure Swedish, and the Academy of Science taking pride in publishing their important papers in the mother tongue. Eric Benzelius, an able critic of the Gothic, and interested in Swedish dialect research, was one of the precursors of Ihre; and so was Olof Celsius, Senior, professor of Greek, later of Oriental languages, who was the first to fix the age of the majority of Runic inscriptions as dating from the Christian era.

John Ihre was born, in 1707, in Lund, where his father was a professor of theology, a talented, witty and learned man. The young Ihre lost his father in 1720, after which time his uncle, Archbishop Steuchius of Upsala, had charge of his education. He later studied modern languages at the University of Jena, made the acquaintance of the contemporary philologists of Holland, and also studied at the universities of London, Oxford and Paris. After an absence of three years he returned, soon to be connected with the University of Upsala, where he remained for forty-two years as professor of rhetoric and politics. Ihre was a liberal, outspoken man, who was severely censured for his opinions upon political and religious subjects, once by the Riksdag being sentenced to pay fines and receiving a warning from the chancellor of the university. When the clergy upon another occasion warned the philosophers not to mix in theological subjects, Ihre defended himself in the following terms in a letter to the chancellor, Count Charles Gustavus Tessin.

"Gracious lord! I teach *eloquentiam*, *politicam* and the states, with all things pertaining to them. To become a heretic I possess neither genius nor stupidity enough, less an evil purpose. Therefore I am willing to forego all theology, if only an allowance of it be made large enough for my private practice and edification in Christianity. I never intended to go any further."

Ihre left religion and politics alone, and received many high distinctions in return for his great scientific merits. When ennobled, he kept his old family name, stating that he was "somewhat known abroad under the name of Ihre," while if he changed it to Gyllenbiorn or Vargstierna, it would take "some time to announce this new disguise." He was renowned for his ready wit, and wielded a considerable influence in academic circles. Ihre was satisfied with his position and his science, and was not willing to exchange them for a political career.

Ihre was led to the study of the Teutonic languages in their oldest forms by his desire to find a consistent spelling and correct understanding of the words in his own language. He was desirous of freeing it from foreign words, but only when those substituted were as expressive and comprehensible as the old. Ihre was a pioneer in the field of dialect lexicographers, publishing the outline of a Swedish dialect dictionary in 1766, and wrote a number of works pertaining to the historic forms of Gothic, Lappish, Finnish and Old Norse. Special importance is due to his epoch-making research concerning the language of the Codex Argenteus. He once for all settled the controversy, proving the Codex to contain the Gothic Bible translation of Bishop Wulfila against the assertions of M. Lacroze of Berlin, who claimed that it was written in Frankish. In regard to the

Edda of Snorre Sturleson, he declared it to be intended as
an introductory study of poesy, a handbook of poetics for
young scalds, an opinion which has been fully established
in a much later time. By these and other theories Ihre
attained a much higher standpoint as a scientific critic than
his contemporaries. He spoke of the resemblance between
the Teutonic and the classical languages, without being able
to find the reasons. He even to some extent anticipated the
great discovery which after its formulator has been called
Grimm's Law, by pointing out "a certain regularity of con-
sonant shift" in the Teutonic languages.

The monumental work of Ihre and the crowning effort
of his life was prepared between the years 1750–1759. This
Glossarium suiogothicum, published at the expense of the
government, is the best Swedish dictionary of the eighteenth century. Ihre by his severe critical method kills
the wild etymologies of the "Rudbeckian philology," turning
to Old Swedish for the derivations, and, where this gave
no satisfaction, to the Old Icelandic, "because this language
nine hundred years ago was separated from our own and
has remained undisturbed by foreign influence." From the
Old Northern dialects he turned to Old High German, Old
English and Gothic, the last mentioned of which he considered the mother of the Teutonic languages. Many of
Ihre's etymologies have not been able to withstand the
scrutiny of later criticism, but his great etymological dictionary is the product of versatile knowledge and unusual
insight, and has not only exerted a profound influence upon
his own period but also served as a model for later epochs
of philological research.

CHAPTER XV

Gustavian Period—Gustavus III. and Gustavus IV. Adolphus

GUSTAVUS III., with his brilliant endowment, one of the most illustrious, and, in spite of his glaring faults, one of the most beloved, of Swedish monarchs, was the first king since Charles XII. who was born in Sweden. For this very reason, and on account of his amiable and charming disposition, he had won for himself the sympathy of the people even before his succession to the throne. This nephew of Frederic the Great of Prussia had inherited the genius, ambition and pride of his gifted mother, all enlarged and intensified, and the gentleness and good nature of his father. He was in every particular a child of his time, and every inch a king. Gustavus was decidedly French in education, taste and superficiality, but had by his first teacher Dalin been inspired with a deep love of his country, its history, language and traditions. He handled the Swedish and French languages with equal skill, and a more eloquent monarch has never graced a throne. He was passionately fond of theatricals and impressive ceremony, and, like his mother and illustrious uncle, he surrounded himself with men of genius. Gustavus was betrothed to Princess Sophie Magdalene of Denmark when only four years of age, and married her when twenty. This union was arranged by the Riksdag, contrary to the wish of Gustavus's parents. Gustavus appeared at first to be deeply in love with the gentle and unpretentious princess, but she soon found herself as neglected by her consort as she was detested by his mother. The crown prince early began to hate the form of government which had brought so much humiliation to his parents. This absolutism of the Riksdag, which could be bought and sold through bribery by foreign powers, he considered dangerous to the independence and welfare of the country, and was resolved to change the balance of power to the hands of the king, of whose dignity and importance he held an exalted opinion.

At the death of his father, Gustavus was in France, returning with the agreement of a secret alliance. At the Riksdag of 1771, where the Caps once more came into power, Gustavus III. signed a pledge with new restrictions of the royal authority. But while the king officially seemed to desire a pacification of both parties, and his time was principally occupied with theatricals, embroideries and costumes, he was secretly arranging a conspiracy. He was crowned in May, 1772, and in August the news of a revolt in Scania, led by John Christian Toll, reached the capital. The king feigned surprise, but waited for similar news from Finland, whence Jacob Magnus Sprengtporten was to bring troops to Stockholm. As Sprengtporten's movements were somewhat delayed, the king had to take action himself. In the morning of August 19th he entered the officers' hall of the body-guards, where he delivered a patriotic address, asking the officers to follow him as their ancestors had followed Gustavus Vasa and Gustavus Adolphus. He was greeted with an enthusiasm which soon spread throughout the capital, assuring the king of perfect loyalty. The state councillors were quickly arrested and order given that no one should be allowed to leave the capital. The Riksdag was called together August 21st, and addressed by the king in an eloquent speech which gave a striking view of the situation and its perils. He declared that he was not going to touch liberty, only to abolish misrule by the establishment of a firm administration. Then was read the proposition for a constitution which the king had prepared. The king alone was to be the executive, appointing higher officials and councillors, making alliances with foreign powers, but not commencing any war of attack without the consent of the Riksdag. The state council was to consist of seventeen members with deliberative, but no executive, power. The Riksdag was to convene at the order of the king, taxation and legislation to be decided on by the king and Riksdag in common. The judicial power of all committees was to be abolished. The Riksdag accepted the royal propositions, and one of the most smoothly and skilfully managed *coups d'état* ever attempted was accomplished, much to the dismay of Russia, Prussia and Denmark. During half a score of years the country enjoyed a happy peace, the king winning the love of his people and being active in administrative improvements.

Gustavus III. was intensely interested in literature and art, and a writer of considerable ability, composing dramatic works of French pattern but with patriotic subjects. In his best creations he is influenced by Shakespeare. Among the poets whom he encouraged were Kellgren, Leopold, Creutz, Gyllenborg, Oxenstierna, Adlerbeth, the creators of a classical school of Swedish poetry and drama, influenced by the contemporary French writers. Above these towers Charles Michael Bellman, who, with his composite and rich endowment, became the first great national poet, and of an originality as remarkable as that of any genius in the literature of the world. The humor introduced into Swedish literature through the contact with the songs of the Edda, in Bellman reaches its perfection, while his poetry in exquisite and triumphant grace of form outrivals that of his classical contemporaries. His poems were almost all produced under the inspiration of the moment, even if later remodelled, and sung to the lute to melodies of the day, or of his own composition. His impressionistic power of description leads the thought to the modern artists, while his ambition to unite the arts of poetry, music and plastics makes him a precursor of Neo-Romanticism. There is not one accent of chauvinism, not even a note of patriotism, in his songs, yet he is the most beloved of Swedish poets, recognized as the highest exponent of the lyrico-rhetorical temperament of his people, a mixture of melancholy humor and exuberant joy in a graceful yet stately form. Anne Marie Lenngren was a highly talented poetess, who preserves the classic form for her verse, in which she ridicules the faults and vices of her period. Thorild and Lidner were men of great genius, but of somewhat bizarre and neglected literary form, influenced by contemporary Romanticism in Germany. Sweden continues to add a number of names to the galaxy of men distinguished in the service of natural science, those of Bergman and Scheele, the founders of modern chemistry, being the most renowned. To the Academy of Science and Academy of Art, established during the Period of Liberty, Gustavus added a Swedish Academy and a National Theatre for the encouragement of poetry, eloquence, music and drama. It is during this period that the Swedish language developed the beauty and plasticity for which it holds the first rank among Teutonic dialects, and is considered one of the most musical languages of the world. Of artists, the painters Hœrberg, Hillestrœm and Roslin rose to great continental fame, while Sergel, through the genius and tendencies of his works one of the most remarkable sculptors of modern times, won renown for his name, but hardly the very highest perfection within his possibilities. His statue of Gustavus III. is the finest monument of Stockholm.

Sweden, so rich in great poets, artists and scientists, is poor in philosophers, content with the systems of thinkers in more favored countries. Swedenborg is an important exception to this rule. Not satisfied with an original system, with pure reason as the fundamental principle, he divined a system in which philosophy and religion are inseparably united. Kant, when made acquainted with Swedenborg's earlier system, was utterly astonished, expressing fear that he himself had been an object of thought-transference, when writing his celebrated work, "Kritik der reinen Vernunft." The system of Descartes was followed by Swedish philosophers of the Carolinian epoch. During the Period of Liberty and the reign of Gustavus III., Locke, Voltaire and Diderot were supreme. At the close of the eighteenth century, Kant began to exert great influence, Benjamin Hœijer being his talented and individualistic disciple, and enjoying the reputation of having been Sweden's greatest original thinker. Charles August Ehrensverd, an able warrior and statesman of the Gustavian epoch, devised an attractive and novel, although slightly dilettantic, system of his own, the Philosophy of Fine Arts.

The suspicions that Gustavus III. was not satisfied with the share of power which he obtained in 1772, and that he was anxious to gain fame by the means of war, were found to be justified. In 1786 he called a Riksdag, at which most of his propositions, to his great surprise, were stubbornly opposed. Catherine II. of Russia was intriguing with the Finnish nobles for the purpose of establishing the independence of Finland under Russian protection. But she was careful not to commence hostilities. Attempts made by Gustavus III. to bring the Norwegian people in revolt against Denmark failed. And so Gustavus, who had no authority to begin a war of attack, arranged for a simulated Russian assault on the Finnish boundary, executed by Finnish peasants in disguise. He declared war on Russia, in June, 1788, although nobody was found willing to believe in the feigned cause of it. The actual hostilities were opened by a brilliant naval battle at Hogland, fought with success by the Swedish fleet under command of Prince Charles, the brother of the king, against the Russians. The king had arrived in Finland resolved to attack St. Petersburg, which plan he was obliged to change. All further operations came to a sudden standstill through mutiny among the Finnish officers in the royal camp at Anjala, 113 of them signing a document in which they pledged themselves to force the king to make peace and to convoke the Riksdag. Another document offering peace and a union of Finland to Russia was despatched to St. Petersburg with Jægerhorn, one of the leaders. The officers received a favorable answer from Russia, which was handed to the king, and the whole army was made acquainted with the proceedings. The king found himself in a most perilous position, out of which he was saved as by a miracle. Denmark declared war, and the king hastened to embrace the opportunity to leave with honor the trap in which his life and liberty were in danger.

Gustavus III. sent word to several provinces, asking the inhabitants to rise in defence of their country. He went himself to Dalecarlia, where he addressed the peasants when coming from church, as had Gustavus Vasa. Everywhere the population rose in arms. The king hastened to Gothenburg, which was threatened by the Danes, and had the city strongly fortified. England and Prussia sided with Sweden, and the Danes found it best to retire from Swedish territory.

Gustavus had won the game. Now for the stakes! He called a Riksdag in 1789. Through his personal courage and patriotism, Gustavus III. had recaptured the love of his people. The nobility was hated and despised on account of its responsibility for the mutiny at Anjala and for its intrigues with Russia. Gustavus III. consequently stood exceedingly well with the three lower Estates of the Riksdag, but lost their respect through the many violations of the law which he committed in forcing upon the Riksdag a new constitution which made him a ruler with almost absolute power. The nobility stubbornly refused to accept any change in the constitution. There were many stormy scenes, both among the nobles and in the presence of the king, who also paid a visit to the Riddarhus, which he left with the statement that the nobles were willing to subscribe, the latter loudly protesting. Axel von Fersen the Elder and several other aristocratic leaders were held in a prolonged arrest. Archbishop Troil told the king that he did not wish to be the first archbishop after Gustavus Trolle to sell the liberty of his country, and begged to be excused from being present at the deliberations. The poet and royal favorite

Adlerbeth, himself a nobleman, pleaded in the Riksdag the right of his Estate to take action on the royal propositions. These were in private signed by the speakers of the four Estates and pronounced by the government as accepted, and were called an "Act of Union and Security." This new constitution gave almost absolute power to the king. The state council was once more, and forever, swept away and not even mentioned in the constitution. It was divided into a supreme court and a department for "the preparation of public affairs." By taking half of their members only from the nobility, the greatest privilege of that class was annulled. To the peasants was extended the privilege of buying land originally belonging to the nobility. By hard pressure, and in opposition to the nobles, the king forced the Riksdag to take the responsibility for the state debt, which had increased considerably.

Gustavus III. opened the Riksdag as the most popular man of the country. He closed it as an absolute sovereign who had lost the love of his people and aroused the revengeful hatred of the nobility. Gustavus III. was now enabled to continue the Russian war at will. His sub-commander Stedingk won a victory over the Russians at Porosalmi, the latter being led by Sprengtporten, the former supporter of Gustavus III., now a soldier of Empress Catherine. He was killed in the battle. Prince Charles won a victory at Œland, but was by negligence of his sub-commander detained from reaping its benefits. Charles August Ehrensverd defeated a superior Russian naval force at Svensksund with the "Skerry Fleet," the creation of his father, Augustinus Ehrensverd. At the order of the king, he then met a still larger fleet and was defeated. Dissatisfied with the king and the result, the valiant hero and philosopher made his report in the following laconic phrase: "Your majesty has no longer any Skerry Fleet," and resigned from his position as admiral-general. In the following year, 1780, the combined naval forces of Sweden were shut up by the Russian fleet in the bay of Viborg, and seemed doomed to destruction. But the king gave orders that all the ships should force a passage, and this heroic effort was successfully made, through the lines of colossal Russian warships chained together. The Russian losses were great, and also those of the Swedes, on account of an explosion on board one of the ships. The Russians were anxious to gain the victory that escaped them at Viborg, and decided on July 9th, the day of Empress Catherine's coronation, as an appropriate date. The battle was fought at Svensksund, and turned into a humiliating defeat, the Russians losing 53 ships, 643 cannon and 14,000 men, and the imperial flag of state; twenty-six of these ships were entered in the Swedish navy. Peace was made at Værælæ a month later. No change of territory was involved, but an end was put to Russian intrigues, and Sweden had once more and forever demonstrated her power of taking care of her independence.

The revolution in France made a deep impression upon the factions which in Sweden were secretly continuing their struggle. The nobility, in their aristocratic republicanism, sided with the revolutionists, while the king, an intimate friend of Louis XVI., tried to save the monarchy. Gustavus III. left Sweden in the summer of 1791, in order to receive Louis XVI. and his family at the frontier, while Count Axel von Fersen the Younger, a son of the old aristocratic party leader who had taken part with distinction in the American revolutionary war, was very near to saving the royal family through a flight from Paris. King

Gustavus III. waited in vain for the royal fugitives, but commenced active operations for the forming of an alliance between Sweden, Russia, Prussia, Austria and Spain against republican France. Sweden and Russia made a treaty of mutual defence, but the negotiations for a general alliance were not at a favorable point when Gustavus III. himself fell by the aristocratic republicans of his own country.

A conspiracy between the nobles had been formed, the majority being men of the highest station. Jacob John Anckarstrom, a retired officer, was found willing to commit the deed of killing the hated despot. After several unsuccessful attempts, the act was accomplished at a mask ball in the Royal Opera, the king being shot through the hip. All of the accomplices present were arrested, and, much to their disappointment, the king not dying instantly, their plan for a revolution was thus frustrated. Gustavus III. was shot March 16, 1792, and died March 26, 1792, suffering his fate with fortitude and great presence of mind. He appointed his brother Charles and his favorite, Charles Gustavus Armfelt, members of the government during the minority of his son, Gustavus Adolphus.

The devotion of his country returned to Gustavus III. at his deathbed, never to leave him. In spite of his superficiality, violation of the law, disregard for a constitutional government, and adventurous and expensive wars, solid reasons remain to love and respect his memory. His noble patriotism, frank heroism, brilliant genius and great generosity are worthy of high praise. His revolution of 1789 brought disastrous consequences, but he furthered the progress of democracy by annihilation of the aristocratic republic and saved his country from the tragic fate of

Poland. Even if the Period of Liberty is to be credited for a great deal of the cultural development during his reign, Gustavus has a large share therein, and Esaias Tegnér is right in his eulogy when he says:

> "There rests o'er Gustav's days a golden shimmer,
> Fantastic, foreign, frivolous, if you please;
> But why complain when *sunshine* caused the glamour?
> Where stood we now if it were not for these?
> All culture on an unfree ground is builded,
> And barbarous once the base of patriotism true;
> But wit was planted, iron-hard language welded,
> The song was raised, life more enjoyed and shielded,
> And what Gustavian was, is, therefore, Swedish too."

In the mixture of patriotism and unreserved cosmopolitanism, true genius and superficiality, earnestness and recklessness in the character of Gustavus III., the Swedes have recognized peculiarities of their own national temperament, for which they are tempted to love him as dearly, although not considering him to be as great, as his two predecessors and namesakes on the Swedish throne. By his eloquence, wit and amiability, his personality charmed even his enemies. In contrast to the sombre autocrats of the Barocco period, Gustavus III. was a typical Rococo monarch, and he tried to give the charms and grace of the Rococo epoch to his surroundings. In appearance, he was of middle size, slender and graceful, with a face which bespoke genius, and eyes of unusual size and brilliancy.

Gustavus IV. Adolphus was a boy of thirteen at the death of his father. His uncle, Prince Charles, was regent in name, but Baron Reuterholm, the latter's favorite, was the real head of the government. Compared to the eccentric but energetic, generous and liberal despotism of Gustavus III., Reuterholm's was a rule of pettiness, incapability, revenge and hypocrisy. Prince Charles was a good soldier, but early lost all energy through dissipation and a natural tendency to mysticism, secrecy and simulation. Reuterholm was a good worker, but of no ability as a statesman, sharing and increasing the love of mysticism and superstition characteristic of his master. The new policy was to estrange the friends and favorites of Gustavus III. as much as possible, they all being sent away under various pretexts. Prince Charles had from the start declared invalid the postscript of the king's will, according to which Count Armfelt was to take part in the government. Later a conspiracy, with Armfelt as the leader, was detected, when he, who was abroad and later entered Russian service, was declared to have forfeited his property, rank and life. A young woman, Lady Madelaine Rudenschiold, who was one of the conspirators, was punished by being exhibited to the mob on the place of execution and afterward imprisoned.

Prince Charles was criticised for the leniency shown toward his brother's murderers, perhaps without justice, for the dying king had pleaded clemency in their behalf. Only Anckarstrom was executed, the other conspirators all receiving surprisingly mild sentences. This was contrasted to the petty and revengeful hatred shown the opponents of the new government, and one now recalled the fact that Gustavus III. in his last moments had refused to see the prince. That Charles also had aspirations of his own seems evident from the fact that he had the young king examined by physicians, raising doubt as to his physical and mental fitness to ever take a hand in the government.

Reuterholm made himself hated and ridiculous by his

pettiness. Thus restrictions were placed on extravagance in food and clothing, the use of coffee for some time being entirely prohibited. The Swedish Academy was disbanded because it did not make Reuterholm a member. The liberty of the press was extended and then suddenly restricted. Thorild, the writer and poet, was exiled for agitation against the old division of the Riksdag into four houses, "because its four Estates always have been bringing about one unsettled state." Characteristic of the opinion of Reuterholm's administration are the words which the warrior and philosopher, Charles August Ehrensverd, gave him in the course of a quarrel between the two: "Monsieur is ambitious to govern, but monsieur does not know how." The best things accomplished during this period were the establishment of a military academy at Carlberg, and improvements of the Bible translation and the ritual and hymn-book of the church.

The attitude toward France was changed with the change of government, Sweden being the first power to recognize the French republic. With that country and Denmark close intimacy was formed, which enraged Russia and England. In order to pacify the empress, old negotiations for a marriage between King Gustavus Adolphus and Alexandra, a niece of Empress Catherine II., were reopened and a decision reached. The king left for St. Petersburg. When the great ceremony was to take place, the empress sat there waiting with her brilliant court for several hours. No Gustavus Adolphus appeared. In the last moment he had been asked by a priest to grant his future consort, Alexandra, liberty to practice her Greek Catholic faith in public, which he refused to do, thus dropping the whole matter. The indignant empress was suddenly taken ill and died a few weeks later. Soon afterward the king married the beautiful princess Frederica of Bade.

Gustavus IV. Adolphus was declared of age and took charge of the government when eighteen (in 1796). Reuterholm was dismissed, and Prince Charles retired. The king surrounded himself with the friends of his father, Armfelt and Toll being recalled, the latter taking excellent care of foreign affairs, as far as his authority went. But Gustavus IV. ruled alone, without favorites or influential advisers. This was most unfortunate, for he was entirely without the gifts of a regent. He was a lover of order, economy, justice and pure morals, but through lack of mental and physical strength his good qualities were misdirected. His father's tragic fate had a sinister influence upon his mind, the equilibrium of which was shaken also by the outrages of the revolutionists in France. Of a morbid sensibility, and without inclination to confide in any one, his religious mysticism led him into a state close to insanity. He imagined himself to be a reincarnation of Charles XII., while in Napoleon he recognized the monster of the Apocalypse, which he himself was sent to fight and conquer.

Gustavus IV. went to an extreme in his fear of liberal movements, placing severe censorship on the periodical press, book market and universities. Benjamin Hœijer, the great philosopher, for some time left his chair at Upsala and the country. A man who was resolved to "go even to the doors of hell in search of truth" could not be in sympathy with the bigot despot. Hard times, produced by failure of crops and fisheries, and by maritime losses during the war between England and France, threw added umbrage over the reign of Gustavus IV. He convoked a Riksdag, in 1800, in order to raise money to cover the debts involved by his predecessor. He never repeated the experiment. The nobles sanctioned the absolute rule, but stormy sessions ensued over the royal propositions, six nobles resigning from titles and privileges, six others their seats in the Riksdag. The peasants, almost as unyielding, were pacified by Toll. By his own authority, the king mortgaged the Swedish city of Wismar, in Mecklenburg, to the ruler of said duchy for a period of one hundred years, in receipt for a sum of some two million dollars.

There was no question in which the insanity of the king became more apparent or disastrous than in his foreign policy. An alliance of armed neutrality between Sweden, Russia and Denmark came to naught through the inactivity of Gustavus IV., and he stubbornly refused to accept the repeated offers of Napoleon of an alliance with France in the combat with the powers. Things took a sinister aspect when an intimate alliance was effected between Napoleon and Alexander of Russia, in 1807. Napoleon had lost patience with the lunatic king, and tried to call forth a catastrophe by urging Alexander to capture Finland, which he at first was unwilling to do. The French invaded Swedish Pomerania, and Toll was able to save the little Swedish army of 10,000 only by means of a most skilful diplomacy. Denmark, attacked by England, declared war against Sweden. Gustavus IV. made great preparations, sending Armfelt with one army to the Norwegian frontier and Toll with another to Scania. The regular army counted 100,000 men, and a great force of militia was organized. But through gross incapability of the government the majority of troops were never used, the militia suffering immensely through neglect and hunger.

Czar Alexander at last decided to capture Finland. He

called it himself an act of bad faith and treason against a relative and ally, and in a treacherous way he carried on his preparations. The Swedish ambassador was misled as to the object of the latter, and when informed received exaggerated accounts as to the force which was to invade Finland. Gustavus IV. was alarmed and gave the old and incapable field-marshal, Klingspor, appointed to command the army in Finland, directions to save his troops in the best way possible. And so commenced, in February, 1808, the war which after a heroic struggle was to separate the Finns from their Swedish brethren. Not only were the Finnish troops possessed of the noblest patriotic spirit, but they had also courageous and distinguished commanders, who, if duly supported and intrusted with more authority, would probably have been able to ward off the attack. Conspicuous among the latter were C. J. Adlercreutz, born in Finland, the hero of Siikajoki, Lappo and Oravais; G. C. von Dœbeln, the victor of Juutas, and J. A. Sandels, the hero of Pulkkila, Indensalmi and Virta, all three of them veterans from the war of Gustavus III.

The aged General Klercker commanded a Finnish army at Tavastehus, where Klingspor arrived with his royal orders, which were for retreat and evacuation of the country. The troops were deprived of their hopes of a battle and forced to make a retreat of nearly 600 miles, suffering from cold and hunger. The retreat continued without interruption for two months, until the army, in April, found itself between Brahestad and Uleoborg. A battle was fought at Siikajoki, April 18th, the sub-commander, General Adlercreutz, receiving instructions to make a stand against the enemy until the safety of the army supplies could be insured. After five hours of fighting, the Finns won a glorious victory over the Russians. But royal orders for a continued retreat arrived, and the Russians took possession of Siikajoki.

As long as Sveaborg, the Gibraltar of the North, was safe, the final outcome of the struggle must remain undecided. Sveaborg, the creation of Augustinus Ehrensverd, is situated on seven islets and consists of several strong works partly cut out of the rock and in an admirable way protecting and supplementing each other. The fortress was defended by 6,000 men, with 1,000 cannon and ample provisions of all kinds; in the harbor a division of the Swedish navy was at anchor. Olof Cronstedt, the commander, was dissatisfied with the king and a secret supporter of Prince Charles. His sub-commander, Jægerhorn, a brother of the leader of the Conspiracy of Anjala, was a traitor, probably in understanding with the Russians even before the war. A little army of 4,000 Russians under the command of Van Suchtelen was sent against Sveaborg. This force was too small to make a serious attack; it was not able to capture any of the fortifications; the naked rocks made it impossible to build any earthworks. What the Russians could not effect by force they accomplished by treachery, winning over the commanding officers of Sveaborg through threats and promises. When the Swedish and Finnish soldiers saw the queer behavior of their officers they planned a mutiny; but this was not carried out on account of lack of leadership. The officers tried by the most shameful lies to pacify the soldiers, Jægerhorn taking the leading part in these proceedings. Sveaborg surrendered May 3d, all Swedes being made prisoners of war, but the Finns given free leave. When the troops saw the small force of Russians and their miserable equipment, they were enraged, breaking their weapons and tearing their banners to pieces. Cronstedt, Jægerhorn and the other commanding officers became Russian citizens, and received high outward distinctions; but by both Russians and Finns they were ever treated with cold contempt on account of their shameless treason.

With the fall of Sveaborg, all hope of saving Finland was lost. In the summer of 1808, her army fought several glorious battles under the command of Adlercreutz, Dœbeln and Sandels, but in the autumn it was attacked by a superior Russian force and was nearly closed in between Old Carleby and Vasa. Gripenberg stood with one division at Old Carleby, furthest to the north, Dœbeln lay prostrated by illness at New Carleby, and Adlercreutz stood with the central body of troops at Oravais, about twenty miles south from the latter town. The Russian army attacked the force which was with Dœbeln, resolved to cut off Adlercreutz from a retreat. One attack was already made at Juutas, near New Carleby, when Dœbeln, alarmed by the news and heedless of his serious illness, was seen approaching. His men received him with enthusiasm, collected their scattering forces and proved victorious over the attacking enemy. The Russians retreated and Adlercreutz was saved.

The famous battle of Oravais was fought the following day, September 14th. The Swedish army was arranged on a promontory in the sea, with artillery on a hill to the north, close to which a detachment of the regiment of Helsingland was arranged in an excellent position. Another detachment of the same regiment was by a little brook at the south base of the promontory, with two cannon, under the command of Count William von Schwerin, a boy of sixteen years. At this latter point the battle was begun at five o'clock in the morning. The Russians, 8,000 strong, with twenty cannon and commanded by Kamenski, approached a bridge leading over the brook. The 400 Swedes offered a plucky resistance to the overwhelming force. Every time the bridge was filled by Russians, Schwerin swept it clear with the fire from his two cannon. This heroic struggle was kept up for four hours, when the Helsings had no more cartridges for their guns wherewith to support the artillery fire. The aide-de-camp Biornstierna, who was despatched thither by Adlercreutz, saw a pitiable sight. Most of the officers of the 400 Swedes were killed and the Russians were storming across the bridge in heavy masses. "Now, count," cried Biornstierna, "let us see what your artillery amounts to!" Schwerin let the Russians approach until only fifty feet from the cannon, when he ordered: "Fire!" The whole first line of the Russian column fell. Schwerin gave command to have the cannon dragged a hundred yards back and then fired, with the same disastrous effect. Thus the retreat was made from hill to hill. At last the young hero received a mortal wound and his men were surrounded on every side. With a final effort he rose to his feet, broke through the lines with his valiant Helsings, and died in the midst of the Swedish troops.

Adlercreutz closely watched the movements of the Russians, and saw an opportunity to break through their centre, which was successfully done, the enemy turning into flight. It looked like an overwhelming defeat for the Russians, when reinforcements arrived in the last moment, and the exhausted Swedes had to stop fighting on account of the darkness of the night. After a battle of fifteen hours the Swedes had lost 2,600 men, or nearly one-third of their forces, but not one single cannon or banner. The remnants of the army followed the "royal orders of retreat," crossing the Swedish frontier. Finland was lost and Sweden proper in danger.

Only a revolution could save the country. The republican aristocrats were the ones to bring it about. A conspiracy among them was formed, George Adlersparre and Ch. H. Anckarsverd being the leaders. When it was rumored that the former, with the western army division, of which he was the commander, had left the Norwegian frontier and was marching on Stockholm, Gustavus IV. sent order to Toll in Scania to meet him with his troops, while the king seemed to make preparations to leave. Great excitement reigned in Stockholm, and General Adlercreutz, who recently had been received in the capital with enthusiasm, resolved to take action in preventing the king's departure. Accompanied by half a dozen officers, he entered the king's bedchamber the morning of March 13th, and took possession of the king in person, who made a struggle and later a frustrated attempt to escape. The body-guards were persuaded to remain inactive. Prince Charles was proclaimed regent. Neither this fact nor the arrest of the king seemed to impress the population, who received the news with ice-cold reserve. The king was conducted to Drottningholm, and later to Gripsholm, where he signed the document of abdication, finally to be escorted out of the country with his family, never to return. He died in St. Gallen in 1837.

The regent's first duty was to ward off the Russian invasion of Norrland and to obtain peace. Napoleon congratulated Sweden on having got rid of the "supremacy of a fool," and sanctioned an armistice, granted by his general. Marshal Bernadotte, who commanded an army in Seeland, ready to attack Sweden. Peace was made in

GUSTAVUS ADOLPHUS Sweden.

Paris, Sweden receiving back Pomerania in return for a promise to close its own harbors against English ships. Peace with Denmark was made, with no change of territory on either side. Attempts to rout the Russian army of invasion at Ratan, in West Bothnia, were unsuccessful, but it withdrew by its own choice. In the treaty of peace signed at Fredericshamn, September 17, 1809, Finland, the archipelago of Aland and a part of Swedish Bothnia were ceded to Russia, the rivers of Torne and Muonio to form the boundary line.

Finland, since time immemorial in intimate relations with Sweden, from whom she had received a portion of her population, had for 600 years with her mother country formed integral parts of the same realm. Sweden had given to Finland her religion, constitution, laws, privileges and culture, and in return received her fidelity and a host of patriotic men eminent in affairs of war and peace. Together the Swedes and Finns had fought on the battlefields of Europe for the political grandeur of their country and the religious liberty of the world. United to Russia, Finland preserved her institutions and privileges unmolested, and has, up to date, enjoyed a peaceful development greater than would perhaps have been her share under Swedish rule. The mother country was after this great loss forced to concentrate her energy on a more solid material progress, and has, according to the prophecy of Esaias Tegnér, "within the boundary of Sweden reconquered Finland." The Finns have proved themselves to be one of the most talented and energetic of nations. Out of the two million inhabitants of Finland, two-fifths are Swedish, forming the nobility and the majority of the cultured classes. Already at the time of the separation from Sweden was born the national singer of **Finland, John** Ludvig Runeberg, who was to become the greatest poet that ever wrote in the Swedish language and one of the greatest that ever lived. In his immortal songs of "Finland's latest war," the two countries have a great common inheritance. Sweden dreamed of reconquering Finland as soon as a good warrior ascended the throne. This hope was given up forever. But the most intimate sympathy still reigns between the two countries. In case that harm to Finland or her home-rule should be done, and her independence be lost, the Swedish people would not be in a position to avenge such a crime, but it would cause profound grief and indignation, and would be considered a shameful act of violence which the glory of no peace emperor would suffice to cover.

By the revolution of 1789, Sweden for a second time in her history surrendered her liberty into the hands of an energetic and patriotic ruler, only to see the absolute power utterly abused by an incompetent successor. The loss and suffering were almost as great as at the death of Charles XII., but the era of democracy, peace and prosperity so much closer at hand. It was the spirit of the aristocratic republicanism which caused the timely downfall of absolute monarchy, but it was in its turn destined to fall for the spirit of democracy and a constitutional government.

CHAPTER XVI

The Constitutional Monarchy—Charles XIII. and the early Bernadottes

CHARLES XIII. succeeded his nephew. He was chosen king after a new constitution had been formulated and accepted by the Riksdag of 1809. Charles XIII. was one of the most unsympathetic of Swedish kings, but his reign marks a new period in Swedish history, commencing the era of constitutional government. The new constitution to which the king subscribed was not a radical document; it only reduced the power of the king. Hans Jærta, one of the nobles who had renounced their privileges and been active in the conspiracy against Gustavus IV., was the leading spirit of the constitutional committee and was appointed secretary of state in the new cabinet. Urgent appeals of the peasant Estate to reduce or abolish the privileges of the upper classes were of no avail, no reform of state or society yet being made. A proposition by Count von Platen to introduce a compulsory militia defence was voted down. This Riksdag, which lasted for a year, gave fuller liberties to the press, which at once used it to voice the popular dissatisfaction with the state of affairs. It was necessary to select an heir to the throne, as the old king was childless, Prince Christian

(365)

August of Augustenborg being chosen, much in opposition to the nobles, who wanted the son of Gustavus IV. The prince of Augustenborg, who was Danish governor general of Norway, accepted, and was adopted by the king, changing his name to Charles August. He was a plain, resolute and active man, unattractive in appearance, but of a kind and noble character. Beloved by the lower classes, who had effected his selection, he was treated coldly by the Gustavian aristocrats and by Queen Hedvig Elisabeth Charlotte (Princess of Oldenburg), who all favored the selection of young Gustavus, the son of exiled Gustavus IV. Reports of attempts to poison the heir-apparent were in circulation even before he arrived in Sweden. Prince Charles August himself often said that he thought he would die young by some stroke of paralysis, but he paid no attention to the warnings given him. During a parade of troops at Qvidinge, in Scania, he was suddenly seen to lose consciousness and dropped dead from his horse. Peculiarities in the investigation of the corpse, led by his physician, caused a second post-mortem examination, in which the celebrated chemist Berzelius took part. The report seemed in favor of the supposition that the death was caused by poison. The indignation of the populace knew no bounds. The friends of the government tried to coin political money by insinuating that the Gustavians, particularly Count Axel von Fersen the Younger and his sister, Countess Piper, were the responsible parties. At the burial of the dead prince the mob of Stockholm perpetrated one of the most hideous murders of a man who was without doubt innocent. When Count Fersen, in the capacity of marshal of the realm, was to open the procession, he was warned not to do so, but in pride and sense of duty resolved to meet his fate. Approaching the church of Riddarholm, his carriage was pelted with stones, Fersen himself seeking shelter in various places, but being pursued by the mob and killed. Fersen had sought protection in a body of troops, whose officers commanded them to turn him over to the mob. Thus perished a man who, with Curt von Stedingk, had received the order of Cincinnatus from the hands of George Washington, and who once was so near saving Louis XVI. and Marie Antoinette from their cruel fate. Fersen's brother was saved only by mere chance and his sister by a flight in disguise. The mob now was resolved to attack Countess Piper, who was thought to be at the castle, and the queen herself. But the authorities, who had brought shame on themselves by their unwillingness to save Fersen, interfered, directing a few shots of cannon against the mob, dispersing it and killing many (June 10, 1810).

Sweden was once more without an heir-apparent to the throne. Frederic, the brother of Charles August, was favored by the king. Frederic VI. of Denmark was a candidate, but the old national hatred against the Danes was still too strong to make his selection possible. A count of Oldenburg was also mentioned by some. The Gustavians, to whom Adlercreutz belonged, dared not openly push their candidate of the old royal line. The patriotic noblemen in power were anxious to see some great general chosen, regardless of a royal pedigree, who could recapture Finland. King Charles sent two emissaries to Napoleon to notify him of the death of Charles August and the selection of his brother. Then one of the most original and daring schemes ever attempted on such a line was carried through by Count Otto Mœrner, one of the emissaries. On his own responsibility, he inquired of Marshal Bernadotte, one of Napoleon's ablest generals, if he would consent to become heir-apparent to the Swedish throne. Bernadotte consented, and the consent of Napoleon was obtained through the Swedish ambassador in Paris. Upon his return, Mœrner was ordered to leave the capital by the minister of state, who blamed him for his unauthorized action. But from Upsala Mœrner led an eager agitation, with the result that the Riksdag of Œrebro selected Bernadotte, who was represented by a secret emissary. Thus the two generals who, at the abdication of Gustavus IV., were, one in Norway, the other in Denmark, with troops ready to attack Sweden, both within one year were chosen to succeed Charles XIII.

Jean Baptiste Jules Bernadotte was born at Pau, in South France, in 1764. The son of a lawyer, he worked himself up in the army and was by the Revolution enabled to reach the high military stations for which his eminent genius had destined him. Next to Napoleon the ablest of French generals, he opposed the imperial tendencies of the latter, but was later repeatedly used by the emperor to fulfil important duties as a warrior, diplomatist and statesman, receiving the rank of a marshal of France and the title of Prince of Ponte Corvo. Related by marriage, the two were never on terms of intimacy, and the Swedish politicians who thought to please the emperor, and gain a strong point with him by the selection of Bernadotte, were mistaken. Bernadotte joined the Lutheran church at Elsinore and landed in Sweden October 20, 1810. By his impressive appearance, his amiability and his genius, he soon won all hearts. As he never acquired the Swedish language, and as his superior ability as a statesman and warrior was not always comprehended, he suffered often through misunderstandings by his new countrymen, who never ceased to admire his eminent genius. Prince Charles, or Charles Johann, as he called himself henceforward, was of a commanding presence and had an interesting face, surrounded by black curly hair. His fascinating ways and winning disposition held captive the admiration even of his political opponents. Prince Charles refused to submit to the undue influence with which Napoleon tried to fetter him, and always carried high and with patriotic independence the interests of his adopted country.

Napoleon soon found reason to be offended with Sweden. Through the peace of Paris, Sweden had agreed to close its harbors to England, but in Gothenburg, which town had suffered destruction by fire and was recently rebuilt, a lively traffic was secretly carried on, connecting England with Northern Europe and enriching Gothenburg. Napoleon was enraged and forced Sweden to declare war on England, which power, realizing the circumstances, did not open any hostilities, and allowed the commercial traffic to continue, although more secretly. Prince Charles, who from the start exerted a strong influence upon the government, effected an approach to Russia and England to save the dignity of Sweden, much to Napoleon's dismay. He also put the army in a satisfactory condition by recruiting. This caused a revolt in Scania, which was subdued with severity. The Riksdag of 1812 passed a law for the establishment of a compulsory militia, all men between twenty-one and twenty-five years old being registered in classes according to age and instructed in military tactics and discipline.

Napoleon tried by various methods to subdue and humiliate the independence of his Swedish ally, which, when fruitless, led him to acts of hostility. Prince Charles made peace with England and an alliance with Russia, who promised 20,000 men to assist in the conquest of Norway. When Napoleon and Alexander of Russia commenced war against each other, popular opinion in Sweden sided with the former, but Prince Charles, who knew in detail the nature of Napoleon's power and its lack of a solid foundation, tried to make his views clear. He met Alexander personally, agreeing with him on plans of mutual action, at Abo in 1812. After Napoleon's unsuccessful march against Russia, Swedish opinions changed and Bernadotte had free hands to follow up his policy. England formed an alliance with Sweden, agreeing to support the conquest of Norway and ceding the island of Guadeloupe (later sold to France by Sweden). In 1813, 25,000 Swedish troops were sent to Germany, joining the continental allies, who, divided in three armies, were to attack Napoleon, according to plans mostly mapped out by Prince Charles of Sweden. The latter was to command the Northern army of 100,000 men, Swedes, Prussians, Russians and English, but his position was a difficult one, for his superior tactics were misunderstood by his subordinates and by Blucher, the valiant but headstrong commander of 50,000 Prussians, who formed the Silesian army. But through the battles of Grossbeeren (August 23d), Dennewitz (September 6th), and Leipsic (October 16-19), the eminence of Bernadotte's genius was fully brought out, his leadership and the Swedish troops taking honorable part in each. Napoleon and his armies were defeated and pursued by the allies. The monarchs voted a resolution of thanks to Prince Charles, who, with his army, marched northward to carry out the ultimate object of his policy, the conquest of Norway, the plans of which had been made by Count Platen and handed him before he ever left Paris.

Denmark had declared war on Sweden and sided with Napoleon. By turning against Denmark the former Marshal Bernadotte saved himself from the necessity of making an attack on the country of his birth. Lubeck surrendered, the Danes were defeated at Bornhœved, Kiel and Glucksburg were captured, and the whole of Holstein occupied. An armistice was agreed to. Denmark offered the diocese of Drontheim, but Prince Charles was resolved to expel Denmark from the Scandinavian Peninsula. January 14, 1814, peace was made at Kiel, Denmark ceding to Sweden the whole of Norway, except Iceland and Fero Islands, and receiving Swedish Pomerania and the island of Rugen in compensation.

Norway, united with Denmark ever since the days of Queen Margaret, in a relation of more or less neglected conditions, during which her original independence was lost, had of late not been satisfied to remain under Danish supremacy. The governing class of officeholders was to a great extent of Danish origin and tendencies, and the patriotism of the population at large dates from a later period. Among the more cultured classes the revolution in France and close relations with England had fostered a desire for political independence. The Danes made use of this fact in order to try to maintain the relation with Denmark in some way. The Danish crown prince, Christian Fredoric, was in 1813 made governor-general of Norway. He was a man of some brilliant gifts, but without any great ability. By journeys in the country he acquired popularity and adherents. In February, 1814, a meeting was held at Eidsvold by men of prominence, who declared the prince regent. May 17th a constitution was adopted and Christian Frederic elected king of Norway. His courteous offer of extending his rule to Sweden was there met by derision. After a triumphal return to Stockholm, Prince Bernadotte gathered his forces and attacked Norway both by land and sea, the aged King Charles XIII. having command of the navy. An army of 20,000 Swedes entered Norway under command of Von Essen, who captured the fortifications at Svinesund. The navy took possession of the islands in the archipelago outside of Fredericstad, which town was captured, with the fortress Kongsten, 100 cannon and considerable stores of weapons and provisions. The Norwegian army of 30,000 men was located in various places with the central body of troops at Moss. The plan of Prince Charles was to enclose it from all sides. A smaller Swedish force of 3,000 men was repulsed by the Norwegians in two conflicts at Lier and Medskog, celebrated by the latter as important victories. In the meantime the Swedish army proceeded northward and the fleet penetrated to the bay of Christiania. The plan to enclose the Norwegian army at Moss was being carried into effect in order to finish the war by one single battle, when negotiations for peace were begun.

Prince Charles was anxious to have the conflict brought to a rapid close because he feared that the powers, envious of Sweden's good fortune and dissatisfied with the refusal of Prince Charles to join in an attack on France, might take unfavorable decisions at the approaching congress of Vienna. Prompted by these reasons, and perhaps influenced by his experience of revolutionary movements, Prince Charles offered to sanction Norway's constitution only with such changes as were necessary for a union with Sweden, besides demanding the abdication and speedy departure of Christian Frederic. On these terms peace was made at the convention of Moss, August 14, 1814. At the first meeting of the Norwegian Storthing, or Diet, the terms of peace were sanctioned and Charles XIII. chosen king of Norway. At the Congress of Vienna, in 1815, treaties were signed between Sweden and Prussia and between Denmark and Prussia, according to which Swedish Pomerania and Rugen were ceded to Prussia on the payment of about $2,000,000, and the duchy of Lauenburg ceded to Denmark. In the relation between Sweden and Norway no change was made, and Denmark lost all hope of the restitution of the latter country.

The great moderation shown by Prince Charles in the acquisition of Norway has been criticised in various ways, but none of the arguments used against it have themselves been able to bear a critical test. The idea of uniting the two countries as independent states was older in Sweden than the very constitution of Norway which Prince Charles accepted. It was the idea of the leading men in Sweden who had dethroned Gustavus IV. in 1809. The Scandinavian Union is not the best imaginable, has brought Sweden no added power or security, and has placed her king in a difficult position. The only bond of union is the king, the two countries each having their constitution, diet and cabinet. There is only one department in common, the one of which the Swedish minister of foreign affairs is the head and which settles all relations with other countries for both Sweden and Norway. Three members of the Norwegian cabinet are residents of Stockholm, to prepare affairs pertaining to the Norwegian administration and to partake in affairs involving both countries. These stipulations are made by the Act of Union, accepted in 1815 by the Diets of both countries. According to the Norwegian constitution, the king can use no greater force than 3,000 men outside the Norwegian boundary, except with the special consent of the Diet. Thus Sweden cannot in case of war expect any solid support from her sister country. The loose connections of the Union did not become apparent during the reigns of Charles XIII. and his successor, and the powers of Europe were not aware of them. Thus the Union served its purpose as offering a solid front of unity and strength to the powers who were dividing and redividing almost every territory on the map of Europe.

Charles XIII. died in February, 1818, at the age of seventy, and his talented queen followed him a few months later.

Charles XIV. Johann was fifty-four years of age when ascending the throne, but a man in his prime. To the dignity of the crown he brought a great personal influence, and his fame as a warrior, which spread throughout Europe. The firm diplomatic relations with Russia were continued, but approaches to England were also made. Charles XIV. gave close personal attention to the administration, being especially interested in the defence, finances, canals and roads. With his brilliant genius, quick temper and sense of superiority, the king sometimes reigned more alone and by his own decision than was considered advisable; but in the majority of cases he was influenced by the able men of his cabinet—Wetterstedt, Rosenblad, Skjœldebrand, Cederstrom and Wirsén. An intimate friend of the king was Count Magnus Brahe, who, though not a member of the cabinet, influenced the government more than was thought compatible with its dignity. Count Brahe, the head of one of the most distinguished of aristocratic families, used his great influence over the king mostly in a noble way, himself being raised to the highest dignities of the state. He was blindly devoted to the king, followed him like a shadow, taking infinite care of him during his last illness, and dying only a few months after his royal friend.

One of the most remarkable works carried on during the reign of Charles XIV. was the Gotha Canal system, which was brought to completion. The old bishop Brask had spoken of a connection between the lakes of Venar and Vetter, and the great Oxenstierna thought of a canal between the North Sea and the Baltic across Sweden. Charles XII. had ordered Polhem to make a trafficable passage around the waterfalls of Trollhetta, which was done after new plans during the reign of Gustavus IV. During the Period of Liberty, Daniel Thunberg had made plans for the whole canal system. But Count Balzar von Platen was the man to make the great work a realized fact, devoting his whole life to it, conquering distrust, opposition and lack of funds. He spent six years in preliminary surveys before taking up the agitation for the realization of his plans. During the whole progress of the work, his efficient activity in looking after every detail could only be compared to his constant agitation in the Riksdag for the support of the immense enterprise and his scrupulous attention to the financial part of it. When the great canal was opposed as an unpatriotic scheme, endangering the defence of the country, Platen answered by completing plans for a colossal fortress in the heart of the canal system, which, when erected, became the strategic stronghold of Sweden, and was named Carlsborg. Platen died as governor-general of Norway, seeing his great life-work nearing completion. The Gotha Canal is the most remarkable of its kind in Europe, being 259 miles long, with 74 locks, many of which have been cut out of solid granite hills. It is of great value to commerce and affords a most picturesque scenic tour.

Charles XIV. met with a power in politics which, from the start not strong enough to carry away victory, ended by attaining its goal. It was the liberal opposition in the Riksdag, supported by a liberal press. Charles XIV., in his native country, had seen to what an infamy the abuse of liberal forms of government could lead, and he was sternly resolved to antagonize any movement which aimed to introduce more democratic principles in the handling of state affairs and in the remodelling of the system of representation. Charles XIV. was in a delicate personal position. He was the only one of the Napoleonic marshals who preserved his throne after the fall of the emperor, and the strong continental reaction looked askance at this new man who wore one of the oldest crowns of Europe. But his great reputation as a warrior and statesman, and his persistent peace policy, ought to have been to him sufficient guarantees of the fidelity of his subjects. Charles XIV., in the agitation against the self-willed cabinet, saw an enmity against himself. By a network of secret detectives, the king tried to uncover conspiracies and plots which existed in his imagination only, or in that of those who were aware of his weakness and sought to gain personal favors by making use of it. The severity with which the press was censured and its members punished created a bitterness against the king personally, which ceased only during the few last years of his reign. With the new constitution a law establishing full liberty of public utterance in print was enacted, but a temporary restraint had been placed on this liberty, in 1812, on account of violent newspaper attacks upon Russia. The government still made use of this restraint, which caused many severe legal sentences and subsequent bitterness.

Among the press organs of that period the "Argus" and "Aftonbladet" were the most conspicuous in their attacks upon the conservative government; Lars Hierta, one of the ablest of Swedish editorial writers, was the publisher of the latter. His paper was repeatedly confiscated. Anders Lindeberg was the publisher of "Stockholmsposten." In an agitation against the royal monopoly in theatrical affairs, Lindeberg threw out the accusation that the king, for purely economical reasons, opposed a reform in those matters. He was arraigned and a sentence of death passed upon him, which was commuted to three years' imprisonment. But Lindeberg refused to accept any clemency, declaring himself ready and resolved to die. The government, who dared not take his life, was in a delicate predicament, but saved itself and Lindeberg by announcing pardon of "political criminals," at the anniversary of the king's first arrival in Sweden. Jacob Crusenstolpe, a novelist and writer of note, was one of the intimate friends and supporters of the government, but turned liberal, attacking the king in a pamphlet. He was sentenced to three years' imprisonment, which created great commotion and a revolt, in Stockholm, not subdued except after a bloody conflict with the troops (July, 1838). Crusenstolpe continued writing from his prison.

The principal leaders of the opposition in the Riksdag were L. Boye, F. B. von Schwerin and C. H. Anckarsverd among the nobles, and Anders Danielsson among the peasants. This opposition criticised the government for negligence, extravagance and incompetency. Its policy was an entire reconstruction of the state, politically, socially and financially, on the basis of a constitutional government. The opposition commenced by establishing the right of free deliberations in the Riksdag. At the Riksdags of 1827 and 1828 the government was severely taken to task on account of the sale of ships to the Spanish insurgents in South America. The king was inclined to join England against Spain, but had to recede on account of pressure from Russia and the continental powers. The sales were partly annulled and the Swedish government experienced a considerable financial loss. Cederstrom was the responsible party, but upon his resignation his able successor Wirsén was able to cover up his tracks.

If Sweden was forced to change her policy in the South American affair she was found unyielding in the settlement of the boundary questions with Russia. This power was anxious to obtain a slice of the Norwegian Finnmark, with excellent ice-free harbors at the bay of Varanger. In the ultimate settlement with Russia, in 1826, a great territory was ceded, but not any of the important harbors.

In 1840 the opposition had waxed strong enough to effect one of its most desired reforms, the constitutional reconstruction of the cabinet. This body was made to consist of ten members, of whom seven were to be the heads of the various state departments, those of justice, foreign affairs, army, navy, civil service, finance and ecclesiastics.[1] As a consequence of this change in the constitution, several cabinet members resigned and were succeeded by men more in touch with the opposition.

---

[1] The ecclesiastic department is also the department of education.

The greatest of contemplated reforms was a new system of representation, but the opposition was not able to carry it through. At the first revolution of Gustavus III., Stedingk favored a reconstruction of the Riksdag after the model of the English parliament. Gustavus III. was afraid to cause complications by the introduction of such a novelty, but considered it gravely at the time of his second revolution. In 1830, the idea was taken up by the opposition, and Anckarsverd and the eminent lawyer Richert made up a plan for a new Diet, according to the plan of the Norwegian Storthing. This plan, with the idea of one chamber, instead of two, was repeatedly discussed at the Riksdag of 1840, but not adopted. This remarkable Riksdag, which lasted seventeen months, did considerable for the improvement of education and was ultimately dismissed by Charles XIV., in a speech of a conciliatory spirit, which went far toward restoring the old popularity of the king.

Charles XIV. died March 8, 1844, at the age of eighty-one. During the last years of his reign he received strong and repeated evidence of the love of his people, especially upon the occasion of his twenty-fifth anniversary as king of Sweden. "No one has made a career like mine," he said shortly before his death. He was a child of the revolutionary epoch, favored by its opportunities to receive a high station, without being sullied by any of its vices. If it be true that his position often was made difficult through lack of appreciation by his new subjects, it is not less true that he, through lack of intimacy with the Swedish language, national character and traditions, was unable to further the development of his new country, in the same degree as would a native provided with such rich endowment. The sun of Charles XIV., which rose in brilliancy, set in the glory of full appreciation.

The reign of Charles XIV. produced a new line of eminent scientists and was the golden age of Swedish literature. The remarkable genius of J. J. Berzelius remolded the science of chemistry, placing it on a basis where there are hardly any limits to its scope. Elias Fries devised a new system of botany. Sven Nilsson, a distinguished zoölogist, also became the founder of a new science, comparative archæology. K. J. Schlyter edited a complete collection of the old provincial laws, a work of equal importance to philology and jurisprudence. P. H. Ling invented the Swedish system of gymnastics and founded the Central Institute of Gymnastics in Stockholm, where the Swedish massage or movement cure has won a scientific development worthy of its world-wide fame. E. G. Geijer, as a philosopher, was a noble follower of Hœijer, while as a historian he is the greatest genius of his country. As a poet and composer Geijer is also noteworthy. Professor of history at Upsala, he was once accused of heterodoxy, but acquitted. His political career was remarkable. Geijer was a firm supporter of the government and conservative principles, until fifty-seven years of age, when he joined the opposition.

The world of letters was divided in parties as bitterly opposed to each other as those of the political world. The old Gustavian school, of which Leopold remained the last representative, was attacked by the "New School," which, inspired by German Romanticism, was brimful of inspiration, imagination and feelings, but very little that was original, clear or national. Of this so-called "phosphoristic" school Atterbom was the distinguished leader. Stagnelius, a poet of rare attainments, but who died early, belongs in this group. The New School was in turn attacked by the "Gothic Society," a school of national Swedish Romanticism, which introduced a cult of the Old Northern spirit of individuality, terseness and power. Ling and Geijer were among the leading men of this school, whose enthusiasm for everything national had a lasting influence upon the research for, and gathering of, folk lore, songs, traditions, customs, and every trait of the popular culture of bygone days. In Franzén and Wallin, Sweden had two religious poets of the very first rank. More famous than any of these was Esaias Tegnér, the second great national poet of Sweden, whose "Frithiof's Saga" was destined to become the most celebrated literary work of all Europe in its day, appearing in a vast number of translations in a great number of languages. Tegnér was in sympathy with the old Gustavian school, but a member of the Gothic Society, and by his choice of subjects in harmony with the national school. There is a wonderful richness of sparkling life and wit in Tegnér's poems, but they are sometimes overladen by the vivid ornamental images in which they abound. Tegnér was a man of extremely broad and liberal views on every phase of human life and effort. He hated with the whole power of his fiery soul the mysticism, obscurantism and morbid sensualism of his age. He was the sworn enemy of the "Holy Alliance" and the reactionary powers in state, church and literature. In his chivalrous spirit and love of the great individuals, he became the admirer of Charles XIV., whose policy he therefore supported. Tegnér is not the one who in the grandeur and faultlessness of his creations has attained the very highest rank among Swedish poets, but is the greatest and most unbiased thinker among them, **and has as** such exerted a beneficial influence upon the national consciousness and cultural development. Tegnér's judgment upon one of his Gustavian precursors may be repeated in his own case: "Perchance the greatest not as poet, but as genius."

Oscar I. was forty-five years of age at the death of his father. He was the only son of Charles XIV. and Queen Desideria, the latter a daughter of a French merchant by the name of Clary. Oscar was, in 1823, married to Princess Josephine of Leuchtenberg, a granddaughter of the French empress of the same name. It was a difficult position, the one held by the heir-apparent. Charles XIV. was jealous of his own power and popularity and suspected his son of being in sympathy with the opposition. The prince, distanced as far as possible from the affairs of state, devoted himself to the study of social and economic subjects. He gave a great deal of attention to the study of prisons and the care of prisoners, seeking by pamphlets to spread his sympathies for the latter and to improve their conditions. Oscar I. was fondly devoted to the fine arts, himself a talented painter and composer. He did not possess his father's brilliant genius or power of personal influence, although an upright man of great talent and exceedingly prepossessing in appearance. Oscar was of a mild, sagacious disposition, who liked to go into detail and take time for investigation and decision. He was not a man of action, and lacked somewhat consistency in carrying out plans of a wider scope. Oscar I. had a little of the autocrat of the father in him and often acted on his own judgment, without taking the advice of his cabinet. Being the loyal, highly cultured and patriotic man that he was, he in various ways furthered the development of his country.

Few kings have ascended a throne under such enthusiasm and joyful aspirations on the part of the people as King Oscar I. Several important reforms were enacted at the Riksdag which met in 1844, and the king gave his sanction to them all. It was decided that the Riksdag should meet every third instead of every fifth year, the liberty of the press was augmented, and to women were given equal rights in the stipulations of inheritance and marriage. The last-mentioned reform was bitterly opposed by the nobles, who feared it would, to a great extent, annul their privileges. The law was passed by the three lower Estates, in spite of the nobles, and was sanctioned by the king. Oscar I. took great pains to have the industries freed from the restraint under which they had been suffering during the reign of his predecessor.

King Oscar surrounded himself with men of a more modern type than his father's advisers. They were in touch with the principles of the opposition, although far from radical, and more respected for their character than for their ability. The opposition, which had been so harsh during the administration of Charles XIV., was toned down considerably; but complaints were soon heard that the new government was neither consistent nor resolute in its liberal policy and that courtiers and young officers won an unduly rapid promotion. Soon an opposition of a new order was organized against the administration. The conservatives, finding that it leaned too much on the liberal principles, attacked it for this reason. A powerful conservative party at the Riksdag was organized, with Hartmansdorff as the leader among the nobles and Archbishop Wingard among the clergy. Attacked by liberals and conservatives alike, and not supported by either, the government was of an undecided and vacillating tenor.

The French revolution of 1848 influenced Swedish politics in several ways. The "friends of reform," viz., the party desiring a parliamentary reorganization, were incited by the republican tendencies. The masses of Stockholm on one occasion gave vent to their feelings by demonstrations which were of a menacing character. Great crowds collected outside the place where a "reform banquet" was held. There it was resolved to attack the houses of Hartmansdorff and several other leading conservatives. The owners placed themselves in safety, but the windows of the houses were broken by the mob, who also threw stones at the troops. The tumult was quenched, but not without bloodshed. The press was greatly agitated for a long time afterward, using language against the government that was by no means choice. The liberals in the Riksdag commenced to take an attitude as decided as the one held by the conservatives. From this time on King Oscar showed great coldness to the liberals, and surrounded himself with advisers more in harmony with the conservatives.

The proposition for a reorganization of the Riksdag, made in 1840, was not accepted, but a committee was appointed in 1848 to make a new proposition, which failed to please either government or Riksdag. The king then had a new proposition prepared, based upon general elections. The liberals did not think the royal proposition democratic enough and offered one of their own. Both of these were defeated at the Riksdag of 1850, thanks to the opposition of nobility and clergy. A third one was made by Hartmansdorff, but also failed to please, not being conservative enough for the nobles. Hartmansdorff aroused so much hatred among his fellow nobles that they refused to be seated on the same bench with him during the sessions. After a period of perfect isolation the old conservative leader was judged with greater leniency by his former followers. Shortly before his death, in 1856, he sent them the following greeting: "Ask the nobles not to stand up so long for their privileges, they will lose nothing by surrendering them." It seemed as if the interest for parliamentary reform had died out during the latter part of King Oscar's reign, but such was not the case; it only gathered force in the quiet, and the king was right when defining it as a "question which could never fall."

The influence of the revolution of 1848 also was felt in the foreign relations of Sweden. The German population of Holstein and Schleswig tried to sever their connections with Denmark in order to effect a union with Germany, Prussia taking upon herself to liberate said provinces. Denmark made various efforts to gain the active support of Sweden. The so-called "Scandinavism" was a good means to obtain this end. This movement, which aimed at the establishment of a closer union between the three Scandinavian countries, based upon the fact of the common origin of their inhabitants, had originated at the University of Copenhagen. The meetings of scientists and students, in 1842 and 1843, at Stockholm, had given growth to this movement, which was of a very high-strung nature, but, as far as the Danes were concerned, also of an egotistical motive. Charles XIV. had been averse to this "students' policy," but Oscar I. was sympathetically impressed by it. "Scandinavism" rose high in 1848, especially at the universities, and King Oscar sent a communication to the Prussian government to the effect that he was resolved to oppose any attack on the

Danish isles. An army of 20,000 men was ordered to
Scania to give weight to this statement. A smaller division
of it was even for a time quartered in the island of Funen.
The German troops which had invaded Jutland soon retired
and hostilities ceased for some time. King Oscar effected
an armistice of seven months, in August, 1848. As a result
of the war between Denmark and Germany during the next
few years an agreement followed, according to which Holstein and Schleswig would for some time remain under
Danish supremacy.

King Oscar had, from the commencement of his reign,
tried to meet all demands for reform made by his Norwegian subjects, who were anxious to demonstrate to the
world the perfect independence of their country. The king
himself took the initiative steps to give Norway a national
flag of its own, the two countries up to the reign of Oscar
having had one common official flag. He also instituted the
Norwegian knightly order of St. Olaf in resemblance to
the older Swedish orders of Seraphim, Vasa, etc., and gave
permission to place the name of Norway before that of Sweden in the Norwegian royal title. For these reasons public
opinion in Sweden expected Norwegian concessions in regard to the Act of Union, which seemed in need of revision.
A committee of men from both countries was appointed to
make the revision, but the Norwegian members opposed all
measures involving any change, expressing themselves in
such emphatic terms that it was found best to leave the
deliberations of the committee unpublished. In 1854 the
Norwegian Storthing decided to abolish the office of a governor-general. King Oscar refused to sanction this law,
but allowed the office to remain vacant during the rest of
his reign.

Intemperance had grown to be an evil from which the Swedish people greatly suffered since the reign of Gustavus III., when alcohol began to be produced in great quantities by the common people. The king encouraged the temperance movement, which was very fruitful in results. In 1853 the Riksdag abolished the free and unrestrained production of alcohol, which was changed into a regular industry and placed under heavy taxation. From 1855 onward, the principles of free trade were adopted for commerce and trade through the influence of J. A. Gripenstedt, the minister of finance, and seemed to have beneficial results in every branch of industrial and commercial activity. The state revenues were greatly increased and the surplus spent in improvements of the widest scope. The means of interior communications were vastly improved. In 1853 the network of the state electric telegraph began to spread and now embraces every part of the country. The agitation for the construction of railways had long been an active one. The first one constructed was a private railway between Œrebro and Arboga. In 1854 the Riksdag decided on the construction of trunk lines in Southern Sweden, to be built and controlled by the state. The Riksdag of 1856 appropriated a sum of $5,000,000 for that purpose. The railways were rapidly and solidly built under the supervision of Baron Nils Ericsson, the highly talented brother of John Ericsson, the world-famous inventor of the propeller, the caloric engine, the steam hose and the "Monitor."

The relations with Russia were not the best during the latter part of King Oscar's reign. The Russian claims on the harbors at the bay of Varanger were repeated in 1847, and when deliberations for a settlement were opened, in 1851, Russia showed a tendency to take possession of the desired places. In the conflict between Russia, on one hand, and Turkey, supported by England and France, on the other, Sweden sided with the latter, especially after Russia had failed to recognize an alliance of neutrality under arms formed by Sweden-Norway and Denmark. In 1855 Sweden entered an agreement with France, promising not to cede any territory to Russia in case of a conflict. In 1856 peace was made at Paris; the only favor won by Sweden was a pledge made by Russia not to fortify the archipelago of Aland.

King Oscar was a very hard worker and also fond of the pleasures of life. His health was injured through illness, in 1857, and he never recovered. The premature death of his second son, Prince Gustavus, a talented composer and highly popular, had a disastrous influence on him. King Oscar I. died July 8, 1859, after a long illness, beloved by the two nations who, during his reign, had enjoyed the happiest epoch of their history.

Romanticism in literature had an important second blossom during the reign of King Oscar I. and his successor. With the exception of Runeberg and Almquist, it offers no name of the very first rank. But Runeberg, the Homer of the North, does not belong to Sweden alone, and Almquist, the only great Romanticist, had made his appearance during the preceding epoch. Charles John Ludvig Almquist was a genius of great versatility and exceptional endowment. He wrote with equal force in all branches of literature; besides the poet, dramatist and prosaist, being a good philologist and well versed in a number of practical pursuits. He anticipated the ideas of which George Sand became a champion, and wrote charming peasant idyls long before Auerbach and Bjœrnson. His most important work is an ambiguous creation, conceived somewhat in the form of Boccaccio's "Decamerone," but much larger, and containing productions in every imaginable artistic form. It is called *Tœrnrosens bok* (The Book of the Wild Rose). Almquist has not, like Bellman and Tegnér, crystallized the Swedish national character in a lyrical form, but he remains, in spite of glaring defects, the most versatile and supremely gifted genius of Swedish literature.

Nybom, Bœttiger, Malmstrœm, Sætherberg and Strandberg were talented lyric poets of this epoch, Von Braun, Sturzen-Becker and Sehlstedt good humorists, while Bœrjesson, Blanche, Jolin, Dahlgren and Frans Hedberg wrote successfully for the stage. Swedish women were destined to win fame for themselves by bringing the novelistic form to a richer development; principal among whom were Frederica Bremer, Sophie von Knorring, Emilie Carlén and Sophie Schwartz, while the men Crusenstolpe, Sparre, Mellin, Ridderstad and Starbæck cultivated the field of historical fiction, for which Swedish history offers such a wealth of appropriate subjects.

Swedish composers of note were becoming numerous, although the field in which they chiefly excel is the rather limited one of lyric song, the most spontaneous medium of expression for the lyrico-rhetoric Swedish temperament. As the composer of "lieder" or *visor*, Adolphus Lindblad, an intimate friend of Mendelssohn, occupies a revered place in the history of music. Close to him stand Crusell, Nordblom and Josephsson, while Hæffner, Otto Lindblad, one of the noblest composers in this line, Prince Gustavus and Vennerberg are famous principally for their part songs.

The cultivators of dramatic and orchestral composition

have as yet been comparatively few. Chief among them is Bervald; further, Norman and Hallstrœm. In a later contemporary epoch, Hallén, Aulin, Sjœgren, Stenhammar have considerably brightened this aspect of cultural development. Gunnar Vennerberg occupies an honored place as a poet, humorist and composer in one. There seems to be a deeply rooted tendency in the Swedish national temperament to unite the various branches of artistic creation, which would stamp it as romantic in its very essence if there did not run a vein of stunningly realistic portrayals through the works of such composite nature. In the art of Bellman this tendency has found its highest exponent. Bellman selected for his subjects the life of the lower middle classes in the Swedish capital of his day. His Fredman sings of the experiences of himself and his friends. Vennerberg has chosen the student's life at the University of Upsala as the subject of his duets between two students, "Gluntarne," in which are mirrored as faithfully, and sometimes as artistically, as by Bellman the humorous and pathetic scenes which have fascinated the poet and composer.

Swedish song for the first time acquired universal fame through Jenny Lind, who has had many successors, but no peer as a dramatic singer. Contemporaneous with Jenny Lind were a number of highly talented histrionic artists, principal among whom were Lars Hjortsberg, Nils William Almlœf, Olof Ulric Torsslov, Emilie Hœgquist and Carl Georg Dahlquist. The Swedish stage has set a good example for the preservation of the highest standards of the language, and in this line exerted a great cultural influence.

CHAPTER XVII

Parliamentary Reform—Charles XV

CHARLES XV., the eldest son of Oscar I., succeeded his father, having for two years presided over the government during king Oscar's last illness. King Charles was of gigantic stature, exceedingly handsome and of a manly and noble bearing. There dwelt a fiery soul within him, conscious of its power, longing for heroic deeds and in sympathy with all that was noble in life and art. The king possessed an abundance of youthful energy and vivacity. He was a passionate hunter and a gay companion, who surrounded himself with men equally boisterous and gay. He was fond of jokes and merry pastimes, and took no pains to hide his weaknesses, which were of a convivial nature. In his social intercourse the king was exceptionally open and frank, treating everybody alike in a good-natured, hearty manner, winning the whole heart of his people. He understood better than any king since Charles XI. how to put himself in cordial relation with the masses of the people. But fond of playing practical jokes on high and low, he did not like to receive in the same measure. Charles XV. was devoted to the pursuits of art. Especially in his youth, he wrote poetry and distinguished himself as a landscape painter through his love for typical Swedish sceneries. Sweden did not at first know what to expect of her new ruler, and no one was able to predict the course of his policy. There were fears that his youthfulness and his fiery southern temperament might lead him to feel satisfied with the exterior of things or that he might give way to the impulses of the moment. These fears soon proved to be without foundation. The king had chosen as his maxim "Land shall with law be built," from the old provincial law of Upland, and he remained, with very rare exceptions, true to the constitutional spirit of these words. He had the good fortune to find highly capable advisers, in whose hands he placed the details of the administration, and, in contrast to his father, was satisfied to give his attention exclusively to matters of a more general importance. He gave his unreserved support to his cabinet, occupying a position above all party interests. Charles XV. often sacrificed, sometimes only after considerable internal struggle, his own personal sympathies and inclinations at the request of the advisers when he saw that the welfare of his country and his own royal dignity demanded such a sacrifice. On account of this, his true constitutional spirit, he deserved as a ruler the blind adoration of his people. His summer residence, the castle of Ulricsdal, in the neighborhood of Stockholm, he changed into an artistic abode, with choice collections in various lines. Charles XV. had, in 1850, married Princess Louise of the Netherlands, of the royal house of Orange. Their daughter, Louise, was married to the crown prince of Denmark, and is still in life, while King Charles had to suffer the premature losses of his only son and of his consort.

The cabinet which surrounded Charles XV. was one of the strongest bodies of its kind that ever controlled the government of Sweden. During his regency, Crown Prince

Charles appointed Baron Louis de Geer minister of justice and Ludvig Manderstrœm minister of foreign affairs. These men continued their duties during the reign of Charles XV., while Gripenstedt, as minister of finance, followed up his beneficent activity for the emancipation and development of the national industries. The historian, Frederic Ferdinand Carlson, had been the teacher of King Charles and had successfully continued the monumental work of Swedish history, left unfinished by Geijer. Carlson occupied, during the greater part of the reign of Charles XV., the position of minister of ecclesiastics (church and education), in which capacity he did great work for the improvement of educational affairs. The high schools and colleges were reorganized through new regulations of 1859, being the work of Carlson before his appointment to the cabinet. Carlson also improved the public, or common, schools. King Charles was a warm friend of public instruction. In one of his speeches from the throne he said: "This is my ambition that a true and living culture shall penetrate our people and with its blessings reach the humblest of its cottages."

The relations between Sweden and Norway, during the first few years of the reign of Charles XV., were strained. The Norwegian Storthing once more voted the abolition of the office of a governor-general. It was thought that the king, who earlier, as viceroy of Norway, had spoken in a spirit of acquiescence upon this question, would sanction the vote of the Storthing. But in Sweden great indignation was felt. It was known and understood that the Act of Union contained nothing in regard to the office in question, but was created by a stipulation in the constitution of Norway which admitted the possibility of its being filled by a Swede.

The Norwegian view was that the Storthing had exclusive right to decide the question, while the Swedish view was that it was a question concerning the Union and to be decided on by the diets of the two countries. Practically the Swedes were right; theoretically, and from a purely patriotic standpoint, which considered necessary the development of a perfect national independence even at the expense of the Union, the Norwegians were right. Ankarsverd, well known since the days of Charles XIV., made a motion, at the Swedish Riksdag of 1859, for the revision of the Act of Union on the basis of the treaty of Kiel, which motion in Norway was accepted as an insult. V. F. Dalman made a motion that the Estates should ask the king not to render a decision in the question of a Norwegian governor-general before the Riksdag had had an opportunity to look into the international aspect of the question. Great was the commotion caused by this issue, both in the diets and the press of the two countries. Swedish pamphlets were circulated which accepted the possibility of a dissolution of the Union. But in Norway, where the security of a union with Sweden had become apparent, especially during the conflict with Russia, such utterances were repudiated. Both of the motions in question were passed by the four Estates of the Riksdag, but put in such a shape that a request to have a revision of the Act of Union made was sent up to the king, with the demand for a royal proposition on that issue. The king was then asked to consider the question of a Norwegian governor-general in connection with that revision. As there was a difference of opinion also in the cabinets of the two countries, the final decision rested with the king alone. The sagacity and discernment of which King Charles gave evidence saved the situation and is worthy of praise. He declared in the Norwegian cabinet that he could not sanction the abolition of the office of a governor-general Shortly afterward, he gave in the Swedish cabinet as his opinion the advisability of postponing, for the time being, all deliberations of a revision of the Act of Union. By doing so, the king quieted the high feelings in both countries, and peace returned. It had become apparent to both Swedes and Norwegians that the Union was the result of great political foresight because it was preserved through the increasing feeling of faith and of the necessity of mutual protection. That great obscurity existed in regard to the affairs regulating the Union had also become evident.

The reforms and improvements which were effected during the reign of Charles XV. were highly important. New criminal and maritime codes were made at the Riksdag of 1862, and sanctioned by the government. Through the new regulations passed in the same year the foundations for increased municipal home rule were laid. Such home rule was as old as the country itself, but, in the same degree as the state organization, had attained a higher development, and the centralization of the administration was realized; it had weakened and was in peril of being entirely lost. Now the time was come for the powers of state to give municipal home rule new strength, adapting its old forms and creating new ones, in accordance with modern requirements. Laws were made which gave the towns the right to elect members to local assemblies (*stadsfullmæg-tige*), with authority to act in behalf of their communities. Similar institutions (*kommunalstæmmor*) were arranged for the country communities. *Landsting* were instituted in every governmental district, or *læn*, at which representatives, elected by the people, were to take action on the public affairs of the district, especially on such that pertained to sanitary conditions, communications, etc. The conditions for suffrage and elective franchise in municipal affairs were based on personal income. The old class distinctions were thus disregarded and a return made to the still older democratic institutions of the ancient Teutonic communities, in which every free man is entitled to his word and vote in public affairs. But those only are considered "free" who by their work can gain enough to pay their taxes in return for the privileges of a citizen. The church got a representation of its own in the clerical assembly (*kyrkomœtet*), which meets every fifth year and consists of equal numbers of ministers and laymen.

The government in the municipal reforms found a basis for the reorganization of the Riksdag. The royal proposition for a new parliamentary representation, placed before the Estates in 1862, was built upon the municipal suffrage and the Landstings or district assemblies, the latter being authorized to elect the members of the senate, or First Chamber. The old system of representation corresponded as little with the new municipal home rule as with the general tendencies in politics and social life. The nobility had lost its old importance. It was no longer advisable for the clergy to take a leading part in political affairs. A new industrial class of wealth and prominence had formed and demanded a representation in the burgher class. The peasants had ever since 1809 been carrying on their agitation for a reduction of taxes and abolition of the class privileges. They had met with an overwhelming opposition, which would fall with the old system of representation. A parliamentary reform had been fervently discussed ever since 1840. The municipal home rule reforms of 1862 had brought the question closer to a solution. The burghers and peasants at the Riksdag of 1860 petitioned the government to present a royal proposition for the reorganization of the Diet. Baron Louis de Geer, the minister of justice, was the author of this proposition, which was presented in 1862 and placed on the table until the next Riksdag. The great question was acted upon at the Riksdag of 1865. There was a great deal of commotion on account of the opposition which was expected from the nobility and clergy. The discussions in the periodical press and in pamphlet form were lively. The country population preserved its peaceful and sensible demeanor, but the excitement in the towns was considerable and increased as the decision drew nearer. The majority of towns and several rural communities in their close proximity sent deputations to Stockholm, who tendered their best wishes to the able minister of justice for the success of his proposition. The commotion in Stockholm was so great that troops were ordered ready in case of an emergency. The 4th of December the proposition was voted on by the burghers and peasants. At the question of the speaker, whether they were willing to accept the royal proposition, the peasants rose to their feet in a body and gave their answer with one laconic yea. A few of the burghers spoke against the proposition, but it was carried also in their Estate, and by an overwhelming majority. Long and heated discussions took place among the nobility and clergy. The clergymen were generally opposed to the parliamentary reform, but feared to be found remaining as the only opponents in the storm of disapproval which would follow. For this reason they postponed their decision until the nobility had taken action upon the proposition.

There rested a spirit of real grandeur over the deliberations at the Riddarhus upon this occasion, when the question of a voluntary surrender of the aristocratic privileges was to be decided. The Swedish nobility had its class instincts and prejudices, but very rarely it had been found lacking in men of the loftiest patriotism and highest attainments, ever ready to take the lead in the defence of the independence of their country or to follow up faithfully the ambitions of their great rulers. Arrangements had been made to allow noblemen from distant parts and of very limited means to be present, if not during the time of the discussions, which lasted four days, at least at the casting of the vote. Never in the memorable history of the knightly chapterhouse had more eloquent language or loftier thoughts been heard than upon this occasion. Both supporters and opponents of the royal proposition spoke with great sagacity and discernment. The former spoke of the inadvisability of a representation by Estates and by hereditary privileges, and of the dangers of a further postponement of the needed reform. The latter nicely scrutinized the royal proposition, which was considered to give too great influence to the peasants, to weaken the executive power and to depend upon municipal reforms as yet untried. They further considered the upper house, or First Chamber, too homogeneous with the Second to be able to exert the conservative or retaining power expected from it. The members of the cabinet all spoke with fervor and persuasive power in favor of the royal proposition, especially De Geer, Gripenstedt and Carlson. The outcome was that the royal proposition was accepted by a vote of 361 yeas against 294 nays. The nobility as a class thus left the political arena voluntarily and with honor. Now the turn was come to the clergy, who unanimously accepted the royal proposition without further discussion. The result was accepted with outbursts of enthusiasm from all over the country, but especially from the towns. The four Estates adjourned June 22, 1866, forever, and the law of the new system of parliamentary representation was sanctioned the same date.

The royal proposition, which became the law of a new Diet, is based upon the principle of general elections. The Riksdag meets at the commencement of every year. It is divided into two houses or Chambers. The members of the First Chamber, or upper house, are elected for a term of nine years, partly by the Landstings, or district assemblies, partly by the assemblies of towns which do not take part in a Landsting. Elective to the First Chamber are those who have a yearly income of at least $1,000 from some business or enterprise, or as the interest on a capital of their own. These members, or senators, must be at least thirty-five years of age; they do not enjoy any compensation. The members of the Second Chamber, or lower house, are elected by every judicial district in the country which has no more than 40,000 inhabitants and by every 10,000 inhabitants of a town. Towns which have a population of less than 10,000 inhabitants are joined into election districts of from 6,000 to 12,000 inhabitants. Elective to the Second Chamber are those who pay taxes on an income of at least $200 a year and who are twenty-five years of age. These members are compensated for the time spent at the Riksdag. The ordinary Riksdag, which meets every year, lasts for a period of at least four months. The extraordinary Riksdag is called by the king whenever he finds it necessary. The members of the cabinet are elective as members of the Riksdag, and should, during all sessions, be present at the deliberations of the Chambers. The standing committees remain the same as during the time of the old system. Special and temporary committees are appointed when considered necessary. When the two Chambers end in a conflicting vote upon one and the same subject, the committee which prepared it for discussion should try to obtain a satisfactory solution. If such fails, the question is dropped for that year. The expenses of state, the state appropriations and the management of the national bank, when involved, form exceptions to this rule and are voted upon by both Chambers together, the majority of votes from both making the decision.

A new era in Swedish history opens up with the acceptance of the parliamentary reform. The constitution itself had suffered no change, except in points of contact with the new rules of the Riksdag. But the powers of state no longer held to each other the same position as of yore. The government hitherto had, in the very division into four Estates, a support against powerful class and party interests. An equally solid support was not to be expected from a Riksdag of only two Chambers, which in questions of state appropriations is practically one. For this reason many would have preferred the establishment of a system which, instead of abolishing the mediæval arrangement of four Estates, would have added as many classes as there are really extant in the modern state, to gain the desired equilibrium through a manifold and dynamically operating representation. As things shaped themselves after the two Chamber system, the government ought more than ever to have a conservative, retaining power in order to preserve the proper balance. But such was not the case, for the Riksdag had been placed in a position to watch and control the executive power much closer than before, thanks to its authority to fix for each year the appropriations and expenditures of the state. The stipulation that the members of the cabinet are to take part in the deliberations of the Chambers gives another pillar of strength to the Riksdag. If the ministers of state are to exert any influence upon the decisions of the Riksdag, it is requisite to have its full confidence. The king is forced to select for his cabinet such members as are supposed to have an influence with the representatives of the people. The influence of the Riksdag has been steadily increasing ever since 1867.

While the issue of a parliamentary reform occupied the attention of all public-spirited men, the interest in the political situation of Europe was hardly less intense. The sympathy with the unhappy Poles was almost feverish. In 1863 two motions were made at the Riksdag to petition the government to take an active part in the restoration of the kingdom of Poland, by means of diplomatic intervention. The position of the government was a difficult one. The complications between Denmark and Germany had recommenced, and it was important to stand in good relations to Russia. The Swedish public did everything to make these relations precarious, by demonstrations of various kinds in favor of Poland, warlike newspaper articles and subscriptions of money to the leaders of the revolt. Thanks to the sagacity and tactful demeanor of Manderstrœm and the common sense of the Riksdag the motions in question were defeated and a dangerous conflict avoided. Complications of a more serious nature arose on account of the reopened conflict between Denmark and Germany. The Danish government had failed in its efforts to make a satisfactory arrangement in the relations between the crown and the duchies of Schleswig and Holstein. The Germans repeatedly mixed themselves up in the interior affairs of Denmark, and the Danes themselves were divided into several parties. King Frederic VII. at last concluded to give up the idea of gathering in the duchies as integral parts of the kingdom, satisfied to sacrifice the ultimate connection of Holstein and Lauenburg with the crown, but resolved to connect the originally Danish Schleswig with Denmark. The purely German parts were, through the so-called "March Patent" of 1863, separated from the rest of the monarchy, while Schleswig was reunited with it, according to the constitution. This policy was approved by the Scandinavian party in Sweden and Norway, supported by Swedish diplomacy, and, in the first place, by Charles XV. himself. King Charles was inspired by general sympathy with the Scandinavian movement and by personal friendship for Frederic VII. to follow up the Scandinavian policy of his father. The two Scandinavian monarchs met twice during the summer of 1863 and influenced the Swedish-Norwegian and Danish cabinets to draw the outline of a treaty of defence on the basis of the river Eider as the Danish boundary to the south. The Danish government made the proposition for a new constitution according to which Schleswig was to be united to Denmark. This was contrary to the promise made by King Frederic to the German powers in 1852. The proposition for a new constitution was placed before the Danish Diet and accepted. Two days later, November 15, 1863, King Frederic suddenly died, before he had sanctioned the new law. This was a severe blow. The popular king left his beloved people in a most inopportune moment, fraught with peril and disastrous mistakes. The people of Schleswig and Holstein renewed an old contention in regard to the right of succession. The new Danish king, Christian IX., gave in to the pressure brought to bear on him by his cabinet and the inhabitants of Copenhagen. He signed the new constitution, which gave to the German powers a valid excuse to interfere. The Prussian and Austrian troops crossed the river Eider to make good the agreements of 1852.

The Swedish-Norwegian government was placed in an embarrassing position. The alliance of defence that was planned was to a great extent based upon the relations of personal friendship between Charles XV. and Frederic VII. Sweden was not legally pledged to shield Denmark as a consequence of the acceptance of the new constitution. But Sweden had taken a conspicuous part in the deliberations, for which reason a change of policy could not be made without considerable difficulty. The liberal organs of the Swedish press, headed by "Aftonbladet," whose editor was August Sohlman, did everything in their power to make such a change an impossibility. But Sweden was not prepared to make war on two of the great powers of Europe, especially as no other power was willing to join in an alliance in behalf of Denmark. The change must be made; and was effected, principally because of the persuasive arguments and resolute demeanor of Gripenstedt. King Charles resolved to take the painful measures of a retreat. The standpoint of his government he gave to the Riksdag in the following words: "It cannot be expected from us that we should place our sword on the scale of justice without considering if the object can be attained with the resources at our command." It was a supreme sacrifice that Charles XV. made when, for the safety of his countries, he was forced to draw back the hand of support and comradeship which he had offered a brother in distress. The noble-hearted king, in one of his poems, has given a touching expression of the sorrow he felt in being unable to assist Denmark in her hour of peril. King Charles might, with proper resources at his command, have proved a formidable enemy. He had given evidence of possessing all the qualities requisite for the make-up of a great general, without doubt an inheritance from his two grandfathers, Prince Bernadotte and Eugene Beauharnais. A few hundred Swedish and Norwegian volunteers took an honorable part in the Danish war, which was the only practical result of the Scandinavian policy. The Swedish press was violent in its attacks upon the government for its change of policy. In March, 1864, the mob of Stockholm assailed the residences of Manderstrœm, Gripenstedt and other cabinet members, breaking the windows with stones.

Poor Denmark was left alone. Napoleon III. made the mistake of not attempting to defeat Prussia before she had reached her climax of strength. He was tied up with his Mexican adventure and unwilling to help Denmark. Charles XV. could not endure to see Denmark thus deserted. Privately he offered Christian IX. an alliance which stipulated that the three Scandinavian kingdoms should be joined into a union with one common foreign policy and common defence. Charles was also willing to make the succession one, if necessary. This alliance was to embrace only such parts of Denmark which were not to enter the German union. Sweden-Norway would do their utmost to prohibit a separation between Denmark and Schleswig. Denmark refused to accept this offer. Her leading statesman, Monrad, held stubbornly to the idea of an undivided Danish monarchy. For this reason, Denmark was for a second time abandoned to fight out alone her uneven battle. It ended in the loss of Holstein, **Lauenburg and** the greater part of Schleswig, through the treaty of Vienna, October 30, 1864. In Denmark a hard feeling against the Swedes and Norwegians sprang up as a consequence of the disastrous war fought without allies; and the Scandinavian policy and enthusiasm had received a blow from which they have never fully recovered. Charles XV. did all in his power to revive them. He had the pleasure of uniting the efforts of Sweden, Norway and Denmark in a peaceful work of great significance, the first Scandinavian Exposition of Industry and Art, which was opened at Stockholm in June, 1866. The consequence was a perfect Norwegian conquest of Sweden, in a cultured sense. The painters Tidemand and Gude captured the prizes. The composers Kierulf and Nordraak took the lead in song and music. Ibsen and Bjornson became the craze in literature. The literary contact with Norway was begun in 1861, when Lorenz Dietriechson was appointed a docent at the University of Upsala, and for the first time made the contemporary Norwegian and Danish poets acquainted in Sweden. What Sweden received from Norway was a quaint, late-born Romanticism of a strong national flavor. When this Romanticism was changed into stern Realism its influence upon Swedish culture, especially her literature, was only increased, Swedish literature receiving strong realistic impulses from the neighboring Scandinavian countries. The Norwegian influence ceased, when the Swedes at last became aware that there was in it a deeply pessimistic trait, akin to the stern Norwegian and Scotch Christianity, which is incompatible with the Swedish national temperament, slightly inclined to melancholy, but of a robust and irrepressible desire to live and enjoy.

Charles XV. followed up his practical Scandinavian policy by marrying his only daughter Louise to Crown Prince Frederic of Denmark. King Charles was as unsuccessful in his noble efforts to unite more closely his two kingdoms as in his foreign policy. The king allowed some time to pass in order to let the ill-feeling, caused by the conflict of 1859 and 1860, die out. In February, 1865, he considered that the moment had arrived to institute the review of the Act of Union. He appointed a committee of Swedes and Norwegians to prepare the proposition of a new Act of Union, on the basis of perfect equality and right to decide separately all matters, except such pertaining to the Union. The committee performed the work, but their proposition was defeated at the Norwegian Storthing of 1871, at the instigation of John Sverdrup and K. Motzfeldt. The Swedish Riksdag for this reason also failed to accept it. At the close of the Riksdag, King Charles made the following utterance in regard to the defeated proposition: "What has now failed to attain success shall perhaps win out without difficulty when the two nations once have learned to place confidence in each other, as the result of a more intimate intercourse." He saw with great satisfaction the completion of a railway which forever unites the Swedish and the Norwegian capitals with ties of steel.

The administration of Charles XV. persevered in its liberal policy concerning questions of economy and jurisprudence. This was particularly noticeable in commercial matters. The idea of free trade had won ascendency in Europe. Napoleon III. had entered a treaty of commerce with England, in strict opposition to the protective system. Other nations were one by one admitted into the free-trade system by means of new treaties. Sweden made a treaty of commerce and navigation in 1865. This step was severely criticised by the Riksdag of 1865-1866, both from a constitutional and financial point of view. Gripenstedt was accused of leading the way over demolished industries, but he defended his position with great eloquence. The treaty was ratified in spite of the powerful opposition in the Riksdag. The press condemned both the treaty and the government in the most violent language.

The first Riksdag of the new parliamentary system met January 19, 1867. The "Landstings" had sent to the First Chamber the most prominent men of the country. It was a truly representative gathering, a house of peers elected by the people. Lagerbielke, the landtmarshal of the preceding Riksdag, was appointed speaker. The Second Chamber counted a larger number of peasants as representatives than of any other class. Anton Nicolaus Sundberg, then bishop of Carlstad, now archbishop of Sweden, was made speaker of the Second Chamber. The power of the peasants made itself felt at once. There was formed a strong and influential party, the *landtmanna*, or countrymen's party, consisting of small landowners. The peasants constituted the majority, but the party also counted many titled and untitled country gentlemen in interests united with them. The founder of the party was Count Arvid Rutger Posse, later minister of state. Emil Key and the peasants Charles Ifvarsson and Liss Olof Larsson were among the leaders of the party. The policy of the Landtmanna party demanded simplification of the administration, economy in the matter of appropriations and a solution of the questions of the defence and taxation in harmony with the interests of the owners of the soil. The party followed up its policy with stern consistency from Riksdag to Riksdag, until in perfect control of the whole government. The opposition consisted of "the Intelligence" or intellectual party, which, without a solid constitution or a fixed policy, has in vain fought the spreading influence and power of the Landtmanna party. The latter has gone almost too far in its endeavors for economical reform, but has also given evidence of appreciation of the material needs of a cultural development, appropriating large sums for the benefit of science and education.

The army question was the most important issue of Swedish politics. The events of 1866 had made it evident that a strengthening of the defences was necessary. King Charles was anxious to have the question solved in a satisfactory manner, finding therein the only reliable safeguard for the future independence of Sweden. It was apparent that any attempts to settle the question in accordance with the system adopted by Charles XI. would be devoid of result. It was based upon direct taxation of the soil and must be opposed by the strong majority of small landowners of the Landtmanna party. A compromise policy was for this reason begun in 1867, the question of an abolition of the land tax being connected with the army question, although the two ought to have had no connection. The question was started with promises of a reduction or exemption of the duties of the old army system as compensation for the acceptance of a new arrangement for the country's defence. The government made an army proposition to the Riksdag of 1869, promising several reductions to the landowners who furnished soldiers according to the old system (*indelningsverket*). The proposition was prepared by a committee, of which the new minister of war, Gustavus Rudolph Abelin, was the chairman. It was based upon the preservation of the old system for the furnishing of the body force of officers and men. The larger force was to be provided for through militia. The militia was to be drilled in the neighborhood of their various homes during sixty days of the year. The proposition was not accepted. The militia compulsory service, as the duty of every citizen for the defence of his country, had nothing to do with the regular army as provided by the stipulations of the old system. But the majority of the Second Chamber confused the two and refused to allow the establishment of the former on a wider basis, because the offers made to reduce the burdens of the old system did not appear to them liberal enough. In 1871 another proposition was made by Abelin to the Riksdag. It was similar to the first one, and its cause was eloquently pleaded by Abelin, Axel Gustavus Adlercreutz, minister of justice, Peter Axel Bergstrœm, minister of civil service, and Gunnar Vennerberg, minister of ecclesiastics. They warned against the mistake of attaching impossible conditions to the acceptance of the proposition. The proposition for an extended militia service was accepted by both Chambers. But when the Second Chamber raised, as a condition for its acceptance, the suspension, for fifteen years, of the old system which provided for the regular army, the government found it impossible to grant this, and the proposition was dropped.

King Charles was grieved and vexed with the fate of the army bills. The Franco Prussian war made it, in his opinion, of added importance to Sweden to have her defences remodelled. He called an extraordinary session of the Riksdag, in the autumn of 1871, when Abelin brought out a third proposition. It was chiefly of the same contents as the preceding ones. But a remarkable change in the public opinion had now taken place, as to the advisability of retaining the old system. Men who looked upon the question more from a military than an economic point of view entertained doubts as to the practical value of the old regular army as the body force of a compulsory militia. Military officers commenced to attack the old system as the basis of a new army. The Landtmanna party persevered in the request for an abolition of the old system, and this killed the army bill at the extraordinary Riksdag.

Together with the request for an abolition of the old army system, demands for redemption from other burdens placed upon the owners of the soil made themselves heard. The land-tax was the principal one of these burdens and caused as much difference of opinion as the army system. The Landtmanna party considered the land-tax to be of the same nature originally as other taxes, which ought to be more evenly distributed and shared by all classes in the same proportion. The Intelligence party was of the opinion that the land-tax in the course of time had come to be rents or mortgages which always were taken into consideration at the exchange of property, as reducing the stock value of the property in question. To free a present generation from the payment of land-tax, was in the eyes of the opposition, an injustice to the other classes whose taxes thereby were to be increased. The Landtmanna party had, in 1869, commenced an agitation for the reduction of the land-tax for shorter periods and on a small scale at first, but with increasing demands at every new Riksdag.

The government, whose members had been the champions of parliamentary reform, was soon disregarded by the triumphant party, while its old opponents never forgot it. The earlier advisers of the king retired one by one when they saw their influence in the Riksdag vanish. King Charles himself took the defeat of the army bills deep at heart. His health commenced to fail in 1871, and when his faithful consort died, in the same year, having exposed her own health in her attempts to improve the condition of the king, the latter grew worse. After a trip abroad for his health, King Charles XV. died at Malmœ, September 18, 1872, deeply mourned by the two nations. In the following year his youngest brother Nicolaus August, duke of Dalecarlia, died, leaving only two of the children of Oscar I., Oscar Frederic, duke of East Gothland, and Princess Eugenie. The history of Charles XV. carries the principal traits of his character. His sweeping reforms in social, political and economical matters, and his great plans for the future, even if sometimes immature, or high-strung, were always characterized by loftiness of purpose. A typical Swede both in his merits and his faults, this was the secret of the immense popularity of King Charles, which always followed him, although he never sought it.

The philosopher Christian Jacob Bostrœm is the most popular of Swedish thinkers and the first who founded a national system and school of philosophy, idealistic and rational, and in strict opposition to the system of Hegel. Bostrœm was born in Pitea, in 1797, was the teacher of the sons of Oscar I., and succeeded the able philosopher Samuel Grubbe, a talented follower of Hœijer, as professor of philosophy at the University of Upsala. Bostrœm was a highly fascinating and suggestive teacher, while he neglected his literary production, which is neither exhaustive nor quite representative of his philosophy. He exerted a considerable influence by his outline of a philosophical state, which pleased the conservatives, while a much more widespread and lasting impression was produced by his criticism of the doctrines of a hell and a devil. A whole literature sprang into life, discussing vehemently the existence or non-existence of the fiend. To this literature and the works and writings of Bostrœm is to be credited the spirit of religious tolerance which characterized life and literature during the reign of Charles XV. It fostered in the cultured few a leaning toward Unitarianism or Theosophy, while it gave rise to a shallow materialism and religious indifference in the less cultured classes and individuals.

The artistic, literary and musical life bore a decided resemblance to the intellectually interested but dilettantic king. Charles XV. was surrounded by a great number of painters who, although possessing a good deal of talent, succeeded only in the smaller field of genre painting. Remarkable exceptions are J. F. Hœckert, Marcus Larsson and C. H. L. D'Uncker, who possessed sterling genius and acquired great fame. Several promising painters, like George von Rosen, developed later the full scope of their power. The sculptor J. P. Molin was highly talented, a worthy follower of B. E. Fogelberg, who had enriched Swedish art with a number of highly important sculptures.

In the world of letters, the spirit of dilettantism was more strongly felt than in art, Swedish literature, after its several glorious epochs, experiencing one of its most stagnant periods. A veritable giant among pygmies was Victor Rydberg, whose remarkable novel, "The Last Athenian," appeared in 1859, but whose principal productivity as a poet and scientist belongs to a later period. So do, to a great extent, the best works of the poets Eduard Beckstrœm, also an able dramatist, and Count Carl Snoilsky. Zacharias Topelius, the Walter Scott and Hans Christian Andersen of Finland, must be mentioned here. Writing in the Swedish language, and for his principal work using subjects of Swedish history, he was as highly beloved in Sweden as in Finland. His excellent series of historical novels, called "The Surgeon's Stories," have been translated into several languages. His juvenile stories are not characterized by the same degree of inventive power as are the tales by Andersen, but Topelius had the latter's ability of placing himself in intimate contact with the pure minds of all ages.

In the most national of Swedish cultural elements, the song, the epoch of dilettantism found its most beautiful and lasting expressions. The quartet and chorus singing at the universities of Upsala and Lund was cultivated to the highest standards of excellence and had a splendid repertory in the songs of Otto Lindblad, Vennerberg, Prince Gustavus, Josephsson, Crusell, Cronhamn, etc. The Upsala students caused a great sensation by their singing at the Paris Exposition of 1867, and have repeated their successes at the Paris Exposition of 1878, and in Berlin in 1898. Swedish quartets of men's and women's voices have travelled all over the world and made a lasting fame for this minor but bewitching branch of musical art. As dramatic singers of the first rank, Louise Michaëli and Christine Nilsson have been the worthy successors of Jenny Lind. To this period, as well as to the next, belongs Elisa Hvasser, the greatest and most versatile actress Sweden has ever had. This artist was equally at home in the farce and melodrama, but excelled in the tragic parts of the Shakespeare, Schiller, and Ibsen repertory. Indispensable in their positions at the Royal Theatre of Stockholm, Michaëli, the songstress, and Hvasser, the tragedienne, did not travel, thereby losing the fame a world would have been only too glad to give them.

CHAPTER XVIII

Progress and Prosperity—Oscar II

OSCAR II. ascended the throne at a moment when universal peace was restored after the great conflict between France and Germany, and when an age of commercial prosperity for Sweden seemed to have begun. King Oscar had received the same superior education as his older brothers, is as brilliantly gifted as they were and of a more scholarly mind. As a writer on scientific subjects, a poet and an orator, Oscar II. had distinguished himself before his succession to the throne. The new king offered the best of securities for a sound administration in his thorough and versatile knowledge, wide experience in public affairs, and rich and harmonious endowment. Oscar II. still did not find it easy to gain the love and admiration of the Swedish people, of which he is so eminently worthy. He was the successor of one of the most popular of rulers that the country ever saw, but King Oscar has lived to see his own popularity almost outrival that of his predecessor. King Oscar is, at seventy, a handsome, spirited gentleman, with that dignity which age, rare attainments, high intelligence and a noble soul grant their common possessor. This the most learned and popular monarch of Europe is of a tall, commanding figure, six feet three inches in height, of a handsome, expressive face, with cheeks of a ruddy color and mild blue eyes.

Oscar II. has shown great discernment in his arrangement of dynastic matters. Himself married to the fervently religious Princess Sophie of Nassau, the king has married his oldest son, Crown Prince Gustavus Adolphus, to Princess Victoria of Bade, a granddaughter of Emperor William I. of Germany, and a great-granddaughter of Gustavus IV. of Sweden. His third son, Prince Charles, duke of West Gothland, is married to Princess Ingeborg of Denmark, a granddaughter of Charles XV. of Sweden. These unions are well calculated to accentuate the increasing political, commercial and cultural intimacy with Germany, the Scandinavian policy of his predecessor and the desire of King Oscar to see the descendants of the old royal line of Sweden as heirs to the crown. In giving his consent to the marriage of his second son, Prince Oscar (Bernadotte), to Lady Ebba Munck, of the Swedish nobility, King Oscar has given evidence of the fact that he is not a matchmaker regardless of the feelings of the parties involved. Prince Oscar, formerly Duke of Gothland, upon renouncing his share of inheritance to the two thrones, was allowed to marry the choice of his heart. King Oscar has tried to heal the wounds of the past by opening the vaults of the church of Riddarholm to the sarcophagi of Gustavus IV. and his son, and by giving Queen Carola of Saxony, the only living granddaughter of the former, repeated proofs of esteem and considerate distinction.

King Oscar with his crowns had received as an inheritance two important problems to be solved—the reorganization of the Swedish army and the settlement of the difficulties in the relations between the two states of the Union.

The latter has not yet found a satisfactory solution, although the king has devoted to it his most strenuous attention and the best of his efforts, in honest application to his royal motto: "The Weal of the Brother Nations "

The reorganization of the Swedish army was not effected until after twenty years of parliamentary struggle. The road of a compromise policy which was opened in 1867 was followed up at the Riksdag of 1873, in all the long chain of years royal army bills being repeatedly rejected. In 1885 the government and Riksdag agreed on a remission of thirty per cent of the military taxes of landowners in exchange for new regulations for the militia compulsory service. In 1887 the Riksdag sanctioned the total abolition of the "indelta," or cantoned troops, as far as the navy was concerned, which was the first step toward the reorganization of the navy, and the same year the militia law of 1885 went into effect.

The old Landtmanna, or agrarian party, in 1888 gave place to a new protectionistic party. A contested election of twenty-two members from Stockholm gave a sudden majority to the protectionists, O. R. Themptander, the able minister of state, resigning. The army bill did not fare well at first. In spite of the fact that the Landtmanna party was brushed aside, the old enemies of an army reform, the landowners, nobles and peasants alike, still being strong enough to successfully oppose it. The Riksdag of 1888 passed a grain tariff, which went into effect February 14th of the same year, enforcing several other points of a protective tariff system.

King Oscar called an extraordinary, or special, session of the Riksdag, October 18, 1892, when royal propositions were offered and accepted. The land-tax was abolished and a new army bill passed. According to the stipulations of the latter, the *beværingstid*, or period of liability for every citizen to bear arms, was extended to embrace twenty years instead of twelve, viz., eight years in the first ban of the *landtværn*, or militia, four years in the second ban, and eight years in the *landstorm*, or final levy. The first ban of militia is in time of war to form an integral part of the first fighting line, the second ban forming a reserve for the first fighting line. The final levy is to be called out for garrison duty exclusively, and for the defence of the country against foreign invasion. Six military districts have been established, five distributed along the entire coast of Sweden, the sixth inland in the western provinces to be a reserve ready to be used at the point and moment most needed. The reorganized army in active service is composed of *værfvade*, or enlisted troops, and *indelta*, or cantoned troops, the expenses also of the latter being paid by the government. The royal guards, chasseurs, hussars, artillery, and engineers are enlisted for two years up to eight. The militia troops are distributed among both the enlisted and the cantoned troops, the length of service with the colors being ninety days in time of peace. The infantry in which all the cantoned troops serve consist of twenty-six regiments and two battalions. The line is armed with Remingtons of 8.8 millimetres calibre. There are eight regiments of cavalry and six regiments and six batteries of field artillery, forty batteries in all, with 240 cannon. The effective of the active army, in 1896, was 1,953 officers, 571 employees, 1,779 non-commissioned officers, 1,641 musicians and 38,802 men, with 6,852 horses. The war effective is 272,994 men, besides 180,000 in the *landstorm*. The chief fortifications of Sweden are Carlscrona, on the south coast; two fortresses outside of Stockholm, viz., Vaxholm and Oscar Fredericsborg; and, in the interior, Carlsborg, near Lake Vetter. The navy comprises 4 turret ships, with 10 inch armor, armed each with 2 10-inch and 4 5.9-inch guns, and having a total displacement of 12,450 tons; 4 armor clad monitors, 9 armored gunboats, 3 corvettes, 9 first-class and 5 second-class gunboats, 2 torpedo cruisers, 7 first-class and 9 second-class torpedo boats, 5 torpedo launches, and 12 school ships. The navy is manned by 267 officers and about 4,500 sailors, not including conscripts to the number of 8,500 men. The entire cost of the defence of Sweden exceeds ten million dollars a year.

The movement for a reorganization of the defences has not been caused by any change in the policy of peace, which has faithfully been carried out by all the rulers of the Bernadotte dynasty. The ruler of Sweden and her people desire peace, but not as a gift of mercy from the great powers, but as a self-chosen right which can be effectively defended if necessary. The ever-increasing armament of the European powers has made a strengthening of the Swedish arms unavoidable, but the Swedish government was the first to announce its readiness to accept the invitation of Czar Nicholas II. of Russia to a conference for the discussion of a general reduction of the regular armies. Germany was made the pattern for the reorganization of the army and navy, the Swedish government having followed the German also in the treatment of the labor question, with schemes of accident and old-age insurance, accepted by the Riksdag.

King Oscar, at his succession to the throne, gave evidence of his desire to meet the reasonable demands of his Norwegian subjects. He sanctioned, in 1873, the abolition of the office of a governor-general of Norway, the government at Christiania to be presided over by a Norwegian minister of state. To the later Norwegian demands for a separate flag, consular service and ministry of foreign affairs, King Oscar has been unyielding. The flag question is of subordinate importance. King Oscar, in 1899, has refused to sanction the resolution of the Storthing, three times passed, for a flag without the mark of Union, for the reason that the flag with that mark was offered to Norway by his father, Oscar I., and gratefully accepted when the country had no colors at all, except the Swedish. The Swedish people will carry their old flag with the mark of Union, irrespective of any changes made in the Norwegian colors. More serious are the questions of consular and diplomatic service. In 1893, the Swedish government offered to compromise by establishing a common ministry of foreign affairs whose head might be indifferently a Swede or a Norwegian. This was rejected by the Norwegian Storthing. The same offer was made in 1837, when the dispute first arose, provided that the Norwegian troops should share the duty of the common defence of both kingdoms. The Swedish Riksdag of 1893 passed a resolution, in compliance with which King Oscar for a second time refused to sanction the bill of Norwegian consulates.

The diametrically opposite views which are held in regard to the relations of Sweden and Norway are, to a great extent, caused by a misconception of the nature of the Union. In lack of a Union parliament, it has by many been considered to be only a personal union of two countries under the same king. Such is not the case. It is true that the two countries are both free and independent states and that the king is the only visible bond between them, according to the Act of Union, but the Union is nevertheless an *actual* and not a *personal* one. If it was only personal, the king could at will, or when forced to do so, resign his power in one of the countries and continue his reign in the other. The Act of Union cannot be changed except upon a resolution, enacted in both of the respective diets, and with the sanction of the king in behalf of the Union. A change can be made at the same Swedish Riksdag at which it is proposed, at the Norwegian Storthing not until the next regular session. As a consequence the Union cannot be dissolved by the representatives of either country alone, and the king cannot dissolve it by exercising any power of his own. The king cannot abdicate one throne without abdicating the other, for the first paragraph of the Act of Union stipulates that the two countries shall be indissolubly and irrevocably united under the rule of the same king. No abdication can be granted, except by common consent of the two diets in joint session. When the two thrones are empty, without an heir-apparent, a new king shall be elected by the two diets in common. What underlies the Norwegian claims of a separate foreign ministry is, besides to own an outward sign of the country's independence, a desire for a closer constitutional control of diplomatic affairs. From the Swedish side the desirability of a Union parliament and a greater authority for the Union government has been expressed. The Swedes have been found unwilling to grant any change of the constitution of the Union, except the right be added for the Union government to dispose of the military forces of both countries, in equal proportion, for the common defence. King Oscar's standpoint in the Unionist conflict has contributed much to increase his popularity in Sweden, where his firm refusal to sanction any measure which would cause a weakening to the Union has been received with the highest approval.

A committee to review the relations of the Union and propose a revision of its charter was appointed in 1897, but failed to accomplish anything, the views of the Swedish and Norwegian members differing too radically in their opinions. It is to be hoped that the ultimate solution of the unionist conflict, whensoever it come or whatsoever it be, will bring the two countries of the Scandinavian peninsula closer together, without any great sacrifice on either side, least of all of their independence.

During the more than eighty years of peace which Sweden has enjoyed under the rule of the Bernadotte dynasty, she has developed her constitutional liberty and her material prosperity in a high degree. The dreams of glory by conquest belong to days gone by, but in the fields of peaceable industries she has attained a greatness which the world begins to realize. At the expositions of Paris in 1867, 1878 and 1889, of Vienna in 1873, of Philadelphia in 1876 and of Chicago in 1893, Swedish industry and art have taken part with honor in the international competition. The railways of Sweden have incessantly spun a more and more extended network of steel over the country, opening connections for enterprises in new districts and furthering commerce and industrial art in a wide measure. Oscar II. is an enthusiastic friend of railway improvements, the state having built and acquired a quite considerable length of road at his initiative. The length of Swedish railways, in 1896, was 6,145 miles, of which 2,283 miles belonged to the state, compared to a total of 1,089 miles of Norwegian railways.

The post office, which was made a government department by Axel Oxenstierna, in 1636, annually transmits 130 million letters and parcels. The telegraph lines have not reached a very high state of development; still there are 14,600 miles of telegraph. The telephone has made much more progress, far surpassing that of any other country in Europe. The total length of the connections exceeds 40,000 miles, and the number of apparatus is more than 25,000. Stockholm makes the widest use of the telephone of any city in the world, with her 300,000 inhabitants having a telephone for every thirty. Sweden has developed into a commercial country of no inconsiderable rank, notwithstanding her isolated position. Exports and imports each exceed yearly in value $100,000,000, the imports being 344,290,000 kronor and the exports 311,434,000 kronor in value, in 1895, a Swedish krona being about twenty-eight cents. The commercial value of the foreign trade amounts to thirty-nine dollars in yearly average for each inhabitant of Sweden, which is about as much as in France. The imports chiefly consist of coal, coffee, salt, cotton and wool, while the exports are timber products, about forty per cent of the whole, iron and steel, the best in the world, machinery, butter, cattle, matches, etc. The inland navigation and commerce are very lively. The state finances are in a prosperous condition. The budget of 1898 showed total receipts of 120,086,000 kronor, of which 14,229,000 was surplus from proceeding budgets.

Thanks to the well equipped and regulated system of instruction, the general education has been so highly advanced that Sweden, in this respect, holds the very front rank among the nations. Besides the national universities of Upsala and Lund and the state medical college of Stockholm, city universities at Stockholm and Gothenburg have been recently founded which are quickly developing. All study at the universities consists of post-graduate work, there being about thirty colleges in various parts of the country which lead their pupils as far as the demands requisite for entering the universities. The Swedish university courses are of unexcelled thoroughness and completeness. The so-called Peasant High Schools are peculiar to Scandinavia, having originated in Denmark. There are twenty-five such high schools in Sweden, which give to young men and women of the peasant class a higher education than is available in the common schools, of which latter there are 10,702, with 692,360 pupils and 13,797 teachers.

Scientific research progresses with energy and success, and Sweden possesses to-day a great number of eminent scholars, even if the epoch of men of universal genius appears to be a thing of the past there as elsewhere. Swedish scientists have opened closer relations with their co-workers in all parts of the world. The energy of King Oscar has brought about several congresses of science at Stockholm. In the natural sciences, Sweden still holds an honored place, in physics offering two great names, Eric Edlund and A. J. Angstrœm, the latter celebrated for his work on the solar spectrum, which forms the basis for the spectral analysis. Death has claimed these men and also J. A. H. Gyldén, an eminent astronomer; J. G. Agardh, C. W. Blomstrand, H. O. Nathorst, J. E. Rydquist, able botanist, chemist, agriculturist, and philologist, respectively; Pontus Wikner, the most remarkable of the disciples of the philosopher Bostrœm, and Victor Rydberg, the philosophical poet, novelist and polyhistor.

Among the most noteworthy of living Swedish scholars are Adolph Norén, Axel Koch and Esaias Tegnér, Junior, philologists; Hans Hildebrand and Oscar Montelius, archæologists; P. Fahlbeck, Nils and Magnus Hœjer, Martin Weibull, Ernest Carlson, historians; A. M. Mittag-Leffler, mathematician; Hugo Hildebrandsson, meteorologist; E. A. H. Key, E. O. T. Westerlund, Anton Wetterstrand, F. J. Biornstrœm, T. F. Hartelius, Curt Wallis, prominent in various branches of medical science.

King Oscar with fervent interest and unfailing liberality has encouraged various scientific explorations, and has had the satisfaction to see the greatest geographical discoveries of the century successfully made by Swedes, the circumnavigation of Asia and Europe, and the discovery of the Northeast Passage by Baron N. A. E. Nordenskiold, and the exploration of Central Asia by Sven Hedin, which has forever settled the learned disputes of ages. A third expedition, the most daring of scientific exploits ever attempted, still keeps the world in suspense as to its final outcome. July 11, 1897, S. A. Andrée, a scientifically experienced aëronaut, with two companions, Nils Strindberg and Knut Frænkel, started in a balloon constructed for the purpose, and with provisions for three years, from an island of Spitzbergen, with the purpose of reaching the North Pole. The daring aëronauts have not been heard from since their departure, but authorities like Baron Nordenskiold have expressed the best of hopes that they may have reached Franz Joseph's Land in safety, whence they might regain settled regions.' S. A. Andrée belongs to a class of men, the Swedish engineers, who have won distinction for their ability, and on whom the examples set by Christopher Polhem and John Ericsson have had a stimulating influ-

---

' A. C. Nathorst, an able scientist and explorer, started in the summer of 1899 with an expedition to Greenland in search of Andrée and his companions.

ence. There are among them two inventors of the very first rank, who belong to the reign of Oscar II., Alfred Nobel (d. 1896), the inventor of dynamite, and Gustavus de Laval, the Swedish Edison. The latter is world-famous for his separator and other inventions, which have revolutionized the dairy industry. Alfred Nobel, the disciple of John Ericsson, has not only the glory of having invented one of the most useful helpers of mechanic and industrial progress, but also that of having set aside his vast fortune, amounting to something like $12,500,000, for public purposes. The money is so invested as to constitute a fund the interest of which shall be applied to five equal annual prizes, to be awarded for the most important discovery or improvement in chemistry, physics or medicine, for the work in literature highest in the ideal sense, and to the one who shall have acted most and best for the fraternity of nations, the suppression or reduction of standing armies, and the constitution and propagation of peace congresses. The first prize, physics and chemistry, shall be awarded by the Academy of Science of Sweden; that for physiology and medicine by the Carolin Institute of Stockholm; the literary prize by the Swedish Academy; and that for the propagation of peace by a commission of five members elected by the Norwegian Storthing. He especially directed that in distributing these prizes no consideration of nationality shall prevail, so that he who is most worthy of it shall receive the reward, whether he be Scandinavian or not. It seems that the sum of each of the five annual prizes thus instituted will amount to $75,000. The inventor of dynamite was deeply interested in all that was done to promote peace by congresses and societies. He always considered that by improving war material, and thus increasing the dangers of war, he was contributing his share toward the pacification of the world. Alfred Nobel has, by the manner in which the Norwegian Storthing is made an active party in the disposition of his will, indicated *his* view upon the Union of Sweden and Norway and his hopes for a peaceful solution of their conflicts.

Swedish literature, after the period of dilettantism and epigones, has, during the reign of Oscar II., twice been rejuvenated and continues its development on broadened paths and with a wider scope. The eighties were characterized by a strong realistic movement, which went far in daring truth of description and brought problems of a social, religious and political nature under discussion in works of a novelistic or dramatic form. In naturalism, it never went to the extremes of the other Scandinavian literature. The movement was to a great extent brought on by Norwegian and Danish influence, and soon subsided for want of solid and fascinating art to maintain it. The Swedish champion of this movement, although without the restrictions of any school, was August Strindberg, a genius of extraordinary endowment. Through the versatility and power of his talent, he created new forms for the Swedish drama, novel, short story and essay. In his battle against reactionary conservatism he went too far; an excitable nature, led into extremes, but he has had the manly courage to confess and regret his mistakes. Strindberg, who is an able historian, ethnographer, naturalist and sinologue, is the most versatile and prolific of contemporary writers. In the wide scope of his genius and originality of his methods, Strindberg is one of the most remarkable dramatists that ever lived. His autobiographical works are of supreme importance, both to the students of literature and psychology. Among his masterpieces are "Master Olof," the great historic drama of his youth, "Swedish Fates and Adventures," and "Utopia Realized," two series of short stories, and "The Father," a modern drama of unsurpassed tragic grandeur.

Several women took an active part in the literary discussion of social problems, with more or less justice considered as the champions of women's rights. Among these Anne Charlotte Leffler, duchessa di Cajanello, in spite of her premature death, developed into a novelist of merit who will be placed side by side with Bremer, Knorring and Carlén.

The golden lyres of Romanticism were silenced and the epigones were hushed by the sarcasms of Realism. Count Snoilsky and Victor Rydberg were the only poets of the earlier period who sang with inspiration and were listened to. After the realistic movement of the eighties came a romantic reaction with new lyrics and new novelists, who avoided the ruthlessness of the realists, but had profited by their merits. This new movement cannot be called a school, for it is marked by its great versatility of subjects and great elasticity of treatment. If the definition of realistic art be "a piece of nature seen through a temperament," that of the new movement may be "an artistic temperament attuned to pieces of nature," a sensitive and supple talent which has an almost unlimited capacity to tell every story just in the vein its particular subject demands. Pre-eminent in this movement stand Ola Hansson, Selma Lagerloef, Verner von Heidenstam, Gustaf af Geijerstam, Peter Hallstrœm, Thor Hedberg, Oscar Levertin, all fine novelists, almost all good poets, and Geijerstam, an able dramatist. One of the most interesting and supremely gifted poets

Sweden has ever had is Gustaf Frœding, who generally excels, sometimes abuses, his remarkable versatility in finding a true lyric expression for the very widest range of subjects. Sigurd Hedenstierna is the most popular humorist, witty in his sketches, but impossible as a novelist. The greatest humorists are August Strindberg and Gustaf Frœding. Contemporary Sweden has very few and no great literary critics, but some good literary historians in Henric Schueck, Karl Warburg and Oscar Levertin. She has a number of able journalists, most distinguished among whom is their Nestor, S. A. Hedlund, of Gothenburg, a fiery but dignified champion of a liberal government, religious tolerance, social evolution and cultural progress.

Swedish literature has a long pedigree compared to Swedish art, which is hardly more than two centuries old. All the more remarkable, then, is its rapid growth and high degree of excellence. The first school of Swedish painters was founded by the German Ehrenstrahl, giving to Swedish art the cosmopolitan character it has preserved to this day, influenced by continental but chiefly French art. Swedish painters early attracted attention abroad. Gustavus Lundberg, with a picture of Boucher and his wife, won the greatest success of the Salon of Paris, in 1743. Peter Adolphus Hall, "painter to the king and the children of France," has been called the Van Dyck of the miniature painters. He resided in Paris up to the time of the revolution and took part in the storming of the Bastile. Alexander Roslin was, from the year 1760, installed in the Louvre as painter to the king and councillor of the French Academy. In 1771 he carried home a prize which the immortal Greuze could not capture, much to the dismay of

Diderot, and died as the most famous and wealthy artist of the period. In a later period, Italy attracted many Swedish artists, and later still, in the sixties of the present century, the influence of Germany, especially of the Dusseldorf school, was strongly felt. John Frederic Hœckert won the first prize of the Paris Exposition of 1855 with his large picture "Divine Service in the Lapmark." When the glories of Hœckert were almost forgotten at home, Edward Wahlberg, in the seventies, was ushered into celebrity as one of the greatest landscape painters of modern times, equally appreciated in Germany, as later in France, and new French laurels were won by Hugo Salmson, William von Gegerfelt and August Hagborg. Since then French influences have become solidly established, with a few important artists of the Munich school, like C. G. Hellquist and Julius Kronberg. The climax of artistic honors was reached by Nils Forsberg, whose picture, "The Death of a Hero," carried home the first prize of the French Salon in 1888 (not an exposition medal), a distinction which no Swede and exceedingly few non-French artists ever won. The repeated successes which Swedish painters have won at expositions of Europe were more than duplicated by the enthusiastic approval granted it at the World's Fair in Chicago in 1893. The truth is that Sweden possesses a number of eminent painters in every branch of painting, except the marine, which has been but sparingly represented since the days of Marcus Larsson. The most famous among them are, besides those already mentioned, Richard Bergh, Oscar Biorck, Eva Bonnier, Gustavus Cederstrœm, Prince Eugene, Eugene Jansson, Ernest Josephson, Nils Kreuger, Carl Larsson, Bruno Liljefors, Charles Nordstrœm, Allan Œsterlind, Georg and Hanna Pauli, George von Rosen,

Robert Thegerstrom, and A. L. Zorn. It has been said of the Swedish painters, by way of complaint, that they are not, as their brethren in Denmark and Norway, in any marked degree national. Swedish art has, for its characteristic boldness and superiority in modern technique, loftiness of purpose, great individuality of expression and depth of feeling. Be these characteristics national or cosmopolitan, the Swedish painters are certainly a great credit to their country. To King Oscar it must be in a high degree satisfactory to see the artistic tendencies of his family culminate in the works of his youngest son, Prince Eugene, who, being in the front line of the advance corps of art, paints, from dreamy, inner life, pictures which are the delight of artists and true connoisseurs.

The sculptors are less numerous, but the art of Sergel, Fogelberg and Molin have found worthy perpetuators and innovators in Per Hasselberg, John Bœrjesson, Frithiof Kjellberg, Alfred Nystrœm, Christian Ericsson, Th. Lundberg and Ingel Fallstedt. To the art of metal engraving on coins and medals Sweden has offered some works of the very highest value by J. E. Ericson, P. H. Lundgren, Lea Ahlborn and Adolphus Lindberg.

Architecture cannot boast of any continuous chain of brilliant development. Since the days of Nicodemus Tessin there have been few great architects until in very recent times, when architecture has received a sudden impetus which has made its progress and results as remarkable, or almost more so, than that of the other arts. To Helgo Zettervall a number of elaborate national works of construction and restoration have been intrusted and, as a rule, carried through in a meritorious manner, although sometimes giving occasion for serious criticism. An important influence was exerted by Frederic William Scholander, more by his teaching than by his works. It is principally his pupils who in the last few decades have almost revolutionized the building methods and architectural aspect of the capital, and endowed Gothenburg and other towns with works of architectural distinction. Pre-eminent among modern architects are I. G. Clason, Gustavus Wickman, K. F. von Gegerfelt, Adrian Peterson, Hans Hedlund, Valfried Karlson, A. F. Anderberg, E. Lallerstedt. The Vasa, or Swedish Castle Renaissance, which with good effect has been reintroduced for monumental buildings, seems to lead architecture on to a wholesome national development, combining impressive outlines and solidity with elaboration and grace of interior decoration.

The foremost composers of orchestral music have been mentioned above. Sweden maintains her reputation as being the country of song through the compositions by Hedenblad, Kœrling, Svedbom, Sjœgren and Arlberg, while Sœderman has brought the form of the ballad, based on national folk music, to the highest development. The royal opera of Stockholm recently moved into new and elegant quarters erected on the site of the old opera house built by Gustavus III. It possesses, in Caroline Œstberg, Mathilde Linden, Arvid Œdman, C. F. Lundquist and J. Elmblad, dramatic singers of high rank, while Sweden, in Louise Pyk, Mathilde Grabow-Taube and Solomon Smith, owns concert singers of great eminence. The international firmament of song has two Swedish stars of considerable magnitude in Sigrid Arnoldsson-Fischhoff, a coloratura songstress, and Ellen Nordgren-Gullbrandson, a Wagner singer. The greatest actor is Emil Hillberg, a noble creator of Ibsen and Strindberg rôles, while the country recently lost its ablest comedian in the death of Knut Almlœf.

Sweden of to-day offers an attractive picture of a country in a high degree cultured and prosperous, but no country or period is entitled to reap only benefits or enjoy undisturbed happiness. No progress is obtained without struggle and relapses, and a good must give way for something better. Beneath a surface generally smiling and serene formidable religious and social forces are in motion. The Swedish state church is divided into two camps, which resemble a high and a low church, out of which the whole may come forward strengthened and rejunevated. The various sects are not all satisfied with the degree of liberty they enjoy. A shallow materialistic movement of anti-religious tendencies, which styled itself Utilitarian, caused some sensation in the latter eighties and early nineties, more through the somewhat too severe manner in which it was suppressed than through any of its own merits. There are agitators for a separation of state and church who are opposed by some of the stanchest friends of a constitutional monarchy. A separation of educational and church affairs seems desirable. The yeomen have regained the predominant position in political life which was theirs in the time of the ancient Teutonic communities, using their power in a way which is not always beneficial to the other classes or the state at large. The great class of country population, which has been in vain striving to rise to the privileged class of landowners, if even on the smallest scale, have emigrated in vast numbers. The emigration, which has given America at least 1,200,000 inhabitants of Swedish birth or parentage, is one of the most astounding phenomena of the century. It has, to a large extent, subsided, but may be revived if the pressure for social improvement is found of no avail. The workingmen are resolved to gain a representation and are striving to attain the introduction of general suffrage. The weapons they use are principally strikes, but may also turn to wholesale emigration. In 1893 the advocates of universal suffrage arranged for the election of a convention by popular vote, the first Folksriksdag, which addressed an appeal to the legal Riksdag, to consider an amendment for the extension of the suffrage. The liberals and radicals are interested in this agitation, and brought out their full vote to the Folksriksdag. The conservative party ignores the whole movement, probably not wisely. The towns are seeking an extended representation and bitterly oppose the curtailment of the rights already enjoyed, fearing the reactionary tendencies of the conservatives, who have their strength in the large agrarian population. Anarchism is something unknown in Sweden. The socialistic agitation, which is spreading among the classes without a political representation, is carried on without any great bitterness and entirely without lawless means.

Any practical or theoretical agitation for a republic there is none in Sweden, the population as a whole not finding salvation from the defects of government or society in any outward change of rule. Civil service is enforced to the letter, and the social pressure from above downward is of a nature caused by financial or educational supremacy only and would remain the same under republican rule. The Swedes are proud of their history and the long and unbroken chain of their political and social development. Their neighbors accuse them of having traces of the chauvinism of bygone days, but not altogether with justice. The national anthem of Sweden can be quoted in their justification. It speaks, in one instance, of the country as enthroned on memories of a glorious past when its name filled the world; but that name is the North, to whose grandeur and loveliness of nature the whole song is a panegyric. The name of Sweden is not even mentioned, a fact which does not point to a narrow or antiquated form of patriotism. There is in the nature of the Swedes a tendency to delight in the display of dignified luxury, which was known to Tacitus. The Swedes love to see the crown of one of the oldest states of Europe carried with dignity as an emblem of their ancient independence. The Swedish king has in reality less power than the President of the United States, but the Swedes have an inherited faculty of confidence and loyalty of which their king receives his full share. The Swedes become excellent citizens of a republic for that very reason: reverence for, and loyalty to, the institutions and historial development of the country in which they dwell. Among the Scandinavian nationalities, the Swede has been characterized as the nobleman or aristocrat, on account of his love of luxury and the joys of life, his dignity, diplomatic talent and lyrico-rhetoric temperament. It is true that his dignity seldom forsakes the Swede; when it does, something of the soldier of the Thirty Years' War comes to the surface. To her diplomatic talent, more than to her glorious victories, Sweden owes her superiority in size, prosperity and political importance, as compared to her Scandinavian neighbors.

The fundamental laws of the kingdom of Sweden are: 1. The constitution of June 6, 1809; 2. The amended regulations for the formation of the Riksdag of June 22, 1866; 3. The law of royal succession of September 26, 1810; and on the liberty of the press of July 16, 1812. According to these statutes, the king must be a member of the Lutheran church, and have sworn fealty to the laws of the land. His person is inviolable. He has the right to declare war and make peace after consulting the state council. He nominates to all higher appointments, both military and civil; concludes foreign treaties, and has a right to preside in the supreme court of justice. The princes of the blood royal are excluded from all civil employments. The king possesses legislative power in matters of political administration, but in all other respects that power is exercised by the Riksdag, in concert with the sovereign, and every new law must have the assent of the crown. The right of imposing taxes is vested in the Riksdag. The executive power is in the hands of the king, who acts under the advice of a cabinet or state council, the head of which is the minister of state. It consists of ten members, seven of whom are ministerial heads of departments and three without departments. All the members of the cabinet are responsible for the acts of the government.

Eric Gustavus Boström is minister of state, holding office since 1891, after the protectionists had got into power and the compromise cabinets which followed were a thing of the past. The other ministers without departments, Baron A. L. E. Akerhielm and S. H. Wikblad, have remained in office since the days of compromise cabinets. The other members who have been in office from five to eight years are as follows: Count L. V. A. Douglas, minister of foreign affairs; P. S. L. Annerstedt, minister of justice; Baron A. E. Rappe, minister of war; J. C. E. Christerson, minister of marine; J. E. von Krusenstierna, minister of interior; Count H. Hansson Wachtmeister, minister of finance; G. F. Gilljam, minister of education and ecclesiastical affairs.

King Oscar II., in the jubilee year of 1897, which marked the completion of a quarter of a century of his reign, received innumerable proofs of the love of the two nations under his rule and of the high esteem in which he is held by the governments and citizens of foreign countries. The occasion was celebrated by a large and highly successful Scandinavian exposition at Stockholm in the summer, Russia, with Finland, also taking part, and by a series of festivities about September 21st, the date of his succession to the throne. King Oscar has always given sympathetic attention to the United States, especially to their citizens of Swedish birth. Several deputations from America called upon the king in the jubilee year. Among these was a male chorus of fifty-four members, belonging to the American Union of Swedish singers. The singers were invited to the royal castle and received and feasted by the aged monarch with cordial simplicity, in all royal splendor, without any of its pomp or ceremony. To the hearty songs of his unpretentious guests, King Oscar responded with one of the eloquent speeches for which he is so justly famous, assuring them that, although citizens of another land, they were still followed by the loving interest of their mother country and her monarch. When the singers intoned one of the songs by Prince Gustavus, the king joined them with his sonorous tenor voice, smilingly calling their attention to the fact that he had not forgotten his students' songs. The anniversary of the seventieth birthday of Oscar II. was celebrated January 21, 1899, a slight gloom being cast over it on account of the temporary illness of the king. Oscar II. fully recovered after a few months of rest and recreation and bears every indication of attaining the same advanced age, with the same unimpaired activity, as his grandfather, which would mean another decade added to the era of undisturbed peace. Crown Prince Gustavus Adolphus, who is yet little known in Norway, enjoys great popularity in Sweden, where his harmonious, sagacious nature and resolute energy are highly respected.

The reign of Oscar II. in Sweden has been marked by reactionary movements in Church and State, but the king has been in such close contact with his people that they have recognized in him a sovereign who stands above the parties. The king has used the conservative elements of his country to strengthen her defences and to maintain the Union with Norway, which have been the great goals of his policy of peace. To sum up King Oscar's standpoint in the Norwegian question, he is willing to grant Norway home rule in its fullest extent, but refuses to grant her separate control of foreign affairs, which he considers incompatible with the idea of the Union. In this standpoint King Oscar is backed by the convictions of the overwhelming majority of Swedes, who see in the dissolution of the Union a danger to Sweden, Norway, or both countries, of sharing the fate of unhappy Finland, which the civilized world is now deeply deploring. The danger which menaces the sons of Suomi has touched all Scandinavians to the quick, and it would seem that the new century shall witness a restoration of the Scandinavian policy. If the movement to bring this about meets with success, it is to be hoped that, from the start, it shall have rather the actual wants than the ideal rights of the independent Scandinavian states in view. From the point of view of citizens of the United States we cannot but sympathize with a movement which may establish a union of independent states into a realm of imperial government, less an emperor. Let there rather be two or three kings in the North, with one solid union government and a common and equal defence in case of war, than two or three foreign ministers with as many different policies and a divided and unequal defence.

INDEX

INDEX

A

ABELIN, G. R., 408–410.
Abo, 89, 122, 171, 172, 186, 232, 313, 370; peace treaty (in 1743), 316, 317. University of Abo (see Universities).
Absolutism, Absolute Monarchy, 255–258, 260, 268, 293, 298, 300–301, 302, 308, 309, 310, 314, 344, 349, 350, 357.
Academic style, 339.
Academy, of Antiquities, 235; of Art, 346; of Science, 336–337, 340, 346; Swedish, 346, 355; French, 428; Military, 355.
Adalvard, 68; the Younger, 68.
Adam of Bremen, 63.
Adlerbeth, G. G., 345, 350.
Adlercreutz, C. J., 358, 360–361, 362, 367; A. G., 409.
Adlersparre, George, 362.
Admiral, 189; State, 250.
Adolphus Frederic of Sweden, 303, 316, 317–320, 339.
Adolphus John, Duke, 249.
Adrianople, 297–298.
Africa, 232.
Aftonbladet, 377, 403.
Agardh, J. G., 423.
Agne, 36.
Agnefit, 36.
Agriculture. See Sweden.
Ahlborn, Lea, 430.
Ahlstrœmer, John, 317, 321, 334–337.
Akerhielm, A. L. N., 435.
Akkershus, district of, 248, 307; fortress of, 307.
Aland archipelago, 171, 388; peace deliberations at, 306.

Albrecht the Elder, duke of Mecklenburg, 95; the Younger, king of Sweden, 95, 96–97, 100, 102, 103.
Alemannians, 29.
Alexander I. of Russia, 357-358, 370.
Alexandra, princess of Russia, 355–356.
Alexandria, 27.
Alf, 36.
Alfred the Great, 43.
Alingsos, 217, 334–337.
Alliance, 187, 189, 202, 206, 225, 259, 273, 283, 296, 315, 319, 344, 352, 357, 370, 388, 404; Triple, 252.
Alliterative prose, 66; verse, 61, 66.
Almlœf, N. V., 390; Knut, 432.
Almquist, C. J. L., 388–389.
Alsnœ, meeting at, 86.
Alof, 38.
Alps, 21.
Alrek, 36.
Altmark, armistice of, 203.
Altona, 295.
Alt-Ranstædt, 279–281; peace treaty signed at, 281, 290.
Alvastra, 74, 77.
Ambassadors, 254, 269, 272, 305, 358, 368.
Amber, 17, 24.
America, 232, 324, 332, 351, 432, 436; South America, 378.
American Union of Swedish Singers, 436.
Amsterdam, 323, 326.
Anastasius, 28.
Anatomy, 262, 325; hall of, 262–263.
Anckarstrœm, J. J., 352.

(439)

Anckarsverd, C. H., 362, 377, 379.
Anderberg, A. F., 431.
Andreæ, Laurentius, 141, 150.
Andrée, S. A., 424.
Ane, or Aune, King, 37.
Angermanland, 5.
Angermannus, Abraham, 183, 184.
Anglii, 47.
Anglo-Saxon, 58, 62. See also Old English.
Angstrœm, A. J., 423.
Anjala Conspiracy, 348-349, 359.
Anne of England, 280.
Annerstedt, P. S. L , 435.
Ansgar, 41, 53-55.
Antiquarian, 233, 235. See also Archæology.
Anund, Swedish kings: Brœt-Anund, 39; Anund, 42; Anund, or Jacob, 62-63.
Apocalypse, 356.
Apostles, Swedish, 41, 53-55, 58.
Apraxin, Admiral, 289.
Arabs, 49, 50.
Arboga, 108, 115, 124, 127, 161, 185, 387.
Arboga articles, 161.
Archæan rocks, 6.
Ardan. See Jordanes.
Argus, 377; the Swedish, 338.
Aristocracy, 65, 66, 101, 104, 115, 119, 174, 175, 188, 199, 238-239, 250-251, 256, 257, 314, 375.
Aristocratic republic, republicans, 314, 321, 352. See also Nobility, higher.
Arcana Cœlestia, 325.
Archæology, 20, 235, 265, 423-424.
Archbishop, 54-55, 70, 72, 74, 78, 82, 87, 103, 111, 117, 124, 127, 139, 143, 150, 175, 183, 189, 266-267.
Architecture, 173, 176, 265-266, 302-303, 430-431.
Arctic explorations, 424; Sea, 24; Stone Age, 15, 16.
Ardgard, 54.
Arlberg, Fritz, 430.
Armfelt: Charles Gustavus, 308; Gustavus Maurice, 352, 354, 356, 357.
Army. See Sweden.
Arnoldsson, Sigrid, 431.
Aros, East (see Upsala). Aros, West (see Westeros).
Aryan race, 265. See also Indo-European.

Asa, Princess, 40.
Asa creed, 31-34.
Asia, 16, 34, 424.
Askold, 49.
Aspeboda, 134.
Astrology, 161, 169, 252, 268, 304.
Astronomy, 324, 333.
Asund, Lake, 126; battle of, 151.
Atland, Atlantica, 263-265.
Atlantis, 264.
Atterbom, P. D. A., 380.
Atterdag. See Valdemar.
Attundaland, 39.
Aude, 35.
Audils, 37-38.
Auerbach, B., 388.
Augdof, fortress of, 198.
Augsburgian Confession, 183.
August II., elector of Saxony and king of Poland. 272, 277-279, 281, 290, 295, 297, 299.
August, Prince Nicolaus, 411.
Aulin, Tor, 390.
Aune. See Ane.
Austria: Swedish empire in the Baltic provinces, 40, 51-52.
Austria-Hungary, 172, 223, 245, 247, 253, 279, 319, 352, 403.
Avignon, 97.
Axelsson. See Tott.
Axtorna, battle of, 168, 169.
Aztec, 18.

B

BADE, 356, 415.
Bagge, Jacob, 164-166, 167.
Bailiffs, 88, 103, 104, 106, 107, 109, 114, 137, 138, 150, 151, 197.
Baltic dominion, 40, 51-52, 55, 57, 164, 199, 229, 249, 292, 312.
Baltic Provinces, 52, 78, 198-199, 200, 232, 282, 283, 291-292, 307.
Baltic Sea, 5, 21, 24, 25, 26, 49, 51, 75, 101, 130, 199, 229, 249, 272, 294, 305, 322, 375.
Ban, Militia, 417; Papal, 77, 94, 121, 126.
Banér, Sten, 170, 185, 195; Anne, 176; Eric, 131; Gustavus, 185, 195; Per, 195; John, 207-208, 222-225, 279.
Banner of State, 116, 118, 125, 168.
Barangoi, 52.
Barbro, Stigsdotter, 134-135.
Bark-king, 112.

INDEX 441

Barn-lock, 86.
Barocco, 261, 321, 353.
Bastile, 428.
Barons, Baronies, 162, 200, 238, 251, 257.
Bavaria, 193, 210, 211, 222.
Beauharnais, Eugene, 404.
Beckstrom, Edward, 412.
Behm, Sara, 321.
Bellman, C. M., 345-346, 389, 390.
Bells, revolt of. See Revolts.
Belt, Lille, 245-246.
Belt, Store, 246-247.
Bender, 287, 293, 294, 295; Kalabalik of, 297.
Benedictine monastery, 235.
Bengt, Duke, 86.
Bengtsson, Jœns. See Oxenstierna.
Bentseby, 266.
Benzelius: Eric the Elder, 266; Eric the Younger, 237 note, 266-267, 322, 340.
Benzelstierna. See Benzelius.
Beowulf, 30, 31, 37.
Bergh, Richard, 429.
Bergman, T. O., 346.
Bergstrœm, P. A., 429.
Berlin, 223, 341.
Bernadotte, 365, 367, 418, 421; Prince Oscar, 415. See also Charles XIV.
Bernard of Clairvaux, 71.
Bernhard, duke of Weimar, 211, 214, 216, 217, 221.
Bervald, F. N., 390.
Berzelius, J. J., 325, 366, 380.
Beværingstid, 417.
Bible, 237; Gothic (see Gothic); translations of, 98, 150, 260, 355.
Bielke, Anna, 127, 132; Gunilla, queen, 175; Sten, 170; Ture, 185.
Bielo-Jesero, 47.
Biœrkœ, 55.
Biœrn. Swedish kings, 42, 54, 55.
Biorck, O., 429.
Biornstrœm, F. J., 424.
Biornstierna, M. F. J., 361.
Birger, Brosa, 76, 77, 79; Jarl, 77, 78-83, 86, 88; King, 84, 87, 88-91, 92; Persson, 89, 97.
Birgitta, St., 97-99, 100, 130, 154.
Birka, 42, 55, 71, 75.
Bishops, 71, 78, 86, 87, 112-113, 127, 128, 145-146, 183.
Bjœrnson, B., 388, 405.

Black Death, 94.
Blanche, queen of Sweden and Norway, 93, 97.
Blanche, August, 389.
Bleking, 5, 29, 63, 67, 93, 95, 150, 151, 190, 247, 249, 259, 291.
Blenda, 72.
Blomstrand, C. W., 423.
Blot-Sven, 69, 73.
Blucher, General, 370.
Bo Jonsson. See Grip.
Boccaccio, 163, 413.
Bœclerus, 240.
Bœrhave, 330-331.
Bœrjesson, John, dramatist, 389; John, sculptor, 430.
Bœttiger, C. V., 389.
Bogesund, battle of, 126-127.
Bohemia, 210, 222, 224, 226, 228.
Bohus, fortress of, 196.
Bohuslæn, 5, 13, 17, 46, 58, 62, 196, 229, 247, 249, 254, 307, 308.
Bologna, 117.
Bonaparte. See Napoleon.
Bonde, Charles Knutsson (see Charles VIII.); Tord, 111; Gustavus, 250.
Bonnier, Eva, 429.
Borgannæs, 107.
Boris of Russia, 172.
Bornhœved, battle of, 371.
Bornholm, 21, 164, 247, 248, 250; naval battle of, 168.
Bosphorus, 49.
Bosson, Nils. See Sture.
Bostrœm, C. J., philosopher, 411-412, 423.
Botany, 262, 321, 330, 331-333, 380, 423.
Bothnia, Gulf of, 5.
Bothnia, West, 363.
Bothniensis, N. O., 183, 185.
"Bottomless Purse," 112.
Botvid, St., 58.
Boucher, 428.
Bourgeoisie. See Burghers.
Boye, L., 377.
Brabant, 237.
Brage-bowl, 39.
Brahe, Joachim, 133; Peter, the Elder, 154, 162; Ebba, 194, 235; Nils, the Elder, 214, 217; Peter, the Younger, 231, 232, 240, 250, 251, 257; Nils, the Younger, 257; Eric, 318; Magnus, 374-375.
Brahestad, 258.

Brandenburg, 223, 228, 234, 244, 247, 253, 255; Elector of, 223; Great Elector of, 225, 244, 245, 252.
Brandsœ, 245-246.
Brask, Bishop Hans, 125, 128, 139, 143, 144, 146, 322, 375.
Braun, V. A. D. von, 389.
Braunsberg, 203.
Bravols, battle of, 41, 56.
Breitenfeld, battles of. See Leipsic.
Bremen, 54, 63, 70, 229, 245, 311.
Bremer, Frederica, 389, 427.
Brenner, S. E., 233.
Brennkyrka, battle of, 125, 131.
Bring. See Lagerbring.
Bridget, St. See Birgitta.
Britain, 24, 25, 45, 60.
British Isles, 60; Museum, 331.
Brœmsebro, peace treaty at, 227.
Brœt-Anund. See Anund.
Bronitz, battle of, 198.
Bronze Age, 11, 13, 16-20.
Brunbeck, battle of, 138.
Brunkeberg, 139; battles of, 116, 119.
Buchow, naval battle of, 168.
Buddenbrock, M. H., 316, 317.
Budget. See Sweden.
Buffon, 324.
Bulgaria, 50.
Bureus, John, 232-235.
Burghers, 108, 128, 144, 146, 158, 185, 200, 201, 253.
Burislev, 75.
Byzantium, Byzantine, 22-23, 27, 28, 49, 50, 51.

C

CABINET, 373, 403; Swedish (see Sweden).
Cadet School. See Carlberg.
Calmar. See Kalmar.
Caloric engine, 387.
Calvinism, 183, 189.
Canute the Great, 57, 58, 62.
"Caps," 316. 319, 320, 337, 344.
Carlberg, 355.
Carl. See Charles.
Carelia, 88, 94.
Carleby. Old, 360; New, 360.
Carlen, Emelie, 389, 427.
Carin Monsdotter, queen, 162, 170-173, 177.

Carlsten, fortress of, 311, 312.
Carolin Institute, 425.
Carlsborg, fortress of, 375, 418.
Carlscrona, navy yards at, 259, 305.
Carlson, F. F., 393, 398; Ernest, 424.
Carlstad, 188, 407.
Carnage of Stockholm, 128, 129, 133, 137.
Cartesius. See Descartes.
Casijn, 173.
Caspian Sea, 50.
Cassander, 236.
Castellholm, 171.
Castles, 96, 102, 146, 173, 233, 251, 266.
Catechismus, 183, 260.
Catherine, Countess Palatine, 234, 239.
Catherine (queens of Sweden), of Saxony-Lauenburg, 155, 156, 157; Stenbock, 156, 157, 177, 181; Monsdotter (see Carin Monsdotter); Jagello, 163, 175.
Catherine II. of Russia, 348, 350, 351, 355-356.
Catholicism, Catholic, 98. 172, 173, 174, 182-184, 187, 189, 192, 240, 244, 325, 335.
Cavendish, 325.
Cederstrom, O. R., 374, 378; Gustavus, 429.
Celibacy, 79.
Celsius, Andrew, 321, 333; Olof, Senior, 329, 333, 340; Olof, Junior, 333-334.
Celtic swords, 21; tribes, 21.
Chambers (of the Riksdag), 396, 398, 399-401, 407.
Chancellor, of State, 87, 189, 199, 220, 250 (see also President of the Chancery); king's, 14, 144, 150; of the University, 263, 340; the Great (see Axel Oxenstierna).
Chancery, 297, 298; president of the, 271, 313, 314, 317, 337.
Charles (kings of Sweden): VII. Sverkersson, 73, 74, 75; VIII. Knutsson, 108-114, 121, 339; IX. 155, 157, 158, 163, 167, 170-174, 176, 179, 181-191, 204, 222, 249, 264; X. Gustavus, 239-241, 242-249, 251, 277, 314; XI. 249-268, 269, 270-271. 277, 391, 408; XII. 182, 264, 267, 268-309, 310, 313, 322, 326, 334, 338, 343, 356, 364;

XIII. 348, 350, 352, 353, 356, 362, 365-374; XIV. 367-373, 374-380, 382, 383, 404; XV. 391-413, 415.
Charles, Bishop, 77.
Charles, Jarl, 77.
Charles Philip, son of Charles IX., 190, 194, 198.
Charles, son of Oscar II., 415.
Charles V., emperor, 151, 158.
Charles II. of England, 237.
Charles's Chronicle, 114.
Charles Frederic of Holstein-Gottorp, 295, 301, 310, 311.
Charles Peter Ulric of Holstein-Gottorp, 316.
Chauvinism, 261, 264, 321, 346, 433.
Chemistry, 333, 346, 380, 423, 425.
Chemnitz, battle of, 224.
Chicago, 421, 429.
China, 289.
Chodkiewitz, 187.
Christerson, J. C. E., 435.
Christian (kings of Denmark): I. 111-113, 116; II. 122, 124-129, 131, 132, 133, 137, 138, 140, 148, 151, 158; III. 149, 164; IV. 190, 196-198, 204, 226-227; V. 254, 255; VIII. 371-373; IX. 403-404.
Christian August (Charles A.), Prince, 365-367.
Christian Frederic, Prince. See Christian VIII.
Christiania, 307, 372, 419.
Christianity, 31, 42; influence of, 52; introduction of, 53-55, 58; opposition to, 58-61.
Christianopel, 190.
Christine (queens of Sweden), 189, 194, 204; 196, 204, 220-241, 242, 262, 302, 314.
Christine of Denmark, 120.
Christine of Hesse, 162, 164-165.
Christopher, kings of Denmark, 81, and of Sweden, 110, 111, 112.
Christopher's, King, Land Law. See Sweden, State Law.
Christinehamn, 188.
Chronica regni gothorum, 117.
Chronicles, prose, 114, 131; rhymed, 80, 114.
Church, 76, 77, 78, 85, 87, 88, 89, 111, 115, 117, 125, 140, 141, 142, 144, 146, 149, 152, 174-176, 183, 188, 200, 201, 260, 266, 396, 432, 437; law, 93, 146, 175. See also Clergy, Bishops.

Cimbrian Peninsula, 26, 27. See also Jutland.
Cincinnatus, Order of, 367.
Cistercians, 71.
Civil service, 433.
Clary. See Queen Desideria.
Clason, I. G., 431.
Clergy, 93, 104, 108, 117, 139, 143, 145-146, 156, 158, 183, 185, 186, 200, 239, 251, 334, 340, 341, 396, 397, 398-399.
Codania, Codanian Bay, 25.
Codex Argenteus, 235-238, 266; Bildstenianus, 9; Bureanus, 9.
Coffee prohibited, 355.
Coins, 60, 62; of need, 301-302.
Collard, Claude, 167.
Colleges, 201, 232.
Collegia, 118, 230 note.
Cologne, 117, 236.
Colonies, Commerce, Communities, Constitution. See Sweden.
Constantinople, 295.
Constantine Porphyrogenitus, 48.
Continent. See Europe.
Copenhagen, 129, 131, 227, 274, 385, 403; siege of, 247-248; peace treaty of, 250.
Corvey, 53, 54.
Cossacks, 283, 285.
Council, Councillors, State (or royal), 87, 92, 106, 107, 108, 115, 116, 120, 122, 128, 183, 184, 185, 189, 190, 196, 199, 200, 230, 251, 257, 258, 271, 272, 289, 290, 292-293, 298, 300, 301, 310, 313, 314, 318, 320, 338, 339, 344-345, 350, 435.
Council, Town, 116, 126, 128, 165.
Councillor of Commerce, 337.
Counties, counts, 162, 200, 288, 251, 257.
Courland, 52, 202, 244, 282.
Cracow, 244, 278.
Creutz, G. P., 339, 345.
Croats, 208.
Croi, Duke de, 275.
Cronhamn, J. P., 413.
Cronstedt, Charles, 295; Olof, 359-360.
Crown lands, 238, 255, 257; restitution of, 96, 102, 111, 233, 238, 243, 256-258, 271.
Crown prince, 316, 317, 319, 320, 371, 392, 406, 415, 437.
Crusell, B. F., 89, 413.

Crusenstolpe, M. J., 377, 389.
Crusades, 70, 73, 77, 78, 94, 185.
Czar (see Russia), Czarina, 289.
Czarniecki, Stefan, 244.
Cuno, John C., 326.

D

DACKE "FEUD," 150-151.
Dacke, Nils, 150-151.
Dag, 36.
Dahlberg, Eric, 245-246, 247, 259, 265-266, 277.
Dahlgren, Frederic Aug., 389.
Dahlquist, C. G., 390.
Dal, province of, 5, 107, 308; River, 5, 138.
Dalecarlia, Dalecarlians, 5, 16, 105, 106, 107, 108, 116, 119, 121, 131, 133-139, 146, 147, 148, 149, 155, 185, 317, 349.
Dalin, O. von, 321, 337-339, 343.
Dædalus Hyperboreus, 322.
"Daljunker," 147.
Dalman, V. F., 394.
Danckwardt, Henric, 311.
Danes, Danish. See Denmark.
Danielsson, A., 377.
Dannebrog, 116.
Danube, 22, 28, 224, 228.
Dantzic, 112, 203.
David, St., 58.
Dearth, 118, 176, 261.
Decamerone, 163, 413.
De Geer. See Geer.
De la Gardie. See Gardie.
Delaware River, 232.
Democracy, Democratic, 64, 65, 66, 114, 115, 117, 120, 121, 199, 200, 260, 352, 364.
Demotika, 297, 299
Denmark, 6, 10, 12, 13, 21, 29, 30, 36, 37, 38, 39, 40, 41, 42, 52, 53, 54, 56-57, 58, 60, 62, 63, 70, 72, 76, 77, 81, 83, 89, 90, 91, 95, 100, 103, 105, 106, 108, 111, 116, 117, 120, 121, 122, 124, 125, 126-127, 128, 131, 133, 135, 136, 148, 149, 164, 166, 167, 168, 174, 195-198, 203, 226-228, 244, 245-248, 250, 253-255, 259, 273-274, 290, 295-296, 299, 307, 311, 312, 316, 343, 345, 348-349, 355, 357, 363, 366, 367, 368, 371-373, 385-386, 388, 392, 401, 405, 406, 415, 426, 430.
Dennewitz, battle of, 370.

Descartes, René, 240-241, 347.
Desideria, Queen, 382.
Diderot, 347, 429.
Diet, 374, 379, 392, 402. See also Riksdag and Norwegian Storthing.
Dietriechson, Lorenz, 405.
Dilettantism, 412, 426.
Diplomacy, 252, 259, 313, 315, 367, 402, 434.
Dir, 49.
Dirschau, 202.
Ditmarschen, 120.
Dimitri, 173, 187; false Dimitris, 187-188.
Dniepr River, 284, 286, 287; cataracts of the, 48.
Dœbeln, G. C. von, 358, 360.
Dœmitz, battle of, 233.
Dolmens, 13.
Domalde, 35
Domar, 36.
Dorpat, 200, 281, 282; University of (see Universities).
Dortrecht, 237.
Douglas, L. V. A., 435.
Drama, 345, 346, 388, 389, 390, 412, 413, 426-427, 431-432.
Dramatic singers, 390, 413, 431.
Drontheim, diocese or district of, 58, 112, 247, 248, 250, 308, 311, 371.
Drottningholm, castle of. 303. 362.
Drotsete, Drotset (Riks-), 87, 91, 96, 102, 108, 189, 199, 240, 250.
Duchies, 82, 158, 161, 185-186.
Duenamuende, 292.
Dufnæs, battle of, 131.
D'Uncker, C. H. L., 412.
Dutch, Dutchman. See Holland.
Dusseldorf School, 429.
Dvina, crossing of the, 277.
Dygve, 36.

E

EADGILS. See Audils.
East Gothland. See Gothland.
Ebo, 54.
Ecclesiastics. See Clergy.
Edda, Eddic songs, 61, 66, 157, 283, 270, 346; Snorre's, 34, 342.
Edlund, Eric, 423.
Edsœre laws, 82, 86.
Education, 117, 201, 232, 260, 379.
Eger, 211.

Egil, 37.
Egino, 68.
Ehrenstrahl, D. K., 303; School of Painters, 303, 428.
Ehrensverd, Augustinus, 317, 350, 359; Ch. A., 347, 350–351, 355.
Eider, River, 402.
Eidsvold, meeting held at, 371.
Eka, Cecilia of, 129, 130.
Ekeberg, 156.
Elbing, 203.
Elective kingdom. See Kingdom.
Electricity, 324.
Elfsborg, 152, 166, 174, 188, 196, 197, 198; New, 311.
Elfsson, Swan, 135–136.
Elgaros, battle of, 76.
Elisabeth of Russia, 316.
Elizabeth of England, 98, 162.
Elmblad, Johannes, 431.
Elsass, 221.
Elsinore, 93, 247, 368.
Emigration, 290, 319, 432–433.
Emund, 63, 67, 68.
Engelbrekt, Engelbrektsson, 105–109, 110, 115, 121, 137, 146; song about, 114.
England, English, 22, 40, 52, 58, 82, 98, 187, 189, 237, 245, 252, 259, 283, 299, 305, 306–307, 315, 322, 334, 349, 355, 356, 357, 363, 369, 370, 371, 374, 379, 388.
Eric (Danish kings): Ejegod, 69; Glipping, 83, 84; Menved, 89, 91; of Pomerania (see Swedish King Eric XIII.).
Eric, Norwegian Jarl, 57.
Eric (Swedish kings): 36; 36–37; 54; Edmundsson, 52, 55; Bicernson Segersæl, 55–57; 68; Arsæl, 69, 71; IX. (St. Eric), 73–74, 75, 78, 80, 127, 130; X. 67, 77; XI. 77–79, 80; XII. 94–95, 96; XIII. 101–110; XIV. 155, 157, 158, 161–173, 177, 264, 334.
Eric (Swedish princes): Birgersson, 83; Magnusson, 87, 89–92; Valdemarsson, 83, 84.
Eric's Chronicle, 80, 85, 89, 114.
Ericson, J. E., 430.
Ericsson, Joesse, 106, 137; John, 387, 424, 425; Nils, 387; Christian, 430.
Eriksgata, 71, 93, 138
Erimbert, 55.
Eskil, St., 58.

Eskil's apartments, 170.
Essen, H. H. von, 372.
Esthonia, Esthonians, 39, 52, 75, 77, 98, 162, 174, 198, 201, 282, 307–312.
Ettak, battle of, 84.
Eugene, Prince of Sweden, 429, 430.
Eugenie, Princess, 411.
Europe, 6, 12, 16, 17, 28, 44, 82, 93, 189, 204, 229, 235, 242, 245, 254, 255, 259, 264, 272, 278, 285, 303, 324, 334, 335, 336, 363, 369, 374, 376, 381, 401, 414, 424, 429.
Expositions, Scandinavian, 405, 436; World's, 413, 421, 429.
Eystein, 38.
Eyforr, 48.
Euphemia, Princess, 95.
Estates, 108, 158, 159, 184, 200, 204–205, 238, 240, 249, 256, 271, 278, 293, 310, 314, 318, 338, 349, 350, 355, 383, 394, 398–399, 400.
Ethnography, 265.

F

FAHLBECK, P., 424.
Falkœping, battle of, 97.
Fallstedt, I., 430.
Falster, 247.
Falun, 138, 152.
"Father, The," 427
Father of Swedish Industry, 334.
Fehrbellin, battle of, 252, 253.
Femern, naval battles of, 227.
Ferdinand (emperors): II 193, 202; III. 221, 228.
Fero Islands, 371.
Fersen, Axel von, the Elder, 324; the Younger, 351, 366–367.
Feudalism, 82
Feud of the Counts, 149.
Fiefs, 96, 103, 151, 162, 244.
Finance. See Sweden.
Fine Arts, Philosophy of, 347.
Finland, Finns, Finnish, 10, 15, 26, 35, 36, 48, 55, 71, 73, 75, 78, 81, 88, 89, 93, 111, 113, 118, 119, 122, 152, 163, 171, 172, 184, 185, 186, 187, 188, 193, 199, 200, 220, 231, 232, 238, 283, 292, 307, 312, 313, 316, 317, 348, 357–364, 367, 412–413, 436, 437; language, 8, 341.
Finnmark, 378.
Finnwoods, 136.

Fiedrundaland, 39.
Fiolner, 35.
Fleming, Clas Ericsson, 184; Clas Larsson, 227; Herman, 243, 250.
Flemish art, 173.
Flensburg, 104.
Flower king of the North, 332.
Fogelberg, B. E., 412, 430.
Fogel Grip, 232.
Fogelwick, 118.
Folk lore, 265, 381.
Folkungs, 76, 78, 79, 81, 97, 130.
Folkung dynasty, 80–99.
Folksriksdag, 433.
Forsberg, Nils, 429.
France, French, 22, 45, 52, 68, 72, 152, 187, 189, 206, 221, 222, 229, 233, 245, 252, 255, 270, 271, 315, 318, 322, 331, 339, 343, 344, 345, 351, 352, 355, 356, 357. 368, 371, 372, 382, 388, 414, 422. 428, 429.
Franciscan, convent, 87; Church (see Riddarholm's Church).
Franconia, 221.
Franco-Prussian War, 409.
Franz Joseph's Land, 424.
Frankfurt, 209.
Francke, A. H., 289.
Franks, Frankish, 29, 210, 236, 341.
Frantz, Albrecht, 216.
Franzen, F. M., 381.
Frederic I. of Sweden, 312–317, 318, 335.
Frederic (kings of Denmark): I. 148; II. 164, 166; III. 246, 247; IV. 273–274, 290, 295, 299; V. 316, 317; VI. 367; VII 402. 403
Frederic of Augustenborg, 367
Frederic, crown prince of Denmark, 406.
Frederic of Holstein, 272-274.
Frederic of the Palatinate, 202, 210
Frederic (kings of Prussia): I. 296; II. (the Great), 318, 319, 343
Frederic William, the Grand Elector. See Brandenburg
Frederica, Queen, 356.
Fredericia, fortress of, 245, 248.
Fredericshall, 308, 322.
Fredericshamn, 316; peace treaty at, 363.
Fredericstad, 372
Fredericsten, 308.
Fredkulla. See Margaret.
Fredman, 390.
Free trade, 387, 407–408.

Freinshemius, John, 240.
Frey, 32, 34.
Friedland. See Wallenstein.
Fries, Elias, 380.
Frithiof's Saga, 381.
Frode (Danish kings): 35, 37.
Frœding, Gustaf, 428.
Funen, island of, 227, 246, 248, 386.
Fuxerna, battles of, 69.
Fyris, River, 36.
Fyrisvols, battles of, 36, 37, 56.

G

GAD, DR. HEMING, 121, 122, 126, 127, 129.
Gadebush, battle of, 295, 296.
Gagarin, governor, 289.
Gallia, Gallic, 20
Gardarike, 52.
Gautland. See Gothaland.
Gardie, Pontus de la, 167, 174, 187, 235; Jacob, 187–188, 190, 194, 198–199, 234, 235; Magnus Gabriel, 234–235, 237, 250, 251, 252, 257, 263.
Gauts, 28, 29, 30, 31, 47, 105.
Gauzbert, 54.
Geátas, 30–31.
Gefle, 138.
Gegerfelt, K. F. von, 431; William, 429.
Geijer, Eric Gustavus, 380, 393.
Geijerstam, Gustaf of, 427.
Geirthiof, 38.
Gellandri, 48.
Gellivara. 7.
Gemauerthoff, battle of, 282.
Geology, 324. 325.
George I. of England, 306.
George Sand, 388
Gepidæ, 29.
Gerhard, Count of Holstein, 84.
Germania, 26.
Germans, Germany, 12, 21, 22, 54, 58, 75, 80, 81, 83, 85, 90, 93, 96, 97, 98, 100. 101, 104, 105, 106, 116, 122, 127, 132, 150, 151, 152, 158, 168, 189, 190, 198, 202, 203, 204, 205, 210, 213, 214, 221, 222, 223, 224, 226, 228, 229, 230, 233, 239, 244, 252, 264, 287, 299, 303, 307, 321, 346, 370, 380, 385–386, 401–405, 414–418, 428, 429; emperor, 122, 151, 158, 193, 202, 209, 210,

211, 212, 224, 228, 235, 245, 281, 299, 415; Order, 162-163.
Gestilren, battle of, 77.
Gestrikland, 5, 16, 138.
Gibraltar of the North, 359.
Giljam, G. F., 436.
Gisslan. See Hostages.
Glaciers, 6.
Glipping. See Eric (Danish kings).
Glom River, 307, 308.
Glossarium sviogothicum, 342.
Glucksburg, 371.
Gluntarne, 389.
Goertz, G H., 301-302, 304, 306-307, 311.
Gœtar. See Gauts.
Gold finds, 22-23.
Golumbo, battle of, 244.
Gospel, 53-55, 104, 146, 207.
Gothahamn, 116.
Gotha Canal, 305-306, 322, 375-376.
Gothaland, 5, 14, 19, 24, 25, 28, 42, 43, 68, 83, 84, 185, 230.
Gothland, East, 5, 7, 17, 31, 39, 41, 71, 98, 111, 168, 185, 186; West, 5, 7, 13, 17, 31, 37, 41, 46, 58, 59, 61, 67, 68, 70, 76, 77. 83, 84, 96, 111, 126, 148, 167, 168, 197, 229, 321, 334, 415; Island of, 6, 21, 22, 25, 66, 82, 85, 95, 103, 105. 111, 113, 117, 120, 142, 165, 227, 254, 304, 415.
Gothenburg, 10, 188, 196, 198, 200, 226, 229, 231, 232, 249, 254, 335, 349, 369, 422, 428.
Gothenburg University. See Universities.
Gotha River, 10, 46, 116, 196, 198.
Goths, of Continental Europe, 22, 28, 30, 235-236, 263; of Sweden (see Gauts); Teutons, 43; East, 29, 71; West, 29, 70, 71.
Gothic, 151, 220, 238, 341, 342; Bible, 67 (see further Codex Argenteus); invasions, 28; language, 235, 237-238; society, 381; glossary, 237.
Gothic law, West, 66, 67, 70.
Gotland, 43.
Gottorp. See Holstein-Gottorp.
Government. See Sweden.
Governor, 184, 202, 231, 232.
Governor-general, 199, 203, 229, 231, 290, 291, 371; of Norway, 366, 375, 386, 394-395, 418-419.

Grabow, Mathilde, 431.
Grammar, 40.
Greece, Greek, 49, 50, 52, 235, 237, 265; myths, 53; church, 288, 355.
Geer, Louis de, 201, 226-227, 231; Louis, 393, 397, 398.
Gregory, VII. 69; IX. 78.
Grimm's law, 342.
Grimsted, 246.
Grip, Bo Jonsson, 96. 102
Gripenstedt, J. A., 387, 393, 398, 403, 404, 407.
Gripsholm, 96, 107, 152, 155, 163, 171, 173, 182, 362.
Gross-beeren, battle of, 370.
Grubbe, Sam, 411.
Guadeloupe, island of, 370.
Gualther, 236.
Gude, 405.
Gudlaug, 36-37.
Guinea, African. 232.
Gullberg, fort of, 196-197.
Gullbrandson, Ellen, 431.
Gunilla, Queen. See Bielke.
Gurzo, battle of, 202.
Gustavian period, 337, 339, 343-364.
Gustavus, Adolphus Society, 219.
Gustavus (kings of Sweden): I. Vasa, 125, 126, 128, 129, 130-160, 161, 165, 168, 170, 173, 177, 178, 199, 226, 322, 334, 344, 349; II. Adolphus, 173, 190, 192-219, 220, 222, 225, 230, 232, 234, 240, 243, 250, 258, 314, 344; III. 319-320, 332, 334, 339, 343-353, 354, 379, 387, 431; IV. Adolphus, 352, 353-362, 366, 373, 375, 415.
Gustavus (princes of Sweden): Ericsson (see Vasa); Prince of Vasa, 366; Frans G. Oscar, 388, 389, 413, 436; Oscar G. Adolphus, crown prince, 414, 437.
Guta, Saga, 67.
Gutai, 28.
Gutnic, Guts, 67, 87, 105.
Gutorm, Jarl, 74, 76.
Guttones, 24, 25.
Gyldén, J. A. H., 423.
Gyldenlœve, general, 254; fort of, 308.
Gyllenborg. Charles, 317, 337; G. F., 339, 345.
Gyllencreutz, Charles G., 268, 302.
Gyllenhielm, C. C., 187.
Gyllenstierna, Christine, 127-129,

130, 131, 140, 142, 147, 149, 155, 158; John, 256, 312.
Gymnastics, 380; Central Institute of, 380.

H

HADRIAN IV. See Nicolaus of Alba.
Hæffner, 389.
Hagbard, 36.
Hagborg, A., 429.
Hake, 36-37.
Hakon (Norwegian kings): 79, 81, 91, 92; Magnusson, 94-95, 100.
Hakon, Swedish regent, 68.
Halberstadt, 224.
Haleygians, 36.
Hall, P. A., 428.
Halland, 5, 13, 43, 84, 93, 95, 167, 196, 197, 227, 229, 247, 249, 254, 337.
Hallén, Andreas, 390.
Hallstrœm, Ivar, 390; Peter, 427.
Halmstad, 108, 166, 254.
Halsten, 68, 70.
Hamburg, 54, 63, 70, 81, 82, 83; peace treaty of, 319.
Hammarby, 332.
Handbook. See Ritual.
Hanover, 299, 311.
Hans. See John II.
Hansa, Hanseatic, 81-82, 101, 103, 104, 116, 132.
Hansson, Ola, 427.
Haraker, battle of, 112.
Harald, king of Denmark, 56.
Harald (kings of Norway): Fairhair, 55; Hardrade, 68.
Harald Hildetand, king of Sweden and Denmark, 41, 51.
Hare's Leap, 6.
Hartekamp, 331.
Hartelius, T. J., 424.
Hartmansdorff, J. A. von, 383, 384-385.
Hasselberg, Peter, 430.
"Hats," political party, 316, 317, 319, 320, 337, 338.
Havamal, 157.
Havel River, 206.
Heathen Revival, 59-61.
Hedberg, Frans, 389; Thor, 427.
Hedenblad, Ivar, 431.
Hedenstierna, A., 428.
Hedin, Sven, 424.

Hedlund, S. A., 428; Hans, 431.
Hedvig, queen of Denmark, 100.
Hedvig, Eleonore, of Sweden, 243, 249, 253, 255, 271, 299, 300; Elisabeth Charlotte, 366.
Hedvig, Sophie, Princess, 269, 310.
Heidenstam, V. von, 427.
Heimskringla, 31, 33-41, 265.
Heir-apparent, 316-317, 365-366, 367, 368, 420.
Heinsius, 240.
Helga. See Olga.
Helge. See Oleg.
Helge, Danish king, 38.
Hellquist, C. G., 429.
Helsingborg, 290, 336; battle of, 291, 296.
Heinrich (the Lion), 75.
Helsingfors, 152, 317; battle of, 316; University of (see Universities).
Helsingland, Helsings, 5, 138, 317, 361; regiment of, 360-361.
Helsingœr. See Elsinore.
Hessleholm, battle of, 91.
Helvig, Queen, 84.
Henric, St., 73, 75.
Herger, 54.
Herjedal, 5, 227.
Herredag (-ar), 88.
Herschel, 324.
Herulians, 28, 29, 48, 66.
Hervadsbro, battle of, 81.
Hesse, 205.
Heterodoxy, 380.
Hielmar Lake, 109.
Hierta: Hans (see Jærta); Lars, 377.
Hildebrand, Hans, 423.
Hildebrandsson, H. H., 424.
Hillberg, Emil, 431.
Hillestrœm, Peter, 347.
Hiortsberg, L., 390.
Hising, island of, 188, 196.
Historia de Gentibus Septentrionalibus, 142.
History, Historians, 11, 24-32, 33-34, 44, 46-47, 48, 50, 64, 80, 114, 142, 232, 321, 333-334, 337-339, 380, 389, 393, 412-413, 423, 424, 426.
Hœckert, J. F., 412, 429.
Hœgquist, Emelie, 390.
Hœijer, B. C. H., 347, 356, 380, 411.
Hœjer, Nils, 424; Magnus, 424.

INDEX

Hœrberg, Peter, 347.
Hœrningsholm, 176, 177, 178, 179, 181.
Hœjentorp, 197, 336.
Hofva, battle at, 83.
Hogland, naval battle at, 348.
Holaveden (Holavid), battle at, 111.
Holland, 12, 198, 201, 226, 227, 232, 236-237, 245, 247, 248, 252, 253, 264, 283, 322, 330, 331, 334, 340.
Holmfrid, 58.
Holmgard, 52.
Holmger, 78.
Holmstrœm, 233.
Holstein, 103, 104, 112, 226, 227, 244, 255, 271, 273, 274, 385, 402, 405; counts of, 84, 93, 149, 228, 271, 272.
Holstein-Gottorp, 243, 295, 301.
Holy Alliance, 381.
Holy Virgin, 228.
Holovzin, battle of, 284.
Horn: Clas Kristersson, Baron, 162, 167-168; Henric, 174; Evert, 198; Gustavus, 207-208, 221-222, 226; Arvid Bernhard, 272, 278, 284, 293, 298, 310-311, 312-316, 337; Rudolph, 282; Jacob, 318.
Hotuna, play at, 90-91.
Hoya, counts of, 149.
Huet, 240.
Hugleik (O. E. Hygelâc): Swedish king, 36; Danish king, 38.
Humor, 233, 346, 389, 390, 428.
Hungary, 68, 245, 299, 322.
Husaby, 58, 62.
Hvasser, Elisa. 413.
Hvin. See Tiodolf.
Hygelâc. See Hugleik.

I

IAROSLAF, 48, 51, 62.
Ibn, Fosslan, 50.
Ibsen, H., 405, 431.
Iceland, Icelanders, Icelandic, 33, 52, 56, 60-61, 93, 235; language, 9; sagas, 40, 52, 67, 297; scalds, sagamen, 60-61.
Iddefjord, 322.
Ifvarsson, Charles, 407.
Igor, 48, 51.
Ihre, John, 321, 339-342.
Illrade. See Ingiald.
Imports. See Sweden.

Imperial army: Imperialists, 202, 203, 209, 216, 217, 221, 224, 225, 228; crown lands, 210, 225.
Indelningsverk, Indelta, 258, 408, 417.
Indensalmi, battle of, 358.
Indians, 232.
Indo-European language, 8.
Industry, 176.
Inge (Swedish kings): the Elder, 68-70, 72; the Younger, 70.
Ingeborg, duchesses, 91, 92; princesses, 58, 78, 80, 89, 415.
Ingegerd, Princess, 61-62; Queen, 76.
Ingermanland (Ingria), 174, 199, 231, 273, 274, 282, 307, 312.
Ingemar, 84.
Ingiald, Illrade, 39-40, 42, 64.
Ingria. See Ingermanland.
Ingbar. See Igœ.
Innocent III., 77.
Interchanging dynasties, 74-79.
Intelligence party, 408, 410.
Interdict. See Ban.
Iron Age, 11, 19, 20-24.
Isala, 135.
Isborsk, 47.
Isiaslaf, 68.
Italy, Italians, 22, 98, 106, 121, 236.
Ivar, Master, 131.
Ivar, Vidfamne, 40, 51.
Ivarsson, Ivar, of Strœmstad, 170.

J

JACOB. See Anund Jacob.
Jacobi, Petrus. See Sunnanvæder.
Jægerhorn, G. H., 359-360; J. A., 348.
Jærta, Hans, 365.
Jagello. See Catherine.
Jansson, Eugene, 429.
Jankowitz, battle of, 228, 239.
Japhet, 263.
Jarl, jarls, 42, 57-58, 74, 87; of the realm, 74.
Jaroslaf. See Iaroslaf.
Jedvard, 73.
Jemtland, 5, 63, 70, 227, 308, 311.
Jerusalem, 97.
Jesuits, 175, 183, 184.
Jœnkœping, 120, 230.
Jœns, Bengtsson. See Oxenstierna.
Jœsse, Ericsson. See Ericsson.

John, archbishop, 75; duke, 186, 189, 197; prince, 72.
John (kings): I. 77; II. Hans, 119-120, 122, 130-131; III. 155, 157, 158, 163, 169, 170-172, 173-176, 180, 182, 186, 188, 235.
John, Casimir, count of Palatinate-Zweibrucken, 239.
John, Casimir, king of Poland. See Vasa.
Johannes, Magni (Johannes Magnus), 114, 142-143, 263.
Jolin, J. C., 389.
Jomsborg, 56.
Jordanes, 29, 34, 44, 263.
Jornandes. See Jordanes.
Jorsalafare. See Sigurd.
Jorund, 36-37.
Josephine, Queen, 382.
Josephsson, J. A., 389, 413; **Ernst**, 429.
Juel, Niels, 253, 254.
Justinian, 28.
Jueterbogk, battle of, 228.
Jutland, Jutes, 26. 30, 31, **37, 43**, 131, 132, 226, 245, 248, 386.
Junius, Franziskus, 237.
Juutas, battle of, 359, 360.

K

KÆPPLINGEHOLM, Massacre of, 101.
Kagg. Lars, 250.
Kalabalik of Bender. See Bender.
Kalloe, 132.
Kalmar, 93, 101, 116, 122, 132, 133, 190; Nyckel, 232; Recess of, 119; Union of (see Union).
Kalmucks, 288.
Kamenski, M. K., 361.
Kansler. See Chancellor.
Kant, 324, 347.
Karelen. See Carelia.
Karin. See Carin.
Karl. See Charles.
Karlberg. See Carlberg.
Karleby, 71; see also **Carleby**.
Karlskrona. See **Carlskrona**.
Karlsson. See Carlsson.
Karlson, Valfried, 431.
Karlstad. See Carlstad.
Kasan, 288.
Katarina. See Catherine.
Keksholm. See Kexholm.
Kerkholm, battle at, 187.

Kellgren, J. H., 345.
Kettilmundsson, Mattias, 91, 92.
Kettilsson, Eric, 97.
Kexholm, 174, 188, 199, 292. 302.
Key, Emil, 407; E. A. H., 424.
Kief, 46, 49, 59.
Kiel, 371; Bay of (see Skiel).
Kierulf, Halfdan, 405.
Kingdom, elective, 64, 65, 310; hereditary, 65, 150, 151, 186, 189, 190, 310.
"King Martha." See Leijonhufvud.
Kjellberg, F., 430.
Klercker, Charles N., 358.
Klingspœ, W. M., 358.
Klusina, 188.
Knapnœfde. See Ragnvald.
Knerœd, peace treaty of, 198.
Kniephausen, Dodo von, 214, 216, 218.
Knights, 200.
Knightly Chapter (see Riddarholm); orders, 318.
Knorring, Sophie von, 389, 427.
Knud. See Canute.
Knut (Swedish kings), Ericsson, 74-76; the Tall, 78, 81.
Knut, Folkung, 81; Bishop, 108; Master, 141-143.
Kœnigsmarck, von, H. C., 236, 258; O. W., 258.
Koch, Axel, 423.
Kœping, 107.
Kœrling, Aug., 431.
Kol, king (Eric Arsæl), 69, **73**; pretender, 75.
Kolbrænna. See Anund Jacob.
Kollandsœ, 69
Kommunalstæmmor, 395.
Konungafrid, 86.
Konghæll, Kungkæll, 62, 69.
Kopparberg, 105, 133
Krakow, Morton, 196-197.
Kreuger, Nils, 349.
Kristian, Kristiern See Christian.
Kristina. See Christine.
Kristofer. See Christopher.
Krivitchi, 47.
Kronberg, Julius, 429.
Kronborg, fortress of, 247, 248.
Krusenstierna, J. E. von, 435.
Kyrkomœtet, 396.

L

LAALAND, 246.
Labor question, 418, 433.

INDEX

Lacroze, M., 341.
Ladoga, Lake, 199.
Ladugardsland, battle of, 124.
Ladulas (Barn-lock). See Magnus.
Læn, 7, 231, 395.
Lagerbielke, Gustavus, 407.
Lagerlœf, Selma, 427.
Laholm, 84.
Lallerstedt, E., 431.
Landskrona (in Sweden), battle of, 254 (in Finland). 88.
Landsting, 395-396, 399, 407.
Landstorm, 417.
Landtmanna party, 407-408, 410, 416.
Landtmarskalk, 200, 407.
Landtværn, 417.
Lange, Lorenz, 289.
Langeland, 246.
Languedoc, 167.
La Place, 324.
Lapland. Lapmark, Laps, 5, 10, 15, 16. 104, 330; language, 8, 341; "Divine service in the Lapmark," 429.
Lappo, battle of, 358.
Lars. See Laurentius.
Larsson, Thomas, 195; Liss Olof, 407; Marcus, 412, 429; Carl, 429.
Latin, 98, 117, 142, 220, 265, 328.
Lauenburg, 402, 405.
Laurentius. See Andreæ and Petri.
Laval, Gustavus de, 425.
Lavoisier, 325.
Laws. See Sweden.
League, Catholic, 189.
Lech, battle of, 210.
Leckœ, 187, 251.
Leczinski (see Stanislav), 427.
Leffler, A M. (Mittag-), 424; Anne Charlotte, 427.
Leibnitz, 266.
Leijonhufvud, 282 note; Margaret (see Margaret, queens of Sweden); Martha (King Martha), 155; Sten, baron, 162, 170.
Leire, 38.
Leipsic, 117, 213, 224, 288; first battle of, 206-209; second battle of, 225-226.
Lena, battle of, 76.
Lenæus, J., 239.
Lenngren, Anne Marie, 346.
Leonidas, the Swedish, 224.
Leopold, C. G., 345.

Leopold I., emperor (1640-1705), 225.
Leuchtenberg, 382
Levertin, Oscar, 427, 428.
Lewenhaupt, 282 note; A. L., 282, 283, 284, 285-287; C. E., 316, 317.
Leyden, 331.
Libau, 203.
Liberty, song of, 114; period of, 310-342, 320-321.
Libraries, 99.
Lidner, Bengt, 346.
Liesna, battle of, 285.
Liewen. H. H. von, 298-299.
Liljefors, Bruno, 429.
Lindberg, A., 430.
Lindblad, A. F., 389; Otto, 389, 413.
Lindeberg, A., 377.
Linden, Mathilde, 431.
Lind. Jenny, 390, 413.
Lindholm (-en) in Scania, 97; in Upland, 130.
Lindskiold, E., 270.
Ling, P. H., 380, 381.
Linkœping, 71. 77. 80, 85, 108. 112, 121, 185, 186, 195; conference at, 72.
Linnæus (von Linné), Charles, 327-333.
Lithuania, 284.
Literature. See Sweden.
Liturgia, 175-176, 183.
Liuksiala 173.
Livonia, Livonians, 162, 163, 187, 198, 202, 203, 223, 231, 250, 258, 273, 277, 281, 282. 283, 290-291, 307, 312.
Lober Brook, 207.
Loccenius, John, 240.
Locke, 347.
Lodbrok. See Ragnar.
Lœdœse, 83, 84, 111; New, 116, 152, 196, 197.
London, 267, 323, 326, 327, 331, 334, 340.
Longobardians, 28, 29.
Lord, 200.
Lothringia, 162, 169.
Louis le Débonnaire (the Pious), 48, 53; XIV. 235, 252, 254-255, 259, 280, 305; XVI. 351-352, 367.
Louise, Princess, 406; Queen, 392, 411.
Louise Ulrica, Queen, 217, 338.
Lovisa. See Louise.

Lubeck, 75, 81, 82, 85, 122, 132, 140, 148, 165, 166, 168, 316, 371.
Lucidor, Lasse (Johansson), 233.
Lulea, 266.
Lubetch, 49.
Ludvig Rudolph of Brunswick, 324.
Luitprand, 48.
Lund, 10, 70, 111, 250, 304, 307, 322, 328, 329, 337, 340; battle of. 254; peace treaty at, 255; University of (see Universities).
Lundberg, Gustavus, 428; Theodor, 430.
Lundquist, C. F., 431.
Luther, Lutheran, 98, 140, 183, 184, 186, 190, 204, 214, 312, 327, 368, 435.
Lutzen, battle of, 213-219; battlefield of, 279, 281.
Lybecker, George, 283, 285.
Lymphatic ducts, 262.

M

MÆCENAS of Sweden, 250.
Machiavelli, 121.
Mælar, Lake, 5, 10, 55, 71, 96, 107, 112, 127, 156. 163.
Magdeburg, 205-206.
Magnetism, 324.
Magnus (Danish princes): M. Nilsson, 71; M. Henricsson, 72-74.
Magnus, Bishop, 148.
Magnus (kings of Norway): M. Barfod, 69; M. Lagabœte, 83.
Magnus (kings of Sweden): M. Ladulas, 82-88, 89, 90; M. Ericsson, 84, 92-95, 97; (princes of Sweden): Magnus Birgersson, 92; M. Vasa, 155, 157, 158, 163-164. 169.
Magog, 263.
Main, River, 209.
Malaspina, 183.
Malebranche, 266.
Malmstrœm, B. E., 389.
Malmœ, 10, 411.
Manheim. See Atland.
Manderstrœm, Count, 393, 401, 404.
Marsk, 87, 102, 108, 249.
Margaret, missionary to the Laps, 104.
Margaret Fredkulla, Princess, 69, 71.

Margaret (queens of Sweden), 89; Valdemarsdotter, 95, 96, 98, 100-105, 120, 371; Leijonhufvud, 155, 156, 177, 178.
Margaret of Valois, 162.
Maria, queen of Sweden, 189.
Marie Antoinette, Queen, 367.
Marie Eleonore, Queen, 234.
Marlborough, 280.
Mariefred, 118, 133.
Mariestad, 188.
Marnæs, 186.
Masudi, 50.
Matchless, The, 165-166.
Martha, Dame, 100.
Matérn, J. A., 288.
Massilia, 24.
Mars, 81.
"Master Olf," 427.
Materialism, 412, 432.
Mathematics, 270, 322.
Mattias, Bishop, 128.
Maximilian of Bavaria, 193, 210, 211.
Mazarin, 220.
Mazeppa, 283, 285, 286.
Mayence, 209.
Mechtild, Danish queen, 81.
Mecklenburg, 95, 97, 168, 210, 223, 244, 295, 357.
Mediæval. See Middle Ages.
Medelpad, 5, 24, 303.
Medical science, 262, 331, 333, 424, 425.
Meibom, 240.
Melanchthon, 204.
Melen, Berndt von, 142, 148.
Memel, 203.
Menuet, Peter, 232.
Mendelssohn, 389.
Meri, 47.
Messenius, John, 232; Arnold J., 240; Arnold, the Younger, 240.
Metals, 15, 16, 116.
Mexico, 18, 404.
Middle Ages, 45, 64-129, 134, 192, 400.
Michaëli, Louise, 413.
Midsummer, Midnight, sun, 7.
Miklagard, 52.
Mines, miners, mine owners, 123, 144, 152, 200-201, 305, 323, 335;
Mining, College of, 304-305, 322, 323.
Ministers, church, 175, 183, 253, 287, 304, 327, 337, 396; state

(secretary), 365, 401, 407, 416; of foreign affairs, 373, 393. 435; of justice, 393, 397, 409, 435; of finance, 393, 435, 436; of ecclesiastics, 393, 409, 436; of war, 408, 435; of civil service, 409; of marine, 435; of interior, 435.
Missionaries, 53–55, 58, 104.
Mitan, 202, 282.
Mœrner, Otto, 367–368.
Mohilev, 284.
Molin, Ambjœrn, 289; J. P., 412, 430.
Monitor, 387.
Monrad, D. G., 404.
Montelius, Oscar, 423.
Mora, in Dalecarlia, 136–138, 140; Stone of, in Upland, 92, 95.
Moravia, 226, 228.
Moræus, Maria Elis, 332.
Mons Bengtsson. See Natt och Dag.
Moscow, 172, 188, 284, 288.
Moss, Convention of, 372–373.
Motzfeldt, K., 406.
Muller, J. B., 289.
Munck, Lady Ebba, 415.
Munich School of Painters, 429.
Muonio, River, 363.
Music, 263, 346, 380, 382, 388, 389–390, 412, 413, 431; national folk, 431.
Mutiny, 188.
Mysticism, 98, 99, 161, 169, 321, 354, 356.
Mythology, classical, 31, 265. Swedish (see Sweden).

N

NAKSKOV, 246.
Namur, 93.
Narva, 174, 282; battle of, 274–277; river, 275.
Napoleon I., 356, 357, 362, 367, 368, 369–371.
Napoleon III., 404, 406.
Nassau, 415.
Nathorst, H. O., 423; A. C., 424 note.
Natt och Dag, Mons Bengtsson, 109; Nils Bosson (see Sture); Ake Hansson, 122 (see also Sture).
Nerigon, 25.
Nerike, 5, 13. 39, 97, 116.
Nerschinsk, 289.

Nestor, 46–47, 49, 52.
Netherlands, 98, 152, 189.
Neva, 78, 93, 289.
New Church, 325.
New Rhymed Chronicle. See Charles Chronicle.
New School, 380–381.
Newton, 324.
Nicolaus of Alba, 72.
Nicholaus II. of Russia, 418.
Nils Bosson (Natt och Dag). See Sture.
Nils, king of Denmark, 71.
Nilsson, Mons, 134; Sven, 380; Christine, 413.
Nimwegen, peace treaty of, 254–255
Niord, 34.
Nithard, 54.
Nobel, Alfred, 425–426.
Nobility, Nobles, 76. 86, 87, 88, 92, 95, 96, 102, 105, 108, 110, 113, 115, 117, 119, 120, 126, 127, 128, 144, 148, 150, 151, 158, 166, 169, 173, 174, 185, 186, 193, 199, 200, 231, 233, 238, 239, 243, 250, 255, 256, 258, 271, 302, 304, 310, 314, 349, 350, 352, 357, 365, 367, 383, 384, 385, 396, 397, 398, 416; higher, 200, 251, 256–257, 314; lower, 200, 251, 253, 256, 257, 314, speaker of (see Landtmarskalk).
Nœrdlingen, battle of, 221, 223.
Nœteborg, 282.
Norcopensis. See Nordenhielm.
Nordanskogs, 5.
Nordberg, G., 288.
Nordblom, J. E.
Nordenflycht, Hedvig Charlotta, 339.
Nordenhielm, Andreas, 269, 270.
Nordenskiold. Baron, 424.
Nordgren, Ellen, 404, 406, 431.
Nordraak, 405.
Nordstrœm, Charles, 429.
Norman, Normandie, 48, 52.
Norman, Georg, 149; F. V. L., 390.
Norén, Adolph, 423.
Norrby, Sœren, 122. 139, 140, 142.
Norrkœping, 190, 320.
Norrland, 5, 6, 7. 14, 24, 43, 107, 138, 193, 266, 362.
North, the Scandinavian, 16, 21, 29, 35, 42, 43, 44. 52, 53. 54, 56, 59, 60, 61, 94, 96, 101, 104, 114, 225, 248, 263, 305, 330, 434, 438.

North Pole, 424.
North Sea, 5, 10, 196, 198, 322, 375.
North Star, Order of the, 318.
Northeast Passage, 424.
Northern language, common, 99; oldest form, 8, 22; tribes, 23; industrial arts, 23; literature, 36, 38, 41.
Northmen, 45, 52, 53, 59.
Norway, Norwegians, 5, 6, 10, 13, 21, 25, 33, 36, 38, 41, 43, 45, 52, 55, 57, 58, 60, 61, 62, 63, 67, 68, 69, 70, 75, 76, 79, 83, 89, 90, 91, 92, 94, 95, 96, 100, 111, 142, 147, 164, 166-167, 174, 247, 307, 308, 311, 348, 357, 362, 366, 370, 371-374, 375, 386, 393-395, 402, 404, 405, 418-421, 430; governor-general question, 386, 393-395, 418-419; constitution, 373-374, 393; cabinet, 373, 394-395, 402; consular and diplomatic service, 419, 420, 437; defence, 419; flag, 386, 419; culture, 405; government, 373; king, 373-374; Minister of State, 419; railways, 421; royal title, 386; Storthing, 373, 379, 386, 393-394, 406, 419, 420, 425-426; viceroy, 393.
Novgorod, 47, 52, 62, 188, 190.
Nuremberg, 211-212, 225.
Nurmanni, 47.
Nykœping, 82, 84, 172, 190, 239, 302; Feast of, 90; Restitution of, 102.
Nyslott, 316.
Nyströem, Alfred, 430.

O

ODER, River, 21, 27, 224, 279.
Odin, 31-32, 34, 35, 37.
Œdman, A., 431.
Œland, island of, 5, 21, 22, 111, 254; naval battles of, 165-166, 167-168, 350.
Œrbyhus, 171.
Œrebro, 109, 146, 150, 174, 368, 387.
Œsel, island of, 164, 227.
Œstberg, Caroline, 431.
Œsterlind, A., 429.
Ohio, 7.
Ohthere. See Ottar.
Olaf (Norwegian kings) Tryggvasson, 57-58; Haraldsson, 61-62, 67; Hakonsson, 100.

Olai, Ericus, 114, 117.
Olaus, Petri (Master Olof). See Petri.
Oldenburg, 366; counts of, 149, 367.
Old Chronicle. See Eric's Chronicle.
Old Danish, 8, 22, 99.
Old English, 237, 342.
Old High German, 342.
Old Icelandic. See Old Norse.
Old Norse language, 8, 22, 99, 341, 342; literature, 32, 232, 270; mythology, 265.
Old Swedish language, 8, 9, 22, 24, 48, 49, 99, 342; literature, 8, 9, 66-67, 80, 98, 114, 121; laws, 48, 66-67, 380, 391.
Oleg, 48, 49, 51.
Olga, 48, 51.
Oliva, peace treaty of, 250.
Oligarchy, 309.
Olof (Swedish kings), 40-41, 42, 54, 55; Skœtkonung, 52, 57-62; Næskonung, 69, 70.
Olsson, Lars, 138.
Olustra, battle of, 78.
Opposition, Conservative, 383, 384; Liberal, 376-378, 379, 380, 382, 383, 384. See also Intelligence Party.
Orange, 259, 392.
Oravais, battle of, 358, 360-362.
Ordeals, 82.
Orientalists, 333, 340.
Ornæs, 134.
Orosius, 43.
Oscar Fredericsborg, 418.
Oscar (kings of Sweden): I. 382-390, 391, 411; II. 411, 414-438.
Oscar, Prince. See Bernadotte.
Oslo, 92.
Ottar, 37-38.
Otto, Bishop, 128.
Oxenstierna, Jœns Bengtsson, 112-113; Axel, 199, 203, 204, 220-221, 222, 226, 229, 230, 233, 234, 239, 242, 312, 375, 421; John, 229; Bengt, 259, 271; John Gabriel, 345; Oxford, 340.

P

PALÆOLITHIC CIVILIZATION, 12.
Palatinate-Zweibrucken, 189, 239, 290.

INDEX

Pappenheim, 203, 207–209, 213, 214, 217–218.
Paris, 118, 305, 331, 340, 368, 371; expositions. 413, 421, 429; peace treaties, 362–363, 369, 388; University, 118, 340.
Parliament, Parliamentary Reform, 108, 111, 376, 379, 384–385, 396–401.
Passage-graves, 13.
Patriotism, 104, 114, 120, 130, 131, 200, 201, 235, 244, 247, 248, 250, 258, 309, 352, 358, 367, 398, 434.
Patkul, J. R., 312.
Pau, 368.
Pauli, Emerentia, 196–197; George, 429; Hanna (Hirsch-P.), 429.
Peasant. See Yeoman.
Peasant High Schools, 423.
Peasant-king, 188.
Peene, River, 312.
Peipus, Lake, 199, 282.
Peutinger, Konrad, 149.
Peringskiold, John, 265.
Pernau, 201, 292.
Person, Andrew, 133–134; Arendt, 134–135; Gœran, 162, 170.
Peter Frisk, 299.
Peter's Pence, 72.
Peterson, Adrian, 431.
Peter the Great, 272–273, 277, 282, 283, 284, 285, 287, 288, 289, 296, 306, 307, 311, 316.
Petri, Olaus (Master Olof), 86, 114, 128, 141, 150; Laurentius, 141, 150, 175, 177, 183; Laurentius P. Gothus, 175.
Peru, 336.
Philadelphia Exposition, 421.
Philip, king, 70; Folkung, 81; Duke (see Charles, Princes of Sweden).
Philipstad, 188.
Philology, 67, 237, 265, 266, 320, 339–342, 380, 388, 423.
Philosophy, 240–241, 321, 327, 340, 411–412, 423.
Phosphoristic School, 380–381.
Physical science, 322, 324–325, 333, 423, 425.
Physiology, 325.
Piccolomini, General, 221, 225.
Pillau, 203.
Piper, Charles, 271, 286, 287, 288, 292; Louise Sophie, 366–367.
Pitea, 411.

Plague, 94, 124, 176, 290, 322.
Plato, 264.
Platen, Baltzar B. von, 365, 371, 375.
Pliny, the Elder, 25.
Poland, Polish, 98, 143, 163, 164, 174, 175, 182, 183, 184, 185, 187, 199, 202, 222, 243–245, 247, 250, 252, 273, 278–279, 281, 282, 283, 284, 290, 292, 294, 295, 297, 313, 401.
Polar Circle, 7, 8; Sea, 93.
Polhammar. See Polhem.
Polhem. Christopher, 267, 302, 304–306, 322, 326, 334, 375, 424; Emerentia, 326.
Polianê, 49.
Polotsk, 47.
Pomerania, 5, 7, 205, 224, 229, 232, 245, 255, 258, 294–295, 299, 302, 312, 319, 336, 357, 363, 371.
Pomponius Mela, 25.
Ponte Corvo, 368.
Pope, 69, 77, 78, 94, 97–98, 117, 121, 124, 126, 144.
Porosalmie, battle of, 350.
Porphyrogenitus. See Constantine P.
Portugal, 45.
Posse, Knut, 116, 118; Arvid, 407.
Potatoes, 336.
Powers, Continental, 187, 248, 250, 252, 319, 320, 344, 345, 372, 374, 378, 403, 418.
Prague, 117, 210, 222, 228, 236, 258.
Press, 231, 365, 376–377, 383, 384, 396, 397, 403, 404, 407, 428; law, 434–435.
Pretenders, 55–56, 74, 75, 78, 147, 187–188.
Prisons, 382.
Priestley, 325.
Priests, 98, 144.
Primas of Sweden, 70.
Printz, John, 232.
Prokopios, 28, 31.
Propeller, 387.
Prose Chronicle. See Chronicle.
Protective system, 406, 416; protectionistic party, 416.
Protestantism, 175, 182–184, 189, 192, 202, 204, 221, 279, 281–282, 325.
Province, Provincial, 5–6, 64–65, 66, 86, 89, 93, 105, 149, 249; laws (see Sweden).

Prussia, 172, 202, 203, 222, 223, 244, 296, 299, 311, 345, 349, 352, 370, 385-386, 403.
Pruth, River, 294.
Pskof, 198.
Ptolemy, 27.
Pufendorff, S., 237.
Puke, Eric Kettilsson (see Kettilsson); Eric (Nilsson), 107, 110.
Pulkkila, battle of, 358.
Pultowa, battle of, 285-286, 289, 290, 291, 292, 294, 303.
Pyk, Louise, 431.
Pyteas, 24.

Q

QUATERNARY period, 12.
Qvidinge, 366.

R

RÆFSNÆS, 133.
Ragnar, Swedish king, 41-42; R. Lodbrok, sea-king, 41-42.
Ragnvald, jarl, 58, 61-62, 67; king, 70-71; prince, 70.
Railways. See Sweden.
Ramberg, 226.
Rankhytta, 133.
Rantzau, Daniel, 168; George, 291.
Rappe, A. E., 435.
Raseborg, 113, 129.
Rashutt, 327.
Ratan, 363.
Ratenau, battle of, 252.
Ravius, 240.
Realism, 405, 426-427.
Reform Banquet, 384.
Reform, Parliamentary. See Parliament.
Reformation, Reformers, 98, 140-146, 150, 153, 339; language, 9.
Reformed Church, 312.
Regensburg, 224.
Rehnskiold, C. G., 284, 285-286, 287, 288.
Renaissance, 153, 157, 261; Swedish Castle, 173, 431.
Renat, J. G., 288.
Renata of Lothringia, 162, 169.
Restitution. See Crown Lands.
Rettvik, 136.
Reuterholm, G. A., 353-356.
Reval, 162, 172, 174, 292.
Revolts, 76, 78, 81, 84, 107-108, 121, 141-143, 146-151, 288, 293, 316-317, 344, 369; of Bells, 148-149, 155.
Revolution, French, 351, 368, 384, 428; Swedish, 138, 143, 146, 344, 345, 349-352, 362, 379.
Rheims, 54.
Ribbing, P., 302, 310, 314.
Richelieu, 220, 224.
Riddarholm's Church, 87, 90, 96, 225, 367, 415.
Riddarhus, The, 166, 200, 256, 268, 398.
Ridderstad, C. F., 389.
Riga, 82, 187, 202, 291-292.
Rikissa, princess, 87; queen, 71; Birgersdotter, 79.
Riksdag, 88, 108, 115, 117, 124, 140, 142, 143, 150, 151, 161, 169, 170, 175, 183-184, 200, 201, 202, 222, 238, 240, 243, 248, 249, 250, 254, 256, 257, 258, 271, 293, 298, 310, 314, 315, 316, 317, 318, 319, 335, 336, 338, 340, 344, 345, 348, 349-350, 355, 356-357, 365, 368, 369, 376, 378, 383, 384, 387, 394-395, 396-401, 403, 406, 407-411, 416-418, 420, 433, 435; regulations of the, 434.
Riksdrotset. See Drotsete.
Riksmarsk. See Marsk.
Rimbert, Archbishop, 52, 55.
Ring ("Sigurd Ring"), 41, 51.
Riswick, peace treaty of, 259.
Ritual and hymn-book, 175, 183, 260, 355.
Rococo, 353.
Rock-carvings, 17, 18.
Rœskilde, peace treaties of, 91, 247.
Rolf Krake, 38.
Romanticism (Neo-), 346, 380-381, 388-389, 405, 427.
Rome, Roman, 20, 21, 26, 27, 28, 72, 74, 97, 125, 141, 144, 175, 204, 263, 265.
Rosen, von, 282 note; George von, 412, 429.
Rosenblad, M., 374.
Roslagen, 48-49.
Roslin, Alex., 347, 428.
Rosstjenst. See Russtienst.
Rostock, 121, 147, 165.
Rostof, 47.
Rothman, Dr., 327-328.
Royal offices, 87; sanctity, 77, 85; title, 84.

INDEX 457

Rud, Otto, 122.
Ruden, Island of, 205.
Rudenschiold, Madelaine, 354.
Rudbeck, Olof, the Elder, 261–265; Olof, the Younger, 330.
Rudbeckius, J., 262.
Rudolph, emperor, 172.
Rugen, Island, 229, 294, 371.
Ruhr, River, 236.
Runeberg, J. L., 364, 388.
Runes, 8, 21–22, 340.
Runius, 233.
Runn, Lake, 134.
Ruotsi, 48.
Rurik, 47–49, 51, 52, 187.
Rus, Rûs, 47, 50, 105.
Russia, Russians, 6, 12, 22, 26, 43, 46–52, 62, 63, 67, 68, 69, 78, 81, 88, 94, 105, 112, 118, 119, 122, 143, 152, 153, 162, 171, 172, 174, 176, 184, 187, 188, 190, 198, 199, 203, 244, 250, 272, 273, 274–277, 278, 280, 282–287, 291–292, 294, 295, 306, 311, 315, 316, 317, 345, 348–349, 350–351, 352, 357–362, 369, 370, 374, 377, 378, 387–388, 394, 401, 418, 436; captivity, 287–289; language, 8; names, 48.
Russtienst, Rusttjenst, 86, 143, 162, 174, 188.
Rydberg, Victor, 412, 423.
Rydboholm, 130.
Rydelius, Andrew, 337-338.
Ryssby, 193.

S

SACHSEN (Saxony)-Lauenburg, 155, 216.
Sæfstrom, 325.
Sætherbey, H., 389.
Sætra, 134.
St. Gallen, 362.
St. Olaf, Order of, 386.
St. Peter of Rome, 240.
St. Petersburg, 88, 282, 283, 285, 289, 348, 355.
St. Salvator, Order of, 98.
Sala, 152.
Salestad, 176.
Salon, French, 428, 429.
Salmson, H., 429.
Salmasius, 236, 240.
Salvius, A., 229.
San, River, 244.
Sandels, J. A., 858, 360.

Saxo, 51, 57.
Saxons, Saxonland, Saxony, 29, 38, 40, 206–208, 211, 213, 222, 223, 224, 228, 272, 273, 277, 279–282, 292, 295, 299, 322, 415.
Scandia, 25.
Scandinavia, Scandinavian, 14, 16, 24, 25, 28, 100, 101, 124, 166, 255, 317, 423, 437; languages, 9, 99, 166; peninsula, 5, 12, 25, 27, 93, 312, 325, 371, 421; policy, 247, 402–406, 415, 437–438; religion, 31.
Scandinavism, 385-386.
Scania, 5, 6, 10, 12, 13, 14, 18, 21, 25, 40, 43, 46, 84, 91, 93, 95, 97, 105, 111, 167, 195, 226, 247, 249, 254, 290–291, 307, 325, 336, 344, 357, 362, 366, 369, 386.
Scandza, 30, 44.
Scheele, C. W., 346.
Schefferns, 240.
Schleswig, 104, 112, 126, 245, 385, 386, 402, 404, 405.
Schluesselburg, 282.
Schlyter, K. J., 380.
Schœnstrœm, P., 288.
Scholander, E. W., 431.
Schools, school laws, 117, 146, 175, 393, 423.
Schueck, H., 428.
Schuisky, Vassili, 187–188.
Schwartz, Sophie, 389.
Schwedenstein, 281.
Schwerin, von W., 360–361; F. B., 377.
Scotland, 208, 405.
Scylfingas. See Skilfings.
Secret Committee, 314, 315, 316.
Seeland, 246–247, 291, 302.
Sehlstedt, Elias, 389.
Semiramis of the North, 104.
Separator, 425.
Seraphim, Order of the, 318.
Seven Years' War, of the North, 164–168; Continental, 319.
Siberia, 287–289.
Sigfrid, St., 58.
Sigismund of Sweden and Poland, 174, 182–186, 187, 188, 202.
Signe, 36.
Signjótr. See Sineus.
Sigrid Storrada, 57.
Sigtuna, 35, 62, 68, 71, 75.
Sigurd, King, 41.
Sigurd Jorsalafare, 70.
Siikajoki, battle of, 358–359.

Silesia, 202, 222, 225, 226, 279, 281-282.
Siljan, Lake, 136.
Simon. See Gauzbert and Stenfi.
Sineus, 47, 48.
Sjœgren, Otto, 390, 431.
Skara, 59, 68, 84, 128, 148, 321.
Skee Finns, 28.
Skenninge Conference, 78; meeting, 86.
Skerry fleet, 350, 351.
Skialf, 36.
Skiel (Kiel), Bay of, 226
Skilfings, 33, 35, 37, 39, 40.
Skjœldebrand, A. F., 374.
Skokloster, 251.
Skytte, Johan, 193, 232.
Slavs, 28, 47-50, 54.
Sloane, Hans, 331.
Smaland, 5, 14, 29, 70, 72, 84, 111, 126, 133, 150, 166, 195, 215, 291, 327, 329.
Smith, S., 431.
Smolensk, 49, 188, 284.
Snaphaner, 226.
Snoilsky, 412, 427.
Snorre Sturleson, 33, 34, 35, 40, 41, 52, 266, 349.
Socialism, 433.
Sœderman, August, 431.
Sœdermanland, 5, 9, 13, 23, 39, 58, 107, 133, 174.
Sœderkœping, 116, 183.
Sohlman, Aug., 403.
Soop, Eric, 303.
Sophia (queens of Sweden), 81; 415.
Sophie Magdalene, queen of Sweden, 343.
Sound, the, 10, 93, 227; naval battle of, 248.
South Company, 232.
Spain, Spanish, 45, 97, 209, 221, 352, 378.
Sparre, P. G., 389.
Sparrsætra, battle of, 78.
Spectator, 338.
Spitzbergen, 424.
Sprengtporten, J. M., 344, 350.
Squire, 106, 131, 200.
Stade, 295.
Stadsfullmægtige, 395.
Stæket, 124, 125, 131.
Stagnelius, E. J., 380-381.
Stanislav of Poland, 279, 281, 290, 295, 313.
Starbæck, George, 389.

Steam hose, 387.
Stedingk, C. von, 350, 367.
Stefan, 74.
Stegeborg, 139, 185.
Stenbock (see Catherine, queens of Sweden), Brita, 156; Gustavus, Baron, 156, 162, 181; Olof, 171; Eric, 176-182, 296; Magdalen (see Sture); Cecilia, 178-180; Beatrix, 180; Anne, 181; Gustavus, 182; Gustavus Otto, 250; Magnus, Count, 182, 277, 284, 290, 291, 294-296.
Stenfi (Stephan), 58.
Stenhammar, W., 390.
Stenkil, 67-68, 70.
Stensœ, 132.
Stephan of Poland, 174.
Stellin, 312.
Steuchius, Archbishop, 340.
Stiklastad, battle of, 62.
Stiernhielm, Georg, 233, 235, 237.
Stiernhœk, 232.
Stobeus, Chilian, 329.
Stockholm, 10, 36, 74, 75, 82, 84, 87, 90, 92, 95, 96, 100, 101, 107, 108, 109, 112, 116, 119, 121, 124, 125, 126, 127, 130, 133, 139, 140, 141, 143, 150, 158, 165, 169, 173, 180, 186, 190, 193, 199, 231-232, 272, 313, 317, 320, 321, 334, 338, 344, 362, 366, 373, 377, 384, 391, 397, 405, 418, 422; Royal Palace, 303; City University (see Universities); Exchange, 337; Posten, 377; Royal Theatre, 346, 352, 413, 431.
Stolarm, Arvid, 185.
Stolbova, peace treaty of, 198.
Stolhandske, Torsten, 216-217, 218.
Stone Age, 11-16; cists, 13.
Stongebro, battle of, 185.
Strahlenberg, J. von, 288.
Strandberg, C. W. A., 389.
Stralsund, siege of, 299-300.
Strengnæs, 71, 114, 128, 140.
Strindberg, August, 426-427, 428, 431; Nils, 424.
Strœmstad, 307, 322.
Strole, Olof, 197.
Stromberg, Nils, 291-292.
Stuhm, battle of, 202-203.
Sturzen-Becker, O. P., 389.
Suchtelen, von, 359.
Succession, Royal, 150, 151, 190, 310; law of, 434.

Stuart, Mary, 162; Charles Magnus, 270, 277.
Sture, 130, 140, 146, 181, 182; original line: Sten Sture, the Elder, 113, 114–120, 121, 123, 130–131; Natt och Dag branch: Nils Bosson, 108–109, 116, 118, 120, 123; Svante Nilsson, 118–123, 141; Sten Sture, the Younger, 123–129, 131, 142; Nils Stensson, 147; Svante Stensson, Count, 149, 151, 155, 156, 162, 168, 169–170, 177; Nils Svantesson, 168, 169; Eric, 170; Martha (see Leijonhufvud); Sigrid, 176–182; Magdalen, 176–182, 296; Anne, 177; Margaret, 177, 179; Christine, 177.
Sture Chronicles, 114.
Styrbiœrn Starke, 55–56.
Subsidies, 252, 316, 319.
Sud, 49.
Suevian Sea, 26.
Suiones, 26.
Sundberg, Archbishop, 407.
Sunnanskogs, 5.
Sunnanvæder, Peder, 141–143, 147.
Suomi, 437.
Supreme Court. See Sweden.
"Surgeon's Stories," 413.
Sværdsbro, 179.
Sværdsjœ, 135.
Svartsjœ, 155, 173.
Sveaborg, fortress of, 317, 359–360.
Svealand, 5, 14, 19, 24, 27, 58, 68, 69, 83, 185.
"Svecia," 265–266.
Svedberg, Jesper, 321.
Svedbom, 431.
Sveijder, 35.
Svein, Norwegian jarl, 57–58.
Sven. See Blot-Sven.
Svend (Danish kings): Tjufvuskægg, 57; Estridsen, 63; Grade, 72.
Svendborg, 246.
Svensksund, naval battles of, 350–351.
Sverdrup, J., 406.
Sverker, the Old, 71–73, 75; the Younger, 74, 75–77.
Sviar, 27, 35, 47, 64.
Sviatoslaf, 51.
Svinesund, 307, 372.
Svithiod, 34, 35, 37, 38, 39, 40, 41.
Svolder, battle of, 57–58.

Swabia, 29, 213.
Sweden, 5, 11, 21, 26, 27, 31, 34, 42, 58, 64, 75, 90, 105, 126, 188, 192, 214, 221, 222, 223, 229–230, 250, 265, 272, 289, 291, 296, 298, 300, 309, 320–321, 363–364, 374, 403, 418, 432–434; administration (see Government); agriculture, 15, 117, 152, 260, 306, 317, 423; alcohol industry, 387; architects (see Architecture); army, 152, 186, 201–202, 203, 231, 258–259, 283, 290, 296, 307, 408–410, 415–418; art, 261, 303, 347, 382, 391, 412, 421, 428–431; botanists (see Botany); broadcloth, 335, 336, 337; budget, 422; cabinet, 365, 374, 376, 378, 382, 383, 391–392, 394–395, 399–400, 402, 404, 435, 436; canals (see Gotha Canal); civilization (see Cultural Development); climate, 7; colonies, 232; commerce, 81–82, 85, 105, 116, 152, 176, 188, 198, 200, 260, 288, 302, 376, 387, 406, 407, 414, 421, 422; communications, 374, 387, 406, 421; communities, 39, 42, 64, 105, 396, 432; composers (see Music); constitution, 64, 65, 105, 255–258, 268, 292–293, 302, 310, 314, 318, 344, 349–350, 366, 378, 400, 434; court, 87, 146, 154, 189, 240, 255, 318, 319, 338, 339; court party, 318–320, 338; criminal code, 395; crown, 144, 149, 174–175, 201, 239, 255 (see also Crown lands, restitution of); cultural development, 14, 18, 23, 30–31, 59–61, 68, 71–72, 98–99, 105, 114, 117–118, 141–142, 173, 188, 201, 232–233, 261–267, 302–306, 313, 320, 321–341, 345–347, 353, 380–381, 382, 388–390, 393, 405, 408, 411–413, 422–433; dairy industry, 152, 425; defence, 254, 260, 293, 374, 375, 408, 417–418; departments, state, 199, 230, 298, 314, 378, 421, 435 (see also Cabinet and Ministers); dialect research, 340, 341; electric telegraph, 387, 422; emblem, 156, 197; engineers, 424–426; estates (see Estates); exports and imports, 422; finance, 94, 187, 239, 243, 301–302, 306, 311, 313, 315, 319, 374, 407, 408, 422; forests,

7, 18; fundamental laws, 434–435; geographical discoveries, 288, 424; geology, 8, 12, 325; government, 64. 65, 74, 85, 87, 88, 91, 92, 93, 96, 101–104, 108, 114, 115, 123, 149–150, 152–153, 161–162, 174, 176, 188, 189, 190, 203, 230, 233, 249–252, 253, 256–257, 258, 259–260, 271, 292–293, 300–302, 310–311, 312, 313, 315, 316, 317, 319, 320, 345, 354–355, 374, 378, 383–384, 390, 391, 395–401, 403, 404, 407, 409, 410–411, 416, 418, 419, 435; graves, 13, 14, 16, 17, 19, 23, 27; historians (see History); industries, 302, 306, 317, 319, 334–337, 383, 387, 393, 407, 421; inland seas, 305, 325; inventors, 304, 321, 322, 425–426; kings, 26, 31, 40, 41, 42, 64–65, 67, 84, 85, 87, 92, 96, 99, 115, 125, 145, 150, 158, 189, 190, 191, 201, 242, 249, 253, 263, 268, 300, 308, 343, 382–383, 391, 401, 411, 414, 415, 434–435; land-tax, 408, 410, 416; language, 8, 9, 15, 47–48, 99, 153. 237, 238, 330, 340, 346–347, 390; legislation, 82, 85–86, 89, 93, 105, 110, 314, 315, 383, 395–401, 416–418; literature, 66–67, 80, 89, 98, 99, 121, 155, 233, 237, 261, 263, 337–339, 345–347, 380–382, 388–389, 405, 412–413, 414, 426–428; loanwords, 8, 47; manufactures, 306, 317, 335–336; maritime code, 395; metal engraving (see Art); migrations, 34; military districts and divisions, 417–418; militia, 357, 365, 369, 409, 410, 416, 417; mining industry, 82, 116, 152, 188, 201, 230–232, 260, 336; municipal government, 395–396; mythology, 31–32, 53; national anthem, 434; national character and temperament, 9, 10, 98, 354, 389–390, 405, 433–434; naturalists (see Science); navigation, 407, 422; navy, 94, 149, 168, 226–227, 231, 253, 258–259, 416, 418; one realm, 39, 43, 64–65, 105; painters (see Art); philologists (see Philology); philosophers (see Philosophy); political grandeur, 191, 192–309; population, 5, 8, 16, 94, 176, 193; possessions, 253, 272, 292, 293, 299, 312 (see also Territory, Finland, and Baltic Dominion and Provinces); postal service, 231, 421; proper names, 32, 47, 48; provincial laws, 8, 66–67, 70, 89, 93, 380, 392; railways, 387, 406, 421; regent, 68, 79, 88, 91, 108, 109, 113, 115. 120, 122, 124, 126, 140, 184, 353–356, 362–364, 391, 392–393; scenery, 6, 98, 330, 391; Riksdag (see Riksdag); seal of state, 164; science, 9, 232, 240, 261, 265, 288, 302, 304–306, 321, 324–325, 332, 339, 340, 346, 380, 408, 414, 421, 426; sculptors (see Art); sects, 432; singers, song (see Music); sloyd, 287; state, 8, 64–65, 151, 192, 199, 230; state law, 67, 93, 105, 110, 315; state treasurer, 189, 250; statesmen, 82, 87, 89, 146, 192, 199, 204, 220, 251, 312, 315–316, 317, 368, 392–393, 437; suffrage, 396, 399, 433; supreme court, 162, 174, 199, 200, 230, 350; taxes, taxation, 76, 88, 103, 107, 201, 233, 238, 240, 279, 290, 293, 314. 317, 387, 396, 408, 410; telephone system, 422; territory, 6, 93, 104; 434; towns, 10, 75, 82, 85, 116, 152, 176, 188, 311, 395. 397, 399; town laws, 116; tribes, 66, 105.

Swedenborg, E., 321–327, 332, 347.
"Swedish Fates and Adventures," 427.
Swinhufvud. See Barbro Stigsdotter.
Sword, Order of the, 318.
Systema Naturæ, 330, 333.

T

Tacitus, 26, 27, 30, 434.
Tartars, 285.
Taube, Mathilde. See Grabow.
Tavastehus, 77, 358.
Tavasti, Tavastland, 77, 78, 88.
Tchudi, 47.
Te Deum, 277.
Tegnér, Esaias, 353, 363, 381–382, 389; Esaias, Junior, 423.
Telegraph. See Sweden.
Temperance movement, 387.
Terna, 133.
Tessin, Nicodemus, Senior, 302–303; Nicodemus, Junior, 302–

304, 317, 430; Charles Gustavus, 317, 318, 332, 336, 339, 340.
Teuffel, General, 207.
Teutons, Teutonic, 8, 21, 22, 25, 26, 28, 44; ancestors, 15; languages, 8, 238, 342; communities, 396, 432; migrations, 20, 23, 44; mythology, 30; origin, 30, 265; sea, 25; state, 64-65; traditions, 29-30; tribes, 30, 43.
Thegerstrom, Robert, 430.
Themptander, O. R., 416.
Theology, 340-341.
Theophilus, Emperor, 48.
Theosophy, 325, 412.
Thermometer, Centigrade, 321, 333. See Celsius.
Thing (Assembly), 55, 56, 58, 61, 65, 72, 82, 86.
Thiodulf of Hvin, 33, 35, 41.
Thirty Years' War, 193, 202-229, 231, 236, 261, 281, 312, 434.
Thomas, Bishop, 114, 121.
Thomasius, 266.
Thor, 30-31.
Thorild, T., 346, 355.
Thorn, 172.
Thorvald, Hialte, 56.
Thraldom, 82, 93, 137, 309.
Thule, 24, 25, 28, 29.
Thunberg, D., 375.
Tidemand, 405.
Tilly, 203, 206-209, 210-211.
Timutarsz, 297, 298.
Tiundaland, 39, 62.
Tiveden, 83, 127.
Tobacco, 336.
Tobolsk, 287.
Tœnnig, fortress of, 295-296.
"Tœrnroseus bok," 389.
Toll, J. C., 344, 356, 357.
Tomte Mats, 137.
Topelius, Z., 412-413.
Tordenskiold, Peter, 307, 311, 322.
Toresson. See Ahlstrœmer.
Torgau, retreat from, 224.
Torgny, 62.
Tormentor of Denmark, 122.
Torne, River, 363.
Torpa, 156, 181.
Torsslov, O. U., 390.
Torstensson, Lennart, 223, 225-229, 239, 245, 248.
Tott, Eric Axelson, 113, 117; Ivar Axelson, 113, 117; Ingeborg, 118; Ake, 173; Clas, 175.

Traventhal, peace treaty of, 274.
Tre Rosor, 282 note; Ture Jœnsson, 146, 148, 149, 156; John Turesson, 149, 156, 158; Gustavus Johnsson, Count, 156, 162.
Trolle, Eric, 123, 124; Gustavus, Archbishop, 124-125, 127-128, 129, 139, 142, 148.
Trollhetta, waterfalls of, 306, 375.
Tromp, Admiral, 253.
Truvor, 47, 48.
Tryggve. See Truvor.
Truso, 43.
Turgot, 59.
Turkey, Turks, 283, 287, 293, 294, 296-298, 299, 303, 305, 388.
Tver, battle of, 188.
Tyr, 30.
Tyrol, 6.

U

UBE, River, 206.
Ukraine, 285, 286, 292.
Uleoborg, 358.
Ulf, jarls, 74; 78, 79.
Ulf Gudmundsson, 97.
Ulfhild, 71.
Ulfsson, Jacob, 117, 124, 133.
Ulrica Eleonore, queens of Sweden, 255, 268, 274; 269, 289, 298, 309, 310, 311, 312, 313, 316.
Ulricsdal, 391.
Union, Act of, 4, 92, 93, 94, 101-102, 104, 114, 120, 129, 151, 166-167, 317, 372-374, 393, 395, 420; nature of the, 419-421, 437; revision of the, 386, 394-395, 406, 421.
Union government, 420, 438; defence, 420, 438; parliament, 420, 438.
Unionism, Unionist party, 110, 111, 114, 120, 121, 122, 123, 130, 393-395, 415-416.
Unitarianism, 325, 412.
United States, 436, 437-438 (see also America); President of, 434.
Universities, 117, 131, 153, 183, 189, 230, 235, 250, 304, 322, 327, 329, 339, 340-341, 356, 380, 385, 390, 405, 411, 413, 422-423.
Unne, 55.
Upland, 5, 10, 23, 35, 39, 48, 73, 78, 89, 90, 97, 105, 107, 110, 124, 139, 185, 391.
Uppstrœm, A., 137 note.
Upsala, 10, 33, 35, 37, 38, 39, 42,

51, 68, 71, 74, 107, 120, 131, 134, 139, 142, 143, 147, 153, 157, 161, 175, 183, 201, 235, 240, 262, 264, 304, 322, 323, 329, 330, 331-332, 340, 356, 380, 413; cathedral, 82, 112; meeting, 183; University (see Universities); University Botanical Garden, 329, 362; Library, 201, 235; Observatory, 333; temple, 59, 60, 68, 71.
Uranus, 324.
Usedom, island of, 205, 229, 312.
Utilitarianism, 337, 432.
Utmeland, 137.
"Utopia Realized," 427.

V

VADSTENA, 98-99, 104, 107, 120, 140, 164, 178, 184, 304.
Værælæ, peace treaty of, 351.
Værend, 29, 58, 66, 72.
Værfvade, 714.
Væringar, 49.
Valdemar of Sweden, 80-84, 89.
Valdemar (kings of Denmark): Seier, 76, 77; Atterdag, 95, 100.
Valdemar, Prince, 87, 89-91.
Vandals, 47.
Vanlande, 35.
Varanger Bay, 378, 387-388.
Varberg, 167, 168.
Variagi, Varangians, 46-53.
Varinians, 29.
Vasa dynasty, family, 130, 163, 187, 193, 194, 249; Original line: Krister Nilsson, 108, 110, 130; Kettil Karlsson, 112-113; Eric Johansson, 128, 130; Gustavus Ericsson (see Gustavus I.); Eric (see Eric XIV.); John (see John III.); Magnus (see Magnus, Princes of Sweden); Charles (see Charles IX.); Gustavus Ericsson, 172-173; Sigrid, 172-173, 177; Sigismund (see Sigismund); John, Duke (see John); Charles Philip (see Charles); Catherine (see Catherine, Countess-Palatine); Gustavus Adolphus (see Gustavus II. Adolphus); Christine (see Christine, queens of Sweden); Polish line, 163, 240; Sigismund (see Sigismund); Vladislav, 186, 188, 243; John II. Casimir, 243-244.

Vasa Renaissance. See Renaissance.
Vasa, town, 360.
Vassili, Czar. See Schinsky.
Vaxholm, fortress of, 197, 418.
Venar, Lake, 5, 69.
Vends, Vendish, 57, 63, 75.
Vennerberg, Gunnar, 389-390, 409, 413.
Verden, 229, 235, 312.
Vermland, 5, 40, 41, 43, 55, 68, 83, 107, 111, 116, 174, 194, 229, 307, 308, 335.
Vessi, 47.
"Verzage nicht," 215.
Vettar, Lake, 5, 77, 164, 418.
Vexio, 71, 84, 291, 327, 328, 331.
Viborg, fortress of, 88, 118, 292, 312, 351.
Victoria, crown princess of Sweden-Norway, 415.
Vienna, 203, 226, 299; Congress of, 372-373; Exposition, 421; peace treaty of, 405; siege of, 228-229.
Viken, 46.
Viking Age, Vikings, 8, 24, 41, 44-63, 66, 70.
Vilmanstrand, battle of, 316.
Vincentius, Bishop, 128.
Virdar, 29.
Virta, battle of, 358.
Visbur, 35.
Visby, 85, 95, 304.
Visigoths, 236.
Visingsborg, 251.
Visingsœ, 77, 87, 180.
Vistula, 21, 27, 31.
Vitalen, or Victualen Brotherhood, 101.
Vitesjœ, battle of, 195.
Vladimir, St., 51, 52.
Vladislav. See Vasa, Polish line.
Voldgæstning, 86.
Volga, 50.
Volmar, 187.
Voltaire, 347.
Vordingborg, 247.
Vorskla, River, 285, 286.
Vossius, 236-237.

W

WACHTMEISTER, Hans, 259; Hans Hansson, 435.
Wahlberg, Edward, 429.
Wallachia, 22, 299.

INDEX

Wallenstein, 203, 204, 210-218, 221.
Wallhof, battle of, 202.
Wallin, J. O., Archbishop, 381.
Wallis, Curt, 424.
Walloons, 231.
War of Clubs, 184.
Warburg, K., 248.
Warsaw, battle of, 244; conquest of, 244, 278; diet of, 278.
Washington, George, 367.
Weibule, M., 424.
Weimar. See Bernhard, Duke of Weimar.
Wendland, 43.
Werben, 206.
Westerbotten, West Bothnia, 5, 16.
Westerlund, Dr., 424.
Westeros, 71, 107, 108, 123, 124, 128, 139, 141, 143, 151, 171, 262; Ordinantia and Recess, 145-146; 151.
West Gothland. See Gothland.
Westmanland, 5, 58, 106, 107, 112, 116, 147, 195.
Westphalia, 236; Peace of, 229.
Wetterstedt, G. af, 374.
Wetterstrand, Dr., 424.
Wickman, G., 431.
Wikblad, S. H., 435.
Wikner, Pontus, 423.
William, Bishop of Salima, 78.
William I. of Germany, 415.
William of Orange, 259.
Windau, 203.
Windsor, 237.
Wingard, C. F. af, 383.

Wirsén, G. F. af. 374, 378.
Wismar, 229, 357.
Witches, 251.
Witmar, 54.
Wittelsbachs, The, 249.
Wittstock, battle of, 223.
Wolfenbuttel, battle of, 224.
Wolgast, 222.
Wollin, island of, 56, 229, 312.
Women's rights, 383.
Wrangel, 286; Herman, 202; Charles Gustavus, 227, 229, 248, 250, 251, 252, 257.
Wulfila, 67, 235, 237, 341.
Wulfstan, 43.

Y

YEOMAN, Yeomanry, 72, 73, 78, 106, 108, 111. 114, 136, 144, 146, 149, 158, 192, 199, 201, 233, 238, 251, 253, 255, 258, 260, 314, 316, 318, 350, 357, 397, 407, 416, 432.
Ynglinga Saga, 31, 33-41, 51.
Ynglingatal, 33-41.
Ynglings, Yngling kings, 33-41.
Yngvar, 38-39.
Yngve, Swedish kings, 35; 36.
York, 58.
Yrsa, 38.

Z

ZAMOISKY, 187.
Zettervall, H., 430.
Zoölogy, 380.
Zorn, A. L., 430.

www.ingramcontent.com/pod-product-compliance
Lightning Source LLC
Chambersburg PA
CBHW022056300426
44117CB00007B/485